ANNUAL EDITIONS

Criminal Justice 13/14

Thirty-Seventh Edition

EDITOR

Joanne Naughton

Joanne Naughton is a former member of the NYPD, where she encountered most aspects of police work as a police officer, detective, sergeant, and lieutenant. She is also a former staff attorney with The Legal Aid Society, where she represented indigent criminal defendants. In addition to her hands-on experience in criminal justice, she was an adjunct professor at John Jay College of Criminal Justice and has retired from Mercy College where she was an assistant professor. She received her BA and JD at Fordham University.

Mc Graw Hill
Connect Learn Succeed™

The McGraw·Hill Companies

ANNUAL EDITIONS: CRIMINAL JUSTICE, THIRTY-SEVENTH EDITION

Published by McGraw-Hill, a business unit of The McGraw-Hill Companies, Inc., 1221 Avenue of the Americas, New York, NY 10020.

This book is printed on acid-free paper.

Annual Editions® is a registered trademark of the McGraw-Hill Companies, Inc.
Annual Editions is published by the **Contemporary Learning Series** group within the McGraw-Hill Higher Education division.

1 2 3 4 5 6 7 8 9 0 QDB/QDB 1 0 9 8 7 6 5 4 3

ISBN: 978-0-07-813609-2
MHID: 0-070813609-1
ISSN: 0272-3816 (print)
ISSN: 2159-1032 (online)

Acquisitions Editor: *Joan L. McNamara*
Marketing Director: *Adam Kloza*
Marketing Manager: *Nathan Edwards*
Senior Developmental Editor: *Jade Benedict*
Senior Project Manager: *Joyce Watters*
Buyer: *Nichole Birkenholz*
Cover Designer: *Studio Montage, St. Louis, MO*
Content Licensing Specialist: *DeAnna Dausener*
Media Project Manager: *Sridevi Palani*

Compositor: Laserwords Private Limited
Cover image credits: Brand X Pictures (inset), Ingram Publishing (background)

www.mhhe.com

Editors/Academic Advisory Board

Members of the Academic Advisory Board are instrumental in the final selection of articles for each edition of ANNUAL EDITIONS. Their review of articles for content, level, and appropriateness provides critical direction to the editors and staff. We think that you will find their careful consideration well reflected in this volume.

ANNUAL EDITIONS: Criminal Justice 13/14
37th Edition

EDITOR

ACADEMIC ADVISORY BOARD MEMBERS

Editors/Academic Advisory Board continued

Preface

In publishing ANNUAL EDITIONS we recognize the enormous role played by the magazines, newspapers, and journals of the public press in providing current, first-rate educational information in a broad spectrum of interest areas. Many of these articles are appropriate for students, researchers, and professionals seeking accurate, current material to help bridge the gap between principles and theories and the real world. These articles, however, become more useful for study when those of lasting value are carefully collected, organized, indexed, and reproduced in a low-cost format, which provides easy and permanent access when the material is needed. That is the role played by ANNUAL EDITIONS.

During the 1970s, Criminal Justice emerged as an appealing, vital and unique academic discipline. It emphasizes the professional development of students who plan careers in the field, and attracts those who want to know more about a complex social problem and how this country deals with it. Criminal Justice incorporates a vast range of knowledge from a number of specialties, including law, history, and the behavioral and social sciences. Each specialty contributes to our fuller understanding of criminal behavior and of society's attitudes toward deviance.

In view of the fact that the criminal justice system is in a constant state of flux, and because the study of criminal justice covers such a broad spectrum, today's students must be aware of a variety of subjects and topics. Standard textbooks and traditional anthologies cannot keep pace with the changes as quickly as they occur. In fact, many such sources are already out of date the day they are published. *Annual Editions: Criminal Justice 13/14* strives to maintain currency in matters of concern by providing up-to-date commentaries, articles, reports and statistics from the most recent literature in the criminal justice field.

This volume contains units concerning crime and justice in America, victimology, the police, the judicial system, juvenile justice, and punishment and corrections. The articles in these units were selected because they are informative, as well as provocative. The selections are timely and useful in their treatment of ethics, punishment, juveniles, courts and other related topics.

Included in this volume are a number of features designed to be useful to students, researchers and professionals in the criminal justice field. These include the table of contents, which summarize each article, and features key concepts in bold italics; a *topic guide* for locating articles on specific subjects; a list of relevant *World Wide web* sites; a comprehensive section on crime statistics; a *glossary,* and an *index.* In addition, each unit is preceded by an *overview* that provides a background for informed reading of the articles, emphasizes critical issues and presents *Learning Outcomes* to consider. Then, each article is followed by a section called *Critical Thinking* that contains questions related to the articles.

We would like to know what you think of the selections contained in this edition of *Annual Editions: Criminal Justice.*

Joanne Naughton
Editor

The Annual Editions Series

VOLUMES AVAILABLE

Adolescent Psychology
Aging
American Foreign Policy
American Government
Anthropology
Archaeology
Assessment and Evaluation
Business Ethics
Child Growth and Development
Comparative Politics
Criminal Justice
Developing World
Drugs, Society, and Behavior
Dying, Death, and Bereavement
Early Childhood Education
Economics
Educating Children with Exceptionalities
Education
Educational Psychology
Entrepreneurship
Environment
The Family
Gender
Geography
Global Issues
Health
Homeland Security
Human Development
Human Resources
Human Sexualities
International Business
Management
Marketing
Mass Media
Microbiology
Multicultural Education
Nursing
Nutrition
Physical Anthropology
Psychology
Race and Ethnic Relations
Social Problems
Sociology
State and Local Government
Sustainability
Technologies, Social Media, and Society
United States History, Volume 1
United States History, Volume 2
Urban Society
Violence and Terrorism
Western Civilization, Volume 1
World History, Volume 1
World History, Volume 2
World Politics

Contents

UNIT 1
Crime and Justice in America

The concepts in bold italics are developed in the article. For further expansion, please refer to the Topic Guide.

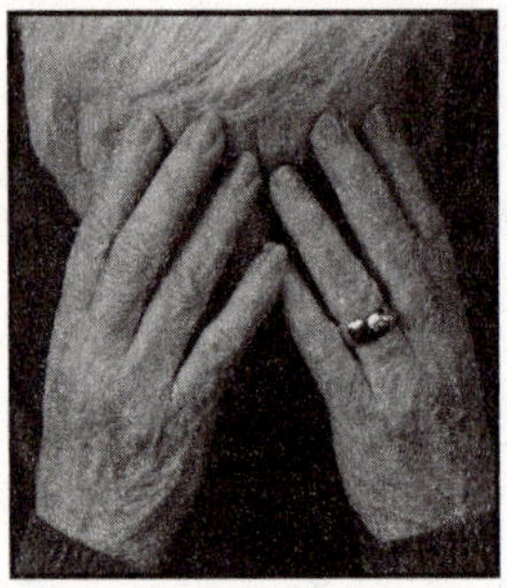

UNIT 2
Victimology

The concepts in bold italics are developed in the article. For further expansion, please refer to the Topic Guide.

UNIT 3
The Police

The concepts in bold italics are developed in the article. For further expansion, please refer to the Topic Guide.

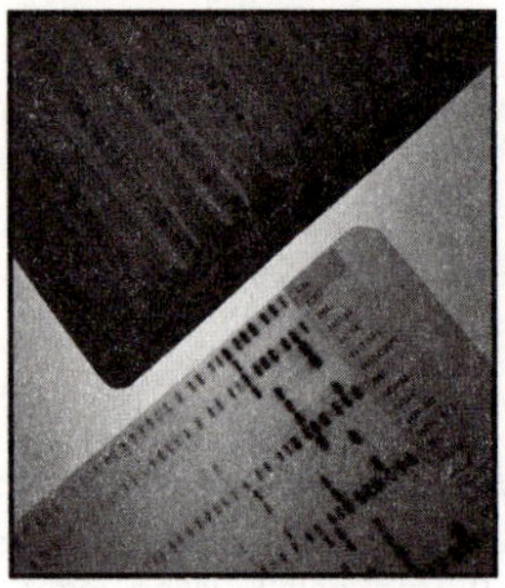

UNIT 4
The Judicial System

The concepts in bold italics are developed in the article. For further expansion, please refer to the Topic Guide.

UNIT 5
Juvenile Justice

The concepts in bold italics are developed in the article. For further expansion, please refer to the Topic Guide.

UNIT 6
Punishment and Corrections

The concepts in bold italics are developed in the article. For further expansion, please refer to the Topic Guide.

The concepts in bold italics are developed in the article. For further expansion, please refer to the Topic Guide.

Correlation Guide

The *Annual Editions* series provides students with convenient, inexpensive access to current, carefully selected articles from the public press. **Annual Editions: Criminal Justice 13/14** is an easy-to-use reader that presents articles on important topics such as *biology, gender, health,* and many more. For more information on *Annual Editions* and other *McGraw-Hill Contemporary Learning Series* titles, visit www.mhhe.com/cls.

This convenient guide matches the units in **Annual Editions: Criminal Justice 13/14** with the corresponding chapters in three of our best-selling McGraw-Hill Criminal Justice textbooks by Adler et al., Masters et al., and Bohm/Haley.

Annual Editions: Criminal Justice 13/14	Criminal Justice: An Introduction, 6e by Adler et al.	CJ: Realities and Challenges, 2e by Masters et al.	Introduction to Criminal Justice, 7e by Bohm/Haley
Unit 1: Crime and Justice in America	**Chapter 1:** Criminal Justice: Introduction and Overview **Chapter 2:** Crime and Criminals	**Chapter 1:** What is the Criminal Justice System?	**Chapter 5:** History and Structure of American Law Enforcement **Chapter 7:** Policing America: Issues and Ethics
Unit 2: Victimology	**Chapter 3:** Explaining Criminal Behavior **Chapter 4:** The Criminal Law	**Chapter 4:** Criminal Law and Defenses **Chapter 14:** Understanding and Helping Victims	**Chapter 2:** Crime and Its Consequences
Unit 3: The Police	**Chapter 5:** History and Organization of the Police **Chapter 6:** Police Functions and Police Culture	**Chapter 5:** Overview of Policing **Chapter 6:** Policing Operations **Chapter 7:** Legal and Special Issues in Policing	**Chapter 5:** History and Structure of American Law Enforcement **Chapter 6:** Policing: Roles, Styles, and Functions **Chapter 7:** Policing America: Issues and Ethics
Unit 4: The Judicial System	**Chapter 7:** The Rule of Law in Law Enforcement **Chapter 8:** The Origin and Role of the Courts **Chapter 9:** Lawyers and Judges	**Chapter 8:** The Courts **Chapter 9:** Pretrial and Trial	**Chapter 8:** The Administration of Justice **Chapter 9:** Sentencing, Appeals, and the Death Penalty
Unit 5: Juvenile Justice	**Chapter 15:** Justice for Juveniles and Victims	**Chapter 15:** Juvenile Justice	**Chapter 13:** Juvenile Justice
Unit 6: Punishment and Corrections	**Chapter 12:** Corrections: Yesterday and Today **Chapter 13:** Institutional Corrections	**Chapter 11:** Overview of Corrections **Chapter 12:** Jails and Prisons **Chapter 13:** Community Corrections	**Chapter 10:** Institutional Corrections

Topic Guide

This topic guide suggests how the selections in this book relate to the subjects covered in your course. You may want to use the topics listed on these pages to search the Web more easily.

On the following pages a number of websites have been gathered specifically for this book. They are arranged to reflect the units of this Annual Editions reader. You can link to these sites by going to www.mhhe.com/cls.

All the articles that relate to each topic are listed below the bold-faced term.

Internet References

The following Internet sites have been selected to support the articles found in this reader. These sites were available at the time of publication. However, because websites often change their structure and content, the information listed may no longer be available. We invite you to visit www.mhhe.com/cls for easy access to these sites.

Annual Editions: Criminal Justice 13/14

General Sources

American Society of Criminology
www.bsos.umd.edu/asc/four.html

This is an excellent starting place for study of all aspects of criminology and criminal justice, with links to international criminal justice, juvenile justice, court information, police, governments, and so on.

Federal Bureau of Investigation
www.fbi.gov

The main page of the FBI website leads to lists of the most wanted criminals, uniform crime reports, FBI case reports, major investigations, and more.

National Archive of Criminal Justice Data
www.icpsr.umich.edu/NACJD/index.html

NACJD holds more than 500 data collections relating to criminal justice; this site provides browsing and downloading access to most of the data and documentation. NACJD's central mission is to facilitate and encourage research in the field of criminal justice.

Social Science Information Gateway
http://sosig.esrc.bris.ac.uk

This is an online catalog of thousands of Internet resources relevant to social science education and research. Every resource is selected and described by a librarian or subject specialist. Enter "criminal justice" under Search for an excellent annotated list of sources.

UNIT 1: Crime and Justice in America

Sourcebook of Criminal Justice Statistics Online
www.albany.edu/sourcebook

Data about all aspects of criminal justice in the United States are available at this site, which includes more than 600 tables from dozens of sources. A search mechanism is available.

UNIT 2: Victimology

National Crime Victim's Research and Treatment Center (NCVC)
www.musc.edu/cvc

At this site, find out about the work of the NCVC at the Medical University of South Carolina, and click on Related Resources for an excellent listing of additional Web sources.

Office for Victims of Crime (OVC)
www.ojp.usdoj.gov/ovc

Established by the 1984 Victims of Crime Act, the OVC oversees diverse programs that benefit the victims of crime. From this site you can download a great deal of pertinent information.

UNIT 3: The Police

ACLU Criminal Justice Home Page
www.aclu.org/CriminalJustice/CriminalJusticeMain.cfm

This "Criminal Justice" page of the American Civil Liberties Union website highlights recent events in criminal justice, addresses police issues, lists important resources, and contains a search mechanism.

Law Enforcement Guide to the World Wide Web
http://leolinks.com

This page is dedicated to excellence in law enforcement. It contains links to every possible related category: community policing, computer crime, forensics, gangs, and wanted persons are just a few.

Violent Criminal Apprehension Program (VICAP)
www.state.ma.us/msp/unitpage/vicap.htm

VICAP's mission is to facilitate cooperation, communication, and coordination among law enforcement agencies and provide support in their efforts to investigate, identify, track, apprehend, and prosecute violent serial offenders. Access VICAP's data information center resources here.

UNIT 4: The Judicial System

Center for Rational Correctional Policy
www.correctionalpolicy.com

This is an excellent site on courts and sentencing, with many additional links to a variety of criminal justice sources.

Justice Information Center (JIC)
www.ncjrs.org

Provided by the National Criminal Justice Reference Service, this JIC site connects to information about corrections, courts, crime prevention, criminal justice, statistics, drugs and crime, law enforcement, and victims.

National Center for Policy Analysis (NCPA)
www.public-policy.org/~ncpa/pd/law/index3.html

Through the NCPA's "Idea House," you can click onto links to an array of topics that are of major interest in the study of the American judicial system.

U.S. Department of Justice (DOJ)
www.usdoj.gov

The DOJ represents the American people in enforcing the law in the public interest. Open its main page to find information about the U.S. judicial system. This site provides links to federal government Web servers, topics of interest related to the justice system, documents and resources, and a topical index.

Internet References

UNIT 5: Juvenile Justice

Gang Land: The Jerry Capeci Page

www.ganglandnews.com

Although this site particularly addresses organized-crime gangs, its insights into gang lifestyle—including gang families and their influence—are useful for those interested in exploring issues related to juvenile justice.

Institute for Intergovernmental Research (IIR)

www.iir.com

The IIR is a research organization that specializes in law enforcement, juvenile justice, and criminal justice issues. Explore the projects, links, and search engines from this home page. Topics addressed include youth gangs and white collar crime.

National Criminal Justice Reference Service (NCJRS)

http://virlib.ncjrs.org/JuvenileJustice.asp

NCJRS, a federally sponsored information clearinghouse for people involved with research, policy, and practice related to criminal and juvenile justice and drug control, provides this site of links to full-text juvenile justice publications.

Partnership Against Violence Network

www.pavnet.org

The Partnership Against Violence Network is a virtual library of information about violence and youths at risk, representing data from seven different federal agencies—a one-stop searchable information resource.

UNIT 6: Punishment and Corrections

American Probation and Parole Association (APPA)

www.appa-net.org

Open this APPA site to find information and resources related to probation and parole issues, position papers, the APPA code of ethics, and research and training programs and opportunities.

The Corrections Connection

www.corrections.com

This site is an online network for corrections professionals.

Critical Criminology Division of the ASC

www.critcrim.org

Here you will find basic criminology resources and related government resources provided by the American Society of Criminology, as well as other useful links. The death penalty is also discussed.

David Willshire's Forensic Psychology & Psychiatry Links

http://members.optushome.com.au/dwillsh/index.html

This site offers an enormous number of links to professional journals and associations. It is a valuable resource for study into possible connections between violence and mental disorders. Topics include serial killers, sex offenders, and trauma.

Oregon Department of Corrections

http://egov.oregon.gov/DOC/TRANS/CC/cc_welcome.shtml

Open this site for resources in such areas as crime and law enforcement and for links to U.S. state corrections departments.

UNIT 1

Crime and Justice in America

Unit Selections

1. **What Is the Sequence of Events in the Criminal Justice System?** *Report to the Nation on Crime and Justice,* Bureau of Justice Statistics
2. **The Never-Ending Drug War: Obstacles to Drug War Policy Termination,** Renee Scherlen
3 **Prison Rips up Families, Tears Apart Entire Communities,** John Simerman
4. **If Convicted Felons Could Vote . . . ,** Eliza Shapiro
5. **After 9/11, A New Era in the Business of Detaining Immigrants,** Chris Kirkham
6. **No Cause for Marijuana Case, but Enough for Child Neglect,** Mosi Secret
7. **Band's Culture of Hazing Flourished at Florida A&M,** David Breen

Learning Outcomes

After reading this unit, you will be able to:

- Name the agencies that make up the criminal justice system.
- State the various steps from the time someone is arrested for a crime.
- Explain how incarceration affects communities and families.
- Consider the value to society of denying convicted felons the right to vote.
- Assess the relationship between private prisons and the U.S. immigration policy.
- Understand how ingrained hazing is in many colleges and universities.

Student Website

www.mhhe.com/cls

Internet Reference

Sourcebook of Criminal Justice Statistics Online
www.albany.edu/sourcebook

Crime continues to be a major problem in the United States. Court dockets are full, our prisons are overcrowded, probation and parole caseloads are overwhelming, and our police are being urged to do more. The bulging prison population places a heavy strain on the economy of the country. Clearly, crime is a complex problem that defies simple explanations or solutions. While the more familiar crimes of murder, rape, assault, and drug law violations are still with us, international terrorism has become a pressing worry. The debate also continues about how best to handle juvenile offenders, sex offenders, and those who commit acts of domestic violence. Crime committed using computers and the Internet also demands attention from the criminal justice system.

Annual Editions: Criminal Justice 13/14 focuses directly on crime in America and the three traditional components of the criminal justice system: police, the courts, and corrections. It also gives special attention to crime victims in the victimology unit and to juveniles in the juvenile justice unit. The articles presented in this section are intended to serve as a foundation for the materials presented in subsequent sections.

The unit begins with "What Is the Sequence of Events in the Criminal Justice System?," an article that reveals that the response to crime is a complex process, involving citizens as well as many agencies, levels, and branches of government.

Following that article, in "The Never-Ending Drug War: Obstacles to Drug War Policy Termination," Renee Scherlen asks the reader to consider that the law enforcement approach to deter or punish illegal drug users, sellers, or producers is a failure. Scherlen discusses why failing programs persist rather than get terminated. In the next article, "Prison Rips up Families, Tears Apart Entire Communities," John Simermann reports on kids growing up in a neighborhood that has one of the highest incarceration rates in New Orleans, in a state that locks up more of its residents, per capita, than any place in the world. And many of those convictions are for nonviolent drug law violations.

Next, Eliza Shapiro discusses the laws in many states that prevent convicted felons from voting, including those who are out of prison and on probation or parole, in her article "If Convicted Felons Could Vote . . ." She writes that half of the convicted felons are serving time for a property or drug crime.

Following that article, Chris Kirkham covers the private prison industry in "After 9/11, A New Era in the Business of Detaining Immigrants." He points out that, because the industry is highly dependent on contracts with the federal government to maintain prisons and detention centers, companies have lobbied Washington extensively in recent years; immigration policy is deeply intertwined with their bottom line.

"No Cause for Marijuana Case, but Enough for Child Neglect," an article by Mosi Secret, describes how parents have faced the loss of their children for child neglect without any further evidence than the possession of small amounts of marijuana or the admission that they used it.

This unit ends with a description by David Breen of the culture of hazing that existed on a school band's bus, in "Band's culture of hazing flourished at Florida A&M." A spotlight was turned onto the practice after the death of a student as a result of the ingrained culture of hazing at the school. In a later article we will learn that hazing is prevalent in many schools.

What Is the Sequence of Events in the Criminal Justice System?

The Private Sector Initiates the Response to Crime

This first response may come from individuals, families, neighborhood associations, business, industry, agriculture, educational institutions, the news media, or any other private service to the public.

It involves crime prevention as well as participation in the criminal justice process once a crime has been committed. Private crime prevention is more than providing private security or burglar alarms or participating in neighborhood watch. It also includes a commitment to stop criminal behavior by not engaging in it or condoning it when it is committed by others.

Citizens take part directly in the criminal justice process by reporting crime to the police, by being a reliable participant (for example, a witness or a juror) in a criminal proceeding and by accepting the disposition of the system as just or reasonable. As voters and taxpayers, citizens also participate in criminal justice through the policymaking process that affects how the criminal justice process operates, the resources available to it, and its goals and objectives. At every stage of the process from the original formulation of objectives to the decision about where to locate jails and prisons to the reintegration of inmates into society, the private sector has a role to play. Without such involvement, the criminal justice process cannot serve the citizens it is intended to protect.

The Response to Crime and Public Safety Involves Many Agencies and Services

Many of the services needed to prevent crime and make neighborhoods safe are supplied by noncriminal justice agencies, including agencies with primary concern for public health, education, welfare, public works, and housing. Individual citizens as well as public and private sector organizations have joined with criminal justice agencies to prevent crime and make neighborhoods safe.

Criminal Cases Are Brought by the Government Through the Criminal Justice System

We apprehend, try, and punish offenders by means of a loose confederation of agencies at all levels of government. Our American system of justice has evolved from the English common law into a complex series of procedures and decisions. Founded on the concept that crimes against an individual are crimes against the State, our justice system prosecutes individuals as though they victimized all of society. However, crime victims are involved throughout the process and many justice agencies have programs that focus on helping victims.

There is no single criminal justice system in this country. We have many similar systems that are individually unique. Criminal cases may be handled differently in different jurisdictions, but court decisions based on the due process guarantees of the U.S. Constitution require that specific steps be taken in the administration of criminal justice so that the individual will be protected from undue intervention from the State.

The description of the criminal and juvenile justice systems that follows portrays the most common sequence of events in response to serious criminal behavior.

Entry into the System

The justice system does not respond to most crime because so much crime is not discovered or reported to the police. Law enforcement agencies learn about crime from the reports of victims or other citizens, from discovery by a police officer in the field, from informants, or from investigative and intelligence work.

Once a law enforcement agency has established that a crime has been committed, a suspect must be identified and apprehended for the case to proceed through the system. Sometimes, a suspect is apprehended at the scene; however, identification of a suspect sometimes requires an extensive investigation. Often, no one is identified or apprehended. In some instances, a suspect is arrested and later the police determine that no crime was committed and the suspect is released.

Prosecution and Pretrial Services

After an arrest, law enforcement agencies present information about the case and about the accused to the prosecutor, who will decide if formal charges will be filed with the court. If no charges are filed, the accused must be released. The prosecutor can also drop charges after making efforts to prosecute (*nolle prosequi*).

A suspect charged with a crime must be taken before a judge or magistrate without unnecessary delay. At the initial appearance, the judge or magistrate informs the accused of the charges and decides whether there is probable cause to detain the accused person. If the offense is not very serious, the determination of guilt and assessment of a penalty may also occur at this stage.

Often, the defense counsel is also assigned at the initial appearance. All suspects prosecuted for serious crimes have a right to be represented by an attorney. If the court determines the suspect is indigent and cannot afford such representation, the court will assign counsel at the public's expense.

A pretrial-release decision may be made at the initial appearance, but may occur at other hearings or may be changed at another time during the process. Pretrial release and bail were traditionally intended to ensure appearance at trial. However, many jurisdictions permit pretrial detention of defendants accused of serious offenses and deemed to be dangerous to prevent them from committing crimes prior to trial.

The court often bases its pretrial decision on information about the defendant's drug use, as well as residence, employment, and family ties. The court may decide to release the accused on his/her own recognizance or into the custody of a third party after the posting of a financial bond or on the promise of satisfying certain conditions such as taking periodic drug tests to ensure drug abstinence.

In many jurisdictions, the initial appearance may be followed by a preliminary hearing. The main function of this hearing is to discover if there is probable cause to believe that the accused committed a known crime within the jurisdiction of the court. If the judge does not find probable cause, the case is dismissed; however, if the judge or magistrate finds probable cause for such a belief, or the accused waives his or her right to a preliminary hearing, the case may be bound over to a grand jury.

A grand jury hears evidence against the accused presented by the prosecutor and decides if there is sufficient evidence to cause the accused to be brought to trial. If the grand jury finds sufficient evidence, it submits to the court an indictment, a written statement of the essential facts of the offense charged against the accused.

Where the grand jury system is used, the grand jury may also investigate criminal activity generally and issue indictments called grand jury originals that initiate criminal cases. These investigations and indictments are often used in drug and conspiracy cases that involve complex organizations. After such an indictment, law enforcement tries to apprehend and arrest the suspects named in the indictment.

Misdemeanor cases and some felony cases proceed by the issuance of an information, a formal, written accusation submitted to the court by a prosecutor. In some jurisdictions, indictments may be required in felony cases. However, the accused may choose to waive a grand jury indictment and, instead, accept service of an information for the crime.

In some jurisdictions, defendants, often those without prior criminal records, may be eligible for diversion from prosecution subject to the completion of specific conditions such as drug treatment. Successful completion of the conditions may result in the dropping of charges or the expunging of the criminal record where the defendant is required to plead guilty prior to the diversion.

Adjudication

Once an indictment or information has been filed with the trial court, the accused is scheduled for arraignment. At the arraignment, the accused is informed of the charges, advised of the rights of criminal defendants, and asked to enter a plea to the charges. Sometimes, a plea of guilty is the result of negotiations between the prosecutor and the defendant.

If the accused pleads guilty or pleads *nolo contendere* (accepts penalty without admitting guilt), the judge may accept or reject the plea. If the plea is accepted, no trial is held and the offender is sentenced at this proceeding or at a later date. The plea may be rejected and proceed to trial if, for example, the judge believes that the accused may have been coerced.

If the accused pleads not guilty or not guilty by reason of insanity, a date is set for the trial. A person accused of a serious crime is guaranteed a trial by jury. However, the accused may ask for a bench trial where the judge, rather than a jury, serves as the finder of fact. In both instances the prosecution and defense present evidence by questioning witnesses while the judge decides on issues of law. The trial results in acquittal or conviction on the original charges or on lesser included offenses.

After the trial a defendant may request appellate review of the conviction or sentence. In some cases, appeals of convictions are a matter of right; all States with the death penalty provide for automatic appeal of cases involving a death sentence. Appeals may be subject to the discretion of the appellate court and may be granted only on acceptance of a defendant's petition for a *writ of certiorari.* Prisoners may also appeal their sentences through civil rights petitions and *writs of habeas corpus* where they claim unlawful detention.

Sentencing and Sanctions

After a conviction, sentence is imposed. In most cases the judge decides on the sentence, but in some jurisdictions the sentence is decided by the jury, particularly for capital offenses.

In arriving at an appropriate sentence, a sentencing hearing may be held at which evidence of aggravating or mitigating circumstances is considered. In assessing the circumstances surrounding a convicted person's criminal behavior, courts often rely on presentence investigations by probation agencies or other designated authorities. Courts may also consider victim impact statements.

The sentencing choices that may be available to judges and juries include one or more of the following:

- the death penalty
- incarceration in a prison, jail, or other confinement facility
- probation—allowing the convicted person to remain at liberty but subject to certain conditions and restrictions such as drug testing or drug restrictions such as drug testing or drug treatment

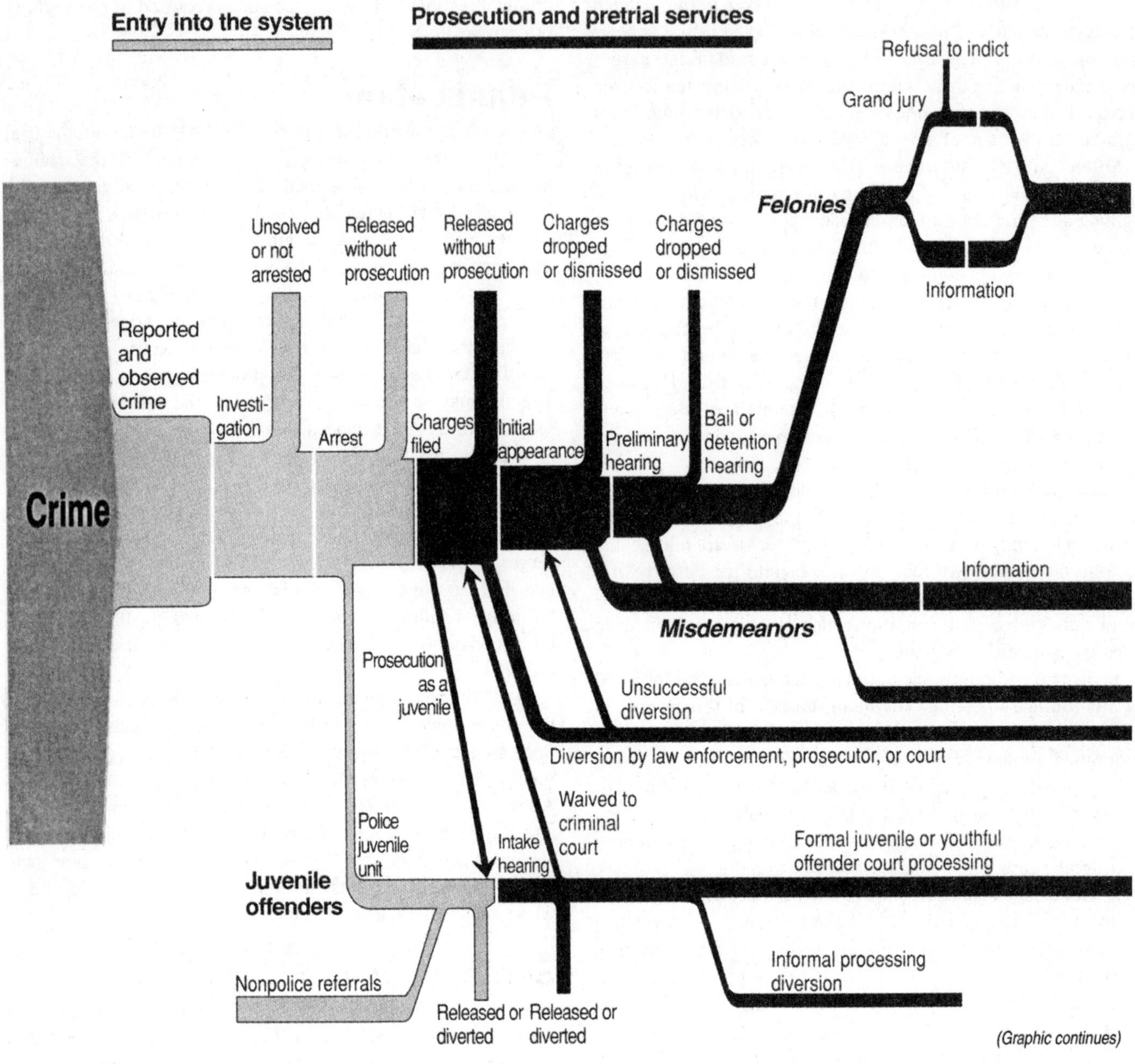

Figure 1

Note: This chart gives a simplified view of caseflow through the criminal justice system. Procedures vary among jurisdictions. The weights of the lines are not intended to show the actual size of caseloads.

- fines—primarily applied as penalties in minor offenses
- restitution—requiring the offender to pay compensation to the victim. In some jurisdictions, offenders may be sentenced to alternatives to incarceration that are considered more severe than straight probation but less severe than a prison term. Examples of such sanctions include boot camps, intense supervision often with drug treatment and testing, house arrest and electronic monitoring, denial of Federal benefits, and community service.

In many jurisdictions, the law mandates that persons convicted of certain types of offenses serve a prison term. Most jurisdictions permit the judge to set the sentence length within certain limits, but some have determinate sentencing laws that stipulate a specific sentence length that must be served and cannot be altered by a parole board.

Corrections

Offenders sentenced to incarceration usually serve time in a local jail or a State prison. Offenders sentenced to less than 1 year generally go to jail; those sentenced to more than 1 year go to prison. Persons admitted to the Federal system or a State prison system may be held in prison with varying levels of custody or in a community correctional facility.

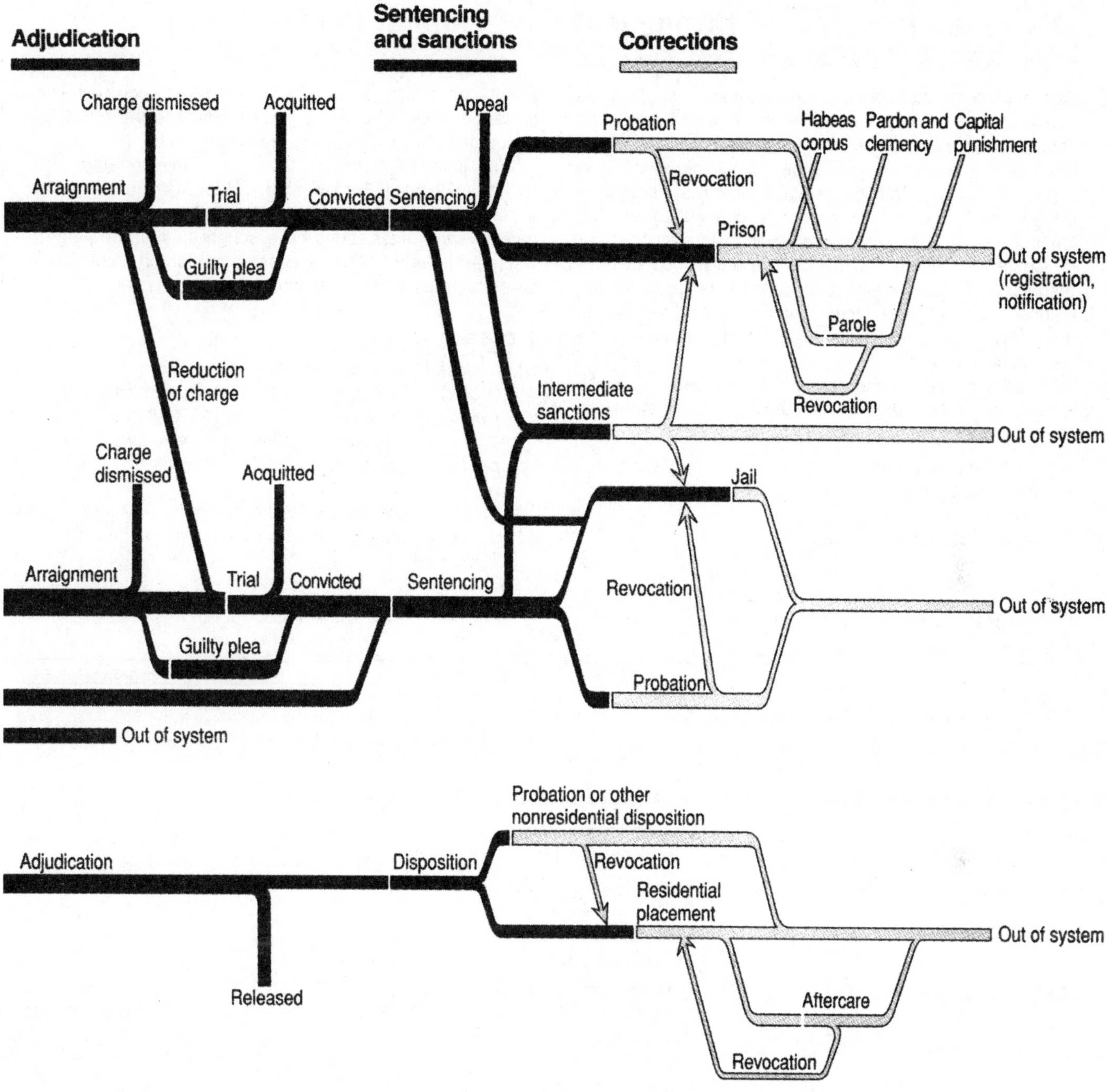

Figure 1 *(continued)*

Source: Adapted from *The challenge of crime in a free society*. President's Commission on Law Enforcement and Administration of Justice, 1967. This revision, a result of the Symposium on the 30th Anniversary of the President's Commission, was prepared by the Bureau of Justice Statistics in 1997.

A prisoner may become eligible for parole after serving a specific part of his or her sentence. Parole is the conditional release of a prisoner before the prisoner's full sentence has been served. The decision to grant parole is made by an authority such as a parole board, which has power to grant or revoke parole or to discharge a parolee altogether. The way parole decisions are made varies widely among jurisdictions.

Offenders may also be required to serve out their full sentences prior to release (expiration of term). Those sentenced under determinate sentencing laws can be released only after they have served their full sentence (mandatory release) less any "goodtime" received while in prison. Inmates get goodtime credits against their sentences automatically or by earning them through participation in programs.

If released by a parole board decision or by mandatory release, the releasee will be under the supervision of a parole officer in the community for the balance of his or her unexpired sentence. This supervision is governed by specific conditions of release, and the releasee may be returned to prison for violations of such conditions.

Discretion Is Exercised throughout the Criminal Justice System

Discretion is "an authority conferred by law to act in certain conditions or situations in accordance with an official's or an official agency's own considered judgment and conscience."[1] Discretion is exercised throughout the government. It is a part of decision making in all government systems from mental health to education, as well as criminal justice. The limits of discretion vary from jurisdiction to jurisdiction.

Concerning crime and justice, legislative bodies have recognized that they cannot anticipate the range of circumstances surrounding each crime, anticipate local mores, and enact laws that clearly encompass all conduct that is criminal and all that is not.[2]

Therefore, persons charged with the day-to-day response to crime are expected to exercise their own judgment within limits set by law. Basically, they must decide—

- whether to take action
- where the situation fits in the scheme of law, rules, and precedent
- which official response is appropriate.[3]

To ensure that discretion is exercised responsibly, government authority is often delegated to professionals. Professionalism requires a minimum level of training and orientation, which guide officials in making decisions. The professionalism of policing is due largely to the desire to ensure the proper exercise of police discretion.

The limits of discretion vary from State to State and locality to locality. For example, some State judges have wide discretion in the type of sentence they may impose. In recent years, other states have sought to limit the judge's discretion in sentencing by passing mandatory sentencing laws that require prison sentences for certain offenses.

Notes

1. Roscoe Pound, "Discretion, dispensation and mitigation: The problem of the individual special case," *New York University Law Review* (1960) 35:925, 926.
2. Wayne R. LaFave, *Arrest: The decision to take a suspect into custody* (Boston: Little, Brown & Co., 1964), pp. 63–184.
3. Memorandum of June 21, 1977, from Mark Moore to James Vorenberg, "Some abstract notes on the issue of discretion."

Bureau of Justice Statistics (www.ojp.usdoj.gov/bjs/). January 1998. NCJ 167894. To order: 1-800-732-3277.

Who Exercises Discretion?

These criminal justice officials . . .	must often decide whether or not or how to—
Police	Enforce specific laws Investigate specific crimes; Search people
Prosecutors	File charges or petitions for adjudication Seek indictments Drop cases Reduce charges
Judges or magistrates	Set bail or conditions for release Accept pleas Determine delinquency Dismiss charges Impose sentence Revoke probation
Correctional officials	Assign to type of correctional facility Award privileges Punish for disciplinary infractions
Paroling authorities	Determine date and conditions of parole Revoke parole

Recidivism

Once the suspects, defendants, or offenders are released from the jurisdiction of a criminal justice agency, they may be processed through the criminal justice system again for a new crime. Long term studies show that many suspects who are arrested have prior criminal histories and those with a greater number of prior arrests were more likely to be arrested again. As the courts take prior criminal history into account at sentencing, most prison inmates have a prior criminal history and many have been incarcerated before. Nationally, about half the inmates released from State prison will return to prison.

The Juvenile Justice System

Juvenile courts usually have jurisdiction over matters concerning children, including delinquency, neglect, and adoption. They also handle "status offenses" such as truancy and running away, which are not applicable to adults. State statutes define which persons are under the original jurisdiction of the juvenile court. The upper age of juvenile court jurisdiction in delinquency matters is 17 in most States.

The processing of juvenile offenders is not entirely dissimilar to adult criminal processing, but there are crucial differences. Many juveniles are referred to juvenile courts by law enforcement officers, but many others are referred by school officials, social services agencies, neighbors, and even parents, for behavior or conditions that are determined to require intervention by the formal system for social control.

At arrest, a decision is made either to send the matter further into the justice system or to divert the case out of the system, often to alternative programs. Examples of alternative programs include drug treatment, individual or group counseling, or referral to educational and recreational programs.

When juveniles are referred to the juvenile courts, the court's intake department or the prosecuting attorney determines whether sufficient grounds exist to warrant filing a petition that requests an adjudicatory hearing or a request to transfer jurisdiction to criminal court. At this point, many juveniles are released or diverted to alternative programs.

All States allow juveniles to be tried as adults in criminal court under certain circumstances. In many States, the legislature *statutorily excludes* certain (usually serious) offenses from the jurisdiction of the juvenile court regardless of the age of the accused. In some States and at the Federal level under certain circumstances, prosecutors have the *discretion* to either file criminal charges against juveniles directly in criminal courts or proceed through the juvenile justice process. The juvenile court's intake department or the prosecutor may petition the juvenile court to *waive* jurisdiction to criminal court. The juvenile court also may order *referral* to criminal court for trial as adults. In some jurisdictions, juveniles processed as adults may upon conviction be sentenced to either an adult or a juvenile facility.

In those cases where the juvenile court retains jurisdiction, the case may be handled formally by filing a delinquency petition or informally by diverting the juvenile to other agencies or programs in lieu of further court processing.

If a petition for an adjudicatory hearing is accepted, the juvenile may be brought before a court quite unlike the court with jurisdiction over adult offenders. Despite the considerable discretion associated with juvenile court proceedings, juveniles are afforded many of the due-process safeguards associated with adult criminal trials. Several States permit the use of juries in juvenile courts; however, in light of the U.S. Supreme Court holding that juries are not essential to juvenile hearings, most States do not make provisions for juries in juvenile courts.

In disposing of cases, juvenile courts usually have far more discretion than adult courts. In addition to such options as probation, commitment to a residential facility, restitution, or fines, State laws grant juvenile courts the power to order removal of children from their homes to foster homes or treatment facilities. Juvenile courts also may order participation in special programs aimed at shoplifting prevention, drug counseling, or driver education.

Once a juvenile is under juvenile court disposition, the court may retain jurisdiction until the juvenile legally becomes an adult (at age 21 in most States). In some jurisdictions, juvenile offenders may be classified as youthful offenders, which can lead to extended sentences.

Following release from an institution, juveniles are often ordered to a period of aftercare that is similar to parole supervision for adult offenders. Juvenile offenders who violate the conditions of aftercare may have their aftercare revoked, resulting in being recommitted to a facility. Juveniles who are classified as youthful offenders and violate the conditions of aftercare may be subject to adult sanctions.

The Governmental Response to Crime Is Founded in the Intergovernmental Structure of the United States

Under our form of government, each State and the Federal Government has its own criminal justice system. All systems must respect the rights of individuals set forth in court interpretation of the U.S. Constitution and defined in case law.

State constitutions and laws define the criminal justice system within each State and delegate the authority and responsibility for criminal justice to various jurisdictions, officials, and institutions. State laws also define criminal behavior and groups of children or acts under jurisdiction of the juvenile courts.

Municipalities and counties further define their criminal justice systems through local ordinances that proscribe the local agencies responsible for criminal justice processing that were not established by the State.

Congress has also established a criminal justice system at the Federal level to respond to Federal crimes such as bank robbery, kidnaping, and transporting stolen goods across State lines.

The Response to Crime Is Mainly a State and Local Function

Very few crimes are under exclusive Federal jurisdiction. The responsibility to respond to most crime rests with State and local governments. Police protection is primarily a function of cities and towns. Corrections is primarily a function of State governments. Most justice personnel are employed at the local level.

Critical Thinking

1. Explain discretion and how it is exercised in the criminal justice system.
2. What are the steps that follow once a suspect is arrested by police and charged with a crime?
3. How are young people who violate the law treated?

U.S. Department of Justice, 1998.

Article 2

The Never-Ending Drug War: Obstacles to Drug War Policy Termination

RENEE SCHERLEN

I co-teach a course on the US drug war that we have offered for almost a decade. In the class, my colleague and I explore both the domestic and international aspects of the drug war. We examine the goals that have been established, the methods used, and actual achievements of the government's drug war policies. Then, we turn to policy analysis: after a cost–benefit analysis, we review policy alternatives. Students begin the semester with many different perspectives and questions. Some strongly support the drug war; others are skeptical. By the end of the semester the most consistent question from and the most vexing problem for students is "Why does the US continue to fight the drug war?" More concretely, the students question the absence of serious policy evaluation in Washington, DC.

The research questions are clear: Why does the United States federal government continue to pursue the war on drugs? Why is policy termination not seriously considered? Before beginning this discussion, however, some points need to be clarified. First, is the current policy inadequate or problematic? Second, what exactly, does "policy termination" mean? After considering these questions, I turn to the literature on policy termination. Over the years it has become clear any policy termination is rare. Indeed, most theories of termination are really theories of nontermination (i.e., explanations for why failing programs, policies, and institutions persist). After surveying the literature, I apply the dominant policy termination findings to the drug war. Unlike other works, however, I explore the benefits of drawing on prospect theory in addition to policy termination theory to understand the rarity of policy termination.

Applying insights from prospect theory to the dilemma of the rarity of policy termination is valuable. Although prospect theory has been used as a framework in international relations and foreign policy decision-making research (see, for instance, Jervis 1992 and Welch 2005), it has little affect on the research on public policy and policy analysis. Prospect theory further clarifies the dynamics of policy change and resistance to termination. Furthermore, prospect theory, along with policy termination theory, can guide the strategies and tactics of activists who want to end the war on drugs.

The Drug War Is a Failure

The term "drug war" refers to the use of a law enforcement approach to deter or punish users, sellers, and producers of illicit drugs. The policy emphasizes incarceration, eradication, interdiction, extradition, and supply reduction. The drug war focuses on supply; the government argues that market disruption and supply reduction will increase drug prices and decrease drug purity. These two elements combined should result in lower drug use among current users and a decrease in the number of new users. While the prohibitionist orientation of the US government dates from the early 1900s (the Shanghai Conference of the Opium Commission and the Opium Exclusion Act of 1909), the current drug war began when President Nixon stated, "America's public enemy number one in the United States is drug abuse. In order to fight and defeat this enemy, it is necessary to wage a new, all-out offensive" (1971a). His administration began a law enforcement prohibitionist policy that has been pursued by US presidents since 1971: Ronald Reagan signed the Anti-Drug Abuse Act of 1986; George H.W. Bush signed the Anti-Drug Abuse Act of 1988, which established the Office of National Drug Control Policy; Bill Clinton signed legislation funding "Plan Colombia"; and, George W. Bush expanded "Plan Colombia" into the "Andean Counterdrug Initiative." Although President Obama's drug czar sought to "banish the idea that the United States is fighting a war on drugs," the actual policies of the United States have not significantly changed (Kerlikowske 2009).

The overall goal of the drug war has been consistent and simple: reduce drug use in the United States. President Nixon sought to "eliminate drug abuse and all the antisocial activities that flow from drug abuse" (Nixon 1971b). President Reagan spoke of "fighting the crusade for a drug free America" (1988). The 1998 National Drug Control Strategy identified specific targets of reducing drug demand by 25 percent by 2002 and by 50 percent by 2007. The 2010 Drug Strategy outlines a "comprehensive approach to reducing drug use . . . [with] a balance of prevention, treatment, and law enforcement" (Office of National Drug Control Policy 2010). Thus, from 1971 to 2011, drug policy has sought to reduce drug use.

What has been accomplished in 40 years? The drug war has not accomplished any specific targets established (such as in the 1998 National Drug Control Strategy). Nor have more general goals, like a drug free America or the elimination of drug abuse, been achieved. Data regarding the degree of drug use in the United States suggest that the drug war has not had a profound impact on drug use.

This trend is echoed in the evidence with regard to drug supply. Contrary to predictions, the price and purity of illicit drugs have not been negatively affected (i.e., price increase and purity decrease). For instance, the 2007 price of 100 percent pure cocaine is substantially lower than in 1990 (earliest date for price/purity data).

The US public also appears to doubt the success of US drug policy. Data across the years indicates that the public does not believe the government to be successful in its drug policy. In 2009, 63 percent of the US public thought that the drug war was either stagnant or losing ground. All of these figures combined indicate that current drug war policy has not achieved its goals. This signals policy failure. And, policy failure should lead to policy termination.

To state that drug war policy has failed and should be terminated does not necessarily signify anything more. Those who agree with this point, however, often draw differing conclusions. The termination of the drug policy might entail creating a new policy of prohibition coupled with harm reduction (rather than law enforcement). Others might argue that policy termination should lead to decriminalization of drugs. Yet others might call for policy termination to result in drug legalization. Some of this disparity might be explained by uncertainty about the concept of policy termination.

Policy Termination

What exactly is meant by the phrase "policy termination"? Does it differ significantly from "policy change" or "policy revision"? Are policy adaptations and modifications variants of policy termination or are they fundamentally different? Looking to the literature on policy termination brings about some clarification. Typically, policy termination "refers to the adjustment of policies and programs that have become dysfunctional, redundant, outmoded, and/or unnecessary" (Brewer 1978, 338). Of course, "adjustment" could encompass policy modifications. Some note that "termination is frequently associated with implementation of a new alternative policy" (Bothun and Comer 1979, 541), suggestive of policy modification. Others speak of termination—"the deliberate conclusion or cessation of specific government functions, programs, policies, or organizations"—and "partial terminations" that lead government agencies programs and/or organizations to "redirect their activities so as to remain operant" (DeLeon 1978, 280). Yet some people remain committed to a strict definition of the term, seeking to exclude instances of cutbacks, reduced size, or scope of policies (Daniels 1997, 5). This article seeks the middle ground. Drug war policy termination entails the deliberate conclusion or cessation of government policies and programs related to the prohibitionist approach to drug use; the continuation of prohibition but with a harm reduction emphasis would be considered partial termination.

Theories of Policy Termination

As noted earlier, policy termination is a rare political phenomenon. Accordingly, little research exists. Some material can be found in the literature on bureaucracy and bureaucratic resistance to change (see, for instance, Wilson 1989). A review of the literature specifically about policy termination reveals a wave-like pattern: articles and books tend to cluster together, separated by years of relatively inactive research. Over the years, however, some points have emerged, been tested, and found to be useful. Peter DeLeon, one of the first scholars of policy termination, has made lasting contributions to the field, especially in the development of a framework for understanding the absence of policy termination (DeLeon 1978, 1983, 1987). Many people (see, for instance, Frantz 1992; Geva-May 2004; and Kirkpatrick, Lester, and Peterson 1999) find DeLeon's schema for explaining the failure of policy termination to be a useful starting point for policy analysis.

DeLeon argues that there are six "reasons why policy termination has been particularly difficult to plan and execute": (1) intellectual reluctance, (2) institutional permanence, (3) dynamic conservatism, (4) antitermination coalitions, (5) legal obstacles, and (6) high start-up costs (1978, 286). For DeLeon, intellectual reluctance encompasses the disinclination of individuals to acknowledge their mistakes as well as a general political tendency to shun contraction of government services. Frantz (1992) notes that the Reagan administration and neoliberal ideology embraced the concept of smaller government; this modifies part of the intellectual reluctance noted by DeLeon. Institutional permanence refers to that well-established characteristic of institutions: longevity. As DeLeon and others (Kaufman 1976; Wilson 1989) noted, bureaucracies are designed to persist; in Kaufman's words, institutions aim for immortality. DeLeon's notion of "dynamic conservatism" is meant to capture the activities of institutions and their supporters as they respond to the political and policy environment that might be detrimental to their survival. Antitermination coalitions are "significant political groups . . . [who] can arise in opposition to termination" (Daniels 1997, 26). Legal obstacles frequently surface; the right to due process means that such challenges often have standing and must be resolved before termination can proceed. Finally, DeLeon argues that pursuit of policy termination demands "the political resources necessary to counter the coalitions . . . that shield organizations and programs from the termination axe" (DeLeon 1978, 291).

Following up on DeLeon's work, Kirkpatrick, Lester, and Peterson (1999) construct a model that creates a conceptual framework for understanding the policy termination process. While using DeLeon as a starting point, the authors draw on additional case studies and policy termination analysis (for example, Behn 1978; Daniels 1997; Frantz 1992) to extract additional variables that shape the dynamics of policy termination. They argue that the process is influenced by three categories of variables: inherent characteristics, the political environment, and constraints (Kirkpatrick, Lester, and Peterson 1999, 211–213).

For these authors, *inherent characteristics* are aspects of the policy that shape its response to termination. The authors note five consistently significant characteristics: (1) the stated mission/ purpose of the policy, (2) the longevity of the policy, (3) the public visibility of the policy, (4) the complexity of the policy, and (5) the distribution of policy benefits (Kirkpatrick, Lester, and Peterson 1999, 213–214). The impact of each characteristic varies. The mission of the policy must be relevant; its purposes must not appear to be out-dated or illegitimate. Clearly, policies that have missions considered critical by the public and politicians are more impervious to termination. Unsurprisingly, the greater the longevity of a policy, the more resistant to termination it proves. Public visibility inversely influences termination; "organizations that are largely invisible to the public have a greater chance of surviving to a ripe old age" (Kirkpatrick, Lester, and Peterson 1999, 214). Likewise, a complex policy dealing with complex issues appears to be more resilient against termination pressures. The last characteristic is one that has long been noted in public policy and political science research: policies with many beneficiaries or with widely dispersed beneficiaries pose a much greater challenge to termination.

The next category of variable influencing policy termination is the *political environment.* Kirkpatrick, Lester, and Peterson identify what they consider to be five key elements of the context within which the effort to achieve policy termination occurs: (1) the prevailing political ideology; (2) the size, strength, and determination of the forces marshaled for termination; (3) the quality and character of the allies arrayed by termination and antitermination coalitions; (4) the existence of possibilities of compromise; and (5) the speed of the termination process (Kirkpatrick, Lester, and Peterson 1999, 215–216).

As with inherent characteristics, the impact of each variable within the category varies. Some variables are relatively self-apparent: if the prevailing political ideology is supportive of change, this increases the possibility of termination. Similarly, when the size, strength, and determination of termination forces are great, the likelihood of termination increases. Allies are critical: which faction has the more powerful allies may determine whether termination or antitermination forces prevail. Kirkpatrick, Lester, and Peterson argue that case studies suggest compromise is a basic survival tactic of institutions and programs; thus, the greater possibility of compromise, the less likely termination becomes. Finally, case study research noted by the authors supports the contention that a speedy termination process is more likely to succeed than a slow one.

The final category of variables is *constraints*. This category draws heavily from DeLeon and follow-up studies that used his framework (Kirkpatrick, Lester, and Peterson 1999, 216–218). The five constraints that limit policy termination are (1) the antitermination coalition, (2) dynamic conservatism, (3) legal obstacles, (4) costs, and (5) fear/uncertainty. Most of these variables are described above. The one variable noted by the authors not discussed by DeLeon is "uncertainty and fear." The authors argue "it is fear of the termination's impact, due to uncertainties, that prevents decisive action from being taken" (Kirkpatrick, Lester, and Peterson 1999, 218). Overall, this variable is not well developed; but, it suggests elements of the decision-making process under conditions of uncertainty analyzed by prospect theory (Kahneman and Tversky 1979).

Figure [1] summarizes the conceptual framework developed by Kirkpatrick, Lester, and Peterson. This framework, coupled with prospect theory, can explain the persistence of drug war policy in the face of its failure to achieve its goals.

Prospect Theory

First presented in a research article in 1979, prospect theory develops a model for understanding decision-making under conditions of risk and uncertainty (Kahneman and Tversky 1979). The theory challenges the assumptions held by expected utility theory and rational choice. The authors are concerned (in part) with understanding peoples' evaluation of loss and gain and how people weigh these assessments in conditions when the outcome is uncertain. In experiments with people, a consistent patterns is revealed: people are risk adverse when they confront choices perceived to involve sure gains; in contrast, people are risk acceptant when they confront choices perceived to involve sure losses. Risk aversion and risk acceptance are not constant; the experiments demonstrated that individuals could not be labeled one or the other, regardless of the circumstances. Rather, people view risk differently depending on whether or not they perceive the situation to be one of gain or loss. Frames are method of establishing the "gain/loss" domain (Kahneman, Knetsch, and Thaler 1991). A policy framed as successful (even mildly so) places it in a gain domain; this is associated with risk aversion and thereby decreases the likelihood of policy termination. In contrast, a frame that placed policy in a loss domain opens the door to a greater possibility of policy change because loss domain in associated with risk acceptance. Thus, framing—creating perceptions of gain or loss—has profound policy termination implications. The frame can generate the fear and uncertainty noted by Kirkpatrick, Lester, and Peterson. Framing should also influence the coalitions that line up in the termination struggle. Prospect theory research suggests that a policy within the gain domain will have more allies; conversely, termination forces will have less support.

Framing is an underdeveloped aspect of prospect theory. The theory accepts, however, that frames are constructed. Thus, forces aligned both for and against termination probably work to frame the policy in a manner that is supportive of their cause.

Explaining the Persistence of the Drug War

Ironically, the war on drugs begun by President Nixon was presented as an emergency response. The policy was seen having a set limit: the Special Action Office of Drug Abuse Prevention (the first federal government agency of the contemporary drug war) was "established to operate only for a period of three years from its date of enactment . . . the President would have the option of extending its life for an additional two years if desirable" ("Excerpts . . . 1971, 22). Forty years later, the drug war continues unabated and unsuccessful. Does the policy termination process detailed above, enhanced by prospect theory, help explain its survival?

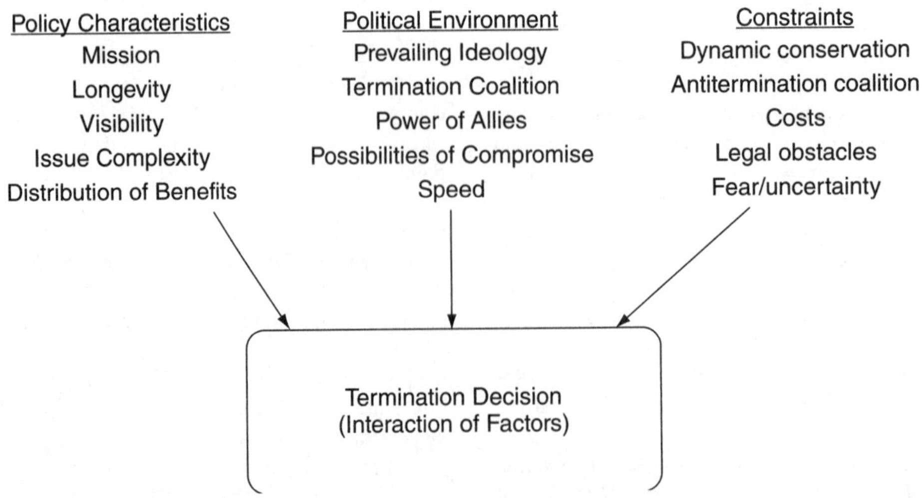

Figure 1 Conceptualizing the Policy Termination Process

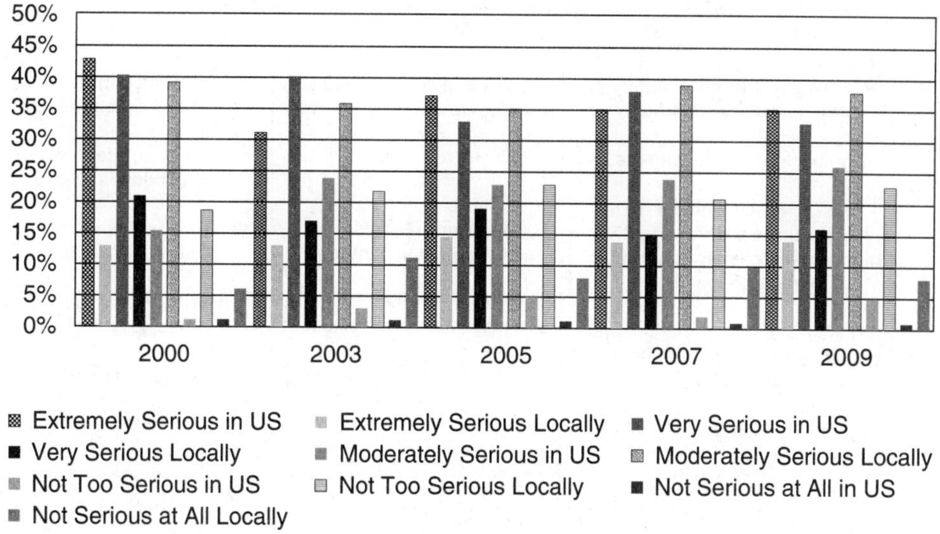

Figure 2 Attitudes toward Drug Problem in the United States and Locally

The Inherent Characteristics of the Drug War

The five characteristics of policy that influence its ability to defy termination suggest that the drug war has a strong foundation to fight against termination. The mission of the drug war is fairly strong and legitimate. For instance, a 2007 national survey found that 73 percent of Americans described the country's problem as either "extremely" (35 percent) or "very" (38 percent) serious (Gallup 2007). As we have seen, the longevity variable favors policy continuation: the offensive against drugs and drug use declared in 1971 by Richard Nixon has been pursued by most presidential administrations. The Office of National Drug Control Policy also has been reauthorized twice (1998 and 2006) since its establishment in 1989.

The public visibility of the drug war is an interesting variable. Research suggests that opinions about the drug war correspond to race, class, and age. Incarceration and adverse consequences from drug war policy also have race, class, and age correlations. This suggests that "negative" visibility is limited to marginal groups, for the most part. The one exception would be members of the law enforcement and judiciary. Law Enforcement against Prohibition (LEAP) and outspoken judicial opponents (such as former judges James Gray and Robert W. Sweet) indicate that familiarity with drug war policy can lead to support for policy termination. Perceptions about the complexity of the drug war are hard to assess. Many people view drugs and drug use in a relatively straightforward (albeit negative) light. However, the public does not appear to have a concrete sense of possible alternatives. The distribution of drug war benefits is extensive. Drug prohibition and its mechanisms are located across all 50 states. It influences city, county, and state law enforcement; asset forfeiture laws make drug war prosecution a key source of law enforcement and judicial funding. People who work in corrections as well as in law enforcement have job security issues to consider when evaluating the continuation of the drug war.

The Political Environment of the Drug War Policy
Termination Process

At present, one could argue that there is a mildly positive prevailing political ideology with regard to drug war termination. Most notably, the drug czar stated in an interview with *The Wall Street Journal* that he was committed to "completely and forever end[ing] the war analogy, the war on drugs" (Kerlikowske 2009). The Obama administration has stated publicly that it will support needle exchange programs and it will no longer support federal raids on medical marijuana facilities in states that have legalized medical use of marijuana. This discussion indicates some openness to change. However, no one in the administration openly supports "policy termination." Much of this change is presented as modifications; this suggests that opposition to the drug war has compromises short of complete termination. Medical marijuana could be considered a compromise move; in terms of the policy termination process, this lessens the likelihood of policy termination. The coalition in favor of termination grows annually; for instance, StoptheDrugWar.org (DRCNet), established in 1997, is now a 27,000-person online network (based on membership figures). The Drug Policy Alliance has 76,619 subscribers. The coalition, however, has yet to attract powerful political allies. A review of the advisers or honorary board members (likely indicators of alliance) show numerous "formers": . . . former governors, former district attorneys, former surgeon generals, and former judges. For instance, the recent "Report of the Global Commission on Drug Policy" issued in June 2011 condemning the war on drugs has an impressive roster of participants: the former president of Brazil, Fernando Henrique Cardoso; the former president of Mexico, Ernesto Zedillo; the former president of Colombia, Cesar Gaviria; and the former U.S. secretary of state, George P. Shultz. Sitting political actors rarely, if ever, voice support for policy termination. The final factor, speed, is clearly not a characteristic of the drug war policy termination process.

At present, one could argue that there is a mildly positive prevailing political idealogy with regard to drug war termination. Most notably, the drug czar stated in an interview with *The Wall Street Journal* that he was committed to "completely and forever end[ing] the war analogy, the war on drugs"

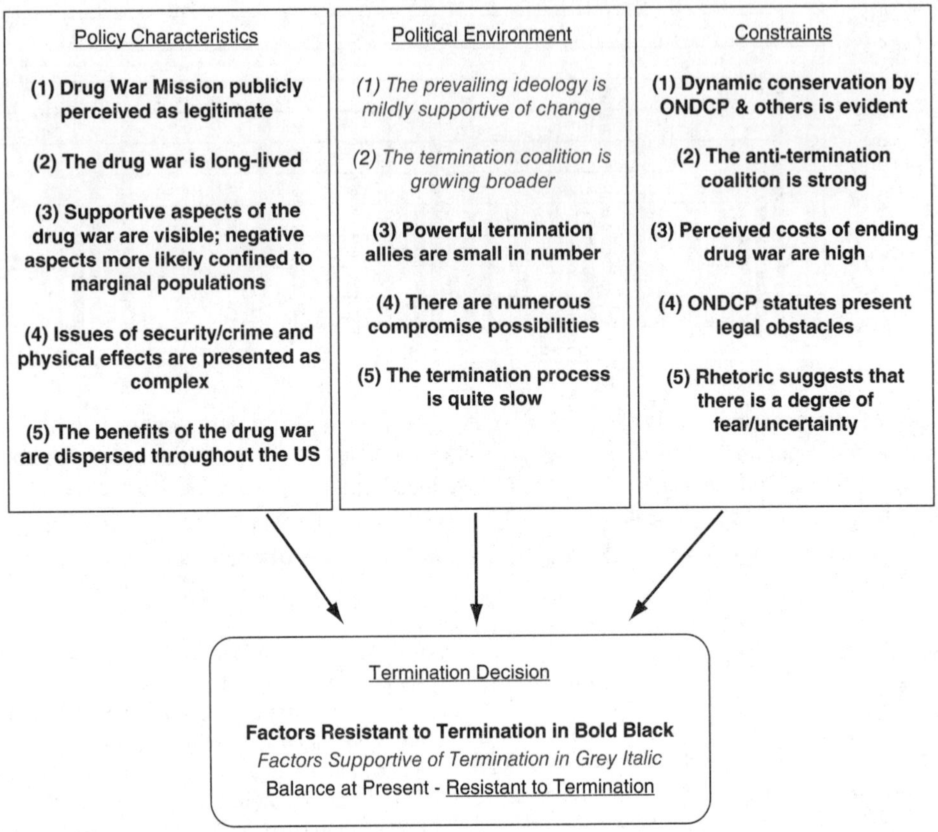

Figure 3 The Drug War Policy Termination Process

All of the constraints noted by DeLeon restrain the drug war policy termination process. The antitermination coalition still has considerable size and strength. Many people might argue that the changes supported by the Obama administration (needle exchange, increased emphasis on public health) are a sign of dynamic conservation. The Office of National Drug Control Strategy is still legally prohibited from considering legalization or decriminalization. The costs associated with policy termination are typically presented as high. The cost-savings of drug war termination (and potential taxation of drugs) is frequently questioned:

> The only way the State can effectively get rid of the black market for marijuana, and thus save these law enforcement dollars, is to take away the substantial profits in the market and allow the price of marijuana to fall to an amount close to the cost of production. Doing so, however, will mean a substantially smaller tax revenue than currently anticipated from this change in policy (Pacula 2009).

Lower price is equated with increased drug use. And, as stated in this testimony to the California State Assembly, "if use increases, known harms will also increase" (Pacula 2009). While opponents of the drug war emphasize the cost of the war, supporters of the war emphasize the cost of legalization.

Increased crime, rising health costs, and other significant costs are all linked to drug policy termination. This framing of the end of the drug war clearly contributes to significant fear and uncertainty. This fear manifests itself in public opinion. A review of Gallup Opinion Poll data (see figure 2) reveals concern about the severity of the drug problems in the United States, although less concern about drug problems within people's own locale is indicated (where you could anticipate that respondents have first-hand information). This suggests that framing of the situation by others is shaping views of the drug war.

The policy termination process model (see figure 3) readily explains the failure of efforts to terminate the drug war. For many, the flaws of the drug war are clear; at a minimum, the failure to achieve its goals after almost four decades calls for policy change. The investigation into the policy termination process highlights that policy termination is a political act rather than a rational policy decision. The political factors—at present—are weighed against policy termination.

Conclusion: So What?

The drug war is expensive, damaging, and ineffective. Yet, as both Behn (1978) and DeLeon (1987) noted, arguments about economics and efficiency are not sufficient to result in termination. Apparently, failure is not sufficient either. This analysis suggests that understanding the causes of the drug war persistence is essential for the design of a victorious termination strategy. What can be done?

The analysis of the drug war policy termination process highlights the role that opinion about drugs, drug use, and the consequences of policy termination are central to the drug war's persistence. In terms of prospect theory, drug war framing is the crucial element. There is presently a low probability of policy termination; the public and politicians prefer the status quo to the risks of policy termination. However, if domain perceptions can be altered, the prospects for termination grow stronger. Policy termination entails risk; the future is an unknown while the present is not. If pursuit of the present course were presented as leading to sure loss (in prospect theory terms, shifting perceptions to the loss domain), then people would become more risk acceptant. Another method would be to offer an alternative policy as a "sure bet." The result would be to place perceptions of policy change into the gains domain. Again, this would lead to greater support for policy change.

How can proponents of policy termination change public perception? Prospect theory experiments review that language is central. Highlighting prospective gains (for example, emphasis on tax revenue to be generated by policy termination) while emphasizing current losses (for example, persistent failure to achieve goals) could prove to be effective.

The policy termination process analysis also suggests reasons for the success of medical marijuana legislation. Technically, medical marijuana laws require policy termination (ending the status of marijuana as a Schedule 1 drug—a drug without medical use). In practical terms, medical marijuana movements have presented themselves as new policy, thus avoiding some of the problems that arise from policy termination. The framing of the issue makes the public and politicians more risk acceptant. Currently, without medical marijuana, people are suffering (a certain loss); the adoption of medical marijuana should help these people (risky). Prospect theory has consistently found that people are more risk acceptant in loss domains (situations of certain loss with maintenance of status quo). The ONDCP efforts to counter medical marijuana (arguments that it will increase youth drug use and drug-related violence; it is ineffective) have not proven effective. The ONDCP is highlighting the risks of change; its failures to understand that the current debate is framed in such a way that participants are more risk acceptant than in other circumstances.

To move toward complete drug war policy termination, the terms of the debate need to be reframed. When the public and politicians become more risk acceptant, support for the status quo will evaporate.

References

Behn, Robert D. 1978. "Closing a Government Facility" *Public Administration Review* 38 (4): 332–38.

Bothun, Douglas, and John C. Comer. 1979. "The Politics of Termination: Concepts and Process" *Policy Studies Journal* 7 (3): 540–53.

Brewer, Garry D. 1978. "Termination: Hard Choices-Harder Questions" *Public Administration Review* 38 (4): 338–44.

Daniels, Mark R. 1997. *Terminating Public Programs: An American Political Paradox.* London: M.E. Sharpe.

DeLeon, Peter. 1987. "Policy Termination as a Political Phenomena." In *The Politics of Policy Evaluation,* ed. Dennis J. Palumbo. London: Sage.

———. 1983. "Policy Evaluation and Program Termination." *Policy Studies Review* 2 (4): 631–47.

———. 1978. "A Theory of Policy Termination." In *The Policy Cycle,* eds. Judith V. May and Aaron B. Wildavsky, 279–300. London: Sage.

"Excerpts from the President's Message on Drug Abuse Control." 1971. *New York Times,* June 18, 22.

Frantz, Janet E. 1992. "Reviving and Revising a Termination Model" *Policy Sciences* 25: 175–89.

Gallup. 2007. *Little Change in Public's View of the U.S. Drug Problem.* www.gallup.com/poll/102061/little-change-publics-view-us-drug-problem.aspx.

Geva-May, Iris. 2004. "Riding the Wave of Opportunity: Termination in Public Policy." *Journal of Public Administration Research and Theory* 14 (3): 309–33.

Kahneman, Daniel, J. Knetsch, and R. Thaler. 1991. "Anomalies: The Endowment Effect, Loss Aversion, and Status Quo Bias" *Journal of Economic Perspectives* 5 (1): 193–206.

Kahneman, Daniel, and Amos Tversky. 1979. "Prospect Theory: An Analysis of Decision under Risk *Econometrica* 47 (2): 263–91.

Kaufman, Herbert. 1976. *Are Government Organizations Immortal?* Washington, DC: Brookings.

Kerlikowske, Gil. 2009. "Q&A with the New Drug Czar" *The Wall Street Journal,* May 14.

Kirkpatrick, Susan E., James P. Lester, and Mark R. Peterson. 1999. "The Policy Termination Process." *Policy Studies Review* 16 (1): 210–36.

Jervis, Robert. 1992. "Political Implications of Loss Aversion." *Political Psychology, Special Issue: Prospect Theory and Political Psychology* 13 (2): 187–204

Nixon, Richard. 1971a. "Remarks about an Intensified Program for Drug Abuse Prevention and Control," June 17, accessed via The American Presidency Project www.presidency.ucsb.edu/ws/index.php?pid=3047&st=Drug+Abuse&st1=.

———. 1971b. "Special Message to the Congress on Drug Abuse Prevention and Control," June 17, accessed via The American Presidency Project www.presidency.ucsb.edu/ws/index.php?pid=3048&st=drug+abuse&st1=.

Office of National Drug Control Policy. 1997–2010. *The National Drug Control Strategy.* http://ncjrs.gov/App/Publications/alphaList.aspx?alpha=N.

Pacula, Rosalie. 2009. "Legalizing Marijuana: Issues to Consider before Reforming California State Law" *Testimony Before the Committee on Public Safety,* California State Assembly, October 28.

Reagan, Ronald. 1988. "Remarks at a Meeting of the White House Conference for a Drug Free America," February 29, accessed via The American Presidency Project www.presidency.ucsb.edu/ws/index.php?pid=35482&st=drug+war&st1=goals.

———. 1986. "Rational Choice and the Framing of Decisions" *Journal of Business* 59 (4), Part 2, S251–78.

Welch, David A. 2005. *Painful Choices: A Theory of Foreign Policy Change.* Princeton, NJ: Princeton University Press.

Wilson, James Q. 1989. *Bureaucracy: What Government Agencies Do and Why They Do It.* NewYork: Basic Books.

Critical Thinking

1. Why does the war on drugs continue after 40 years?
2. Has the war on drugs been largely successful or unsuccessful?
3. If terminated, what would you replace the war on drugs with?

Renee Scherlen is associate professor in the department of government and justice studies at Appalachian State University in Boone, North Carolina. Dr. Scherlen writes on Latin American politics, U.S. foreign policy, and the drug war. She is the co-author, with Matthew Robinson, of *Lies, Damned Lies, and Drug War Statistics.*

Prison Rips up Families, Tears Apart Entire Communities

JOHN SIMERMAN

For Jaymalis Falls, life has come to this: reluctant homebody, confined to a front-door stoop. He sat there one recent sundown, twisting the dark curls above his forehead and trying to ignore the bulky plastic monitor strapped around a sock on his left ankle. He's been caught 26 times for violating his house arrest, he said. A juvenile judge gave him one last chance.

"I hate it. I can't go anywhere," he said. "They can see through walls. I feel like an animal in this."

A few months ago, the 15-year-old was an elusive figure, disappearing to who knows where, attending school or not. He did what he wanted, and often that meant trouble.

A role in a knife-point robbery over an iPod last year landed him in juvenile detention for a month. Another time, he hopped on a bicycle outside a corner store, rode off and quickly got busted.

The KIPP Central City Academy, which has a mission to shepherd disadvantaged kids from the neighborhood into college, booted him from its rolls.

"He's drifting away to the street life," said his great-aunt and caretaker, Desmond Marie Hyman Davis. "He feels like he can whoop the world. Right now on his mind is money. He wants fast money. I said, 'Not all money is good money.' "

Jaymalis—who goes by "J.J."—is meandering toward a cliff that seems always right around the corner in a neighborhood with one of the highest incarceration rates in New Orleans, in a state that locks up more of its residents, per capita, than any place in the world.

Nearly everyone in his immediate family has served time. Family members and others fear the same, or worse, for him.

Jaymalis and his 13-year-old sister, Semaj, have bounced around among relatives since they were little. Their father was murdered, and their mother admits she's been too strung out on heroin to devote herself to raising her kids. Davis, who juggles a responsibility she didn't seek with a drug habit she can't shake, has considered asking a juvenile court judge to revoke Jaymalis' probation. Sending him away for a while, she thinks, might set him straight.

"I'd rather he go in the system," she said, "than be in jail for the rest of his life or sprawled out dead in the middle of the street."

The yellow shotgun double where Jaymalis sleeps, in a room with barren walls and a bed propped up on cinderblocks, sits just three blocks from the columned mansions and oak canopies of St. Charles Avenue. But it feels miles away.

This is "the belt" of Central City, home to an invisible, grating force—the cycling of its residents in and out of prison—that can fray family and community at their roots.

Around here, young men leave home for prison, not college. No one can afford to buy Jaymalis trendy sneakers, MP3 players, the things kids covet. So before his house arrest, he took to hanging out with friends and taking what was there.

Neighborhoods like this one have been particularly hard-hit as Louisiana's prison population has increased exponentially in the past few decades. Nobody here is a stranger to the ripples emanating from the state's stiff sentences, swollen prison rolls and vacuum of resources for convicts who return home.

While the state spends millions of dollars each year locking up Central City residents, it has invested comparatively little in schools, recreation programs, job centers and health clinics. Boys grow up believing that dealing drugs—a daily trade in the few blocks around Jaymalis—is the surest way to cash. Doing time is an expected price, if not a rite of passage.

Schools like KIPP, which arrived in New Orleans after Hurricane Katrina, offer one of the few clean paths out of the neighborhood's crime-pocked streets. As he sits on the stoop, pondering an ill-defined future as a famous rap artist, Jaymalis may already have squandered his best chance.

Police Sweeps

Outside the Uptown Meat Market at Seventh and Danneel streets, drug dealers sling their wares while school-aged kids shoot hoops on a lone, netless rim parked near the curb.

Police swept up several of Ralph Martin's friends about a year ago, the dreadlocked 18-year-old said. Now those buddies are in prison.

"See what we doin' now, lookin' bored? That's how it affects the neighborhood," Martin said of the constant jailings. "They handpick the people they want."

Asked why police busted his friends, he said: "For what else? Stuff that goes on in the neighborhood."

Tameka Franklin, a grandmother at 40, sat on the porch of a model house with solar panels chatting with Martin. Her son, Martin's close friend, is doing two-and-a-half years at Hunt Correctional Center on a marijuana rap.

"Last year they put it on him," Franklin said. "He says it's a place nobody wants to be."

It seems everyone in this neighborhood has a relative or friend in prison. Many have done time themselves.

Residents here see an element of chance to who lands behind bars and who stays out. Who will the cops pick next? Where are the police sweeps on the tony side of St. Charles?

The 6th District police not long ago put a full-court press on a five-block-by-five-block swath of the neighborhood, "marching like Sherman on every porch, on every stoop," said 6th District Commander Robert Bardy. The goal, Bardy said, was not so much arrests as presence.

Bardy said he sees an alarming number of "shameful" knock-down, drag-out fights among girls in the area—and a core group of kids driving crime in the neighborhood. He receives numerous calls from residents and activists who pinpoint trouble spots.

He said he knows police can't arrest their way out of the problem. But he can't rely on "justice reinvestment"—a concept to redirect millions spent on incarceration into Central City programs that might put kids on a different path. Right now, Bardy said, a malignant subset of youth in the neighborhood still needs arresting.

"They are opportunists," he said. "If they're riding a bike from A to B and see a laptop in a car, it's their laptop."

While drug dealing is prevalent here, it's not the most violent corner of the city, at least not right now. Neighbors note that gunfire has subsided since two murders last year, a week apart.

Steven Powell was shot dead while running through Davis' backyard. Then Kendrick Gibbs, who struggled to hold a dishwashing job despite frequent returns to jail, was killed a block up Sixth Street.

Still, no one would be surprised to witness another shooting. The sparsely populated four-block area of Sixth and Seventh streets between Dryades and Danneel streets was home to 98 NOPD arrests in the past two years, including 60 for drug violations, according to police statistics.

Before Katrina, Central City had 4 percent of the overall population but 8 percent of its imprisoned residents, according to a 2009 study by urban planners from Columbia University.

Mostly spared from Katrina flooding, Central City revived relatively quickly, and so did its crime. Within two years, the area's incarceration rate hit 82 percent of pre-Katrina levels, the study showed.

As Louisiana locks up more people for longer periods, Central City—a neighborhood full of children, nephews, girlfriends and grandparents of the imprisoned—feels the sting.

Growing up Angry

Semaj slips inside the house on Dryades, where a small TV blares the latest episode of "First 48," a reality murder-investigation show.

Lately she's been lashing out—"beaucoup fights," Davis said—and her school attendance is spotty. She often runs away, sometimes for days.

In late February, social workers came to the house with clipboards on two straight days. Davis said she called them herself.

Davis has been prodding the children's mother, Troylynn Falls—whom Davis also took in when she was young—to play a bigger role. The kids, Davis said, don't respect her like they might a real mother.

"I can't control them. I'm ready to give up," she said, bleary-eyed and raspy. At 50, her gaunt face reflects years of struggle with crack addiction. "Most of all, they retaliating out on me. It's tearing out at me, inside and out. I can't move on like this here."

Falls served a 30-month prison sentence for cocaine, got out and still struggles with a heroin addiction. She lives a dozen blocks away, toward the river, and comes by every now and then.

The children's father, James "Roper" Dowell, spent years in and out of jail for drugs and car theft until someone killed him months before Katrina. Semaj, his name spelled backward, never saw much of him. "I just know he was shot," she said.

Falls, who occasionally comes by the house, said the task of raising the kids eludes her. On her chest is a scrawled tattoo of Dowell's middle name, Romalis.

"The way for me to get my motherhood back is to really think: What goes and what don't. They love me, but they don't condone the situation," said Falls, a grandmother at 34 after another daughter had a baby at 16.

Davis' fiancé, Irvin McCoy, is the nearest thing to a male figure around the house. He did more than a decade at Hunt on a burglary charge and now roams the neighborhood on his bicycle, picking up occasional yard work. He says he now keeps to liquor, not drugs.

"I told him how it's real," McCoy said, about telling Jaymalis about the threat of prison. "He doesn't listen."

Davis does some housekeeping and gets $400 a month from the state for the kids' upkeep. McCoy helps with the rent, but it's not enough to give the kids what they want, she said.

Jaymalis and Semaj have never met their grandfather, Davis' brother. He's doing life for murder and rape.

Semaj dangles her lanky legs off the bed and picks at a scab. It's an early spring day and she's wearing the same satin sleep cap and the sweatshirt with the butterfly print that she seems to put on almost every day. Her dark eyes wander the walls.

She wants to be a singer and a model someday, she said. She likes Whitney Houston and sings when she's angry. She sings a lot.

"I don't think 'happy' lives here with me. They're always killing people and stuff," she said. "It's hard living without a mom. I see her. We just say, 'Hi.' Every time it's time for her to try, she don't want to try."

'They Have No Way Out'

Dryades Street runs through the center of an incarceration hotbed framed by LaSalle Street on the lake side, St. Charles on the river side, Toledano Street on the uptown end and First

Street on the downtown end. A few blocks removed from leafy St. Charles, the area turns about 94 percent black.

Fewer than one in six children in the neighborhood live in husband–wife households, according to the 2010 census. Like Jaymalis and Semaj, a quarter are not living with either parent.

More than a third of the homes are empty—some of them crumbling shells draped with vegetation—even as new homes and apartment houses rise among them.

The story of the neighborhood is a fairly typical American tale of descent into urban poverty and crime.

It has long been a working-class streetscape but also served as a retail hub for black residents from across the city during the Jim Crow era. Shops and churches along the strip of Dryades now called Oretha Castle Haley Boulevard, east of where Jaymalis lives, thrived at mid-century.

By the 1970s, drugs and prostitution had crept in, and the former retail stretch is now largely occupied by storefront churches, empty windows and bootstrap social services agencies. Attempts to revive it have been halting at best.

In 2009, a group of Columbia University planners found that Central City contains some of the highest incarceration levels, and costs, in the city.

While precise neighborhood-level statistics on incarceration are unavailable, the area's residents are overwhelmingly poor and black. Data show that one in 14 black men from New Orleans is behind bars, compared with one in 141 white men. One in seven black men from the city is either in prison, on probation or on parole. Those rates are substantially higher in depressed areas like Central City.

Several of the apartment houses in the neighborhood where Jaymalis lives are occupied largely by ex-convicts and parolees. Many of them are jobless or lightly employed. They hang out at midday playing dominoes or gather in the morning to drink and swap stories on stoops.

Patricia Farve grew up here and has watched the decline. She serves as a mentor for Jaymalis in a church program for children with incarcerated parents.

"We've had doctors, lawyers, Indian chiefs come out of this neighborhood. The Mardi Gras flavor was in the neighborhood. Anybody could parent you, tell you to get back in that house," said Farve, 53, a licensed child-care provider. "Now you've got churches and barrooms. What's going on? Churches, barrooms and corner stores. And we're not talking fruits and vegetables. It's not a Winn-Dixie or a Walmart."

It's an environment, some say, that breeds nearsightedness, a "see it, take it" mentality: Better to sling drugs than work a fast-food counter for minimum wage.

"They have no way out, and it becomes a hopelessness that permeates these communities because there has been, 'Go to this job training,' and there are no jobs," said Phyllis Cassidy of the Good Work Network, which runs an incubator program in Central City for budding minority business owners.

Compounding the problem is a disturbing indifference at the prospect of prison. Incarceration, for some, has become an expected fate.

"It's hard out here, and it's hard in there," said Brandon Washington, who said he spent a year in the Orleans Parish jail on a drug charge but would rather have done time in a state prison like Hunt. "In state, you get better treatment. You get to go outside."

Washington was hanging out on Seventh Street one recent afternoon with a group of a half-dozen friends. All said they had spent time behind bars.

None of them wanted back in, but none seemed to particularly fear it. "That's a place of longings. I don't want to go back, but I'm not scared," said one woman who just got out after three years in state prison.

In and Out of Trouble

Jaymalis doesn't worry about a life behind bars. It's just not for him, he said. Not now, and not in five years. He has a music career in his future and may want to attend Harvard University, he said.

Lean, with reddish-brown dye fading from his dark hair, Jaymalis has a lithe, 5-foot-7-inch frame and soft eyes that make him seem younger than his 15 years, with a quiet sureness that doesn't. He would rather not talk about his parents, or himself for that matter. But his time on home confinement has given him a chance to think, he said.

"I be making some crazy decisions," he said. "I know how to stay out of trouble. I just can't wait 'til all this is over and I be famous, be a rapper."

Last year, he spent several weeks in juvenile detention. "I didn't want to be there, but it was all right," Jaymalis said. "I had a couple of fights."

KIPP Central City, which Jaymalis attended before his expulsion, is part of a national charter school network specializing in delivering kids from poverty to college.

Principal Todd Purvis said he recruits heavily in the neighborhood, which is home to about 40 percent of its students. All of the 800 students at the school are black, and nearly every one qualifies for a free lunch.

"One of the things we work with kids on is, you need to bring your A-game to school. There's an opportunity to break the cycle here," said Purvis, who would not discuss Jaymalis' removal.

Still, just a few weeks ago, a 15-year-old girl and boy who had gone to another KIPP college prep school both were slain by gunfire. Jaymalis said he and the boy, Brandon Adams, were close friends.

"I figure if those people are getting killed, I gotta watch my back," Jaymalis said. "Don't know who's looking at me. People's dropping like flies. Imagine when summer hits."

Since he left KIPP, Jaymalis has attended a ReNew charter school in Algiers for teenagers at risk of dropping out. He claims the work is easy, although a recent report card was peppered with failing grades. He says he's moving to a different school now, in Jefferson Parish. "I think they want to see if my attitude will change," he said.

Farve, Jaymalis' mentor, laments the lost opportunity of KIPP's rigorous education. "That was a golden ticket. You had a ticket to go to college, and you threw that away," she said.

"This didn't just happen yesterday. He never had a break. They never had a break. He's been thrown to the aunt, thrown here, thrown there. At the end of the day, you have to have some power over your own destiny."

Fathers Locked Up

The number of children who are growing up with one or both parents behind bars has multiplied nationwide along with the incarceration rate. According to one estimate, the total has increased sevenfold in the past two decades. More than 1.7 million children in the United States now have at least one parent in state or federal prison.

According to studies, these children exhibit telltale behavior: aggression, defiance, disobedience, school problems, emotional withdrawal, anger and hostility toward caregivers.

The Rev. Patrick Keen, pastor of Bethlehem Lutheran in Central City, said he knows about a dozen people currently serving time. Almost all have children.

Keen's church runs a mentoring program for children with parents in prison. Jaymalis met Farve there. Mentors organize weekly excursions to the park, the movies, Zephyrs baseball games—anywhere away from the neighborhood.

Like Jaymalis, many of the kids in the program have already come face to face with the law. Keen said success comes in small doses of respect.

"They're challenging their caregivers. They're challenging society. They're reacting, and they have a right to react. It takes on psycho-social ramifications that we have not begun to wrestle with," Keen said.

The troubles do not end after a parent is released from prison. Federal rules prohibit felons from living in government-subsidized housing and from getting food stamps.

With few job prospects and sometimes hefty child support bills, convicts often return on the outs with family, said Ernest Johnson with Families and Friends of Louisiana's Incarcerated Children, not far away on Oretha Castle Haley.

Johnson spent eight years in prison for various offenses. His son is now behind bars awaiting trial for an alleged murder committed when he was 14.

"If you were sustaining a family, and I were to take you for six months or 20 years, it doesn't matter. Six months, you done broke up my family," Johnson said. "Everybody in that house has to carry that burden."

A Kid at a Crossroads

Jaymalis sat on the stoop and shrugged. "I'd like to move out of here. Too much killing," he said.

He likes to play hoops nearby. Now, with the ankle bracelet, he can't do much of anything. He recently had a job painting trim on houses in the neighborhood, he said, but the work meant repeatedly breaking his curfew restrictions and sparked another visit to a juvenile judge.

With his movements restricted to the front stoop and inside the house, Davis said she sees a turnaround. Farve, his mentor, sees a kid at a crossroads, toggling like so many others between promise and prison.

Others wonder whether Jaymalis and Semaj can withstand all the trouble on Dryades. Laquwanda Dowell, an aunt, sometimes falls into the past tense when talking about them.

"They're so far gone. They're allowed to do whatever they want to do, and they don't have to answer to anybody. If they were in a stable home with more discipline, it would have been fine," she said. "[Jaymalis] is kind of falling in the street because he needs things. He wants clothes or whatever. If he's doing it, it's to survive."

Critical Thinking

1. How does Jaymalis Falls see his future?
2. Is he likely to reach his goals?
3. Why would a mother ask the court to revoke her son's probation?
4. Could life be better for the kids in "the belt"?

If Convicted Felons Could Vote . . .

. . . They might decide the presidential election. A new report says a record 5.85 million felons are disenfranchised, twice the number some say the election could come down to.

Eliza Shapiro

A record 5.85 million convicted felons aren't allowed to vote, according to a report out today (PDF) by The Sentencing Project, a criminal justice research and advocacy group. That's about 500,000 more than were disenfranchised in 2004—and potentially enough to decide this year's tightly contested presidential election.

By some estimates, the election could be decided by a margin of roughly two points, or a mere 2.5 million people. The disenfranchised felon voting block is "absolutely enough" to swing an election, says Sasha Abramsky, author of *Conned: How Millions Went to Prison, Lost the Vote and Helped Send George W. Bush to the White House.*

Consider the case of the hanging chads and butterfly ballots in Florida in 2000. Florida's laws preventing convicted felons from voting meant that some 750,000 people, including those still in prison, on probation or parole, didn't get a say in who would be president. Since the election was decided by 537 votes, Abramsky estimates that if just 1 percent of the disenfranchised felon population had voted, 60 percent to 40 percent for Al Gore over George W. Bush, Gore would have won. These are conservative estimates, considering the limited research on voting habits of former and current felons has shown that they swing Democratic. Still, "no one wants to gun for the felon vote," Abramsky says.

The latest numbers on felon disenfranchisement are a crucial piece of a larger debate over voting rights this election cycle. Laws restricting voting are making headlines for the first time in years as states like Florida and Pennsylvania adopt tougher voter identification laws. Voting rights advocates are calling the moves "voting purges" designed to benefit Republican candidates because the bulk of people who would be effectively disenfranchised are Democrat-leaning African-Americans and Latinos. Last month, Pennsylvania House Majority Leader Mike Turzai said that the state's new voter ID laws are "gonna allow Governor Romney to win the state of Pennsylvania."

Laws that keep felons and others away from the polls "have their roots in Jim Crow laws, and were passed along with relics like literacy tests and poll taxes," says Lee Rowland, counsel for the NYU Brennan Center for Justice Democracy Program. This week, Eric Holder called Texas' new voter ID law, which requires people to show an ID every time they vote, rather than do a one-time registration, a "poll tax" in an address at the NAACP national convention.

Felon Disenfranchisement Report Shapiro

Statistics show that felon disenfranchisement disproportionately affect African-Americans, with 7.7 percent of the total African-American population denied the vote as a result, according to the Sentencing Project. That's 1 out of every 13 black Americans. Rowland says stricter felon disenfranchisement laws are often made as "political calculations" that "skew the electorate."

Four million of the 5.85 million disenfranchised are currently out of prison, some on probation and parole. "The murderer behind bars," waiting to cast his vote, "is an atypical case," says Christopher Uggen, professor of sociology at the University of Minnesota and lead author of the Sentencing Project report. The group's director, Marc Mauer, estimates that half of the convicted felons in prison are serving time for a violent offense and the other half for a property or drug crime.

Felon disenfranchisement varies widely between states. On one end of the spectrum, Maine and Vermont don't link voting rights to criminal records. On the other end, Iowa, Florida, Virginia and Kentucky have laws permanently disenfranchising anyone who has been convicted of a felony unless approved on an individual basis by the state government. After the 2010 interim elections, Florida and Iowa's newly elected Republican Governors, Rick Scott and Terry E. Branstad, toughened felon disenfranchisement laws within their first years in office. Scott reversed former Florida governor Charlie Christ's 2007 procedures restoring voting rights to ex-felons and instituted a minimum five-year waiting law before former felons can begin the process of regaining their vote in Florida.

Laws that keep felons and others away from the polls "have their roots in Jim Crow laws."

The report shows that in Alabama, Florida, Kentucky, Mississippi, Virginia and Tennessee, over 7 percent of the adult population is disenfranchised. In Florida, Kentucky and Virginia, more than one in five African-Americans is disenfranchised.

Ex-felons returning from prison struggle to re-enter society when they are stripped of their rights, says Ann Jacobs, the director of John Jay College of Criminal Justice's Prisoner Reentry Institute. "Felony convictions become a life sentence. 'If you do the crime, you do the time' is misleading . . . an ex-felon is forever running into these barriers about voting, housing, and employment that in many cases relate to the worst thing they ever did at some point prior in their lives."

Former felons who have struggled to regain their voting privileges said the process is exhausting and demoralizing. Desmond Meade, a second-year law student at Florida International University College of Law, another ex-felon, says he has been applying for his voting rights—unsuccessfully—since 2006. Even as a law student, he cannot sit for the Florida bar exam.

Pastor Kenneth Glasgow spent fourteen years in an Alabama prison for the possession and sale of crack cocaine. He became a pastor when he was released from prison in 2001. He says he spent three years trying to regain his voting rights. He studied the Alabama State Constitution and cited clauses that possession—rather than sale—of an illegal substance doesn't legally result in the loss of the vote. When he finally got the vote in 2004, he tied a string around his voter registration card and wore it around his neck.

Critical Thinking

1. What, if anything, is wrong with denying the vote to convicted felons?
2. Are there political consequences to disenfranchising ex-cons?

After 9/11, A New Era in the Business of Detaining Immigrants

CHRIS KIRKHAM

"It is clear that since Sept. 11, there's a heightened focus on detention, both on the borders and in the U.S.," Logan, the chief executive of publicly traded prison corporation Cornell Companies, told analysts on a quarterly earnings call. "More people are gonna get caught. . . . So I would say that's positive."

Logan's upbeat assessment of the post-9/11 world would prove true, as the federal government has embarked on an unprecedented campaign to round up, detain and eventually deport illegal immigrants under the guise of bolstering national security. Since Congress brought immigration enforcement under the Department of Homeland Security in 2003, the number of immigrants locked up each year has nearly doubled to more than 390,000, creating a lucrative opportunity for private corporations hired to build and supervise detention centers across the country.

Particularly in the latter half of the Bush administration's tenure, Congress appropriated ever-increasing amounts of federal money toward immigration detention efforts within the Department of Homeland Security—a move that has led private prison executives on a massive buildout, adding beds to increase revenues. Between 2005 and 2010 alone, the amount of money appropriated for immigrant detention and removal more than doubled, from $1.2 billion to more than $2.5 billion.

"There has always been a fear of immigrants, and Sept. 11 really magnified that fear, and allowed fears that were always there to come to the surface," said Alina Das, a supervising attorney at the Immigrant Rights Clinic at New York University's School of Law. "It becomes the drive for numbers: Numbers to prove that the government is doing something about an issue that the public has come to believe is tied to national security and safety."

By 2009, nearly half of all immigrants detained by the federal government were in facilities managed by outsourced private contractors, according to a recent analysis of federal data by advocacy group Detention Watch Network. The growth of private industry tied exclusively to government policy has also led to an extensive federal lobbying campaign, and raised questions about the quality of services provided by businesses seeking returns for investors.

Over time, local and state law enforcement agencies have also been brought into the fold, entering into agreements the Immigration and Customs Enforcement agency to seek out immigration violators independently. Yet while government rhetoric has focused on detaining and deporting immigrants as a means to ensure public safety, the majority of those detained from 2005 through 2009 had no criminal convictions, according to data compiled by the Transactional Records Access Clearinghouse at Syracuse University.

Companies such as Corrections Corporation of America and the GEO Group Inc., which are publicly traded on Wall Street, have come to rely on immigration detention contracts with the federal government as a growing source of revenues over the past decade. According to filings with the Securities and Exchange Commission, the GEO Group's contracts with the Immigration and Customs Enforcement agency grew in value from $33.6 million in 2005 to $163.8 million by the end of 2010.

Contracts are generally structured around the number of inmates housed in a facility on any given day. In public filings, Corrections Corporation of America measures revenue with a term called a "compensated man-day," representing the revenues and expenses incurred by each inmate on a given day.

Yet critics have argued that the government's hard-line approach toward immigration enforcement, coupled with the profit motive for private prison operators, has turned a civil detention program into something that looks exactly like a prison system for criminals.

In many cases, immigrants are detained at facilities originally built as jails to house criminals. A 2009 inspector general's report from the Department of Homeland Security concluded that "immigration detention and criminal incarceration detainees tend to be seen by the public as comparable, and both confined populations are typically managed in similar ways."

"They don't change their practices for immigration detainees, they just change who they bill," said Brittney Nystrom, director of policy and legal affairs for the National Immigration Forum, an immigrants' rights group. "Immigration detention isn't supposed to be punitive. We're not holding them as incarceration for any criminal offenses they have done. This is really just holding people so that they follow through with their immigration processes."

The 2009 report from the Department of Homeland Security's inspector general also found numerous lapses in the way Immigration and Customs Enforcement oversaw standards at private detention facilities. The immigration agency not only outsourced much of prison operations to the private sector, according to the report, but also hired private contractors to do annual inspections and on-site monitoring.

In a particularly shocking revelation in 2009, the Department of Homeland Security admitted that it had miscounted the number of deaths in its detention facilities, acknowledging that there were 104 deaths—10 more deaths than previously reported—between 2003 and 2009 after a suit from the American Civil Liberties Union.

Among other findings over the years: the Homeland Security inspector general discovered in a survey of detention facilities that 20 percent of detainees did not receive a physical medical examination within 14 days, as required by government health standards.

Access to adequate medical care and supervision has been at the center of numerous legal disputes involving privately run immigration detention centers. The American Civil Liberties Union filed a lawsuit in 2007 against the San Diego Correctional Facility, operated by Corrections Corporation of America, documenting how numerous detainees were denied access to medical care for months.

The lawsuit came in response to the case of Francisco Castaneda, who complained from March 2006 to February 2007 of severe pain and bleeding from his groin. He received no medical care for nearly a year until a urologist eventually determined that he had penile cancer. After being released from detention, his penis was amputated in 2007, but he died a year later as the cancer continued to spread.

A spokesman for Corrections Corporation of America, Steve Owen, told *The Huffington Post* that the company could not comment on specific cases, but wrote, "We take the care of every detainee in our care very seriously, and CCA has complied with all required reporting of incidents and detainee deaths to our government partner agencies."

The Obama administration pledged in August 2009 to drastically overhaul the immigrant detention system, shutting down certain facilities and agreeing to provide much more oversight by the immigration agency itself. But the administration is also aggressively pushing ahead with the Secure Communities program, which cross-references the fingerprints of anyone booked into local jails with immigration violation data held by the Department of Homeland Security.

Cori Bassett, a spokeswoman for Immigration and Customs Enforcement, pointed out that the agency is determined to "focus its resources on detaining and removing aliens who pose the greatest risk to our communities. This includes using discretion when making decisions for those aliens who don't pose the greatest risk."

Given that the private prison industry is highly dependent on contracts with the federal government to maintain prisons and detention centers, companies have lobbied Washington extensively in recent years. Statements from the companies' annual filings with the SEC make it clear that immigration policy is deeply intertwined with the bottom line.

"The President recently signed the Homeland Security Appropriations Bill into law, which included an 11 percent increase for U.S. Customs and Border Protection, adding more border patrol agents and funding for detention beds," Corrections Corporation of America noted in a 2005 filing. "We believe these initiatives could lead to meaningful growth to the private corrections industry in general, and to our company in particular."

Since 2001, the amount of lobbying by the for-profit prison industry has skyrocketed.

Corrections Corporation of America bumped its lobbying expenditures more than sevenfold between 2001 and 2005, from $470,000 to nearly $3.4 million. The GEO Group increased federal lobbying spending from $120,000 in 2004 to $660,000 in 2010.

Corrections Corporation of America's Owen wrote in a statement to *HuffPost* that the company's lobbying efforts are "exclusively dedicated to educating decision makers and have escalated as the company's presence has continued to expand nationally into more than half of all states and a dozen municipalities. . . . The goals of our lobbying efforts have not changed over the years or as a result of 9/11."

A spokesman for the GEO Group said the company declined to comment.

National Public Radio further documented the connections between immigration policy and the private prison industry in a piece last fall, noting that representatives of Corrections Corporation of America were present during the drafting of Arizona's controversial immigration law, which gave law enforcement officers wide discretion to determine a person's legal status as a citizen during routine traffic stops or arrests.

A spokesman for Corrections Corporation of America said the company disputes the NPR piece, and has a policy "not to engage in legislation involving crime or sentencing policies."

With the Obama administration's continued focus on immigration enforcement through the Secure Communities program, observers have questioned whether the detention system's expansion is likely to slow any time soon.

"By and large it's very difficult for people to stand up and say, 'We're spending too much money on something that's harming people's lives, and really isn't making us that much safer,'" said Bob Libal, a senior organizer with Grassroots Leadership, an advocacy group that has followed the rise of for-profit prisons and the detention system. "You're defined as being against homeland security somehow."

Critical Thinking

1. How did 9/11 benefit the private prison industry?
2. Do you agree that immigration violators should be treated as criminals?
3. What are some findings of the 2009 DHS inspector general's report?

Acknowledgements—The article was updated to reflect Corrections Corporation of America's disagreement with an NPR piece linking the company to the drafting of Arizona's immigration law.

Article 6

No Cause for Marijuana Case, but Enough for Child Neglect

Mosi Secret

The police found about 10 grams of marijuana, or about a third of an ounce, when they searched Penelope Harris's apartment in the Bronx last year. The amount was below the legal threshold for even a misdemeanor, and prosecutors declined to charge her. But Ms. Harris, a mother whose son and niece were home when she was briefly in custody, could hardly rest easy.

The police had reported her arrest to the state's child welfare hot line, and city caseworkers quickly arrived and took the children away.

Her son, then 10, spent more than a week in foster care. Her niece, who was 8 and living with her as a foster child, was placed in another home and not returned by the foster care agency for more than a year. Ms. Harris, 31, had to weather a lengthy child neglect inquiry, though she had no criminal record and had never before been investigated by the child welfare authorities, Ms. Harris and her lawyer said.

"I felt like less of a parent, like I had failed my children," Ms. Harris said. "It tore me up."

Hundreds of New Yorkers who have been caught with small amounts of marijuana, or who have simply admitted to using it, have become ensnared in civil child neglect cases in recent years, though they did not face even the least of criminal charges, according to city records and defense lawyers. A small number of parents in these cases have even lost custody of their children.

New York City's child welfare agency said that it was pursuing these cases for appropriate reasons, and that marijuana use by parents could often hint at other serious problems in the way they cared for their children.

As states and localities around the country loosen penalties for marijuana, for both recreational and medical uses, they are increasingly grappling with how to handle its presence in homes with children. California, where the medical marijuana movement has flourished, now requires that child welfare officials demonstrate actual harm to a child from marijuana use in order to bring neglect cases, and defense lawyers there say the authorities are now bringing fewer of them.

But in New York, the child welfare agency has not shied from these cases. For these parents, the child welfare system has become an alternate system of justice, with legal standards on marijuana that appear to be tougher than those of criminal courts or, to some extent, of society at large. In interviews, lawyers from the three legal services groups that the city hires to defend parents said they saw hundreds of marijuana cases each year, most involving recreational users.

The lawyers said they currently had more than a dozen cases on their dockets involving parents who had never faced neglect allegations and whose children were placed in foster care because of marijuana allegations.

Lauren Shapiro, director of the Brooklyn Family Defense Project, which defends most parents facing neglect charges in Family Court in Brooklyn, said more than 90 percent of the cases alleging drug use that her lawyers handle involve marijuana, as opposed to other drugs.

"There is not the same use of crack cocaine as there used to be, so they are filing these cases instead," Ms. Shapiro said.

Marijuana is the most common illicit drug in New York City: 730,000 people, or 12 percent of people age 12 and older, use the drug at least once annually, according to city health data.

Over all, the rate of marijuana use among whites is twice as high as among blacks and Hispanics in the city, the data show, but defense lawyers said these cases were rarely if ever filed against white parents.

Michael Fagan, a spokesman for the Administration for Children's Services, said the defense lawyers were offering a simplistic portrayal of these cases.

"Drug use itself is not child abuse or neglect, but it can put children in danger of neglect or abuse," Mr. Fagan said. "We think the argument that use of cocaine, heroin or marijuana by a parent of young children should not be looked into or should simply be ignored is just plain wrong."

Mr. Fagan said most of the cases involved additional forms of neglect, like a child who is not going to school or who has been left unattended.

"In other times, we find that admitted marijuana use masks other substance abuse," Mr. Fagan said.

But lawyers for parents countered that the agency often brought neglect charges based solely on recreational marijuana use, then searched later for other grounds to bolster cases.

"In some cases, there are other allegations, but we think they are add-ons," said Susan Jacobs, executive director of the Center for Family Representation, which works in Manhattan and Queens. "The reason the person is being brought into Family Court is the marijuana use."

Ms. Jacobs cited the case of a former client, Jose Gunnell, 23, of Harlem, who lost custody of his 1-year-old daughter in March after an employee at a homeless shelter where he was staying found a $5 bag of marijuana in his room during an inspection.

Mr. Gunnell said in an interview that he stopped smoking marijuana in 2010 but that he used it again in March after having an infected tooth pulled. "The wound wouldn't close," he said. "I was getting hungry, but I couldn't eat. I bought weed."

The neglect petition that the Administration for Children's Services filed against Mr. Gunnell shows that he admitted to smoking marijuana to develop an appetite.

The agency's petition also said that his daughter did not always have adequate clothing, that shelter workers once smelled alcohol on Mr. Gunnell's breath and that his room was dirty and had an odor.

The agency would not comment on Mr. Gunnell's case or on others described by defense lawyers, citing confidentiality rules.

Ms. Jacobs acknowledged that the Administration for Children's Services might at times correctly determine that marijuana use was one of many serious problems in a family, but she contended that those were only a minority of the cases.

State law makes possession of as much as 25 grams of marijuana—enough for 20 or 30 marijuana cigarettes—a violation similar to a traffic offense, punishable by a fine of up to $100. The Administration for Children's Services does not track the number of parents facing marijuana allegations. It compiles statistics only on the total number of neglect cases for drugs and alcohol, rather than for individual drugs. There were 4,891 such cases in 2010.

State law considers a child neglected if his or her well-being is threatened by a parent who "repeatedly misuses" a drug. But the law does not distinguish marijuana from heroin or other drugs. The law says that if parents have "substantial impairment of judgment," then there is a presumption of neglect, but it does not refer to quantities of drugs.

Furthermore, the law does not require child welfare authorities to catch parents while they are high or with drugs in their possession. Simply admitting past use to a caseworker is grounds for a neglect case.

In marijuana cases, as in all others, caseworkers have the obligation to remove children who they believe are in imminent danger, but they can recommend that the agency file neglect charges against the parents without removing the children. They can also close cases for unsubstantiated allegations.

Neglect findings, while sometimes allowing parents to keep their children, can have serious repercussions. They prohibit parents from taking jobs around children, like driving a school bus or working in day care, or from being foster care parents or adopting. And they make it easier for Family Court judges to later remove children from their homes.

The findings stay on parents' records with the Statewide Central Register until their youngest child turns 28.

The policy of the Administration for Children's Services to pursue marijuana cases is not widely known. But when told of it, some lawmakers said the agency was overstepping its authority.

"I would hope that A.C.S., knowing what a wide-net strategy the N.Y.P.D. is using, would treat marijuana arrests with a grain of salt," said Brad Lander, a Democratic city councilman from Brooklyn. "A neglect charge should not be leveled."

Ms. Harris, the woman briefly held in custody in the Bronx, said the police had searched her apartment because they believed drugs were being sold there, an allegation that she denied. She said the small bags of marijuana the police found belonged to her boyfriend and were for his personal use. She tested negative for drugs after she was released.

The Administration for Children's Services filed neglect charges about a week after Bronx prosecutors declined to press charges. Ms. Harris was represented by the Bronx Defenders, a nonprofit organization that provides legal assistance to Bronx residents.

In a hearing the next day, the agency agreed to return Ms. Harris's son on the condition that her boyfriend not return to the home, that she enroll in therapy and submit to random drug screenings, and that caseworkers could make announced and unannounced visits to her home. Ms. Harris's case was closed in April without a finding of neglect.

Critical Thinking

1. In general, is it in the best interest of children if their parents are investigated for child neglect for possessing small amounts of marijuana?
2. What is the logic behind New York's child welfare agency's pursuit of such cases?
3. What are the ramifications of a finding of neglect?

Band's Culture of Hazing Flourished at Florida A&M

DAVID BREEN

The culture of hazing is so embedded in the fabric of the Florida A&M Marching 100, investigative records show, that the band adopted a language known not just by current and former band members, but even kids in high school aspiring to join the famous ensemble.

In the thousands of pages of investigative documents released by Orange County prosecutors last week in the hazing death of drum major Robert Champion, witness statements were laced with terms such as "Crossing Bus C," the "Hot Seat" and "Crash Position."

These terms were as familiar to Florida A&M's young musicians as the chromatic scale.

University administrators—including the recently retired band director, Julian White—insist they've been battling hazing by holding workshops and punishing members with suspension or expulsion who have been caught participating in the ritual.

Despite those efforts, though, the culture flourished.

The mind-set of some band members was captured vividly when Orange County sheriff's detective Vance Voyles found himself lecturing a witness who said he had undergone hazing because he had hoped to be a leader in the band.

"A leader doesn't condone cr—like this," Voyles snaps at the young witness, captured in an interview transcript. "You shouldn't have to get beat down to play in a band. You shouldn't have to get beat down to do anything unless you're in prison, okay? That's prison warfare.

". . . You're representing the school. And if you want to be a leader, you stop that from happening. That's how you be a leader."

The detective then talked about the mind-set of the percussion section of the band: "Everybody but percussion is going to get it worse because you're not part of the gang. Gang being the operative word here."

White has defended his actions while band director, pointing to the anti-hazing pledges, workshops and suspensions. But it's clear that while individual incidents may have been punished, the underlying culture remained in place.

In White's own words to criminal investigators after Champion's death, it was a culture that was foreign to him.

During his witness interview, White recounted a conversation with one of the band's drum majors the night of Champion's death.

The distraught drum major told him: "It's a Bus C ritual that if you want to be respected by Bus C, which is a majority of the percussion players, you gotta go through this initiation."

White then recalled saying: "What is the, uh, initiation about?" And the young band member replies:

"Well you have to run from the front of the bus to the back of the bus and when you do that they, uh, hit you, kick you."

White responds: "With paddles?"

"No, they just, it's fist, fist, and so you got to get through from the front to the back."

Later, White says to the investigator: "This 'Bus C' thing was a shock to me. I had never heard of it before."

How could such a violent culture thrive, year after year, without the knowledge of university leaders?

It couldn't, according to current and former students and band members. Documents from the Champion investigation paint band administrators as less than eager to root it out.

Band member Marcus Fabre wanted no part of hazing rituals and paid a price for it. He told investigators: "Upperclassmen told the freshmen not to listen to me. Not to respect me because I didn't go through the initiation . . . you have to have self-esteem to do what I did."

Fabre said he told assistant director of bands Shelby Chipman that trouble was brewing between himself and a drummer who rode Bus C, where Champion was later fatally beaten.

"If I ride that bus (Bus C) there's gonna be a problem," he recounted telling Chipman. ". . . Dr. White said he was going to handle it, but he kind of brushed it off, cause it was homecoming."

In interviews with the *Orlando Sentinel,* former Florida A&M University students told similar stories of physical violence and official indifference—or worse—going back years before Champion's death.

Peter McKay was editor of the school paper. He graduated in 1997.

"There are certain details that I guess it's plausible they don't know," he said of administrators. "But the idea that they don't know the broad arc of the problem is not plausible. It's just not true. They knew."

University President James Ammons and White were both at the school during this time, McKay pointed out, then serving as provost and associate band director, respectively.

The culture of hazing in the band "was an open secret on campus even when I was in school," McKay said.

Lawrence Patrick, McKay's roommate at school, grew up in Michigan wanting to be a member of the Marching 100. The prevalence of hazing—and the tacit complicity of the band's directors—came as a shock to him when he arrived on campus in 1993, he said.

It was well known even then, Patrick said, that "on Bus C the band director is not going to protect you."

"If you were on Bus C, the chaperon didn't matter," Patrick said. "The chaperon knew the reputation of Bus C, and they weren't going to do anything, no matter who the chaperon was. It was like the cool kids' bus because everything goes."

Critical Thinking

1. Why would a college student submit to beatings by other students? Would you?
2. Could the school have done anything that might have prevented Robert Champion's death?
3. Did the school paper have any moral or ethical obligation to publicize and take an editorial stand on hazing?

UNIT 2

Victimology

Unit Selections

8. **Telling the Truth about Damned Lies and Statistics,** Joel Best
9. **When a Hazing Goes Very Wrong,** Michael Winerip
10. **The Face of Domestic Violence,** Amanda White, as told to Sarah Elizabeth Richards
11. **Sexual Violence and the Military,** *The New York Times* Editorial
12. **Forensic Interviewing Aids: Do Props Help Children Answer Questions about Touching?,** Debra Ann Poole, Maggie Bruck, Margaret-Ellen Pipe
13. **Human Sex Trafficking,** Amanda Walker-Rodriguez, JD and Rodney Hill, JD
14. **Could the Penn State Abuse Scandal Happen Somewhere Else? Definitely,** Patrick Hruby

Learning Outcomes

After reading this unit, you will be able to:

- Evaluate statistics more critically.
- Explain how hazing can constitute criminal activity.
- Understand how the sexual abuse of students could continue for years at Penn State.
- Outline the scope of human sex trafficking.
- Describe how victims are recruited into the business of human sex trafficking.

Student Website

www.mhhe.com/cls

Internet References

National Crime Victim's Research and Treatment Center (NCVC)
www.musc.edu/cvc

Office for Victims of Crime (OVC)
www.ojp.usdoj.gov/ovc

For many years, crime victims were not considered an important topic for criminological study. Now, however, criminologists consider that focusing on victims and victimization is essential to understand the phenomenon of crime. The popularity of this area of study can be attributed to the early work of Hans Von Hentig and the later work of Stephen Schafer. These writers were the first to assert that crime victims play an integral role in the criminal event, that their actions may actually precipitate crime, and that unless the victim's role is considered, the study of crime is not complete.

In recent years, a growing number of criminologists have devoted increasing attention to the victim's role in the criminal justice process. Generally, areas of particular interest include establishing probabilities of victimization risks, studying victim precipitation of crime and culpability, and designing services expressly for victims of crime. As more criminologists focus their attention on the victim's role in the criminal process, victimology will take on even greater importance.

This unit provides a sharp focus on several key issues. The lead article "Telling the Truth about Damned Lies and Statistics" by Joel Best discusses the need for good statistics in order to talk sensibly about social problems. That is followed by "When a Hazing Goes Very Wrong," an article in which Michael Winerip shows how widespread the culture of hazing is on American campuses. He writes about the death of a student at Cornell; since 1970 there have been at least 104 student deaths.

Amanda White's first-person account of her harrowing experience follows next in "The Face of Domestic Violence." In a *New York Times* editorial, "Sexual Violence and the Military," the Pentagon is criticized for the intolerably high rate of sexual assaults on American women in the military by American men in the military, despite repeated vows of "zero tolerance." The *Times* seems skeptical that the Pentagon can reform itself without some help from Congress.

In "Forensic Interviewing Aids: Do Props Help Children Answer Questions About Touching?," Debra Ann Poole, Maggie Bruck, and Margaret-Ellen Pipe discuss the use of dolls and diagrams when interviewing child victims of sexual abuse. Next,

© Randy Faris/Corbis

"Human Sex Trafficking" by Amanda Walker-Rodriguez and Rodney Hill is about the epidemic of children and teens living on the streets of the United States who are involved in commercial sex activity.

The final article in this section, "Could the Penn State Abuse Scandal Happen Somewhere Else? Definitely," Patrick Hruby interviews the director of a documentary about sexual abuse in sports, Chris Gavagan. Gavagan says that victims are the last priority; the drive to keep it quiet and put it "behind us" is paramount, especially at schools whose pristine reputation is paramount. Rather than making a successful coach go away, the accuser or the accusations are made to go away.

Telling the Truth about Damned Lies and Statistics

JOEL BEST

The dissertation prospectus began by quoting a statistic—a "grabber" meant to capture the reader's attention. The graduate student who wrote this prospectus undoubtedly wanted to seem scholarly to the professors who would read it; they would be supervising the proposed research. And what could be more scholarly than a nice, authoritative statistic, quoted from a professional journal in the student's field?

So the prospectus began with this (carefully footnoted) quotation: "Every year since 1950, the number of American children gunned down has doubled." I had been invited to serve on the student's dissertation committee. When I read the quotation, I assumed the student had made an error in copying it. I went to the library and looked up the article the student had cited. There, in the journal's 1995 volume, was exactly the same sentence: "Every year since 1950, the number of American children gunned down has doubled."

This quotation is my nomination for a dubious distinction: I think it may be the worst—that is, the most inaccurate—social statistic ever.

What makes this statistic so bad? Just for the sake of argument, let's assume that "the number of American children gunned down" in 1950 was one. If the number doubled each year, there must have been two children gunned down in 1951, four in 1952, eight in 1953, and so on. By 1960, the number would have been 1,024. By 1965, it would have been 32,768 (in 1965, the F.B.I. identified only 9,960 criminal homicides in the entire country, including adult as well as child victims). By 1970, the number would have passed one million; by 1980, one billion (more than four times the total U.S. population in that year). Only three years later, in 1983, the number of American children gunned down would have been 8.6 billion (nearly twice the earth's population at the time). Another milestone would have been passed in 1987, when the number of gunned-down American children (137 billion) would have surpassed the best estimates for the total human population throughout history (110 billion). By 1995, when the article was published, the annual number of victims would have been over 35 trillion—a really big number, of a magnitude you rarely encounter outside economics or astronomy.

Thus my nomination: estimating the number of American child gunshot victims in 1995 at 35 trillion must be as far off—as hilariously, wildly wrong—as a social statistic can be. (If anyone spots a more inaccurate social statistic, I'd love to hear about it.)

Where did the article's author get this statistic? I wrote the author, who responded that the statistic came from the Children's Defense Fund, a well-known advocacy group for children. The C.D.F.'s *The State of America's Children Yearbook 1994* does state: "The number of American children killed each year by guns has doubled since 1950." Note the difference in the wording—the C.D.F. claimed there were twice as many deaths in 1994 as in 1950; the article's author reworded that claim and created a very different meaning.

It is worth examining the history of this statistic. It began with the C.D.F. noting that child gunshot deaths had doubled from 1950 to 1994. This is not quite as dramatic an increase as it might seem. Remember that the U.S. population also rose throughout this period; in fact, it grew about 73 percent—or nearly double. Therefore, we might expect all sorts of things—including the number of child gunshot deaths—to increase, to nearly double, just because the population grew. Before we can decide whether twice as many deaths indicate that things are getting worse, we'd have to know more. The C.D.F. statistic raises other issues as well: Where did the statistic come from? Who counts child gunshot deaths, and how? What is meant by a "child" (some C.D.F. statistics about violence include everyone under age 25)? What is meant by "killed by guns" (gunshot-death statistics often include suicides and accidents, as well as homicides)? But people rarely ask questions of this sort when they encounter statistics. Most of the time, most people simply accept statistics without question.

Certainly, the article's author didn't ask many probing, critical questions about the C.D.F.'s claim. Impressed by the statistic, the author repeated it—well, meant to repeat it. Instead, by rewording the C.D.F.'s claim, the author created a mutant statistic, one garbled almost beyond recognition.

But people treat mutant statistics just as they do other statistics—that is, they usually accept even the most implausible claims without question. For example, the journal editor who accepted the author's article for publication did not bother to consider the implications of child victims doubling each year. And people repeat bad statistics: The graduate student copied the garbled statistic and inserted it into the dissertation prospectus. Who knows whether still other readers were impressed by the author's statistic and remembered it or repeated it? The article remains on the shelf in hundreds of libraries, available to anyone who needs a dramatic quote. The lesson should be clear: Bad statistics live on; they take on lives of their own.

Some statistics are born bad—they aren't much good from the start, because they are based on nothing more than guesses or dubious data. Other statistics mutate; they become bad after being mangled (as in the case of the author's creative rewording). Either way, bad statistics are potentially important: They can be used to stir up public outrage or fear; they can distort our understanding of our world; and they can lead us to make poor policy choices.

The notion that we need to watch out for bad statistics isn't new. We've all heard people say, "You can prove anything with statistics." The title of my book, *Damned Lies and Statistics*, comes from a famous aphorism (usually attributed to Mark Twain or Benjamin Disraeli): "There are three kinds of lies: lies, damned lies, and statistics." There is even a useful little book, still in print after more than 40 years, called *How to Lie With Statistics.*

We shouldn't ignore all statistics, or assume that every number is false. Some statistics are bad, but others are pretty good. And we need good statistics to talk sensibly about social problems.

Statistics, then, have a bad reputation. We suspect that statistics may be wrong, that people who use statistics may be "lying"—trying to manipulate us by using numbers to somehow distort the truth. Yet, at the same time, we need statistics; we depend upon them to summarize and clarify the nature of our complex society. This is particularly true when we talk about social problems. Debates about social problems routinely raise questions that demand statistical answers: Is the problem widespread? How many people—and which people—does it affect? Is it getting worse? What does it cost society? What will it cost to deal with it? Convincing answers to such questions demand evidence, and that usually means numbers, measurements, statistics.

But can't you prove anything with statistics? It depends on what "prove" means. If we want to know, say, how many children are "gunned down" each year, we can't simply guess—pluck a number from thin air: 100, 1,000, 10,000, 35 trillion, whatever. Obviously, there's no reason to consider an arbitrary guess "proof" of anything. However, it might be possible for someone—using records kept by police departments or hospital emergency rooms or coroners—to keep track of children who have been shot; compiling careful, complete records might give us a fairly accurate idea of the number of gunned-down children. If that number seems accurate enough, we might consider it very strong evidence—or proof.

The solution to the problem of bad statistics is not to ignore all statistics, or to assume that every number is false. Some statistics are bad, but others are pretty good, and we need statistics—good statistics—to talk sensibly about social problems. The solution, then, is not to give up on statistics, but to become better judges of the numbers we encounter. We need to think critically about statistics—at least critically enough to suspect that the number of children gunned down hasn't been doubling each year since 1950.

A few years ago, the mathematician John Allen Paulos wrote *Innumeracy*, a short, readable book about "mathematical illiteracy." Too few people, he argued, are comfortable with basic mathematical principles, and this makes them poor judges of the numbers they encounter. No doubt this is one reason we have so many bad statistics. But there are other reasons, as well.

Social statistics describe society, but they are also products of our social arrangements. The people who bring social statistics to our attention have reasons for doing so; they inevitably want something, just as reporters and the other media figures who repeat and publicize statistics have their own goals. Statistics are tools, used for particular purposes. Thinking critically about statistics requires understanding their place in society.

While we may be more suspicious of statistics presented by people with whom we disagree—people who favor different political parties or have different beliefs—bad statistics are used to promote all sorts of causes. Bad statistics come from conservatives on the political right and liberals on the left, from wealthy corporations and powerful government agencies, and from advocates of the poor and the powerless.

In order to interpret statistics, we need more than a checklist of common errors. We need a general approach, an orientation, a mind-set that we can use to think about new statistics that we encounter. We ought to approach statistics thoughtfully. This can be hard to do, precisely because so many people in our society treat statistics as fetishes. We might call this the mind-set of the awestruck—the people who don't think critically, who act as though statistics have magical powers. The awestruck know they don't always understand the statistics they hear, but this doesn't bother them. After all, who can expect to understand magical numbers? The reverential fatalism of the awestruck is not thoughtful—it is a way of avoiding thought. We need a different approach.

One choice is to approach statistics critically. Being critical does not mean being negative or hostile—it is not cynicism. The critical approach statistics thoughtfully; they avoid the extremes of both naïve acceptance and cynical rejection of the numbers they encounter. Instead, the critical attempt to evaluate numbers, to distinguish between good statistics and bad statistics.

The critical understand that, while some social statistics may be pretty good, they are never perfect. Every statistic is a way of summarizing complex information into relatively simple numbers. Inevitably, some information, some of the complexity, is lost whenever we use statistics. The critical recognize that this is an inevitable limitation of statistics. Moreover, they realize that every statistic is the product of choices—the choice between defining a category broadly or narrowly, the choice of one measurement over another, the choice of a sample. People choose definitions, measurements, and samples for all sorts of reasons: Perhaps they want to emphasize some aspect of a problem; perhaps it is easier or cheaper to gather data in a particular way—many considerations can come into play. Every statistic is a compromise among choices. This means that every definition—and every measurement and every sample—probably has limitations and can be criticized.

Being critical means more than simply pointing to the flaws in a statistic. Again, every statistic has flaws. The issue is whether a particular statistic's flaws are severe enough to damage its usefulness. Is the definition so broad that it encompasses too many false positives (or so narrow that it excludes too many false negatives)? How would changing the definition alter the statistic? Similarly, how do the choices of measurements and samples affect the statistic? What would happen if different measures or samples were chosen? And how is the statistic used? Is it being interpreted appropriately, or has its meaning been mangled to create a mutant statistic? Are the comparisons that are being made appropriate, or are apples being confused with oranges? How do different choices produce the conflicting numbers found in stat wars? These are the sorts of questions the critical ask.

As a practical matter, it is virtually impossible for citizens in contemporary society to avoid statistics about social problems. Statistics arise in all sorts of ways, and in almost every case the people promoting statistics want to persuade us. Activists use statistics to convince us that social problems are serious and deserve our attention and concern. Charities use statistics to encourage donations. Politicians use statistics to persuade us that they understand society's problems and that they deserve our support. The media use statistics to make their reporting more dramatic, more convincing, more compelling. Corporations use statistics to promote and improve their products. Researchers use statistics to document their findings and support their conclusions. Those with whom we agree use statistics to reassure us that we're on the right side, while our opponents use statistics to try and convince us that we are wrong. Statistics are one of the standard types of evidence used by people in our society.

It is not possible simply to ignore statistics, to pretend they don't exist. That sort of head-in-the-sand approach would be too costly. Without statistics, we limit our ability to think thoughtfully about our society; without statistics, we have no accurate ways of judging how big a problem may be, whether it is getting worse, or how well the policies designed to address that problem actually work. And awestruck or naïve attitudes toward statistics are no better than ignoring statistics; statistics have no magical properties, and it is foolish to assume that all statistics are equally valid. Nor is a cynical approach the answer; statistics are too widespread and too useful to be automatically discounted.

It would be nice to have a checklist, a set of items we could consider in evaluating any statistic. The list might detail potential problems with definitions, measurements, sampling, mutation, and so on. These are, in fact, common sorts of flaws found in many statistics, but they should not be considered a formal, complete checklist. It is probably impossible to produce a complete list of statistical flaws—no matter how long the list, there will be other possible problems that could affect statistics.

The goal is not to memorize a list, but to develop a thoughtful approach. Becoming critical about statistics requires being prepared to ask questions about numbers. When encountering a new statistic in, say, a news report, the critical try to assess it. What might be the sources for this number? How could one go about producing the figure? Who produced the number, and what interests might they have? What are the different ways key terms might have been defined, and which definitions have been chosen? How might the phenomena be measured, and which measurement choices have been made? What sort of sample was gathered, and how might that sample affect the result? Is the statistic being properly interpreted? Are comparisons being made, and if so, are the comparisons appropriate? Are there competing statistics? If so, what stakes do the opponents have in the issue, and how are those stakes likely to affect their use of statistics? And is it possible to figure out why the statistics seem to disagree, what the differences are in the ways the competing sides are using figures?

At first, this list of questions may seem overwhelming. How can an ordinary person—someone who reads a statistic in a magazine article or hears it on a news broadcast—determine the answers to such questions? Certainly news reports rarely give detailed information on the processes by which statistics are created. And few of us have time to drop everything and investigate the background of some new number we encounter. Being critical, it seems, involves an impossible amount of work.

In practice, however, the critical need not investigate the origin of every statistic. Rather, being critical means appreciating the inevitable limitations that affect all statistics, rather than being awestruck in the presence of numbers. It means not being too credulous, not accepting every statistic at face value. But it also means appreciating that statistics, while always imperfect, can be useful. Instead of automatically discounting every statistic, the critical reserve judgment. When confronted with an interesting number, they may try to learn more, to evaluate, to weigh the figure's strengths and weaknesses.

Of course, this critical approach need not—and should not—be limited to statistics. It ought to apply to all the evidence we encounter when we scan a news report, or listen to a speech—whenever we learn about social problems. Claims about social problems often feature dramatic, compelling examples; the critical might ask whether an example is likely to be a typical case or an extreme, exceptional instance. Claims about social problems often include quotations from different sources, and the critical might wonder why those sources have spoken and why they have been quoted: Do they have particular expertise? Do they stand to benefit if they influence others? Claims about social problems usually involve arguments about the problem's causes and potential solutions. The critical might ask whether these arguments are convincing. Are they logical? Does the proposed solution seem feasible and appropriate? And so on. Being critical—adopting a skeptical, analytical stance when confronted with claims—is an approach that goes far beyond simply dealing with statistics.

Statistics are not magical. Nor are they always true—or always false. Nor need they be incomprehensible. Adopting a critical approach offers an effective way of responding to the numbers we are sure to encounter. Being critical requires more thought, but failing to adopt a critical mind-set makes us powerless to evaluate what others tell us. When we fail to think critically, the statistics we hear might just as well be magical.

Critical Thinking

1. Why are there bad statistics?
2. How can one approach statistics critically?
3. What was wrong with the following statement made in 1995: "Every year since 1950 the number of American children gunned down has doubled"?

Joel Best is a professor of sociology and criminal justice at the University of Delaware. This essay is excerpted from *Damned Lies and Statistics: Untangling Numbers from the Media, Politicians, and Activists,* published by the University of California Press and reprinted by permission.

When a Hazing Goes Very Wrong

MICHAEL WINERIP

In the early-morning hours of that Friday in February 2011, at around 3 A.M., George Desdunes and another Cornell sophomore were sitting on a couch blindfolded, their wrists and ankles bound with zip ties and duct tape.

They had been kidnapped and driven to a townhouse somewhere on campus, one of the annual hazing rites of the Sigma Alpha Epsilon fraternity. This particular ritual worked in reverse of most hazing. It was the freshman pledges who kidnapped older students.

The two S.A.E. brothers were asked trivia questions about the fraternity. If they gave a wrong answer they were supposed to drink a shot of vodka. As George Desdunes's roommate would later tell the police, "The purpose is to tie up the brother and get him drunk."

The young man sitting on the couch beside Mr. Desdunes recalled downing four or five shots of vodka in 20 minutes and then vomiting into a garbage pail. The two were fed Pixy Stix, chocolate powder, strawberry syrup, a bite of a sandwich, hot sauce. "Something that felt like dish soap was dripped on my face," said the 20-year-old sophomore, whose name was redacted from the police report. He drank more shots and vomited again.

Students later provided differing opinions on how threatening it was to be kidnapped. Some said Mr. Desdunes could have been cut loose at any time just by asking. "It was meant to be fun," Edward Williams, a freshman pledge who was one of the kidnappers, told the police. Others wanted no part of it. Before going to bed, Mr. Desdunes's roommate at the fraternity had locked their door, to guard against being kidnapped.

Eventually, Mr. Desdunes passed out and was loaded into the back seat of a Honda Pilot belonging to one of the brothers. At the fraternity, it took several people to carry him to his room, but when they found it locked, he was brought to the library and left on a leather couch.

They tilted his head, said Mr. Williams, so "he would vomit onto the floor" and not choke. Then they walked downstairs to the kitchen, made themselves something to eat and went to bed.

The S.A.E. house was quiet a few hours later, at 6:45 A.M., when the cleaning man and his father arrived for work. The place was worse than usual. There had been a beer pong tournament that night. Plastic cups were strewn all over. Furniture was broken. The room smelled like stale Keystone Light. After finishing the toilets, the younger cleaner walked by the library and noticed a student in a brown hoodie lying still. "I could see what looked like vomit or mucous on his mouth," he told the police. "I tried to wake him by grabbing his foot to make sure he was O.K. There was no response." Mr. Desdunes's right pant leg was rolled up. One of the zip ties was around his ankle; a second zip tie with duct tape lay on the floor beside the couch.

The cleaners called 911.

When the police and firefighters arrived, they found an unresponsive male. He was not breathing, had no pulse and was cold to the touch. They laid him on the floor, cut off his sweatshirt, suctioned his throat and applied CPR. He was put on a stretcher and taken to a hospital in an ambulance.

The rescue workers remarked later that there was not a single fraternity brother in sight, just the cleaners, who told the police what they knew, then went downstairs to finish the kitchen.

Hazing is common on American campuses. A 2008 University of Maine study concluded that 55 percent of students who join fraternities, sororities, sports teams or other student groups experience it. On Wednesday night, officials at Binghamton University of the State University of New York, citing "an alarmingly high number of serious hazing complaints this spring," halted all recruiting and pledging for the rest of the semester while it investigates. Binghamton has more than 50 fraternity and sorority chapters.

Hank Nuwer, a professor at Franklin College in Indiana who has written four books on the subject, says that as long as there have been universities, there has been hazing: in 1657, two Harvard upperclassmen were fined and suspended for hazing. Mr. Nuwer has counted 104 deaths involving hazing since 1970. In one high-profile case, a drum major in Florida A&M's Marching 100 was beaten to death in November during a hazing on the band bus. While no arrests were made in that case, seven band members have been arrested since then in two other hazing incidents. At Cornell, four students have been charged with hazing in connection with the Desdunes case and are scheduled to go on trial May 21.

Douglas Fierberg has built a law practice by suing fraternities involved in hazing cases. In 2010, he won a multimillion-dollar settlement for the family of Carson Starkey, a freshman at California Polytechnic State University, who had pledged the S.A.E. chapter there.

According to the police, the pledges were put in a garage, given large quantities of liquor and told to drink quickly while the brothers chanted "Puke and rally." When Mr. Starkey passed out, fraternity members drove him to the hospital, but turned around for fear of being arrested. Mr. Starkey, 18, was placed on a mattress at the house, where he died. His blood alcohol level was about .40, five times the legal limit to drive.

As a condition of that settlement, S.A.E. officials agreed to post on their Web site every case in which a local chapter was put on probation, suspended or expelled by universities from 2007 to 2011. In five years, disciplinary action has been taken against nearly 80 of S.A.E.'s 223 chapters. A spokesman for S.A.E., Brandon Weghorst, declined to comment for this article, citing continuing litigation. (In the spirit of full disclosure: one of my sons belonged to an S.A.E. chapter for two years, and enjoyed his experience.)

Last June, Mr. Fierberg filed a $25 million lawsuit against S.A.E. on behalf of Mr. Desdunes's mother, Marie Andre. A widow and Haitian immigrant living in Brooklyn, she worked as a nanny, hospital aide and AIDS counselor so her only child, George, could go to private schools.

In his essay for the Common Application, Mr. Desdunes wrote: "My family consists of two people. My Mom, Marie, and myself. Over the years I have come to realize the sacrifices that she has made for me in order to help me achieve something with my life."

Alcohol is often the not-so-secret ingredient that turns pledging into hazing. Four of five fraternity and sorority members in this country are binge drinkers, according to a 2000 Harvard study. Mr. Nuwer estimates that 80 percent of hazing deaths have involved alcohol.

At least two national fraternities, Phi Delta Theta and Phi Kappa Sigma, have mandated that all their chapter houses be alcohol free. It makes a big difference, said James Favor, president of James R. Favor & Company, which sells insurance to 15 national fraternities. In the decade before Phi Delta Theta became alcohol free, the fraternity averaged 12.3 liability claims a year that paid out an average of $812,951 in settlements, Mr. Favor said. After the fraternity went dry in 2000, there were three claims a year at an average annual cost of $15,388.

In 2006, Mr. Favor's firm was bought by a partnership of seven national fraternities, including S.A.E. Asked whether he recommends that fraternity houses ban alcohol, he said, "I make them aware of the effects of going from wet to dry."

The fraternity has debated getting rid of alcohol. In a proposal submitted to the S.A.E. Eminent Supreme Recorder in 2010, Frank Ginocchio (S.A.E. Northwestern '66) recommended that the constitution be amended to require that all chapters be alcohol free by Aug. 1, 2014. "This proposal takes into account that approximately two-thirds of our members are under the age of 21 and that most of our risk management incidents involve the abuse of alcohol," he wrote. "Beneficial consequences of this change will be a better maintained housing facility, and a better environment for studying."

Last July, at S.A.E.'s 155th national convention in Memphis, the 450 fraternity brothers present failed to give the measure the two-thirds majority needed for passage. "A big mistake," said Mr. Fierberg. "These decisions ought to be made by experts in risk management, not underage drinkers."

Three freshman pledges in the Cornell case—Mr. Williams, Max Haskin and Ben Mann—have been charged with misdemeanor hazing, a penalty that carries up to a year in jail.

The records of a fourth pledge, who was 18 at the time and considered a juvenile, have been sealed. In addition to hazing he has been charged with tampering with evidence. After the police arrived at the fraternity house that morning, it was that fourth pledge who called his roommate and asked him to get rid of evidence of the kidnapping, according to court papers.

The authorities subpoenaed his cellphone records and made a transcript: "I need you to do me a favor. It's extremely urgent. Throw out all the zip ties and duct tape in the room, please. ASAP."

Response: "All right, I'm heading back to the room. Is everything all right?"

"No, I can't really talk right now. Please just get rid of it."

Response: "Are they going to be searching our room? Should I take stuff out of the freezer?"

"Maybe."

The police also recovered a receipt for six rolls of duct tape that was bought for $53 at Home Depot on the afternoon before Mr. Desdunes was kidnapped.

Raymond M. Schlather, who is representing Max Haskin, has requested that the case be dismissed. In a brief filed last June, he noted that Mr. Haskin has no criminal record, that his grade-point average was 3.779 and that he was a member of the college tennis team.

He argues that Mr. Desdunes was drinking heavily before the kidnapping, had a history of binge drinking, willingly went along with the prank and, as an older frat member who dealt with pledges, could have ended it at any time.

There is considerable evidence for this theory.

The fraternity's scholarship chairman told the police that Mr. Desdunes was carrying a partly filled bottle of Captain Morgan rum and that from about 11:30 to midnight they had drinks together at the house. He said that Mr. Desdunes had two rum and Pepsi drinks with two to three shots in each. Witnesses saw him 15 minutes later at Dino's, a local bar, and said he was there until closing at 1 A.M. His roommate at the fraternity told the police: "George drinks harder than other people do but he doesn't do it frequently. You would check on him because he may be keeled over in the bar." He said that Mr. Desdunes, who was 19 years old, carried a fake ID.

In his brief, Mr. Schlather wrote that Mr. Desdunes "voluntarily consumed at least 10 to 12 ounces and perhaps as much as 15 to 20 ounces of alcohol before going to Dino's." He wrote that any alcohol Mr. Desdunes consumed after he was kidnapped by the pledges "was relatively insignificant compared to what Desdunes apparently had consumed earlier."

There is also considerable evidence that Mr. Desdunes was not intoxicated before being kidnapped. His roommate from freshman year, who was at Dino's that night, told the police that Mr. Desdunes did not buy anything from the bar.

"I have known George for around two years and have seen him intoxicated," he said, "and he was not at all last night."

When the bar closed, according to the police report, the two walked to Collegetown Pizza, where at about 1:15 Mr. Desdunes met a young woman, who would tell the police they "hooked up" at her apartment. He was not drunk, she said.

He left her about 2:15 A.M., she said, and shortly after was picked up by the pledges.

At least two factors will make it difficult to sort out what happened. Most of the fraternity brothers declined to be interviewed by investigators. Within hours of the death, according to the police, Mr. Mann "informed us that he had received a text from the Fraternity, that the Fraternity had retained a lawyer and that no one should talk to the police without counsel."

The other obstacle to getting at the truth is all that alcohol. One fraternity brother, who did not live at the house, did talk to the police, and told them that he was there playing beer pong until 1:30 A.M. "I went home, got in the shower, threw up, drank some water and went to bed. I imagine either a sober brother or a pledge drove me home, but I don't remember."

Mr. Desdunes's blood alcohol level that night was about .40.

The S.A.E. frat house, founded in 1891, was the biggest at Cornell. Forty brothers, about half the membership, lived in the three-story Tudor known as Hillcrest, which literally sits far above Cayuga's waters. In March 2011, the university revoked recognition of the chapter for five years and the house, which is owned by Cornell, was vacated. It has been renovated and is now used as a coed dorm.

The four defendants in the criminal case, along with six others involved, have left Cornell. Several have attempted to transfer but have been told by admissions officers at other universities that their applications will not be considered until the charges are resolved.

Susan Murphy, Cornell's vice president of student and academic affairs, criticized S.A.E. shortly after the episode, telling reporters that "even though the members and associate members recognized the condition Mr. Desdunes was in, they failed to call for medical care."

There is a good possibility that the lawyers representing the four pledges will seek to have the charges reduced from a first-degree to a second-degree misdemeanor. That would carry a fine of a few hundred dollars. It is equivalent to pleading guilty to disturbing the peace. The four would have no criminal record.

In an Op-Ed piece in *The New York Times* last August, David J. Skorton, the president of Cornell, wrote that the Desdunes tragedy "convinced me that it was time—long past time—to remedy practices of the fraternity system that continue to foster hazing."

He does not intend to get rid of fraternities and sororities, which serve about a quarter of Cornell's 14,000 undergraduates. "The Greek system is part of our university history and culture, and we should maintain it because at its best, it can foster friendship, community service and leadership."

The most concrete change to date has been to prohibit freshmen from attending fraternity parties that serve alcohol. A committee is expected to make recommendations in the next few weeks for ways to improve the pledging process.

Long before the Desdunes case there were many troubling signs at Cornell. Though hazing has been illegal at the university since 1980 and in New York State since 1983, 60 percent of the university's fraternities and sororities were found responsible for hazing activities over the last decade. In 2006, the S.A.E. chapter was suspended for a semester for hazing violations.

Though most hazing involves alcohol, in the fall of 2009 Cornell's Greek oversight council approved the use of alcohol at 181 social events. In the spring of 2010, alcohol use was approved at 244 events. That hasn't changed much. Last fall, there were 156 Greek events with alcohol.

In 2010, 13 percent of all Greek social events resulted in complaints, more than double the percentage from five years before. The number of disciplinary cases, a large portion of them involving hazing, also rose, to 108 from 88.

Many people, including the lawyers for the accused, believe that Cornell officials should have foreseen problems but looked the other way because the Greek system is so popular. "It's a shame Cornell is scapegoating freshman pledges to cover up its own historic failure to effectively deal with alcohol use in the Greek system," said Mr. Schlather.

Many immigrants never move beyond their own ethnic communities. Marie Lourdes Andre came here with little, yet was able to.

She worked as a nanny for Dr. Robert Fischer, an ophthalmologist, and his wife, Mary, and though Ms. Andre left that job long ago, they remain close. She is also close to John Sheehan, an information technology consultant who once lived across the hall from her.

They helped navigate the way for the mother and son. "George had no father," said Ms. Andre. "He needed men to look up to."

From sixth to 12th grade, George Desdunes attended Berkeley Carroll, an elite Brooklyn private school. He was an altar boy, a counselor at an overnight camp and an excellent swimmer, and he played trumpet in the school jazz band. He began music lessons at age 5. He was not permitted to watch television on school nights. "You didn't have to tell him to do homework," she said. "He knew this was his responsibility."

When it was time for him to look at colleges, Mr. Sheehan drove him to see Cornell; Dr. Fischer took him to visit Williams.

The essay for Williams asked applicants to imagine looking through a window and, in 300 words, reflect on what they saw. George wrote that he saw his mother climbing through a window to come from Haiti to the United States, but that was as far as she could go. He wrote that because of her, he was able to climb through the window and become an American.

George was accepted to Williams, but chose Cornell. He wanted to be a doctor.

"He told me he joined a fraternity so when he graduates college, they help him get a job," Ms. Andre said.

Midday on Friday, Feb. 25, 2011, Ms. Andre was working at her job as an AIDS counselor at SUNY Downstate Medical Center in Brooklyn when she got a call to come to the human resources department. She worried she was going to be laid off, but was told that a police officer was waiting to see her.

"Do you have a son named George at Cornell?" he asked.

The drive from Brooklyn to the medical examiner in Binghamton is five hours. The morgue was in a hospital basement.

Ms. Andre, accompanied by several friends for support, walked down a hallway to an examining room. A nurse asked them to please wait a moment, disappeared inside, then opened the door.

The body was face up, on a gurney, covered by a sheet that reached to the shoulders. It was George, but everything that made him George was gone—the intellect, the sense of humor, the smile, the life in his eyes.

Ms. Andre let out a horrible wail.

Critical Thinking

1. How is alcohol a problem for fraternity and sorority members?
2. Does hazing have a legitimate purpose for today's students?
3. Does the fact that a student, who is seriously injured or killed, voluntarily engaged in the hazing absolve everyone else of any ethical or moral culpability?

The Face of Domestic Violence

How could Amanda White have stayed with a husband who beat her over and over again? A young mom opens up about what she went through and why she believed it would all get better.

AMANDA WHITE, AS TOLD TO SARAH ELIZABETH RICHARDS

First Signs of Trouble

I sat in my mom's house not knowing what to do.

My body still ached from being beaten by my husband a day earlier. But he kept pleading through the door: "I was drunk. I'm sorry. I'll never do that to you again. I know I need help." I had a 2-week-old baby. I wanted to believe him. I opened the door.

I had a crush on Dietrich White back in junior high. When I ran into him almost a decade later in 1997, I was 21 and even more attracted to his sexy smile and blue eyes. I was thrilled when he asked me out. I was living with my mom in Hot Springs, Arkansas, while I took time off from college to heal from complications of endometriosis surgery. I tried to fill my time by running a booth-rental business in a crafts mall, but many of my friends were away at school and I was lonely.

Dietrich and I became a couple and spent nearly every day together. He said we were soul mates, brought me flowers, and took me on a trip to Florida. Two months later we were engaged. We moved in together in Little Rock (about an hour away from my mom), where Dietrich owned a carpet-cleaning business. I intended to return to school, but Dietrich said he earned enough to support us, so I could spend my time decorating our home and planning my dream wedding.

Dietrich and I rarely argued, but sometimes he got jealous and claimed I looked at other men. I was flattered that he was so in love with me that he couldn't stand the idea of me being with someone else. I wish I had known then that jealousy is often a warning sign of an abusive personality.

Our idyllic life didn't last long. Within a few months Dietrich had lost many of his customers and became distant. We had our first fight when I couldn't find him at his jobsite one afternoon; I smelled beer on his breath when he came home. "Where the hell have you been?" I demanded. He lied that he had been working and headed for the shower. I got so mad I threw a glass-covered candle at the bathtub. Dietrich stormed over and slapped me hard across the face. No one had ever hit me before, and I was stunned. "Did you just hit me?" I screamed.

"You made me do it!" I remember him shouting back. "You have no right to attack me when I've been working."

Later I apologized, and he said, "We never need to do that again." I tried to forget about the incident, but the next day my mother saw my black eye. "He was drinking, and I started it," I tried to explain. She exploded. "I don't care about the circumstances," she said. "No man can do that!"

Dietrich's irrational jealousy erupted again a month later when he accused me of sleeping with a friend of his. He canceled our wedding, which was just two weeks away, and asked me to move out. My parents lost thousands of dollars, but my mother was relieved. I was devastated.

On what would have been our wedding day I found out I was pregnant. After my endometriosis surgery, my doctor had told me I was infertile, so we hadn't been using birth control. The timing was terrible, but I was thrilled to learn I could have kids. My mom urged me to have the baby on my own, but I didn't want to be a single mother. Besides, I believed that a child would complete our little family and make things better.

Pain and Denial

When I was eight months pregnant we finally got married—in a judge's office. Then, after our son was born, Dietrich's business tanked and we had to move in with my mom. After she left for work one morning he said he had overheard us talking about my high school boyfriend and accused me of planning to see him. When I denied it he called me a liar and punched me several times in the face. I fell and the baby started screaming. I had never seen Dietrich this enraged. "Please stop!" I begged hysterically as I tried to reach the baby. He'd calm down and let me nurse the baby, but then he'd explode and come at me again.

At first I had white flashes in front of my eyes and a pounding pressure in my head, but my adrenaline kicked in and I felt dazed and couldn't tell where I'd been hit. Seven long hours later he told me to wash the blood off my face. I thought the nightmare was over, but as soon as I climbed into the tub he came into the bathroom and started choking me under the water until I passed out. I was sure I was going to die. He must have pulled my head out of the water in time because I came to, stumbled out of the bathroom and discovered that he'd taken the baby. By the time I called my sister-in-law to come get me, Dietrich had returned. He had calmed down, told me the baby was at his mother's house and took me to the hospital.

My mom found me in the ER, where they examined my black eyes and bruises. When the doctor asked what happened, I said I fell down a flight of stairs. He didn't ask any more questions and I was released. When we got home, Dietrich had brought back the baby, but my mom made him leave. She called the police the next day, but they said you have to call within four hours of a domestic-violence incident in order for them to make an arrest (the state law has since been changed to 12 hours). That evening Dietrich came over to apologize. He said he'd been drunk the night before. He swore he'd go to Alcoholics Anonymous. He promised we'd go to couples counseling. Three days later I let him back in.

My mom was furious. It's hard to explain how anyone could stay with someone after being hurt like that, but I had convinced myself it was because of the alcohol and that this one incident had gotten out of control. I knew that Dietrich loved me. I wanted to believe he was truly sorry and would never harm me again.

A Fresh Start?

I felt reassured when Dietrich made good on his pledge to attend a couple of AA meetings. He thought we needed a clean slate, so in the fall of 1998 we moved almost 1,000 miles away to Tampa, Florida. Those days were the best of our marriage. He found work laying down tile; I helped out while the baby slept. We took our son swimming in the ocean, and Dietrich toted him around in a baby carrier. He also fussed over me and bought me a beautiful silk bathrobe and diamond bracelet. I really thought he had changed.

But six months later Dietrich couldn't get any more work. That's when he started to abuse me again. During an argument he pushed me and broke my arm. Again I lied to doctors at the hospital and said I had fallen down the stairs. And to my surprise I found out I was pregnant. We eventually ran out of money and moved back to Arkansas. After our second son was born, in November 1999, Dietrich attacked my mom when she tried to stop him from driving drunk with the baby in the car.

In 2001, three years into our marriage, I finally got up the courage to leave. My parents were so relieved and rented me a house. Dietrich begged me to come back, but even though I learned I was pregnant for the third time, I stayed strong and filed for divorce. He said there was no way I could care for three kids on my own, and that scared me. So by the time I delivered a third son, Dietrich and I were back together.

Hitting Rock Bottom

I know it sounds crazy now, but I really didn't think I was a battered woman—at least not yet. Then one May night in 2002 Dietrich beat me so badly with a child's chair that he broke my nose, shattered my knuckles, and fractured several bones in my face. My mom called the police. My hair was full of blood and my body was covered in gashes and bruises. I needed 65 stitches; Dietrich was arrested and charged with domestic battery in the first degree. The court added child endangerment charges since he had attacked me with the kids around. While he spent some time in jail, he was released on bond.

You'd think the severity of that beating would have been the last straw. This time, though, I thought jail had really scared him. During Thanksgiving at his parents' house that year he acted as if he had really missed me and the boys. I was moved by his sincerity and, during a weak moment, yes, we had sex. As luck would have it, since Dietrich would never let me use birth control, I got pregnant for the fourth time.

As the Arkansas trial drew closer, Dietrich started to unravel under the pressure and, afraid of jail time, fled to Ohio. He threatened that if I didn't join him, he would kill my family. Now that I knew what he was capable of, I was terrified he would do it. So I told my parents I was taking the kids to see friends but instead left for Ohio. They frantically called Dietrich's relatives and hired a private investigator but couldn't find me for more than a year. I wasn't surprised that the beatings continued in Ohio, but I was shocked when one night in 2004 someone called the police, and they arrested Dietrich *and* me. We had a fourth son by then, and I was charged with child endangerment for allowing the kids to witness the violence.

A New Life

The threat of losing my kids was the turning point. I had no idea how much they had suffered. I was devastated when I looked through their coloring books and saw they had scratched out all the faces. I thought I had protected them by making sure they were in another room or sleeping. But who was I kidding? Of course they heard the fighting and saw the bruises. Of course they lived in constant fear, too.

I knew I had to make it up to them and prove myself as a mom. So I completed all the court's required parenting classes and attended a domestic-violence support group. Dietrich begged me to drop the charges from the beating in Arkansas, which would increase his sentence. But I wouldn't do it. My mom was so proud. In the end he was sentenced to serve 18 years in prison. After seven years of marriage, our divorce became final in 2005.

At age 30 I returned to Arkansas to start over. Now I work for the Saline County Safe Haven, a local domestic-violence shelter. I've testified before the state legislature to raise money, and I speak to women to help them recognize the signs of abuse. I was proudest, though, when I completed my training to be a police officer. I was recruited to handle domestic-violence calls, and it feels great to help women find a shelter or get legal help. More than anything, I try to make them understand that they're choosing to continue the cycle of abuse every time they go back. I wish I had learned that lesson sooner.

The boys know their father is in jail and isn't allowed to contact them. They don't talk about him much, but occasionally one might say, "I wish our dad wasn't so mean so he could be with us." I put them each in counseling for about a year, and except for some minor anger issues they all seem to have recovered. I'm proud of them. They're all so loving, get good grades, and play school sports. I spend as much time as possible with them and organize my schedule so I can be home when they get out of school.

Dietrich will be eligible for parole in June, and I know he'll get out eventually. He may try to find me and get me to come back as he did before, but I'm a different person now. I won't let anyone hurt us ever again.

Critical Thinking

1. Is it sometimes OK for a woman to hit a man, especially if he has provoked her?
2. Should the wife in Ohio in 2004 have been arrested?
3. Is there anything more doctors should have done?

Sexual Violence and the Military

The rate of sexual assaults on American women serving in the military remains intolerably high. While an estimated 17 percent of women in the general population become victims at some point in their lives, a 2006 study of female veterans financed by the Department of Veterans Affairs estimated that between 23 percent and 33 percent of uniformed women had been assaulted. Those estimates are borne out in other surveys, and a recent Pentagon report on sexual assaults at the service academies found that in the 2010–11 academic year, cadets and midshipmen were involved in 65 reported assaults.

Too often victims are afraid to come forward. Defense Secretary Leon Panetta estimated that the number of attacks in 2011 by service members on other service members—both women and men—was close to 19,000, more than six times the number of reported attacks.

The problem has outlasted decades of Pentagon studies and task forces and repeated vows of "zero tolerance." Mr. Panetta has promised that this time will be different. In February, he told Congress, "We have got to get our command structure to be a lot more sensitive about these issues, to recognize sexual assault when it takes place and to act on it, not to simply ignore it."

Mr. Panetta has announced welcome reforms, including more money for training military investigators and judge advocates to prosecute sexual assault cases, more opportunity for victims to report crimes and request transfers and a system to collect and monitor assault cases. The director of the Pentagon's Sexual Assault Prevention and Response Office, or Sapro, Maj. Gen. Mary Kay Hertog of the Air Force, has pledged to enact the reforms and provide more outreach and support for victims.

There is a lot of tough work ahead. A continuing poster campaign by Sapro, which had started before General Hertog took over, is disturbingly clueless. It carries the tag line, "Ask Her When She's Sober," as if predation could be combated through a grotesque parody of an etiquette poster.

The Defense Department's record of prosecuting assault cases is dismal. In 2010, fewer than 21 percent of cases went to trial, for a number of reasons, including decisions by commanding officers not to prosecute or to impose nonjudicial or administrative punishments. About 6 percent of the accused were discharged or allowed to "resign in lieu of court-martial"—quit their jobs. Only about half the cases prosecuted resulted in convictions.

There are also serious problems in the civilian world. It is even harder for military women to get away from abusers they work with or for; they can't just quit their jobs or leave a combat zone. They must rely on commanding officers who act as investigators, judges and juries, in an extremely tight-knit workplace.

Members of Congress of both parties are trying to address these problems.

A bill from Representative Bruce Braley, Democrat of Iowa, would strengthen military penalties for rape, sexual assault, harassment and domestic violence and end the practice of giving convicted attackers nonjudicial or administrative punishment. It would ensure that allegations of rape and assault are referred to higher-ranking officers to address concerns that lower-level ones are too close to the accused and the victims. It would also allow service members to seek redress in federal court for the military's failure to investigate or prosecute a sexual crime.

The Pentagon insists that it can reform itself, and we are aware of the perils of civilian intrusion into the military justice system. But for "zero tolerance" to become a reality, Congress may have to push reform forward.

Critical Thinking

1. Why do you think women are at such risk in the military?
2. Why do you think so few cases are prosecuted by the Defense Department?
3. What is "clueless" about the poster campaign by Sapro?

Forensic Interviewing Aids: Do Props Help Children Answer Questions about Touching?

DEBRA ANN POOLE, MAGGIE BRUCK, AND MARGARET-ELLEN PIPE

When allegations of sexual abuse arise, informed decisions about child protection and criminal prosecution depend on the ability of forensic interviewers to help children provide accurate, detailed reports of events that might have involved touching. This goal is hampered by the myriad reasons children may fail to report experienced touches, including motivational factors (e.g., embarrassment and the desire to protect loved ones), linguistic issues (e.g., children's restricted understanding of the word "touch" and their limited vocabularies to describe abuse), and memory phenomena (e.g., failures to cue target memories). To address these concerns, clinicians and forensic interviewers sometimes question children with nonverbal props, such as anatomically detailed dolls and body diagrams. Supporters of props believe that children are "concrete thinkers" who often miss the point of questioning without props, that props allow children to respond without verbalizing embarrassing information, and that props are effective retrieval cues (Russell, 2008).

Researchers became interested in dolls and body diagrams because there was no evidence for the incremental validity of these assessment tools (Wolfner, Faust, & Dawes, 1993). That is, dolls and body diagrams gained popularity in the absence of data on whether props produced more accurate details than traditional verbal interviewing without an unacceptable increase in false reports. The resulting research was illuminating, revealing developmental, theoretical, and methodological insights into the nature of children's reports of significant events involving bodily contact.

Anatomically Detailed Dolls

Dolls were imported into forensic interviewing from clinical practice, where it was thought that interactions with dolls revealed children's emotional issues and themes in their lives. It was only after the use of dolls had been firmly engrained in forensic practice that researchers began to ask two important questions: (a) Are children's reports of touching during doll-assisted interviews sufficiently accurate for forensic purposes? and (b) Do dolls help children provide more information than verbal questions alone? After years of research, the resulting answers were "no" and "no."

Children must have three cognitive skills to report past events accurately with anatomical dolls: an understanding that the dolls are simultaneously objects *and* symbols representing themselves (i.e., dual representation, which permits "representational insight"; see DeLoache, 2000), the ability to map past events onto the dolls, and the ability to stay on task and not drift off into play. There is a frequent misunderstanding that dolls are developmentally appropriate for children ages 3 and older due to the oft-cited finding that representational insight is "achieved" around 3 years of age. In fact, 3-year-olds perform accurately only 75 percent to 90 percent of the time on dual-orientation tasks involving three-dimensional objects (DeLoache, 2000), so the error rate is too high for forensic purposes. When representational tasks are more complicated, even 4-year-olds fail to pass a significant number of trials. In one study, for example, 12 percent of 4-year-olds failed to accurately place at least three out of four stickers on a doll when demonstrating where stickers had been placed on their bodies—even though most of the children still wore visible stickers (DeLoache & Marzolf, 1995).

Children who have achieved representational insight will still have problems using dolls to report events if the intriguing appearance of dolls, with novel genitalia and holes that permit exploration, cause them to ignore the purpose of interviews. In a field study with suspected victims of abuse, children provided with dolls engaged in more play and "reported" proportionately more fantastic details than children questioned without dolls (Thierry, Lamb, Orbach, & Pipe, 2005). Even immediately after medical examinations, dolls increased false reports of genital and anal touching among 3- and 4-year-old children, and some children who had been lightly touched by the doctor falsely showed insertions into anal or vaginal cavities (Bruck, Ceci, & Francoeur, 2000). Other evidence has confirmed that 3- to 6-year-olds produce more errors without a corresponding increase in accurate information when interviewers use dolls (Pipe & Salmon, 2009).

But there are some optimistic findings. For example, direct questions ("Did the doctor touch you here?") paired with a doll greatly increased true reports of vaginal touching by 5- and 7-year-old girls who had experienced medical examinations, without a similar increase in false reports (i.e., only 3 percent of children who had not experienced vaginal touching falsely said that they had; Saywitz, Goodman, Nicholas, & Moan, 1991). The encouraging cost–benefit ratio in this study likely reflected several factors: The girls were school-aged, were not in an atmosphere of concern about touching, and had not been suggested possible answers by being asked to label various body parts. There are other studies showing that additional questioning with dolls elicits more reports of experienced touching, but these conclusions are unclear because the designs rarely included comparison groups of untouched children or children who were similarly questioned without the dolls.

By the mid 1990s, researchers and policy groups had arrived at three conclusions: (a) that children's interactions with dolls were not diagnostic of abuse, (b) that interviewers should not use dolls in ways that ask children to demonstrate abuse prior to verbal reports of abuse (e.g., Boat & Everson, 1996), and (c) that dolls were especially risky with children under 5 years of age. Facing mounting concerns about dolls and the risk of false reports from direct questions, interviewers were advised to use dolls mainly to help children clarify and elaborate on their verbal reports of abuse.

However, analyses of actual forensic interviews (involving children from 2 to 12 years of age) have not consistently found that dolls help children describe abuse, partly because dolls tend to inhibit children from talking (Dickinson, Poole, & Bruck, 2005). Using a laboratory paradigm to provide more control over the ways interviewers used the dolls, Malloy, MacKay, Salmon, and Pipe (2010) questioned 5- to 7-year-old children 1 week after they had experienced bodily contact that was central to several activities (e.g., getting a pirate badge). After the children had spontaneously reported touch, interviewers asked them to elaborate either with or without a doll. Children interviewed with the dolls did not report more information than children who were asked to elaborate verbally (e.g., "You said he put it on your arm. Tell me more about that.").

In short, dolls have not lived up to expectations as a means of helping children recount important abuse-relevant information. As anatomical dolls were gradually disappearing from forensic assessments, some professionals responded by replacing them with another prop: body diagrams.

Body Diagrams

Forensic interviewers who endorse body diagrams typically use realistic drawings of children and adults to elicit names for body parts, prompt disclosures of abuse, and/or clarify verbal disclosures. When used to prompt disclosures, interviewers display a body diagram, ask children to label specific parts on the diagram (including the genitals, breasts, and buttocks), and then attempt to raise the topic of abuse with a question such as, "Has anyone touched you in any of these places?" A more common practice is to use diagrams after children have already disclosed touching, often to make sure that interviewers understand children's body part names and descriptions of events.

Similar to the history of doll use, diagrams enjoyed popularity without evidence that they were developmentally appropriate or added value to interviews. Supporters of body diagrams have argued that young children appreciate the symbolic nature of pictures, so it is safe for interviewers to elicit disclosures by asking questions with a diagram (e.g., Russell, 2008). As with dolls, however, symbolic understanding is not a sufficient condition for children to use diagrams appropriately because there are other potential sources of error, such as the demand characteristics of the diagram.

In investigative interviews, adding diagram-assisted questions after other questions does lead children to recall additional information (e.g., Aldridge et al., 2004), including elaborations of bodily contact (Teoh, Yang, Lamb, & Larsson, 2010), but the accuracy of this information and the reason children recall more (i.e., diagrams vs. additional retrieval attempts vs. more specific questions) are unclear. Controlled laboratory studies that provide accuracy assessments do not support the use of body diagrams to elicit disclosures. Just as anatomical dolls permit children to inspect genitals and insert fingers in holes, body diagrams make it easy for children to point to body parts that were not touched during target experiences. Consequently, body diagrams elevate false reports of touching—even among children who actually experienced some touching (i.e., prompting them to report additional touches that had not occurred), and even among school-aged children (Poole & Dickinson, 2010). Moreover, some false reports are forensically meaningful (e.g., 7 percent of children falsely reported genital touching and 24 percent falsely reported touching to their breasts in Willcock, Morgan, & Hayne, 2006, Experiment 2). It is difficult to justify this risk when studies have failed to prove that diagrams elicit a greater number of true disclosures than identical questions delivered without diagrams (Brown, Pipe, Lewis, Lamb, & Orbach 2007; Bruck, 2009).

What about using body diagrams to clarify disclosures? In one study, there were no differences in the amounts of accurate or false information provided by children questioned for clarification with body diagrams and by children asked to elaborate without the diagrams (Malloy et al., 2010). Moreover, there is evidence that the introduction of body diagrams leads interviewers to use a more specific questioning style than is recommended by forensic protocols (Aldridge et al., 2004; Malloy et al., 2010).

Why Are Touch Reports Sparse among Children Who Have Not Yet Disclosed?

A consistent message in the studies reviewed here is the lack of evidence that dolls and diagrams produce increases in accurate details of touching compared to verbal questions alone. Furthermore, these studies also found that, in general, the children reported few of the experienced touches, whether they were genital/anal touches (which are memorable but embarrassing to report; e.g., Steward & Steward, 1996) or less salient touches (which are less memorable and emotionally neutral). These findings thus prompted related investigations to explore why young children have difficulty reporting actual touches when there are no obvious motivational barriers to reporting.

There appear to be several sources of difficulty. First, young children do not always understand that the word "touch" can refer to common touching actions, such as patting and hugging (Bruck, 2009; Bruck & Landau, 2009). Second, children may not readily encode touching actions that occur in complex activities. Although children can identify touching when shown still photographs of touching actions, they are poor at remembering touch when these actions are embedded in a sequence of interesting actions (Bruck & Landau, 2009; Poole & Dickinson, 2010). Of course, laboratory studies focus on innocuous and socially sanctioned touches, not the type of painful or embarrassing touching we would expect children to process differently. Still, many actions of sexual abuse are not painful and take place while children are engaged in other activities, rendering them less likely to be recalled when interviewers unexpectedly ask about touch. If children's failure to provide complete and accurate reports of touching partly reflects semantic and attentional difficulties, then it is not surprising that dolls or diagrams do not enhance performance, as these aids were not designed to overcome such difficulties.

Barriers to Policy Change and Future Directions

As in other professions, there are numerous barriers to policy change in the field of forensic interviewing. For example, the admission that a technique is prone to false positive findings may call prior case decisions into question, and the adoption of new procedures requires enormous retraining efforts. Most important, basic assumptions are deeply rooted (e.g., that props help children tell).

Two conceptual barriers also limit the speed with which research informs practice. One barrier is a tendency to use findings based on one group of children to render conclusions regarding another. Forensic interviewers do not question only abused children (including those who have disclosed and those who have not); they also interview nonabused children who do not believe they were abused and nonabused children who have received false suggestions about abuse. It is important to keep in mind that the reporting patterns of one of these groups may not generalize to others. For example, an interview technique may elicit few false reports from nonabused children who have not been misled about abuse, yet this same technique might have great risks when nonabused children are in an environment of concern about possible abuse. Because individual studies address only some groups and forensic interviewers usually do not know what proportion of their case assignments represents each group, it has been challenging for policymakers to agree on which interviewing techniques are appropriate for eliciting touch reports.

A second barrier is the "missing perfect study" problem. Three types of studies have contributed the majority of evidence on props, each with different strengths and limitations. First, there are field studies of actual interviews with suspected victims of abuse. Because there is usually no evidence to verify these children's actual experiences, it is not possible to determine the accuracy of their reports. As a result, these studies only tell us if nonverbal props produce more details (e.g., Aldridge et al., 2004). Second, there are studies in which children described medical examinations (e.g., Bruck et al., 2000; Steward & Steward, 1996). Although some of these studies asked children to recall anal or genital touch, conclusions are limited because the social acceptability and emotional associates of these touches are quite different from what occurs in abusive scenarios. Finally, there are laboratory studies where touching occurred in the context of games or educational events (e.g., Brown et al., 2007). Although these studies offer control over the types and numbers of touches, they do not involve inappropriate touching.

It is easy for advocates of interviewing aids to dismiss unwanted findings by mentioning the limits of each type of study in turn. But of course, the most definitive conclusions summarize findings that are consistent across study types—and there are consistent findings. For example, touched children who have not previously disclosed tend not to report all touches (whether those touches were actual abuse or laboratory analogs), specific questions elevate rates of false touch reports (whether children have experienced actual medical evaluations or playful events), and there is no collective evidence that interviewing props improve the quality of children's testimony compared to verbal questions alone (whether children have participated in actual or simulated forensic interviews).

In response to these findings, investigators are beginning to explore new ways of encouraging children to discuss inappropriate touching that abandon old ideas about the natural compatibility between children and props. One line of thought is based on the fact that nondisclosing children behave differently from disclosers even before sensitive topics are raised, which suggests that reticent children need more acclimation time and perhaps more extensive use of relatively safe memory retrieval techniques (e.g., questions that reinstate the context of key events) prior to addressing abuse issues (Orbach, Shiloach, & Lamb, 2007). If laboratories begin exploring creative solutions, the next decade of research could provide an answer to the ultimate challenge of forensic interviewing: the need to encourage disclosures without dramatically elevating false reports.

Recommended Readings

DeLoache, J.S. (2005). Mindful of symbols. *Scientific American, 293,* 72–77. A brief explanation of why symbols are not intuitive to children, with applications to interviewing and education.

Dickinson, J.J., Poole, D.A., & Bruck, M. (2005). (See References). A summary of concerns about anatomically detailed dolls, including the effects of dolls on child and interviewer behavior.

Kuehnle, K., & Connell, M. (Eds.), *The evaluation of child sexual abuse allegations: A comprehensive guide to assessment and testimony.* Hoboken, NJ: Wiley. Essays on issues in child sexual abuse allegations, including the logic of indicators and research on forensic interviewing techniques.

Lamb, M.E., Hershkowitz, Y.O., & Esplin, P.W. (2008). *Tell me what happened: Structured investigative interviews of child victims and witnesses.* Hoboken, NJ: Wiley. Summaries of research on the value of structured interviewing protocols.

Pipe, M.-E., & Salmon, K. (2009). (See References). A chapter on how props influence the amount of accurate and inaccurate details in children's reports of events.

References

Aldridge, J., Lamb, M.E., Sternberg, K.J., Orbach, Y., Esplin, P.W., & Bowler, L. (2004). Using a human figure drawing to elicit information from alleged victims of child sexual abuse. *Consulting and Clinical Psychology, 72,* 304–316.

Boat, B.W., & Everson, M.D. (1996). Concerning practices of interviewers when using anatomical dolls in child protective services investigations. *Child Maltreatment, 1,* 96–104.

Brown, D.A., Pipe, M.-E., Lewis, C., Lamb, M., & Orbach, Y. (2007). Supportive or suggestive: Do human figure drawings help 5- to 7-year-old children to report touch? *Journal of Consulting and Clinical Psychology, 75,* 33–42.

Bruck, M. (2009). Human figure drawings and children's recall of touching. *Journal of Experimental Psychology: Applied, 15,* 361–374.

Bruck, M., Ceci, S.J., & Francoeur, E. (2000). Children's use of anatomically detailed dolls to report genital touching in a medical examination: Developmental and gender comparisons. *Journal of Experimental Psychology: Applied, 6,* 74–83.

Bruck, M., & Landau, B. (2009, May). *Children's reports of touching experiences.* Paper presented at the annual meeting of the Association for Psychological Science, San Francisco.

DeLoache, J.S. (2000). Dual representation and young children's use of scale models. *Child Development, 71,* 329–338.

DeLoache, J.S., & Marzolf, D.P. (1995). The use of dolls to interview young children: Issues of symbolic representation. *Journal of Experimental Child Psychology, 60,* 155–173.

Dickinson, J.J., Poole, D.A., & Bruck, M. (2005). Back to the future: A comment on the use of anatomical dolls in forensic interviews. *Journal of Forensic Psychology Practice, 5,* 63–74.

Malloy, A., McKay, K., Salmon, K., & Pipe, M.-E. (2010). *Do dolls and human figure diagrams increase the effectiveness of a protocol-guided interview in eliciting touch reports from young children?* Manuscript submitted for publication.

Orbach, Y., Shiloach, H, & Lamb, M.E. (2007). Reluctant disclosers of child sexual abuse. In M.-E. Pipe, M.E. Lamb, Y. Orbach & A.-C. Ceberborg (Eds.), *Child sexual abuse: Disclosure, delay, and denial,* (pp. 115–134). New York, NY: Routledge.

Poole, D.A., & Dickinson, J.J. (2010). *Evidence supporting restrictions on uses of body outlines in forensic interviews.* Manuscript submitted for publication.

Pipe, M.-E., & Salmon, K. (2009). Dolls, drawings, body diagrams, and other props: Role of props in investigative interviews. In K. Kuehnle & M. Connell (Eds.), *The evaluation of child sexual abuse allegations: A comprehensive guide to assessment and testimony.* (pp. 365–395). Hoboken, NJ: Wiley.

Russell, A. (2008). Out of the woods: A case for using anatomical diagrams in forensic interviews. *Update, 21*(1), 2–6. Retrieved from www.ndaa.org/pdf/update_vol_21_no_1_2008.pdf.

Saywitz, K.J., Goodman, G.S., Nicholas, E., & Moan, S.F. (1991). Children's memories of a physical examination involving genital touch: Implications for reports of child sexual abuse. *Journal of Consulting and Clinical Psychology, 59,* 682–691.

Steward, M.S., & Steward, D.S. (with Farquhar, L., Myers, J.E.B., Reinhart, M., Welker, J., Joye, N., Driskill J., & Morgan, J.). (1996). Interviewing young children about body touch and handling. *Monograph of the Society for Research in Child Development* (Serial No. 248, Volume 61, Nos. 4–5).

Teoh, Y.-S., Yang, P.-J., Lamb, M.E., & Larsson, A.S. (2010). Do human figure diagrams help alleged victims of sexual abuse provide elaborate and clear accounts of physical contact with alleged perpetrators? *Applied Cognitive Psychology, 24,* 287–300.

Thierry, K.L., Lamb, M.E., Orbach, Y., & Pipe, M.-E. (2005). Developmental differences in the function and use of anatomical dolls during interviews with alleged sexual abuse victims. *Journal of Consulting and Clinical Psychology, 73,* 1125–1134.

Willcock, E., Morgan, K., & Hayne, H. (2006). Body maps do not facilitate children's reports of touch. *Applied Cognitive Psychology, 20,* 607–615.

Wolfner, G., Faust, D, & Dawes, R.M. (1993). The use of anatomically detailed dolls in sexual abuse evaluations: The state of the science. *Applied & Preventive Psychology, 2,* 1–11.

Critical Thinking

1. What did researchers learn about the accuracy of children's reports of touching during doll-assisted interviews?
2. Why are props still being used when interviewing children about sexual abuse?
3. Why do young children have difficulty reporting that they have been touched?

Debra Ann Poole—Department of Psychology, Central Michigan University.

Maggie Bruck—Division of Child and Adolescent Psychiatry, Johns Hopkins University.

Margaret-Ellen Pipe—Department of Psychology, Brooklyn College, The City University of New York.

Human Sex Trafficking

AMANDA WALKER-RODRIGUEZ, JD AND RODNEY HILL, JD

Human sex trafficking is the most common form of modern-day slavery. Estimates place the number of its domestic and international victims in the millions, mostly females and children enslaved in the commercial sex industry for little or no money.[1] The terms *human trafficking* and *sex slavery* usually conjure up images of young girls beaten and abused in faraway places, like Eastern Europe, Asia, or Africa. Actually, human sex trafficking and sex slavery happen locally in cities and towns, both large and small, throughout the United States, right in citizens' backyards.

Appreciating the magnitude of the problem requires first understanding what the issue is and what it is not. Additionally, people must be able to identify the victim in common trafficking situations.

Human Sex Trafficking

Many people probably remember popular movies and television shows depicting pimps as dressing flashy and driving large fancy cars. More important, the women—adults—consensually and voluntarily engaged in the business of prostitution without complaint. This characterization is extremely inaccurate, nothing more than fiction. In reality, the pimp *traffics* young women (and sometimes men) completely against their will by force or threat of force; this is human sex trafficking.

The Scope

Not only is human sex trafficking slavery but it is big business. It is the fastest-growing business of organized crime and the third-largest criminal enterprise in the world.[2] The majority of sex trafficking is international, with victims taken from such places as South and Southeast Asia, the former Soviet Union, Central and South America, and other less developed areas and moved to more developed ones, including Asia, the Middle East, Western Europe, and North America.[3]

Unfortunately, however, sex trafficking also occurs domestically.[4] The United States not only faces an influx of international victims but also has its own homegrown problem of interstate sex trafficking of minors.[5]

The United States not only faces an influx of international victims but also has its own homegrown problem of interstate sex trafficking of minors.

Although comprehensive research to document the number of children engaged in prostitution in the United States is lacking, an estimated 293,000 American youths currently are at risk of becoming victims of commercial sexual exploitation.[6] The majority of these victims are runaway or thrown-away youths who live on the streets and become victims of prostitution.[7] These children generally come from homes where they have been abused or from families who have abandoned them. Often, they become involved in prostitution to support themselves financially or to get the things they feel they need or want (like drugs).

Other young people are recruited into prostitution through forced abduction, pressure from parents, or through deceptive agreements between parents and traffickers. Once these children become involved in prostitution, they often are forced to travel far from their homes and, as a result, are isolated from their friends and family. Few children in this situation can develop new relationships with peers or adults other than the person victimizing them. The lifestyle of such youths revolves around violence, forced drug use, and constant threats.[8]

Among children and teens living on the streets in the United States, involvement in commercial sex activity is a problem of epidemic proportion. Many girls living on the street engage in formal prostitution, and some become entangled in nationwide organized crime networks where they are trafficked nationally. Criminal networks transport these children around the United States by a variety of means—cars, buses, vans, trucks, or planes—and often provide them counterfeit identification to use in the event of arrest. The average age at which girls first become victims of prostitution is 12 to 14. It is not only the girls on the streets who are affected; boys and transgender youth enter into prostitution between the ages of 11 and 13 on average.[9]

The Operation

Today, the business of human sex trafficking is much more organized and violent. These women and young girls are sold to traffickers, locked up in rooms or brothels for weeks or months, drugged, terrorized, and raped repeatedly.[10] These continual abuses make it easier for the traffickers to control their victims. The captives are so afraid and intimidated that they rarely speak out against their traffickers, even when faced with an opportunity to escape.

Today, the business of human sex trafficking is much more organized and violent.

Generally, the traffickers are very organized. Many have a hierarchy system similar to that of other criminal organizations. Traffickers who have more than one victim often have a "bottom," who sits atop the hierarchy of prostitutes. The bottom, a victim herself, has been with the trafficker the longest and has earned his trust. Bottoms collect the money from the other girls, discipline them, seduce unwitting youths into trafficking, and handle the day-to-day business for the trafficker.

Traffickers represent every social, ethnic, and racial group. Various organizational types exist in trafficking. Some perpetrators are involved with local street and motorcycle gangs, others are members of larger nationwide gangs and criminal organizations, and some have no affiliation with any one group or organization. Traffickers are not only men—women run many established rings.

Traffickers represent every social, ethnic, and racial group.

Traffickers use force, drugs, emotional tactics, and financial methods to control their victims. They have an especially easy time establishing a strong bond with young girls. These perpetrators may promise marriage and a lifestyle the youths often did not have in their previous familial relationships. They claim they "love" and "need" the victim and that any sex acts are for their future together. In cases where the children have few or no positive male role models in their lives, the traffickers take advantage of this fact and, in many cases, demand that the victims refer to them as "daddy," making it tougher for the youths to break the hold the perpetrator has on them.

Sometimes, the traffickers use violence, such as gang rape and other forms of abuse, to force the youths to work for them and remain under their control. One victim, a runaway from Baltimore County, Maryland, was gang raped by a group of men associated with the trafficker, who subsequently staged a "rescue." He then demanded that she repay him by working for him as one of his prostitutes. In many cases, however, the victims simply are beaten until they submit to the trafficker's demands.

In some situations, the youths have become addicted to drugs. The traffickers simply can use their ability to supply them with drugs as a means of control.

Traffickers often take their victims' identity forms, including birth certificates, passports, and drivers' licenses. In these cases, even if youths do leave they would have no ability to support themselves and often will return to the trafficker.

These abusive methods of control impact the victims both physically and mentally. Similar to cases involving Stockholm Syndrome, these victims, who have been abused over an extended period of time, begin to feel an attachment to the perpetrator.[11] This paradoxical psychological phenomenon makes it difficult for law enforcement to breach the bond of control, albeit abusive, the trafficker holds over the victim.

National Problem with Local Ties

The Federal Level

In 2000, Congress passed the Trafficking Victims Protection Act (TVPA), which created the first comprehensive federal law to address trafficking, with a significant focus on the international dimension of the problem. The law provides a three-pronged approach: *prevention* through public awareness programs overseas and a State Department-led monitoring and sanctions program; *protection* through a new T Visa and services for foreign national victims; and *prosecution* through new federal crimes and severe penalties.[12]

As a result of the passing of the TVPA, the Office to Monitor and Combat Trafficking in Persons was established in October 2001. This enabling legislation led to the creation of a bureau within the State Department to specifically address human trafficking and exploitation on all levels and to take legal action against perpetrators.[13] Additionally, this act was designed to enforce all laws within the 13th Amendment to the U.S. Constitution that apply.[14]

U.S. Immigration and Customs Enforcement (ICE) is one of the lead federal agencies charged with enforcing the TVPA. Human trafficking represents significant risks to homeland security. Would-be terrorists and criminals often can access the same routes and use the same methods as human traffickers. ICE's Human Smuggling and Trafficking Unit works to identify criminals and organizations involved in these illicit activities.

The FBI also enforces the TVPA. In June 2003, the FBI, in conjunction with the Department of Justice Child Exploitation and Obscenity Section and the National Center for Missing and Exploited Children, launched the Innocence Lost National Initiative. The agencies' combined efforts address the growing problem of domestic sex trafficking of children in the United States. To date, these groups have worked successfully to rescue nearly 900 children. Investigations successfully have led to the conviction of more than 500 pimps, madams, and their associates who exploit children through prostitution. These convictions have resulted in lengthy sentences, including multiple 25-year-to-life sentences and the seizure of real property, vehicles, and monetary assets.[15]

Both ICE and the FBI, along with other local, state, and federal law enforcement agencies and national victim-based advocacy groups in joint task forces, have combined resources and expertise on the issue. Today, the FBI participates in approximately 30 law enforcement task forces and about 42 Bureau of Justice Assistance (BJA)-sponsored task forces around the nation.[16]

In July 2004, the Human Smuggling Trafficking Center (HSTC) was created. The HSTC serves as a fusion center for information on human smuggling and trafficking, bringing together analysts, officers, and investigators from such agencies as the CIA, FBI, ICE, Department of State, and Department of Homeland Security.

The Local Level

With DOJ funding assistance, many jurisdictions have created human trafficking task forces to combat the problem. BJA's 42 such task forces can be demonstrated by several examples.[17]

- In 2004, the FBI's Washington field office and the D.C. Metropolitan Police Department joined with a variety of nongovernment organizations and service providers to combat the growing problem of human trafficking within Washington, D.C.
- In January 2005, the Massachusetts Human Trafficking Task Force was formed, with the Boston Police Department serving as the lead law enforcement entity. It uses a two-pronged approach, addressing investigations focusing on international victims and those focusing on the commercial sexual exploitation of children.
- The New Jersey Human Trafficking Task Force attacks the problem by training law enforcement in the methods of identifying victims and signs of trafficking, coordinating statewide efforts in the identification and provision of services to victims of human trafficking, and increasing the successful interdiction and prosecution of trafficking of human persons.
- Since 2006, the Louisiana Human Trafficking Task Force, which has law enforcement, training, and victim services components, has focused its law enforcement and victim rescue efforts on the Interstate 10 corridor from the Texas border on the west to the Mississippi border on the east. This corridor, the basic northern border of the hurricane-ravaged areas of Louisiana, long has served as a major avenue of illegal immigration efforts. The I-10 corridor also is the main avenue for individuals participating in human trafficking to supply the labor needs in the hurricane-damaged areas of the state.
- In 2007, the Maryland Human Trafficking Task Force was formed. It aims to create a heightened law enforcement and victim service presence in the community. Its law enforcement efforts include establishing roving operations to identify victims and traffickers, deputizing local law enforcement to assist in federal human trafficking investigations, and providing training for law enforcement officers.

Anytown, USA

In December 2008, Corey Davis, the ringleader of a sex-trafficking ring that spanned at least three states, was sentenced in federal court in Bridgeport, Connecticut, on federal civil rights charges for organizing and leading the sex-trafficking operation that exploited as many as 20 females, including minors. Davis received a sentence of 293 months in prison followed by a lifetime term of supervised release. He pleaded guilty to multiple sex-trafficking charges, including recruiting a girl under the age of 18 to engage in prostitution. Davis admitted that he recruited a minor to engage in prostitution; that he was the organizer of a sex-trafficking venture; and that he used force, fraud, and coercion to compel the victim to commit commercial sex acts from which he obtained the proceeds.

According to the indictment, Davis lured victims to his operation with promises of modeling contracts and a glamorous lifestyle. He then forced them into a grueling schedule of dancing and performing at strip clubs in Connecticut, New York, and New Jersey. When the clubs closed, Davis forced the victims to walk the streets until 4 or 5 A.M. propositioning customers. The indictment also alleged that he beat many of the victims to force them to work for him and that he also used physical abuse as punishment for disobeying the stringent rules he imposed to isolate and control them.[18]

As this and other examples show, human trafficking cases happen all over the United States. A few instances would represent just the "tip of the iceberg" in a growing criminal enterprise. Local and state criminal justice officials must understand that these cases are not isolated incidents that occur infrequently. They must remain alert for signs of trafficking in their jurisdictions and aggressively follow through on the smallest clue. Numerous websites openly (though they try to mask their actions) advertise for prostitution. Many of these sites involve young girls victimized by sex trafficking. Many of the pictures are altered to give the impression of older girls engaged in this activity freely and voluntarily. However, as prosecutors, the authors both have encountered numerous cases of suspected human trafficking involving underage girls.

Local and state criminal justice officials must understand that these cases are not isolated incidents that occur infrequently.

The article "The Girls Next Door" describes a conventional midcentury home in Plainfield, New Jersey, that sat in a nice middle-class neighborhood. Unbeknownst to the neighbors, the house was part of a network of stash houses in the New York area where underage girls and young women from dozens of countries were trafficked and held captive. Acting on a tip, police raided the house in February 2002, expecting to find an underground brothel. Instead, they found four girls between the ages of 14 and 17, all Mexican nationals without documentation.

However, they were not prostitutes; they were sex slaves. These girls did not work for profit or a paycheck. They were captives to the traffickers and keepers who controlled their every move. The police found a squalid, land-based equivalent of a 19th-century slave ship. They encountered rancid, doorless bathrooms; bare, putrid mattresses; and a stash of penicillin, "morning after" pills, and an antiulcer medication that can induce abortion. The girls were pale, exhausted, and malnourished.[19]

Human sex trafficking warning signs include, among other indicators, streetwalkers and strip clubs. However, a jurisdiction's lack of streetwalkers or strip clubs does not mean that it is immune to the problem of trafficking. Because human trafficking involves big money, if money can be made, sex slaves can be sold. Sex trafficking can happen anywhere, however unlikely a place. Investigators should be attuned to reading the signs of trafficking and looking closely for them.

Investigation of Human Sex Trafficking

ICE aggressively targets the global criminal infrastructure, including the people, money, and materials that support human trafficking networks. The agency strives to prevent human trafficking in the United States by prosecuting the traffickers and rescuing and protecting the victims. However, most human trafficking cases start at the local level.

Strategies

Local and state law enforcement officers may unknowingly encounter sex trafficking when they deal with homeless and runaway juveniles; criminal gang activity; crimes involving immigrant children who have no guardians; domestic violence calls; and investigations at truck stops, motels, massage parlors, spas, and strip clubs. To this end, the authors offer various suggestions and indicators to help patrol officers identify victims of sex trafficking, as well as tips for detectives who investigate these crimes.

Patrol Officers

- Document suspicious calls and complaints on a police information report, even if the details seem trivial.
- Be aware of trafficking when responding to certain call types, such as reports of foot traffic in and out of a house. Consider situations that seem similar to drug complaints.
- Look closely at calls for assaults, domestic situations, verbal disputes, or thefts. These could involve a trafficking victim being abused and disciplined by a trafficker, a customer having a dispute with a victim, or a client who had money taken during a sex act.
- Locations, such as truck stops, strip clubs, massage parlors, and cheap motels, are havens for prostitutes forced into sex trafficking. Many massage parlors and strip clubs that engage in sex trafficking will have cramped living quarters where the victims are forced to stay.
- When encountering prostitutes and other victims of trafficking, do not display judgment or talk down to them. Understand the violent nature in how they are forced into trafficking, which explains their lack of cooperation. Speak with them in a location completely safe and away from other people, including potential victims.
- Check for identification. Traffickers take the victims' identification and, in cases of foreign nationals, their travel information. The lack of either item should raise concern.

Detectives/Investigators

- Monitor websites that advertise for dating and hooking up. Most vice units are familiar with the common sites used by sex traffickers as a means of advertisement.
- Conduct surveillance at motels, truck stops, strip clubs, and massage parlors. Look to see if the girls arrive alone or with someone else. Girls being transported to these locations should raise concerns of trafficking.
- Upon an arrest, check cell phone records, motel receipts, computer printouts of advertisements, and tollbooth receipts. Look for phone calls from the jailed prostitute to the pimp. Check surveillance cameras at motels and toll facilities as evidence to indicate the trafficking of the victim.
- Obtain written statements from the customers; get them to work for you.
- Seek assistance from nongovernmental organizations involved in fighting sex trafficking. Many of these entities have workers who will interview these victims on behalf of the police.
- After executing a search warrant, photograph everything. Remember that in court, a picture may

be worth a thousand words: nothing else can more effectively describe a cramped living quarter a victim is forced to reside in.
- Look for advertisements in local newspapers, specifically the sports sections, that advertise massage parlors. These businesses should be checked out to ensure they are legitimate and not fronts for trafficking.
- Contact your local U.S. Attorney's Office, FBI field office, or ICE for assistance. Explore what federal resources exist to help address this problem.

Other Considerations

Patrol officers and investigators can look for many other human trafficking indicators as well.[20] These certainly warrant closer attention.

General Indicators

- People who live on or near work premises
- Individuals with restricted or controlled communication and transportation
- Persons frequently moved by traffickers
- A living space with a large number of occupants
- People lacking private space, personal possessions, or financial records
- Someone with limited knowledge about how to get around in a community

Physical Indicators

- Injuries from beatings or weapons
- Signs of torture (e.g., cigarette burns)
- Brands or scarring, indicating ownership
- Signs of malnourishment

Financial/Legal Indicators

- Someone else has possession of an individual's legal/travel documents
- Existing debt issues
- One attorney claiming to represent multiple illegal aliens detained at different locations
- Third party who insists on interpreting. Did the victim sign a contract?

Brothel Indicators

- Large amounts of cash and condoms
- Customer logbook or receipt book ("trick book")
- Sparse rooms
- Men come and go frequently

Conclusion

This form of cruel modern-day slavery occurs more often than many people might think. And, it is not just an international or a national problem—it also is a local one. It is big business, and it involves a lot of perpetrators and victims.

Agencies at all levels must remain alert to this issue and address it vigilantly. Even local officers must understand the problem and know how to recognize it in their jurisdictions. Coordinated and aggressive efforts from all law enforcement organizations can put an end to these perpetrators' operations and free the victims.

Notes

1. www.routledgesociology.com/books/Human-Sex-Trafficking-isbn9780415576789 (accessed July 19, 2010).
2. www.unodc.org/unodc/en/human-trafficking/what-is-human-trafficking.html (accessed July 19, 2010).
3. www.justice.gov/criminal/ceos/trafficking.html (accessed July 19, 2010).
4. Ibid.
5. www.justice.gov/criminal/ceos/prostitution.html (accessed July 19, 2010).
6. Richard J. Estes and Neil Alan Weiner, *Commercial Sexual Exploitation of Children in the U.S., Canada, and Mexico* (University of Pennsylvania, Executive Summary, 2001).
7. Ibid.
8. http://fpc.state.gov/documents/organization/9107.pdf (accessed July 19, 2010).
9. Estes and Weiner.
10. www.womenshealth.gov/violence/types/human-trafficking.cfm (accessed July 19, 2010).
11. For additional information, see Nathalie De Fabrique, Stephen J. Romano, Gregory M. Vecchi, and Vincent B. Van Hasselt, "Understanding Stockholm Syndrome," *FBI Law Enforcement Bulletin,* July 2007, 10–15.
12. Trafficking Victims Protection Act, Pub. L. No. 106–386 (2000), codified at 22 U.S.C. § 7101, et seq.
13. Ibid.
14. U.S. CONST. amend. XIII, § 1: "Neither slavery nor involuntary servitude, except as a punishment for crime whereof the party shall have been duly convicted, shall exist within the United States, or any place subject to their jurisdiction."
15. U.S. Department of Justice, "U.S. Army Soldier Sentenced to Over 17 Years in Prison for Operating a Brothel from Millersville Apartment and to Drug Trafficking," www.justice.gov/usao/md/Public-Affairs/press_releases/press10a.htm (accessed September 30, 2010).
16. www.fbi.gov/hq/cid/civilrights/trafficking_initiatives.htm (accessed September 30, 2010).
17. www.ojp.usdoj.gov/BJA/grant/42HTTF.pdf (accessed September 30, 2010).

18. http://actioncenter.polarisproject.org/the-frontlines/recent-federal-cases/435-leader-of-expansive-multi-state-sex-trafficking-ring-sentenced (accessed July 19, 2010).
19. www.nytimes.com/2004/01/25/magazine/25SEXTRAFFIC.html (accessed July 19, 2010).
20. http://httf.wordpress.com/indicators/ (accessed July 19, 2010).

Critical Thinking

1. Do you believe prostitutes are victims of human sex traffickers?
2. How can sex traffickers compel anyone to become a sex worker against his or her will?
3. What laws have been enacted to deal with sex trafficking?

From *FBI Law Enforcement Bulletin* by Amanda Walker-Rodriguez and Rodney Hill, March 2011. Published by Federal Bureau of Investigation. www.fbi.gov.

Could the Penn State Abuse Scandal Happen Somewhere Else? Definitely

An interview with Chris Gavagan, director of a documentary about sexual abuse in sports.

PATRICK HRUBY

With the release of a damning, 267-page investigative report compiled by former FBI director Louis Freeh, the ongoing child sex abuse scandal engulfing Penn State University and former football coach Joe Paterno went from bad to worse, with possible negligence involving the sex crimes perpetrated by former defensive coordinator Jerry Sandusky giving way to a probable cover-up.

For Chris Gavagan, however, the contents of the Freeh report were hardly surprising.

A Brooklyn-based filmmaker, Gavagan is working on *Coached Into Silence*, a documentary about sexual abuse in sports that includes interviews with experts, victims, and a roller hockey coach Gavagan claims abused him when he was a teenager.

To understand how Penn State fits into the larger context of sexual abuse by coaches—as well as how the university's leaders could display what Freeh termed a "total disregard for the safety and welfare of Sandusky's child victims"—*The Atlantic* spoke with Gavagan about the report, Paterno, and where the school goes from here.

What Similarities Do You See Between the Penn State Depicted in the Freeh Report and the Cases of Child Sex Abuse by Sports Coaches Documented in Your Film?

You could white out every proper name in the Freeh report and apply it to institutions all over this country that have failed in their responsibility to protect children. Time after time, the evidence has shown the most powerful and influential decision-makers circling the wagons and conspiring to decide, "How are we going to handle this?"

Victims are the last possible priority. Over and over, you see the drive to keep it quiet, to put it "behind us" with the fewest possible people being aware of it. In many cases—particularly at schools whose pristine reputation is paramount—rather than making a successful coach go away, they have made an accuser or the accusations go away.

In one elite prep school featured in the film, several students who came forward about abuse they suffered were quietly dismissed. In other cases, there have been payments handed out, "hush money" to convince a parent pushing the issue to relent.

It would shock me if the same tactics have not been put into play with Penn State over the decades of Jerry Sandusky's involvement with the program, which began in the late 1960's.

What Differences Do You See Between Penn State and the Cases You've Covered?

The difference is the documentation. In most other cases, there will never be a report. We will never see this evidence. We will never be privy to these discussions. Without the national spotlight, most of these institutions have been able to avoid the scrutiny of such an investigation. Often, a loophole in the law—such as widely varying state-by-state statutes of limitations—can provide another shield. If an institution can avoid, delay and intimidate long enough, they can make Penn State [vice president Gary] Schultz' 1998 email wish "I hope it is all behind us" a legal reality.

Prior to the ubiquity of email, an institution would have just solved much of this problem with payoff for an accuser and a shredder for the incriminating documentation. In some ways, we are fortunate that technology has created more of a trail in these cases.

Generally Speaking, How Does Something Like This Happen?

It takes a village to enable a sexual predator to continue unfettered for so long. The combination of ignorance of warning signs and willfully hidden information are necessary for these abuses to go on for decades.

Pillars of the community are given much more of a benefit of the doubt, but what has been demonstrated, unfortunately, is that nobody can be considered beyond reproach. The greatest masks of all are apparent good intentions and a smile. This is one of the most insidious aspects of these crimes. The stranger in the trench coat preying on children is the rarest of cases—the overwhelming majority are perpetrated by someone who is both trusted and known to the child.

In our film, we discussed with former *Sports Illustrated* editor Don Yaeger his process of researching his 1999 cover article "Every Parent's Nightmare." In our interview, he quotes a pedophile as calling coaching "the last great candy store of opportunity." Not only did the most powerful men at Penn State choose not to shut down Sandusky's candy store when it was brought to their attention, but by allowing his continued access to all things Penn State they went above and beyond to ensure that it remained open for business and that the shelves were stocked with the sweetest bait a young boy could imagine.

Which Specific Details of the Freeh Report Most Stood Out to You, and Why?

The coded, callous discussions of incidents that Schultz called "at worst sexual improprieties"—and the talk of needing to clarify to Sandusky his "guests' use of the facilities"—is appalling. They refer to a child victim of rape as if he were a kid being punished for peeing in the pool. It shows a complete and utter disregard for other human beings.

The nameless boy in the shower was someone's child.

Also, the fact that information was withheld from the board right until the last possible moment, time and time again, demonstrates the danger of a lack of accountability and oversight. [Penn State president Graham] Spanier, [athletic director Tim] Curley, and Schultz come across as the last men shouting that the *Titanic* is unsinkable, even as their lungs are filling with frigid water of the North Atlantic.

How Does the Disregard for Children Happen?

More often than not, this kind of disregard occurs in tiny dehumanizing increments. For a human being, no matter what is at stake to professionally or financially, to take actions that enable these abuses to continue, they must begin by not seeing the victim as a human. The farther you get away from that flesh and blood child—nameless and faceless—the easier it is for you to proceed.

There is a reason that the prosecutors in the Sandusky trial opened their case by showing photographs of the victims at the ages that they were when these crimes were committed against them—because it works. I was sitting in that courtroom, and to be forced to face the very real, very human toll of these crimes is unbelievably powerful.

The men in power at Penn State did not have to face that. They faced words, they faced an idea, and by facing only that I believe they were able to discount, to some extent, the horrors that were being committed on their watch. There are things that one must lie to themselves about in order to be a part of, if you are to live with yourself. I would imagine that sacrificing a child to the "greater good" of an institution is one such case.

The Freeh Report Concluded That Joe Paterno and Other Top Penn State Officials Covered up the Sex Abuse Allegations against Sandusky Because they were Afraid of "Bad Publicity." Is That Unusual? Why or Why Not?

In the vast majority of these cases, "bad publicity"—and all the considerations that entails, specifically in terms of financial backlash—is the immediate concern.

For example, when you run an elite prep school and charge $33,000 a year for tuition—like one of the schools featured in our film—administrators will go to great lengths to prevent any evidence from coming out that could tarnish their reputation and thereby handicap their ability to charge such an astronomical amount. Schools also rely heavily on alumni donations. How willing do you think their alumni would be to write out generous checks if they were aware that some portion of that donation was going to fight to keep sex abuse cases from going to trial?

Spanier acknowledging in the Freeh report that their decision not to go to the proper authorities leaves them vulnerable is a rare peek behind the curtain of all decision-makers who have chosen the same course of action—or inaction. They explicitly knew the risks, yet they did it anyway.

If there were a fire on campus, there would have been no debate as to "how are we going to handle this?" The proper authorities to handle the specific situation would have been called immediately.

One of the Most Heartbreaking Things in the Freeh Report Involves Janitors Who Saw Sandusky Molesting a Boy in the Penn State Football Showers but did not Report the Incident for Fear of Losing Their Jobs. Was Their Fear Reasonable? What Kind of Reaction do Child Sex Abuse Whistleblowers Typically Face?

Their fears were unfortunate, but more than reasonable. To ask the lowest men on the totem pole to be heroes where "great men" have failed is unfair. The lower you rank, the heavier the pressure of the edifice above you. The little people get crushed—and who can rank lower than a child? Powerless. No money. No influence. The greatest action taken in your defense by anyone at Penn State was a slammed locker.

In a case featured in the film, it was the assistant coach who was the whistleblower, going to his superiors to report what he knew to be credible accusations against his head coach. As thanks for his speaking out, the administration of the school began a smear campaign against the *assistant* in the press, even going so far as to remove the whistleblower's picture from the school's hall of fame, while the picture of the head coach—who would eventually plead guilty to two counts of child rape—still smiled from his plaque within a glass case.

Personally, my own experience of reporting my coach and abuser to the league is both a subjective prism through which I view reporting, and also a glimpse of the pressures that can be brought to bear. Although the director of the league believed me when I reported my coach, the next words out of his mouth were problematic: "I know you love this league too . . . and when this gets out they're going to shut us down." Not so subtly, the victim had been handed responsibility for the potential closing of his beloved league. They dismissed the coach that night, but did no more. During the production of *Coached Into Silence,* I would discover that he took his whistle six miles down the road and continued coaching for years. The statute of limitations in my home state of New York had expired, and there was nothing I could do.

The Freeh Report Also Blamed a "Culture of Reverence for the Football Program." What do You Make of That?

In an interview that we conducted in 2009 with Cardozo law professor Marci Hamilton, she discusses the shadow side of a successful coach. Although a successful coach is wonderful for any organization, there is a danger when that individual's success has begun "a legacy of donations for the institution." Sandusky masterfully exploited the cover provided by his own gridiron success, and those in power who surrounded him willingly provided the ongoing shield with the Penn State imprimatur—with one apparent and unenforced condition: *Don't do it here.*

We have cases in the film where the abusers have not just won many games or championships, but are gold medal-winners or enshrined in their sport's Hall of Fame. For a particular institution or sport to admit and acknowledge abuse or a problem with someone who has risen to these heights and has been given every accolade imaginable takes an extraordinary amount of fortitude.

Unfortunately, that kind of courage is rare. More often than not, a literal or figurative cost benefit analysis is done, an institution tabulates the price of potential lawsuits, and the decision is made to do all that is within their power to make the problem go away without reporting it to the police.

A Report Estimated That the Sandusky Case Could Ultimately Cost Penn State $100 Million in Civil Damages. What is the Psychological and Emotional Cost to Sandusky's Victims?

The true human cost will never be accurately tallied. Having personally lived through the effects of these abuses on a victim—and studied all that there is to study about them—I can say that not all who fall prey will live long enough to be called a "survivor." Among Sandusky's victims, there are bound to be those who have taken their secret shame to the grave, dying by the drugs or alcohol that they took to cope with the abuse, or succumbing to depression and suicide. The suicide rate among victims is many, many times higher than average.

What Lessons can Penn State—and the Rest of Us—Learn from This Tragedy?

When any man—or any college sports program—becomes more powerful than the institution itself, corruption is sure to follow.

As someone who remains a true sports fan and has enjoyed the benefits of being involved, I can't demonize that world. Yet when any aspect of an organization becomes a money-printing machine, the tail begins to wag the dog. For example, Phil Knight's hero worship [of Paterno] cannot be viewed independently of knowing where his bread was buttered.

Penn State remains an incredible educational institution, turning out many of this country's best and brightest minds. But some of the deepest soul searching that must be done at the school regards exactly how much power they have ceded to football. They have sacrificed too much at the altar of the sport.

Should Penn State take down Its on-campus statue of Paterno?

To choose to continue to honor the man as the winningest football coach and the architect of his "grand experiment" is to ignore this truth: For all of the good he may have done, for all the lives that he may have impacted in a positive way, his grand experiment was a failure. The cult of personality, the total lack of accountability, the man who could tell his superiors exactly when he would be stepping down existed in a poisoned atmosphere of his own creation. The power centralized in one man, immortalized in bronze, made a true chain of command, of checks and balances, impossible. When it is a controversial decision to paint over someone's halo, we are ignoring the man's humanity, not honoring it. The disregard for the humanity of the victims—"some Second Mile kid" and "the boy in the shower"—is how this was allowed to occur in the first place.

My wish is for the statue to be taken down and returned to the workshop where it was created, then have Paterno's skyward-pointing index finger repositioned in front of his lips—the exhale of a quiet, craven "Shhhhh." Put that new version on a flatbed truck and tour the nation, with those who have survived childhood sexual abuse speaking at every stop to educate and raise awareness of the issue while warning against the hubris that led a "great man" to believe that his own reputation mattered more than the lives of children.

Critical Thinking

1. In general, are most child abusers strangers to the children or trusted acquaintances?
2. Is it enough to fire a coach who has been abusing his students, making sure he won't bother the kids in that school again, without also having him arrested?

UNIT 3

The Police

Unit Selections

Learning Outcomes

After reading this unit, you will be able to:

- State the differences between the policing environments in 1985 and 2008.
- Relate some of the challenges facing police executives today.
- Show how the growth of private security affects policing.
- Describe the differences and similarities between police and the military.
- Show how dogs can do police work.
- Relate some of the problems with forensic evidence.
- Describe how police officers can reduce the psychological discomfort that might accompany their misconduct.
- Evaluate a police officer's style of writing an incident report.
- Recognize how the loss of mental health resources can directly affect policing.

Student Website

www.mhhe.com/cls

Internet References

ACLU Criminal Justice Home Page
www.aclu.org/CriminalJustice/CriminalJusticeMain.cfm

Law Enforcement Guide to the World Wide Web
http://leolinks.com

Violent Criminal Apprehension Program (VICAP)
www.fbi.gov/wanted/vicap

Police officers are the guardians of our rights under the Constitution and the law, and as such they have an awesome task. They are asked to prevent crime, protect citizens, arrest wrongdoers, preserve the peace, aid the sick, control juveniles, control traffic, and provide emergency services on a moment's notice. They are also asked to be ready to lay down their lives, if necessary.

In recent years, the job of the police officer has become even more complex and dangerous. Illegal drug use and trafficking are still major problems; racial tensions are explosive; and terrorism is now an alarming reality. As our population grows more numerous and diverse, the role of the police in America becomes ever more challenging, requiring skills that can only be obtained by greater training and professionalism.

The lead article in this section, by David H. Bayley and Christine Nixon, "The Changing Environment for Policing," takes an in-depth look at policing over the years 1985 to 2008. Next, in "When the Police Go Military," Al Baker reports on the relatively recent phenomenon of police officers adopting military-style tactics and equipment and behaving more like soldiers as they face down citizens, although American law and tradition have tried to draw a clear line between police and military forces. To blur the roles is to mistake the mission of each. Another police tactic is described by Burkhard Bilger in "Beware of the Dogs." Dogs in the military have a history that goes back to ancient times, and the American military now has some 3000 active-duty dogs. Since 2001 the New York Police Department has nearly doubled its canine force while losing 17 percent of its uniformed officers.

Following is a report by Spencer S. Hsu, "Forensic Techniques are Subject to Human Bias, Lack Standards, Panel Found," part of a series on criminal justice issues in *the Washington Post,* in which he points out the weaknesses in commonly accepted forensic techniques such as hair and handwriting analysis, ballistics evidence, and even fingerprint identification.

In the next article, the problem of police officers who violate their oath is discussed by Brian D. Fitch, in "Understanding the Psychology of Police Misconduct." In "The Art of the Police Report," Ellen Collet shows how a Los Angeles cop writes a report that follows the department's guidelines and presents the facts, yet is also a compelling narrative that engages the reader emotionally.

The last article in this section, "As Mental Health Resources Shrink Police Become Front Line with Lives at Stake" by Henri E. Cauvin, describes how financially strapped state and local governments are putting pressures on police as more people with mental health problems are cut off from treatment.

Article 15

The Changing Environment for Policing, 1985–2008

DAVID H. BAYLEY AND CHRISTINE NIXON

Introduction

In 1967, the President's Commission on Law Enforcement and the Administration of Justice published *The Challenge of Crime in a Free Society.* This publication is generally regarded as inaugurating the scientific study of the police in America in particular but also in other countries. Almost 20 years later, the John F. Kennedy School of Government, Harvard University, convened an Executive Session on the police (1985–1991) to examine the state of policing and to make recommendations for its improvement. Its approximately 30 participants were police executives and academic experts. Now, 20 years further on, the Kennedy School has again organized an Executive Session. Its purpose, like the first, is to combine professional with scholarly appraisals of the police and their contribution to public safety.

So the question naturally arises, what are the differences in the environment for policing between these two time periods? Are the problems as well as the institution of the police similar or different from one period to the next? Our thesis is that policing in the mid-1980s was perceived to be in crisis and there was a strong sense that fundamental changes were needed in the way it was delivered. In contrast, police are considered to be performing well 20 years later by both practitioners and outside observers. Crime has been falling for almost 18 years and any new challenges, including terrorism, appear to be manageable without the invention of new strategies for the delivery of police services. Past experience contains the lessons needed for the future. In our view, this assessment may be mistaken, not because existing policies are defective in controlling crime but because the institutions that provide public safety are changing in profound ways that are not being recognized.

The Policing Environment in 1985

Policing in the United States was under siege in the 1980s for two reasons: (1) crime had been rising from the early 1960s, and (2) research had shown that the traditional strategies of the police were ineffective at coping with it. In 1960, the serious crime rate was 1,887 per 100,000 people. In 1985 it was 5,224, almost a threefold increase. This trend peaked in 1990 at 5,803. Violent crime (i.e., murder, rape, robbery and aggravated assault) rose from 161 per 100,000 people in 1960 to 558 in 1985, on the way to quadrupling by 1991 (Maguire and Pastore, 2007). Crime was, understandably, a big issue, feeding what could properly be called a moral panic.

Prompted by the President's Commission on Law Enforcement and the Administration of Justice in 1967, researchers in universities and private think-tanks began to study the effectiveness of standard police strategies. In the ensuing two decades, studies were published showing that crime rates were not affected by:

- Hiring more police (Loftin and McDowell, 1982; Krahn and Kennedy, 1985; Koenig, 1991; Laurie, 1970; Gurr, 1979; Emsley, 1983; Silberman, 1978; Reiner, 1985; Lane, 1980).
- Random motorized patrolling (Kelling et al., 1974; Kelling, 1985; Morris and Heal, 1981).
- Foot patrols (Police Foundation, 1981).
- Rapid response to calls for service (Tien, Simon and Larson, 1978; Bieck and Kessler, 1977; Spelman and Brown, 1981).
- Routine criminal investigation (Laurie, 1970; Burrows, 1986; Greenwood, Petersilia and Chaiken, 1977; Eck, 1982; Royal Commission on Criminal Procedure, 1981).

These conclusions, despite challenges to some of them on methodological grounds, were considered authoritative. They were so well accepted, in fact, that Bayley could say in 1994 that "one of the best kept secrets of modern life" was that the police do not prevent crime. "Experts know it, the police know it, and the public does not know it" (Bayley, 1994:3).

No wonder, then, that the first Executive Session concluded that fundamental changes were needed in police strategies. The Session took the lead in developing and legitimating a new model for the delivery of police services—community policing. The key recommendation was that police needed to be reconnected to the public in order both to enhance their crime-control effectiveness and to increase public respect. The strategy for doing this was community policing, including problem-oriented policing (Trojanowicz and Bucqueroux, 1990; Goldstein, 1990). Of the 17 studies published by the first Executive Session as *Perspectives on Policing,* eight featured "community" or "community policing" in the title, and several others discussed the importance of community. George Kelling and Mark Moore, members of the session, argued that the evolution of American policing could be described as movement from a politicized system to professionalism, then to constitutionalism, and ultimately to community policing (Kelling and Moore, 1988).

The first Executive Session also encouraged a new management style for policing, namely, one based on the analysis of crime and disorder problems and the evaluation of remediation programs. This process of description and analysis was to be carried out jointly by police and outside experts, such as academic scholars and management consultants.

The Policing Environment in 2008

When the second Executive Session met in January 2008, crime in the United States had declined dramatically since 1990. The serious crime rate (Part I crimes) had fallen to 3,808 per 100,000 people by 2006, a decline of 34 percent (Maguire and Pastore, 2007).[1] Even though the violent crime rate was still three times higher in 2006 than in 1960 (474 versus 161 per 100,000 people), it had declined by 37.5 percent since its peak in 1991, a huge change for the better. The police, in particular, feel that the decline vindicates their crime-control efforts, notably the strategy attributed to Bill Bratton of New York City, of the strict enforcement of laws against disorder and the management technique known as *zero tolerance,* managed through COMPSTAT (Bratton and Knobler, 1998; Eck and Maguire, 2000).

The decline has been so dramatic that it offset the continued questioning by analysts of the importance of police action in controlling crime (Eck and Maguire, 2000). Furthermore, there are now positive findings about the efficacy of certain police strategies. The most authoritative summary of this research comes from a panel of the National Research Council (Skogan and Frydl, 2004).

Reviewing all research conducted since the President's Commission (1967) and available in English, the panel reaffirmed the findings of the 1970s and 1980s that the standard practices of policing—employing more sworn officers, random motorized patrolling, rapid response and criminal investigation—failed to reduce crime when applied generally throughout a jurisdiction. It should be noted that most of the research on these topics, except for analysis of the effect of the number of police employees on crime, dated from the earlier period. At the same time, the panel found that police could reduce crime when they focused operations on particular problems or places and when they supplemented law enforcement with other regulatory and abatement activities.

The strongest evidence for effectiveness was some form of problem solving, especially when focused on "hot spots," that is, locations accounting for a high volume of repeat calls for police service. Nonenforcement options included changing the physical design of buildings and public spaces, enforcing fire and safety codes, providing social services to dysfunctional families, reducing truancy and providing after-school programs for latch-key children.

By 2008, police executives could feel much happier about their efforts to control crime than they had 20 years before. Scholars, too, agreed that strategies used since the 1980s were efficacious, by and large.

This is not to say that police leaders currently feel that they can rest on their laurels nor that the environment for policing is entirely benign. Police executives understand that they are confronting several challenges, some new and some old:

- **Declining budgets and the rising cost of sworn police officers.** The cost of policing has quadrupled between 1985 and 2005, according to the Bureau of Justice Statistics (Gascón and Foglesong, 2009). The causes are rising labor costs for both sworn officers and civilian personnel, increased demand for police services and the growing complexity of police work. As a result, police budgets are increasingly at risk, with some cities reducing the number of police officers per capita.
- **Terrorism.** The primary impact of the Sept. 11 terrorist attack on state and local policing in the United States has been to improve their capacity for risk assessment of local vulnerabilities and first-responding in the event of terrorist incidents (Bayley and Weisburd, 2009). Although threat assessment and first-responding are understood to be core responsibilities of local police, their role with respect to counterterrorism intelligence gathering and analysis is more problematic. At the moment, most intelligence about terrorism comes from federal sources. Some observers take the view that local law enforcement, especially in the United States with its radically decentralized police system, does not have the personnel or skills to collect operational intelligence in a cost-effective way. Others argue, however, that local general-duties police who work among the population are essential for detecting precursor terrorist activities and building cooperative relations with the communities in which terrorists live (Bayley and Weisburd, 2009). Many police executives are critical of the federal government, therefore, for downgrading its law enforcement attention from nonterrorist crime and for reducing its support for local community-responsive and crime-prevention activities.
- **New immigrants, both legal and illegal.** Until recently, most American police departments took the view that enforcing immigration was a federal rather than a local responsibility. They took this view, in part, because they wanted illegal immigrants to feel free to approach police when they were victims of crime, particularly when they were exploited by employers. Police executives felt that even people who were in the country illegally deserved protection under the law. Recently, however, driven by growing anti-illegal immigration feelings in their jurisdictions, some police departments have begun to enforce immigration regulations. As anticipated, this has alienated these communities at the very moment when the importance of connecting with immigrants—legal as well as illegal—has become imperative as a response to terrorism. Not only may foreign terrorists take cover in immigrant communities but these communities, especially if they are disadvantaged and marginalized, may produce their own home-grown perpetrators. Great Britain and France have both experienced this phenomenon. Thus, the threat of terrorism raises difficult questions about the scope, intensity and methods of law enforcement in immigrant communities.
- **Racial discrimination.** Charges of unequal treatment on the basis of race have been a continual problem for police since the rise of civil rights consciousness in the 1960s. Concerns raised about the substantial amount of discretion possessed by frontline police was one of the first issues taken up by police researchers more than 40 years ago. Various aspects of policing have been implicated—arrests, use of force, shootings, street stops, search and seizure,

offense charging and equality of coverage (Fridell et al., 2001; Skolnick and Fyfe, 1993; Walker, 2003). Not only is racial discrimination an enduring issue for police executives to manage but its potential for destroying the reputation of police agencies and the careers of officers is hard to exaggerate. It is the allegation that every police chief dreads.

- **Intensified accountability.** Oversight of police performance, with regard to effectiveness in controlling both crime and personal behavior, has grown steadily in the past few years. The monitoring of institutional performance has been part of a governmentwide movement to specify measurable performance indicators. External oversight of individual behavior has involved complaints commissions, citizen review panels and ombudsmen. Many would argue that the quality of policing with respect to crime control and personal behavior has improved over the last half of the 20th century as a result of these developments. The public, however, seems more skeptical, especially with respect to the behavior of individual officers. At least that would be a fair reading of the fact that in the United States as well as other English-speaking countries, the demand for greater oversight of police behavior continues to grow, fed by the media's insatiable appetite for stories about police misdeeds.

  There are two aspects to what is being asked for: (1) holding the police to account for performing the services for which they were created—crime prevention and criminal investigation and (2) disciplining officers who behave improperly in the course of their duties. Today, more than 100 of America's largest cities have some sort of civilian oversight of police behavior compared with only a handful in the early 1990s (Walker, 2003). Independent civilian review of complaints against the police has been established in the last three decades in Great Britain, New Zealand, Australia and Canada. But this is only the most visible tip of a larger iceberg. Oversight has also intensified in the form of tighter financial auditing, performance indicators mandated by governmental and quasi-governmental bodies, enactment of more stringent legal standards and federal consent decrees. This is in addition to what seems to police to be an unappeasable media appetite for revelations about police, and even ex-police, misbehavior.
- **Police unions.** While acknowledging the reasons that led to the growth of police unions, police executives complain about its impact on management. In particular, they criticize the reflexive defense of work rules that inhibit strategic innovation and organizational change, the elaborate procedures required to discipline poorly performing officers, and the inculcation of an occupational culture preoccupied with tangible rewards.

Although all of these current challenges certainly complicate their work, police executives do not view them as a crisis for policing as was the case in the mid-1980s. These challenges are complex and difficult but manageable within the competence of experienced executives. With the arguable exception of terrorism, they do not require a shift in the strategies of policing.

Embedded in this sense of achievement among police professionals is frustration with the gap between objective measures of public safety and public perceptions. Although crime may have declined, the public's fear has not. Police commonly attribute this discrepancy to the exaggeration of crime by the media and the failure to give credit where credit is due.

The Looming Watershed

We believe that policing may be approaching, if not well into, a period of change that will significantly affect what police do and how they do it. It may be as significant as the period after 1829 when Sir Robert Peel created the London Metropolitan Police. The choice of 1829 as the reference point is not rhetorical. This year marked the beginning of the gradual monopolization of the police function by government. Starting in 1829, governments in Anglo-Saxon countries, much earlier in Europe, assumed responsibility for policing—for hiring, paying, training and supervising. What is happening now is the reverse of that: nation-states are losing their monopoly on policing.

The pressures eroding the monopoly of governments within national boundaries to create and manage policing come from three directions:

- The internationalization of policing.
- The devolution of policing to communities.
- The growth of private policing.

In short, policing is being pushed up, down and sideways from its traditional mooring in government.

The Internationalization of Policing

Policing has shifted away from national governments because of the development of a genuinely international police capacity and increased international collaboration in law enforcement. The United Nations now has more than 11,000 police recruited from about 118 countries and deployed in 13 missions. The United States currently contributes 268 police to UNPOL (formerly CIVPOL). Although UNPOL's primary mission is "to build institutional police capacity in post-conflict environments" (Kroeker, 2007), its officers have been armed in Kosovo, Timor-Leste and Haiti and enforce laws alongside the local police. It is worth mentioning that this is part of a broader development of international institutions of justice, including the development of a portable international criminal code, courts and tribunals authorized to try individuals, and prisons for persons both convicted and under trial.

The United States now collaborates widely with law enforcement agencies abroad. As of February 2010, the FBI has offices in 70 cities overseas and the DEA has offices in almost 90 (see FBI and DEA home pages). The United States trains more than 10,000 police a year at its four International Law Enforcement Training Academies (located in Budapest, Bangkok, Gaborone and San Salvador) and brings many more trainees to the United States. The United States also participates in a host of international task forces and ad hoc law enforcement operations that focus on drugs, terrorism, trafficking in people and, more recently, cyber-crime, including pornography. The United States has also encouraged—some would say "pressured"—countries to bring their laws into conformity with American practice, for example, with respect to wiretapping, the use of informants, asset forfeiture, and the Racketeer Influenced and Corrupt Organizations Act (Nadelman, 1997;

Snow, 1997). American influence, direct and indirect, has been so powerful that Chris Stone says there has been an "Americanization of global law enforcement" (Stone, 2003). The United States, furthermore, has begun to create a reserve force of police and other criminal justice experts that can be deployed at short notice to countries emerging from conflict.

If policing is a fundamental attribute of government, along with external defense, then the world has begun to create a world government of sorts. Although seeds of this movement preceded the first Executive Session, a major impetus was the fall of the Berlin Wall in 1989 and the subsequent implosion of the Soviet Union (Bayley, 2006).

The Devolution of Policing to Communities

The attitude of police generally in the Western world, but especially in its English-speaking democracies, toward collaborating with members of the public who act voluntarily to improve public security has undergone a major change since the 1980s. No longer viewed as nuisances or dangerous vigilantes, these people are now seen as "co-producers" of public safety. This transformation of view is attributable in large part to the acceptance of community policing, which the first Executive Session was instrumental in promoting. Police in democratic countries now actively encourage citizen participation by sharing information, training volunteers, consulting the public about priorities, mobilizing collaborative crime-prevention programs, enlisting the public as informants in problem solving, and soliciting help from city planners, architects and the designers of products to minimize criminal opportunities. Neighborhood Watch is probably the best known police-citizen partnership. Others include Business Improvement Districts, mobile CB-radio patrols, and private-sector programs for providing equipment and professional skills to police departments.

It has become axiomatic in policing that the public should be encouraged to take responsibility for enhancing public safety. As police themselves now recognize, they cannot do the job alone. Public participation is seen by police and academics alike as a critical contributor to police effectiveness and thus to public safety.

The Growth of Private Policing

Policing is being pushed sideways by the growth in the private security industry. Estimates of its strength are not exact because "private security" covers a wide range of activities—e.g., guarding, transporting valuables, investigating, installing protective technology and responding to alarms—and is supplied by companies commercially to others as well as by businesses to themselves. The U.S. Department of Labor estimated that there were slightly more than 1 million private security guards in 2005 (U.S. Bureau of Labor Statistics, 2005). That would be 49 percent more than the number of full-time sworn police officers in the same year (673,146). A report issued by the International Association of Chiefs of Police (IACP) and the Community Oriented Police Services (COPS) Office estimated, however, that in 2004, the number was about 2 million (IACP, 2005). If that were true, there would be almost three times as many private security personnel as full-time police officers. The discrepancy between figures of the Department of Labor and those of IACP-COPS may have arisen because the larger estimate includes in-house security provided by private organizations, whereas the Department of Labor figures only include the personnel of companies providing security services commercially. The larger figure is the one most often cited in commentaries on private policing (Cunningham and Taylor, 1985; Singer, 2003).

The growth of private security appears to be a phenomenon of the last quarter of the 20th century (Nalla and Newman, 1991). It was first documented in *The Hallcrest Report: Private Security and Police in America* (Cunningham and Taylor, 1985), which estimated the number at 1.5 million. This was more than twice the number of public police at that time. Although the use of private security was certainly visible to police officials in the 1980s, the number of *commercial* private security personnel has grown by as much as two-thirds. Their number rose sharply immediately after the Sept. 11 attack, fell in 2003 (although not to pre-Sept. 11 levels) and has continued to increase (U.S. Bureau of Labor Statistics, 2007). It is reasonable to assume that the number of *in-house* private security personnel has also increased, though perhaps not as much.

Worldwide, there are now more private police than government-run police: 348 versus 318 per 100,000, according to a survey by Jan Van Dijk (2008). The highest rates are in the United States, Canada and central Europe. Britain and Australia also have slightly more private security personnel than public police (Australian Bureau of Statistics, 2006; European Union, 2004). In the European Union, only Britain and Ireland have more private than public police (European Union, 2004). Statistics are not available for Latin America, Africa, and South and Southeast Asia, but private security is certainly very visible there.

The point to underscore is that worldwide, and dramatically in the United States, there has been a steady growth in the number of private "police." If visible guardians are a deterrent to crime, as the routine-activities theory of crime asserts and as police themselves strongly believe, then one reason for the decline in crime in the United States since the early 1990s might be the growth in private security. As far as we are aware, analyses of the crime drop in the United States have not tested for this possibility.

The effect of these three changes in the environment for policing is to diversify the providers of public safety. Governments, especially country-based governments, no longer direct or provide public safety exclusively. The domestic security function has spread to new levels of government but, more important, to non-state actors, volunteers and commercial providers. The police role is now shared. This is not simply saying that there are now both public and private police. Public and private policing have blended and are often hard to distinguish. Governments hire private police to supplement their own police; private entrepreneurs hire public police. We are in an era of what Les Johnston refers to as hybrid policing (Johnston, 1992).

Until now, assessments of the police have focused on two questions: How can they be made more effective, and how can the behavior of individual officers be improved? Now, we suggest, a third question has arisen: Who is responsible for policing?

Changes within Public Policing

Not only are changes occurring in the environment that may affect the structure of policing but police themselves are in the process of changing the way they work. The factors driving this are

(1) the threat of terrorism, (2) intelligence-led policing and (3) DNA analysis. Each of these developments transfers initiative in directing operations to specialists who collect and analyze information and away from both general-duties police and the public. Ironically, these changes could undo the signature contribution of the 1980s—community policing.

The Threat of Terrorism

Although many anti-terrorism experts understand the importance of working with communities, especially immigrant ones, counterterrorism centralizes decision making, shifting it upward in police organizations and making it less transparent. In the aftermath of Sept. 11, a new emphasis has been placed on the development of covert intelligence gathering, penetration and disruption. In the United States, the development of covert counterterrorism capacity has been unequally distributed, being more pronounced in larger police forces. Where it occurs, important questions arise about legal accountability as well as operational payoff. These issues are familiar to police, having arisen before in efforts to control illegal narcotics and organized crime.

Intelligence-Led Policing

Intelligence-led policing[2] utilizes crime mapping, data mining and the widespread use of closed-circuit television monitoring, which all rely on analysis based on information collected from impersonal sources. It thereby empowers senior commanders to develop their own agendas for law enforcement rather than consulting with affected communities.

DNA Analysis

DNA analysis allows crimes to be solved without witnesses or confessions. Research in the 1970s showed that the identification of suspects by victims and witnesses was essential to the solving of most crimes (Greenwood, Petersilia and Chaiken, 1977). Detectives, contrary to their fictional portrayals, work from the identification of suspects by the public back to the collection of evidence to prove guilt. DNA changes that, emphasizing forensic evidence over human testimony, promising a technological solution to criminal identification.

The effect of these developments—the threat of terrorism, intelligence-led policing and DNA analysis—impels the police to rely more on their own intellectual and physical resources and on centralized decision making for agendas and strategies. It lessens the importance of consulting with and mobilizing the disaggregate resources of communities. It also favors enforcement as the tool of choice over preventive strategies of regulation and abatement. These changes in orientation may be necessary and may raise police effectiveness, but they also represent a return to the sort of insular professionalism that characterized policing before the 1980s.

The Challenges of Change

The changes described both inside and outside the established police structures and functions create issues that will have to be confronted. With the expansion of private policing, public safety may become more inequitably distributed on the basis of economic class. The affluent sectors of society, especially its commercial interests, may be more protected, and the poor sectors less protected (Bayley and Shearing, 2001). This trend could be exacerbated if the tax-paying public at the same time withdraws its support from the public police in favor of private security. There are indications that this has already occurred in public education, where people with the means to pay for private schools are increasingly reluctant to support public education. If this should occur in policing, a dualistic system could evolve—responsive private policing for the affluent, and increasingly underfunded public policing for the poor (Bayley and Shearing, 2001). The political consequences of this could be calamitous.

Furthermore, who is to hold private policing to legal and moral account? Public police in the United States and other democracies have been made accountable in many ways. Public police executives themselves often argue that they are too accountable, meaning they are scrutinized too closely, too mechanically and at a substantial cost in reporting. Private policing, however, is imperfectly regulated and it is unclear whether existing law provides sufficient leverage (Joh, 2004; Prenzler and Sarre, 2006).

So, an ironic question arises: Is there a continuing role for government in ensuring an equitable and lawful distribution of security at the very time that government is losing its monopoly control? Should it accomplish by regulation what it no longer can by ownership? If so, how should this be done? In particular, what agency of government would be responsible for it?

The internationalization of policing also raises issues of control and legitimacy. Simply put, whose interests will be served by policing under international auspices? Will it be collective interests articulated by constituent states and powerful organized interests, or by the needs of disaggregate populations represented through participative institutions? Democratic nation-states emphasize the needs of individuals in directing police. It is not at all clear that international institutions will do the same, although they have taken impressive steps on paper to articulate comprehensive standards of police conduct (U.N. High Commissioner for Human Rights, 1996).

Finally, we submit that policing may be facing a clash of cultures as the public increasingly demands participation in the direction and operation of policing while at the same time police agencies become more self-directing and self-sufficient in their use of intelligence resources. This issue is not new. It is the same issue that policing faced in the 1980s and that was tackled in the first Executive Session. How important is public legitimacy for police effectiveness and public safety? How can the support of the public be maintained while police take advantage of powerful new technologies that may decrease interaction with them?

Conclusion

In the United States and other developed democracies, changes are occurring that may undermine the monopoly of state-based policing as well as its community-based paradigm. In pointing out these changes between 1985 and 2008, we are not making value judgments about them. These changes may have made the police more effective at providing public safety without infringing human rights in unacceptable ways. We call attention to these changes because their potential effects are enormous and largely unappreciated. They constitute an invisible agenda as consequential as the problems discussed in the 1980s.

Twenty years ago, policing was in the throes of what is now regarded as a revolution in its operating approach. It shifted from a philosophy of "give us the resources and we can do the job" to realizing the importance of enlisting the public in the coproduction of public safety. Policing today faces much less obvious challenges. Current strategies and technologies seem to be sufficient to deal with foreseeable threats to public safety, with the possible exception of terrorism. If this is so, then policing will develop in an evolutionary way, fine-tuning operational techniques according to experience, particularly the findings of evidence-based evaluations. If, however, changes in the environment are reshaping the structure and hence the governance of policing, and adaptations within the police are weakening the connection between police and public, then we may be entering a period of evolutionary discontinuity that could be greater than that of the 1980s, perhaps even of 1829. Both the role of police in relation to other security providers and the soul of the police in terms of how it goes about its work may be in play today in more profound ways than are being recognized.

References

Australian Bureau of Statistics. "2006 Census of Population and Housing, Australia, Occupation by Sex (Based on Place of Employment)." Accessed February 11, 2010, at www.censusdata.abs.gov.au.

Bayley, David H. *Police for the Future.* New York: Oxford University Press, 1994.

Bayley, David H. *Changing the Guard: Developing Democratic Police Abroad.* New York: Oxford University Press, 2006.

Bayley, David H. and Clifford Shearing. *The New Structure of Policing: Description, Conceptualization, and Research Agenda.* Final report. Washington, D.C.: U.S. Department of Justice, National Institute of Justice, July 2001. NCJ 187083.

Bayley, David H. and David Weisburd. "Cops and Spooks: The Role of the Police in Counterterrorism." In *To Protect and Serve: Policing in an Age of Terrorism,* ed. David Weisburd, Thomas E. Feucht, Idit Hakimi, Lois Felson Mock and Simon Perry. New York: Springer, 2009:81–100.

Bieck, William and David A. Kessler. *Response Time Analysis.* Kansas City, Mo.: Board of Police Commissioners, 1977.

Bratton, William and Peter Knobler. *Turnaround: How America's Top Cop Reversed the Crime Epidemic.* New York: Random House, 1998.

Burrows, John. *Investigating Burglary: The Measurement of Police Performance.* Research Study 88. London: Home Office, 1986.

Cunningham, William C. and Todd H. Taylor. *The Hallcrest Report: Private Security and Police in America.* Portland, Ore.: Chancellor Press, 1985.

Eck, John E. *Solving Crimes: The Investigation of Burglary and Robbery.* Washington, D.C.: Police Executive Research Forum, 1982.

Eck, John E. and Edward Maguire. "Have Changes in Policing Reduced Violent Crime? An Assessment of the Evidence." In *The Crime Drop in America,* ed. Alfred Blumstein and Joel Wallman. New York: Cambridge University Press, 2000:207–265.

Emsley, Clive. *Policing and Its Context, 1750–1870.* London: Macmillan, 1983.

European Union. "Panoramic Overview of Private Security Industry in the 25 Member States of the European Union." Presentation at Fourth European Conference on Private Security Services, Brussels, Belgium. Confederation of European Security Services and UNI-Europa, 2004. Accessed February 11, 2010, at www.coess.org/pdf/ panormal.pdf.

Fridell, Lori, Robert Lunney, Drew Diamond and Bruce Kubu. *Racially Biased Policing: A Principled Response.* Washington, D.C.: Police Executive Research Forum, 2001.

Gascón, George and Todd Foglesong. "How to Make Policing More Affordable: A Case Study of the Rising Costs of Policing in the United States." Draft paper submitted to the Second Harvard Executive Session on Policing and Public Safety, Cambridge, Mass., 2009.

Goldstein, Herman. *Problem Oriented Policing.* Philadelphia, Penn.: Temple University Press, 1990.

Greenwood, Peter W., Joan Petersilia and Jan Chaiken. *The Criminal Investigation Process.* Lexington, Mass.: D.C. Heath, 1977.

Gurr, Ted R. "On the History of Violent Crime in Europe and America." In *Violence in America: Historical and Comparative Perspectives,* ed. H.D. Graham and Ted R. Gurr. Beverly Hills, Calif.: Sage Publications, 1979:353–374.

International Association of Chiefs of Police. *Post 9-11 Policing: The Crime Control–Homeland Security Paradigm—Taking Command of New Realities.* Alexandria, Va.: IACP, 2005.

Joh, Elizabeth E. "The Paradox of Private Policing." *Journal of Criminal Law and Criminology* 95(1):(2004)49–131.

Johnston, Les. *The Rebirth of Private Policing.* London: Routledge, 1992.

Kelling, George L. "Order Maintenance, the Quality of Urban Life, and Police: A Different Line of Argument." *In Police Leadership in America,* ed. William A. Geller. New York: Praeger Publishers, 1985:309–321.

Kelling, George L. and Mark H. Moore. *The Evolving Strategy of Policing.* Harvard University, Kennedy School of Government, Perspectives on Policing Series, No. 4. Washington, D.C.: National Institute of Justice, November 1988. NCJ 114213.

Kelling, George L., Antony M. Pate, Duane Dieckman and Charles Brown. *The Kansas City Preventive Patrol Experiment: Summary Report.* Washington, D.C.: Police Foundation, 1974.

Koenig, Daniel J. *Do Police Cause Crime? Police Activity, Police Strength and Crime Rates.* Ottawa, Ontario: Canadian Police College, 1991.

Krahn, Harvey and Leslie Kennedy. "Producing Personal Safety: The Effects of Crime Rates, Police Force Size, and Fear of Crime." *Criminology* 23 (1985): 697–710.

Kroeker, Mark. Informal presentation to biannual meeting of the International Police Advisory Commission, Abuja, Nigeria, January 2007.

Lane, Roger. "Urban Police and Crime in Nineteenth-Century America." In *Crime and justice,* ed. N. Morris and Michael Tonry. Chicago: University of Chicago Press, 1980.

Laurie, Peter. *Scotland Yard.* New York: Holt, Rinehart & Winston, 1970.

Loftin, Colin and David McDowell. "The Police, Crime, and Economic Theory: An Assessment." *American Sociological Review* 47 (1982): 393–401.

Maguire, Kathleen and Ann L. Pastore, eds. *Sourcebook of Criminal Justice Statistics.* Years 2000–2007. Washington, D.C.: U.S. Department of Justice, Bureau of Justice Statistics. Accessed February 11, 2010, at www.albany.edu/sourcebook/about.html.

Morris, Pauline and Kevin Heal. *Crime Control and the Police: A Review of Research.* Research Study 67. London: Home Office, 1981.

Nadelman, Ethan A. "The Americanization of Global Law Enforcement: The Diffusion of American Tactics and Personnel." In *Crime and Law Enforcement in the Global Village*, ed. William F. McDonald. Cincinnati, Ohio: Anderson Publishing, 1997:123–138.

Nalla, Mahesh and Graeme Newman. "Public versus Private Control: A Reassessment." *Journal of Criminal Justice* 19 (1991): 537–549.

Police Foundation. *The Newark Foot Patrol Experiment*. Washington, D.C.: Police Foundation, 1981.

Prenzler, Tim and Rick Sarre. "Private and Public Security Agencies: Australia." In *Plural Policing: A Comparative Perspective*, ed. T. Jones and T. Newburn. London: Routledge, 2006:169–189.

President's Commission on Law Enforcement and the Administration of Justice. *The Challenge of Crime in a Free Society*. Washington, D.C.: U.S. Government Printing Office, 1967.

Reiner, Robert. *The Politics of the Police*. New York: St. Martin's Press, 1985.

Royal Commission on Criminal Procedure. Research Study 17. London: HMSO, 1981.

Shearing, Clifford D. "The Relation Between Public and Private Policing." In *Modern Policing*, ed. N. Morris and Michael Tonry. Chicago: University of Chicago Press, 1992.

Silberman, Charles. *Criminal Violence, Criminal Justice*. New York: Random House, 1978.

Singer, Peter W. *Corporate Warriors: The Rise of the Privatized Military Industry.* Cornell Studies in Security Affairs. Ithaca, N.Y.: Cornell University Press, 2003.

Skogan, Wesley and Kathleen Frydl. *Fairness and Effectiveness in Policing: The Evidence.* Washington, D.C.: National Academies Press, 2004.

Skolnick, Jerome H. and James Fyfe. *Beyond the Law*. New York: Free Press, 1993.

Snow, Thomas. "Competing National and Ethical Interests in the Fight Against Transnational Crime: A U.S. Practitioners Perspective." In *Crime and Law Enforcement in the Global Village,* ed. William F. McDonald. Cincinnati: Anderson Publishing, 1997:169–186.

Spelman, William and Dale K. Brown. *"Calling the Police": Citizen Reporting of Serious Crime.* Washington, D.C.: Police Executive Research Forum, 1981.

Stone, Christopher. "Strengthening Accountability in the New Global Police Culture." Presentation at conference on Crime and the Threat to Democratic Governance, Woodrow Wilson International Center for Scholars, Washington, D.C., 2003.

Tien, James M., James W. Simon and Richard C. Larson. *An Alternative Approach to Police Patrol: The Wilmington Split-Force Experiment.* Washington, D.C.: U.S. Government Printing Office, 1978.

Trojanowicz, Robert C. and Bonnie Bucqueroux. *Community Policing: A Contemporary Perspective.* Cincinnati: Anderson Publishing, 1990.

United Nations High Commissioner for Human Rights. *International Human Rights Standards for Law Enforcement: A Pocket Book on Human Rights for Police.* Geneva, Switzerland: UNHCHR, 1996.

U.S. Bureau of Labor Statistics, U.S. Department of Labor. "May 2005 Occupational Employment and Wage Estimates." Accessed February 11, 2010, at www.bls.gOv/oes/oes_dl /htm#2005_m.

U.S. Bureau of Labor Statistics, U.S. Department of Labor. "Security Guard Employment Before and After 2001." Summary 07–08 (August 2007). Accessed March 22, 2010, at www.bls.gov/opub /ils/pdf/opbils61.pdf.

Van Dijk, Jan. The World of Crime. Los Angeles: Sage Publications, 2008.

Walker, Samuel. "The New Paradigm of Police Accountability: The U.S. Justice Department 'Pattern or Practice' Suits in Context." *St. Louis University Public Law Review* 22(1) (2003):3–52.

Notes

1. The FBI, which provides the statistics on crimes known to the police, stopped calculating a rate for the entire Part I index after 2001. It did, however, continue to publish rates for both violent and property crime, from which a total rate for all Part I crime can be calculated.
2. Intelligence-led policing may be confused with evidence-based policing. Intelligence-led policing refers to the targeting of operations on the basis of specific information, whereas evidence-based policing refers to shaping of operational strategies on the basis of evaluations of their efficacy.

Critical Thinking

1. Why was community policing developed?
2. What factors are affecting the way policing is done today?
3. Does the increase of private policing present the possibility of problems?
4. What has been the public's reaction to the fact that crime has declined?

David H. Bayley is Distinguished Professor in the School of Criminal Justice at the State University of New York, Albany. **Christine Nixon** is APM Chair, Victorian Bushfire Reconstruction and Recovery Authority, and State Commissioner of Police, Victoria, Australia (Retired). The authors acknowledge valuable research assistance provided by Baillie Aaron, Research Assistant, in the Program in Criminal Justice and Police Management, John F. Kennedy School of Government, Harvard University.

When the Police Go Military

AL BAKER

Riot police officers tear-gassing protesters at the Occupy movement in Oakland, Calif. The surprising nighttime invasion of Zuccotti Park in Lower Manhattan, carried out with D-Day-like secrecy by officers deploying klieg lights and a military-style sound machine. And campus police officers in helmets and face shields dousing demonstrators at the University of California, Davis with pepper spray.

Is this the militarization of the American police?

Police forces undeniably share a soldier's ethos, no matter the size of the city, town or jurisdiction: officers carry deadly weapons and wear uniforms with patches denoting rank. They salute one another and pay homage to a "Yes, sir," "No, sir," hierarchical culture.

But beyond such symbolic and formal similarities, American law and tradition have tried to draw a clear line between police and military forces. To cast the roles of the two too closely, those in and out of law enforcement say, is to mistake the mission of each. Soldiers, after all, go to war to destroy, and kill the enemy. The police, who are supposed to maintain the peace, "are the citizens, and the citizens are the police," according to Chief Walter A. McNeil of Quincy, Fla., the president of the International Association of Chiefs of Police, citing the words of Sir Robert Peel, the father of modern-day policing.

Yet lately images from Occupy protests streamed on the Internet—often in real time—show just how readily police officers can adopt military-style tactics and equipment, and come off more like soldiers as they face down citizens. Some say this adds up to the emergence of a new, more militaristic breed of civilian police officer. Others disagree.

What seems clear is that the terrorist attacks of Sept. 11, and the federal Homeland Security dollars that flowed to police forces in response to them, have further encouraged police forces to embrace paramilitary tactics like those that first emerged in the decades-long "war on drugs."

Both wars—first on drugs, then terror—have lent police forces across the country justification to acquire the latest technology, equipment and tactical training for newly created specialized units.

"There is behind this, also, I think, a kind of status competition or imitation, that there is positive status in having a sort of 'big department muscle,' in smaller departments," said Franklin E. Zimring, a professor of law at the University of California, Berkeley. "And then the problem is, if you have those kinds of specialized units, that you hunt for appropriate settings to use them and, in some of the smaller police departments, notions of the appropriate settings to use them are questionable."

Radley Balko, a journalist who has studied the issue, told a House subcommittee on crime in 2007 that one criminologist found a 1,500 percent increase in the use of SWAT (special weapons and tactics) teams in the United States in roughly the last two decades.

The Posse Comitatus Act of 1878 generally bars the military from law enforcement activities within the United States. But today, some local and city police forces have rendered the law rather moot. They have tanks—yes, tanks, often from military surplus, for use in hostage situations or drug raids—not to mention the sort of equipment and training one would need to deter a Mumbai-style guerrilla assault.

Such tactics are used in New York City, where Police Commissioner Raymond W. Kelly (whose department has had armored vehicles for decades) has invoked both the 19th-century military strategist Carl von Clausewitz and the television series "24" in talking about the myriad threats his city faces—both conventional and terrorist. After the would-be Times Square bomber Faisal Shahzad was arrested aboard a plane at Kennedy Airport in 2010, Mr. Kelly calculated the plot-to-capture time: slightly more than 53 hours.

"Jack Bauer may have caught him in 24," said Mr. Kelly, who served as a Marine commander in Vietnam. "But in the real world, 53's not bad."

In truth, a vast majority of Mr. Kelly's 35,000-member force are not specialized troops, but rank-and-file beat cops. But that did not stop Mayor Michael R. Bloomberg from sounding like Patton at the Massachusetts Institute of Technology last week, when he boasted, "I have my own army in the N.Y.P.D.," suggesting his reasons for preferring City Hall to the White House. More disturbing than riot gear or heavy-duty weapons slung across the backs of American police officers is a "militaristic mind-set" creeping into officers' approach to their jobs, said Timothy Lynch, director of the criminal justice project at the Cato Institute, a libertarian think tank. "It is in the way they search and raid homes and the way they deal with the public," he said.

The more the police fail to defuse confrontations but instead help create them—be it with their equipment, tactics or demeanor—the more ties with community members are burned, he said. The effect is a loss of civility, and an erosion of constitutional rights, rather than a building of good will.

"What is most worrisome to us is that the line that has traditionally separated the military from civilian policing is fading away," Mr. Lynch said. "We see it as one of the most disturbing trends in the criminal justice area—the militarization of police tactics."

Police officials insist they are not becoming more militarized—in their thinking or actions—but merely improving themselves professionally against evolving threats. This is the way to protect citizens and send officers home alive at the end of shifts in an increasingly dangerous world, they say. Of course, in the event of a terrorist attack, they have to fill the breach until federal or National Guard troops can rush in.

"If we had to take on a terrorist group, we could do that," said William Lansdowne, the police chief in San Diego and a member of the board of the Major Cities Chiefs Association. Though his force used federal grants to buy one of those fancy armored vehicles—complete with automatic-gun portals—he said the apparatus was more useful for traditional crime-busting than counter-terrorism.

"We are seeing suspects better armed than ever before," Chief Lansdowne said.

Now the Occupy movement and highly publicized official responses to it are forcing the public to confront what its police forces have become. But analysts say that even here the picture of policing is mixed. While scenes from Oakland were ugly, the police in Los Angeles and Philadelphia last week evacuated Occupy encampments relatively peacefully; Los Angeles officers used a cherry picker to pluck protesters from trees.

Police officers are not at war, said Chuck Wexler, the executive director of the Police Executive Research Forum, and cannot imagine themselves as occupying armies. Rather, they must approach any continuing Occupy protests, now or in the spring, with a respect for the First Amendment and a realization that protesters are not enemies but people the police need to engage with up the road.

"You can have all the sophisticated equipment in the world, but it does not replace common sense and discretion and finding ways to defuse situations," Mr. Wexler said. "You can't be talking about community policing one day and the next day have an action that is so uncharacteristic to the values of your department."

Critical Thinking

1. What's wrong with police adopting some of the tactics of the military?
2. Are police becoming more militarized, or just improving?

Al Baker is a metropolitan reporter for *The New York Times*.

Beware of the Dogs

Can New York's canine units keep the city safe from terrorism?

BURKHARD BILGER

The weapons were housed in Long Island City, in a low-slung, prefabricated building on Northern Boulevard. I could hear them growling and yammering in the dark. I'd arrived well before dawn on a wet, chilly October morning, and still wasn't sure how to proceed. A police officer had told me to meet him there at five-forty-five, but there was no bell to ring, no intercom to buzz. The building was surrounded by a ragged chain-link fence edged with spools of razor wire and posted with warnings. When I tested the gate, it was unlocked, but the entrance lay across an empty parking lot and up a wooden ramp. I wasn't sure that I could make it to the door in time.

I've never been much good around dogs. In the town where I grew up, about an hour north of Oklahoma City, every other house seemed to be patrolled by some bawling bluetick or excitable Irish setter, and the locals liked to leave them unchained. When I'd fill in for my brother on his paper route, or ride my one-speed bike to a friend's house, I could usually count on a chase along the way, some homicidal canine at my heels. The dogs didn't seem to give my friends as much trouble. And my father had a way of puffing himself up and waving his arms that would send them scampering. But I never figured out how to show them who's boss.

One of the satisfactions of city life has been turning that relationship around. A pet here is always on probation, its instincts curbed or swiftly incarcerated. A hound that chases children around would be considered a public menace, and even the little yappers have to be kept on a leash. In the past ten years, though, that balance of power has shifted. Since the attacks on September 11th, New York's subways and train stations, parks and tourist destinations have been prowled by police dogs—large, pointy-eared, unnervingly observant beasts deeply unconvinced of our innocence. They sniff at backpacks and train their eyes on passersby, daring us to make a move. It's a little unsettling but also, under the circumstances, reassuring. There are worse things to fear than getting bitten.

The New York City subway has more than four hundred stations, eight hundred miles of track, six thousand cars, and, on any given weekday, five million passengers. It's an anti-terrorism unit's nightmare. To sweep this teeming labyrinth for bombs would take an army of explosives experts equipped with chemical detectors. Instead, the city has gone to the dogs. Since 2001, the number of uniformed police has dropped by seventeen per cent. In that same period, the canine force has nearly doubled. It now has around a hundred dogs, divided among the narcotics, bomb, emergency-response, and transit squads.

A good dog is a natural super-soldier: strong yet acrobatic, fierce yet obedient. It can leap higher than most men, and run twice as fast. Its eyes are equipped for night vision, its ears for supersonic hearing, its mouth for subduing the most fractious prey. But its true glory is its nose. In the nineteen-seventies, researchers found that dogs could detect even a few particles per million of a substance; in the nineties, more subtle instruments lowered the threshold to particles per billion; the most recent tests have brought it down to particles per trillion. "It's a little disheartening, really," Paul Waggoner, a behavioral scientist at the Canine Detection Research Institute, at Auburn University, in Alabama, told me. "I spent a good six years of my life chasing this idea, only to find that it was all about the limitations of my equipment."

Just as astonishing, to Waggoner, is a dog's acuity—the way it can isolate and identify compounds within a scent, like the spices in a soup. Drug smugglers often try to mask the smell of their shipments by packaging them with coffee beans, air fresheners, or sheets of fabric softener. To see if this can fool a dog, Waggoner has flooded his laboratory with different scents, then added minute quantities of heroin or cocaine to the mix. In one case, "the whole damn lab smelled like a Starbucks," he told me, but the dogs had no trouble homing in on the drug. "They're just incredible at finding the needle in the haystack."

The New York police have two kinds of canines: detection dogs and patrol dogs. The former spend most of their time chasing down imaginary threats: terrorist attacks are so rare that the police have to stage simulations, with real explosives, to keep the dogs on their toes. Patrol dogs, on the other hand, have one of the most dangerous jobs in public life. Canine police are often called when a criminal is on the loose, and they're far more likely than others to have a lethal encounter. "The crimes I get called out on are always in progress," one officer told me. "The suspects are armed. They're known to be violent. So, by the mere nature of that call, it's going to be more dangerous." He shrugged. "I guess I'm an adrenaline junkie. I got into canine to hunt men."

The dogs in Long Island City were heirs to an ancient and bloodthirsty line. Their ancestors, descended from the great mastiffs and sight hounds of Mesopotamia, were used as shock troops by the Assyrians, the Persians, the Babylonians, and the Greeks. (Alexander the Great's dog, Peritas, is said to have saved his life at Gaugamela by leaping in front of a Persian elephant and biting its lip.) They wrought havoc in the Roman Colosseum, ran with Attila's hordes, and wore battle armor beside the knights of the Middle Ages. In 1495, when Columbus sailed to what is now the Dominican Republic, he brought Spanish mastiffs almost three feet high at the withers and greyhounds that could run down an enemy and disembowel him. At the battle of Vega Real, each hound killed a hundred natives in less than an hour, according to the Dominican friar Bartolomé de las Casas. "They carry these dogs with them as companions wherever they go," he later wrote. "And kill the fettered Indians in multitudes like Hogs for their Food."

It took a while to break them of the habit. The colonists used dogs against Indians and slaves—"They should be large, strong and fierce," Benjamin Franklin recommended, "and will confound the enemy a good deal"—and the Confederates sent them after escaping Union prisoners at Andersonville. And though the U.S. Army opted for more modern weaponry abroad, attack dogs were still used at home, for crowd control. "Up until the nineteen-seventies, the police just wanted dogs that would bite everyone," Jim Matarese, the treasurer of the United States Police Canine Association, told me. "They'd go to the pound and get dogs that were fear biters—just scared to death of people. Or someone would call in and say, 'I've got a real aggressive dog. He'll bite!' Well, we saw what happened at the marches from Selma: those dogs just ate people up."

In Europe, police dogs were a more refined lot, though not always to their benefit. The German shepherd, first registered as a breed in 1889 by a former cavalry captain, Max von Stephanitz, was selected for intelligence and steadiness as well as power. The Germans fielded thirty thousand dogs in the First World War, and used them for everything from transporting medicine and wounded soldiers to shuttling messages between trenches. When the war was over, the animals were mostly killed, discarded, or consumed by the starving populace. "Dog meat has been eaten in every major German crisis at least since the time of Frederick the Great, and is commonly referred to as 'blockade mutton,'" *Time* noted, in 1940. "Dachshund is considered the most succulent."

The survivors went on to second careers in law enforcement or as guide dogs for the blind, and their breeding and training grew ever more sophisticated. In Germany, registered shepherds have to pass rigorous physical and behavioral tests, and their puppies are trained by nationwide networks of volunteers. *Schutzhund* competitions, in which dogs are tested for their ability to track, obey orders, and protect their owners, are a national passion, and the largest ones fill stadiums. "They just have a different dog culture over there," Steve White, a dog trainer and former canine officer in the Seattle area, told me. "If you look at North America, there are maybe five thousand German shepherd breeders. If you go to Germany, it's probably got fifty-five thousand."

It took the Lockerbie bombing, followed by the attacks at Columbine and Oklahoma City, to galvanize interest in police and military dogs in America. Auburn's canine program began as an attempt to build a better bomb detector. "In the eighties, we thought, Let's build a machine that can mimic the dog!" Robert Gillette, the director of the university's animal-health and performance program, told me. "But you can't mimic a dog. It's just a superior mechanical working system. So in the nineties we began to think, Hmm, let's put some of that research into the animals." The Department of Defense has apparently come to the same conclusion. Since 2006, it has spent close to twenty billion dollars searching for explosives in Iraq and Afghanistan. "The detection rate has hung stubbornly at around fifty per cent," Lieutenant General Michael Oates told the magazine *National Defense* two years ago. When the same patrols use dogs, he added, the success rate leaps to eighty per cent: "Dogs are the best detectors."

The American military now has some three thousand active-duty dogs in its ranks, but good animals are hard to find. The American Kennel Club requires no proof of health or intelligence to register an animal—just a pure bloodline—and breeders are often more concerned with looks than with ability. "We breed for the almighty dollar here," one trainer told me. Programs like the ones at Auburn and at Lackland Air Force Base, in San Antonio, are trying to reverse that trend. But their graduates are still the exceptions. "Some of these dogs, they couldn't find a pork chop if it was hanging around their neck," a dog broker in Minnesota told me.

The upshot is that many, if not most, American police dogs now come from Europe. Those in the New York subway were mostly born in Hungary, Slovakia, or the Czech Republic—descendants of the powerful border-patrol dogs bred during the Cold War. Other police dogs come from brokers in Holland and Germany, and still respond to Dutch and German commands: *Sitz! Bleib! Los! Apport!* "Europeans have more dogs than they can use, so they sell the excess to us," White told me. "We subsidize their hobbies."

When I'd finally summoned the nerve to sprint across the parking lot and up the ramp, that morning in Long Island City, I stumbled in on six patrolmen strapping on their gear. They were all with the transit squad, which safeguards the subway: four recruits and two trainers. A dry-erase board hung on the wall, scrawled with notes. One side listed explosives that the dogs could detect, including C-4, TNT, ammonium nitrate, and several others. The other side listed fines for canine misbehavior: five dollars for urinating in the subway, twenty-five for biting someone ("must draw blood").

Wayne Rothschild, one of the trainers, had just finished adding his weight to another list on the board—part of a contest to see who could lose the most pounds by the end of the week. (Canine police tend to be more active than others, but their dogs do most of the running.) The men in his squad averaged more than two hundred pounds, topping out at two hundred and thirty-six, for the sergeant, Randy Brenner.

"One pound?" a recruit was asked. "You've lost one pound?"

"I swallowed a lot of aggression."

"And pizzas."

Rothschild laughed. At one eighty-one, he was among the fittest men in the group. He and Brenner had first met in junior high and later played football together for the Hicksville Comets—Rothschild at quarterback and Brenner at center. Twenty years later, they still looked their parts: Rothschild square-jawed and decisive, with jet-black hair close-cropped on the sides; Brenner stolid, round, and reliable—the immovable object. Technically, Brenner was now Rothschild's boss, but their relationship hadn't changed much. "I was blocking for him then and I'm still blocking for him," Brenner said.

Like many of the men in the squad, Rothschild and Brenner had been around police dogs most of their lives. Rothschild's father, uncle, brothers, and cousins were in law enforcement, as were Brenner's father and grandfather. After high school, Rothschild spent two years at a community college and another two working construction, before joining the force. Brenner took his police-academy entrance exam at sixteen. When the transit canine unit was formed, six years ago, they each put in for it unbeknownst to the other, and found themselves back on the same team. "I'd rather be a cop in canine than a sergeant somewhere else," Brenner said. "It's all I ever wanted."

He and Rothschild led the recruits to the kennel behind the offices, to get their new partners. A week earlier, each recruit had been paired with an equally green police dog, a little over a year old. "We want the dog to make up for where the handler is weak and vice versa," Brenner said. "But I'll tell you, after a while the person's personality becomes similar to the dog's." Matthew Poletto, a rangy recruit with the jutting cheekbones and cut biceps of a bodybuilder, had been matched with Ranger, a skinny, high-strung Belgian Malinois—"like a German shepherd on steroids," as one handler put it. Horacio Maldonado, a small, soft-spoken Hispanic, had a sweet female Labrador named Ray. The others had big-boned, lordly shepherds with the contained power peculiar to the breed. The Labrador was a detection dog; the shepherds and the Malinois were patrol dogs—though some, like Rothschild's German shepherd, Danz, did both.

For the next month and a half, the dogs and men would learn to work together, to read each other's cues and idiosyncrasies, as if in an arranged marriage: police dogs and their handlers are usually partnered for life. "He's a great dog. It's just . . . sometimes I'd like to relax a little," Poletto said, sounding like the honeymoon was already over. "You know, watch TV and not have him put the chew toy in my lap."

Inside the kennel, the dogs were in an uproar. They lunged at their cages when they saw their owners, foam flying from their muzzles. They stayed here only when not on patrol or at home with their partners, but even this much confinement was hard to bear. "A lot of them are cage chewers," the unit's other trainer, Richard Geraci, told me. He showed me a photograph on his phone of a ventilation cover that his dog, Chief, had reduced to twisted scrap. "That's quarter-inch steel," he said. A German shepherd's jaw can exert upward of seven hundred and fifty pounds per square inch. "They just chew it up, tear it up. Chief's got broken teeth, but I'm surprised he doesn't have more."

And yet the moment the cages were opened the noises stopped. The dogs trotted silently to their partners' side, then sat back on their haunches—ears erect, eyes focussed forward—and waited. "It's like you've turned on a switch," Brenner said.

Canine police tend to talk about their dogs as if they were mechanical devices. They describe them as tools or technology and say that they're "building dogs" through proper training. They say that their animals need "maintenance" to be "fully operational," and that a "dual-purpose dog"—one that has been taught to both chase down criminals and detect drugs or explosives—has "superior functionality." At home, a police dog may be like a member of the family. But once in the field it's just another piece of gear.

This is more than a manner of speaking. It's a way of thinking about dogs that goes back to the psychologist B. F. Skinner and his work on behaviorism, in the nineteen-forties. Skinner argued that it's pointless to imagine what's going on in an animal's head. Better to treat its mind as a black box, closed and unknowable, with inputs that lead to predictable outputs. Skinner identified four ways to manipulate behavior: four buttons to push—positive reinforcement ("Good dog! Have a biscuit"), positive punishment ("Bad dog!" *Whack*), negative reinforcement ("Good dog! Now I'll stop whacking you"), and negative punishment ("Bad dog! Give me back that biscuit"). Connect an action to an outcome and almost any behavior can be trained. Skinner called this "operant conditioning," and considered it as effective for people as for their pets. "Give me a child," he once said, "and I'll shape him into anything."

By treating animals as clever machines, behaviorists managed some impressive feats: rats navigated mazes, chickens played tic-tac-toe, pigeons played Ping-Pong. During the Second World War, Skinner went so far as to design a pigeon-guided missile. The birds sat in the nose cone, each one pecking at a target on a translucent plate. The setup worked surprisingly well, but the pigeons were never enlisted—no one in the military would take them seriously, Skinner complained. Behaviorism, as a means of animal training, had a long, slow fuse.

The revolution, when it came, began with creatures beyond the reach of regular compulsion. An orca or a dolphin can't be tugged on a leash or stung with a whip. It can't hear what you're shouting most of the time. To make it do what you want, you have to break down the behavior into discrete components—swim over here, pick up that hoop, leap through the air—then offer a reward for each step. At marine parks and aquariums, in the nineteen-sixties, an orca that did something right would hear a whistle blast and get a fish. After a while, each behavior would be associated with a different hand signal, and become so rewarding, in and of itself, that the orca wouldn't always need to get a fish. One of the pioneers in this field, Karen Pryor, once taught a goldfish to swim through a tiny hoop just for the flicker of a flashlight. "It's easy," she told me. "You just have to have a healthy goldfish. And it has to be hungry."

As operant conditioning has spread from aquariums to zoos, what once would have been circus acts have come to seem like ordinary good behavior. Thirty years ago, if a lion needed a flu shot, it had to be tranquillized. These days, it will walk up to its trainer and proffer its paw. "I could give you examples all day," Ken Ramirez, the vice-president of animal training at the Shedd Aquarium, in Chicago, told me. "We have sharks that will swim from tank to tank, and a beluga whale that will present its belly for an ultrasound. Our sea otters hold their eyes open to get drops, and I've had a diabetic baboon submit to regular insulin injections." Not long ago, when a camel broke its jaw at the nearby Brookfield Zoo, it walked up to a table and laid its head on a lead plate for an X-ray. "It makes managing animals so much easier," Ramirez said. "They do things as part of a game that you've taught them."

Dogs were made for this sort of thing. No other animal so loves a game or so diligently aims to please. No other has been shaped so specifically to our needs. Selective breeding has turned *Canis lupus familiaris* into the most physically varied animal on earth. Its genome is the Microsoft Windows of biological programming: layer upon layer of complex function and code, often accreted at cross-purposes. It can produce Great Danes big enough to kill wild boars and Chihuahuas small enough to go down rat holes, beagles that track pythons and collies that catch Frisbees. "When you get to a detection dog that wants to find ammonium nitrate just so that it can play with a rubber ball, that is a very, very complex end point," Auburn's Robert Gillette told me.

The patrol dogs in the transit squad could bark on command (Speak!) and urinate at their handler's discretion (Empty!). They could climb ladders, crawl through drainage pipes, and leap through the open window of a moving car. They were smart, disciplined, extremely capable animals. But the blood of the old war hounds still ran in them, and their most effective ability was intimidation.

"One canine team can do the work of ten or fifteen guys in a gang situation," Lieutenant John Pappas, the head of the squad, told me. "It's 'Fuck you! I'm not going anywhere.' But when you throw in some jaws and paws—holy shit! It changes the landscape." In 2010, one station on the Lexington Avenue line was hit by twenty felonies in a matter of months. Once a canine unit was sent in, the number dropped to zero. "It's like pulling up in an M1 Abrams battle tank," Pappas said.

The commuters at Union Square seemed a peaceable crowd one Wednesday morning. Yet the dogs made even the innocent nervous. When the squad filed into a subway car, I could see backs stiffen all around, eyes focussed on the floor. Each dog and its handler took position at a set of doors, overseen by Rothschild and Brenner. Between stations, the dogs watched the riders. When the doors opened, they pivoted around to study the crowd on the platform. The German shepherds soon settled into the routine, but the Malinois kept twisting about on its leash, registering each face like a laser scanner.

"Malinois just really love bite work," a canine cop from Middletown, New York, had told me. "They have this giant prey drive. Some people call them Maligators." After a while, one of the riders—a tall, spindly man in a yarn prayer cap—began to get uncomfortable. He scooted down the seat, hunching his shoulders, and glared back at the Malinois. "If you tense up, if you're feeling threatened, the dog picks that up and perceives a threat," Brenner told me. Or as my friends used to say when I was a kid, at the worst possible moments, "They can smell your fear."

Times Square is the busiest station in the city, and the main concourse was at its most cacophonous. A band of black bluegrass musicians, called the Ebony Hillbillies, was sprawled in lawn chairs playing an old fiddle tune called "Martha Campbell." The bass and banjo lines skittered from run to run while the washboard chattered underneath, mimicking the commuters around us. "New York is just different," Brenner said, looking around with satisfaction. "Our version of a crowd is different from anywhere else in the world. And these dogs are tuning in to everything. They're trained for handler protection, and they don't know when that threat is going to be upon them."

The squad had been there only a few minutes when one of the German shepherds—a huge black male named Thunder—began to bark at something nearby. I could see a man in a hoodie crouched beside a pillar. An officer was shouting at him to show his hands, but he wouldn't do it. One second, the two were frozen in a standoff, Thunder straining at the leash. Then the suspect lunged, the cop let go, and the dog leaped through the air. "Get this dog off of me!" the man screamed, as Thunder's jaw clamped around his arm. The handler called Thunder back, but then the suspect broke away and the dog was on him again within a few steps, jerking him to the ground.

As it turned out, the suspect was a decoy—another transit cop, posing as a troublemaker. The second attack, though, had been unscripted: the decoy hadn't meant to act as if he were running away. "The dog wasn't wrong," Rothschild said. It's a police dog's job to perceive threats, and the handler's job to keep the dog in check. This is the hardest part of canine work. "You have to put emergency brakes on these creatures," one handler told me. A single loss of control could cause wrongful injury, lawsuits, or even death, but the dog doesn't know that. As Stewart Hilliard, a specialist in animal learning who works with the canine program at Lackland Air Force Base, put it, "You can't think of a reward more desirable to a dog than the opportunity to keep biting that person."

A few weeks earlier, at the National Police Dog Field Trials, in Detroit Lakes, Minnesota, I'd watched several dozen dogs wrestle with their conscience. The field trials are a kind of canine decathlon, modelled on *Schutzhund* competitions. They bring together the best-trained police dogs in the country to test their agility, obedience, and ability to track criminals and catch them. Rothschild and his German shepherd were there to represent New York, along with four other dogs and handlers from their region.

Detroit Lakes sits on a flat, glacier-scoured plain about an hour east of Fargo. Some officers had driven as far as fifteen hundred miles to get there, but were unprepared for the freezing rain and the local fare. ("It's September—I brought all shorts!" Rothschild told me the first night, at a local buffet, while his teammates eyed the bratwurst; "I'm not eatin' those things," one of them said.) The night before, on the drive in from North Dakota, I'd received a speeding ticket on a desolate stretch of road. I later heard that the same thing had happened to two of the police officers—and they were driving their cruisers at the time.

"A lot of people are under the misapprehension that this is a dog show," one of the judges, Gary Pietropaolo, a mustachioed ex-cop from Yonkers, told me the next day. We were sitting in folding chairs on a baseball field, watching the criminal-apprehension trial. By then, I'd seen dogs search for guns in tall grass, and dogs sniff out a suspect hidden in rows of identical wooden boxes. In this case, they had to chase down a gunman, bite his arm, and waylay him until the handler caught up to make the arrest. It was a stylized routine, scored on niceties of execution—sitting slightly askew at a handler's side was enough to earn a deduction—but the dogs seemed deadly serious. At least four dogs had been killed or severely injured in the line of duty in the past year. One was thrown into traffic by an armed robber; another bit into a brick of cocaine; another was stabbed repeatedly; the last barely survived an attempted drowning. "If it's not a violent felon, you typically don't send in the dog," Pietropaolo said. "In the use-of-force scale, it's almost equal to using a nightstick."

Earlier that morning, as I was running across the field to join the judges, I'd suddenly realized that I was being watched. At the other end of the field, a half dozen German shepherds were lined up along a fence, their eyes locked on my every move. To them, I must have seemed like just another target—a man in a turkey suit, dashing through the forest on opening day of hunting season. "You got lucky," Rothschild told me later. Even with a protective sleeve on, an officer he knew was bitten so hard that his arm broke in two places, and Rothschild bore a dozen scars from trials gone awry. "It's just something you have to overcome," he said. "Most of us never got bit before going into canine. But you kind of get the feel of it. It's normal wear and tear."

Danz, Rothschild's dog, was a big, bristling male with something of his handler's swagger. When his turn came in the trial, he sat without a twitch while the decoy shot off a round and ran down the field. Then, at a murmured word from Rothschild, the dog took off—body low to the ground, feet a blur, like a shaggy brown missile. He was halfway across the field, in mid-flight, when Rothschild yelled "Stop!" The effect was immediate: Danz peeled away, circled back to his handler, and sat squarely at his side—a near-perfect routine.

MORE RELUCTANT

It's time for a little chamber music
of Arensky or Borodin, something minor
and enduring, as we imagine ourselves
to be, let that be a wake-up call,
as the man said. When you turned I thought
you've got to stop me, I'm out of control
but mature, so every step I take
counts. Meanwhile you were rumbling on
about something, nobody knows what,
so that behind the wall of the setting sun
the great presences could collect and mutate
as in former times. Wasn't it all a legend
or fictive construction? Why did we
think it mattered for us and not for others?
The whole urban chaos spalls and before
we know it the subject has changed.
What other conversation are you in?
Whose day has spent?
Working in the town,
that lummox was charged with evaluation,
so if groups of young people started off
in an opposite direction there would be a mention
sometimes. The housefronts seem more gaudy this year,
eggshell and pale green and no one
wants to take the responsibility. Moonlighters
observe customs of the spruce of the year
the way tin warriors would keep company with paper
models if others left the square unsupervised.
By the way they have a store in Hartford,
Connecticut. I often pee sometimes.
The awful leaf was congruent,
too. Mothers and hustlers bridled in the choking
dust that afflicts it from everywhere, yet owns
to no thread in the proceedings. They washed
it clean every night. In the mornings the footprints
were back, but no one was wiser. A little
bunny or some kind of ferret was probably
there too, and bore witness as only rodents can.
I could see the guy. Some in lesser hands
say repeatedly, wash it out, the shared indictment
ought to stand if only so they can all go home. Wonderful,
that it is. Now that wasn't so easy, was it?

—John Ashbery

Others weren't so successful. When David Causey, a patrolman from Lake County, Florida, called his animal off, you could almost see the dog weighing his options. He glanced back at Causey, slowed down for a moment, then hunched his shoulders and accelerated toward the target. "That's called 'He fucked you,'" Causey's friend David Williams told me. "Fifty points off. He's out of the competition."

For Causey, the result was made even worse by a sense of déjà vu. The year before, on the last day of the field trials, the same dog had bitten a decoy's hand and then, for good measure, his crotch. It was a case of accidental reinforcement, Causey said. A few weeks earlier, in Florida, his dog had chased a felon into a closet. A rough struggle ensued until the dog, in desperation, bit the man between the legs. Immediate surrender. The next time the dog chased down a suspect, he tried the same trick. Success again! By the time the field trials rolled around, the behavior was locked in.

When Causey and Williams told me this story, we were having breakfast at a coffee shop with Kurt Dumond, the officer who had received the unfortunate bite. Williams, a garrulous Cajun with a life-size revolver tattooed on his hip ("I'm always packing"), pulled out his cell phone and called up some pictures he'd taken at the emergency room: Dumond in a pale-blue hospital gown, followed by several distressing closeups of his scrotum. "That's a mess right there," Dumond said. Williams nodded. "The nurse, when she sees it, she goes, 'Woo woooooo!' Then the doctor comes out and goes, 'That is going to hurt!' Kurt, he'd just told me he had a little laceration. I didn't realize it was thirteen stitches' worth." This year, Williams added, Dumond wore a cup.

How do you keep a dog in line? The answer used to be simple: you smacked it or yelled at it or yanked on its chain. It wasn't pretty, but it could get the job done. Punishment and compulsion are still common in dog training, though usually in more subtle forms—a tug on a leash, for instance, or a mild shock from an electric collar. Traditional trainers, from the monks of New Skete to *Schutzhund* champions like Friedrich Biehler, can produce very accomplished dogs. But, as behaviorism has worked its way from aquariums to kennels, more and more dogs are being taught with positive reinforcement, often using a handheld clicker. "You used to wait until the dog did something wrong, then corrected it," Michele Pouliot, the director of research and development at Guide Dogs for the Blind in Oregon, told me. "Now you're rewarding a behavior you like before it goes wrong."

Like so much else in the dog world, the change mirrors a trend in child rearing—and provokes the same heated debate. ("The only thing two dog trainers can agree about is what the third dog trainer is doing wrong," Steve White told me.) The tough love of Cesar Millan, the Dog Whisperer, and the tender manipulations of Victoria Stilwell, the host of "It's Me or the Dog," have their exact analogues in parenting styles. Hearing Pouliot talk about headstrong, distractible puppies—the kind that usually make good police dogs—is a lot like hearing an elementary-school teacher talk about attention-deficit disorder and the trouble with boys. "If a dog loves squirrels, you have to find something that excites him so much it overpowers the squirrel instinct," Pouliot told me. "If you're constantly on top of him—punishing, punishing, punishing—that behavior is not going away. You have to get that dog to try to figure out what you want."

Canine police are conservative by nature. They have little margin for error or experiment, so they tend to play the Tiger Moms in this debate. "It goes like this," Gary Pietropaolo, the judge from Yonkers, told me. "You always want to use positive motivation first. But, if that was the only thing we used with these animals, we wouldn't have enough shelters in this country. What do you do with the dog that, if you show him the clicker, he shows you his teeth? Do you just kill him?"

It was the third day of the field trials, and Pietropaolo and the other judges were gathered in a conference room at the Holiday Inn, pooling their scores. Kurt Dumond's dog, Erek, held a thin lead over the rest of the field, with Rothschild's Danz in fifth place. (Erek would eventually drop to third, Danz to eleventh, and the championship would go to a dog from Austin, Minnesota, named Ghost—one of only a few Belgian Malinois in a sea of German shepherds.) The best handlers never abuse their dogs, Pietropaolo said, but, like good parents, they make their authority clear. "If you tell your kid to sit down and be quiet at the table, and he doesn't do it, it's over. You have to make it happen. But you don't necessarily have to grab him by the hair and drag him around." The judge beside him grinned. "I still use a choke chain on the kid," he said.

Guide-dog trainers were a lot like the police once, Michele Pouliot told me. Their methods were rooted in military dog training, brought over from Europe after the two world wars. "Everything was steeped in this tradition of very harsh treatment," she said. "Everything was 'You're wrong.'" Then, six years ago, Guide Dogs for the Blind switched over to positive reinforcement. "It was a huge undertaking," Pouliot told me. "We have sixty-five instructors who took years to get good at what they're doing. You're asking them to flip-flop a whole set of technical skills. It's like starting all over."

The benefits are already clear, Pouliot said. Less than half the dogs in her program used to complete their training successfully; now the number is close to three-quarters. "And the dogs are doing things they could never do before, unbelievable things," she said. One of Pouliot's specialties is canine musical freestyle—essentially, dancing with your dog. On YouTube, you can see her Australian shepherd, Listo, doing its best Ginger Rogers: waltzing backward, spinning pirouettes, doing double-takes, handstands, and cancan kicks, all to a medley of TV theme songs. "If you break down that routine and ask a traditional trainer, 'How do you train that?' he'd say, 'Hmm,'" Pouliot told me. "It would be impossible. If I jerk a dog on a leash, I can make him sit. I can make him cringe. But I can't make him show his natural joy."

Police dogs, though, aren't like other animals. Their work is inherently harsh and contradictory. Joy is often beside the point. "We have to have an animal that's willing to consummate its aggression on a living, breathing human, then contain it enough to come back to you," one trainer told me. "That's a lot to ask of any being, much less a dog." Positive reinforcement may be better at coaxing dogs into dancing figure eights and giving high fives, as Pouliot's partners do. But a certain amount of stress could inure an animal to the rigors of the street or the battlefield. "Dogs that are trained in a completely positive way, you deploy them in Afghanistan with the bombs going off—I think they'll crumble," a trainer at Auburn told me.

The program at Auburn is like boot camp for dogs. The Canine Detection Research Institute occupies part of an old military base in Anniston, Alabama, in the foothills of the southern Appalachians. When I visited, two weeks after the national field trials, I was taken to a low metal building across the road from the main offices. Inside, a narrow corridor was flanked by rows of steel cages, each with a small door that led to a dog run, outside. The air was edged with traces of ammonia and feces and reverberated with near-constant barking. Overhead, a loudspeaker system piped in still more noise: equipment clanking, boots stomping, engines roaring, bombs exploding.

"That's a Spook Less soundtrack," my guide explained. The system was first developed for stables, he said, and was used by police to get their horses ready for riot squads and other unsettling duties. The recordings could be swapped out to simulate thunderstorms, fireworks, screaming crowds, or construction sites. At one point, after a bombing raid—"I think that's 'Saving Private Ryan' "—I heard some bagpipes playing. When I asked what they were for, I was told that police have to attend a lot of funerals.

Auburn specializes in detection dogs. It has twenty-five trainers, who supply about a hundred animals a year to Amtrak, Federal Protective Services, and police departments around the country, including the N.Y.P.D. (Rothschild and his German shepherd, Danz, both trained there.) The average canine graduate costs twenty-one thousand dollars, including ten weeks of lessons for the handler. An élite Vapor Wake dog—"They're like the Michael Jordans of dogs," one of the trainers told me. "They can pick fragments out of the air"—costs thirty-two thousand, with an extra six weeks of training.

Detection dogs tend to vary by country and by national temperament. The French like standard poodles, the English springer spaniels. The Russians, in the Moscow airport, use a strange little breed called a Sulimov dog—a mixture of wild jackal, Lapland herding dog, and other breeds—which is said to be the world's best bomb sniffer. Bloodhounds have long been used as trackers in the South. But at Auburn, as at most canine-detection programs in the country, the cages were filled with Labrador retrievers. They were good-natured, highly driven animals, and less liable to bite than pointy-eared dogs. They were in such demand, in fact, that Auburn was also experimenting with other breeds, including springer spaniels and German pointers. "The country is almost out of Labs for detection work," one broker told me. "They're gone. And they don't have any Labs in Europe, either. I had a department wait ten months for one before I found it."

Dogs have such good noses that almost any breed can detect explosives. "If there are differences among them, they're probably well within the margin of error for our ability to measure them," Paul Waggoner, the behavioral scientist at the institute, told me. "The big key is trainability." Waggoner, who is forty-five, is a bearded, bearish figure with an unnerving habit of rolling his eyes back in his head as he talks, like a psychic. Bloodhounds are usually too single-minded for detection work, he said. Once they've hit a trail, they can seem "brutally stupid" when asked to change gears. Border collies can be too smart for their own good: they follow their handlers' cues rather than their own noses. Coonhounds like to go off crittering; dachshunds are too small and stumbly underfoot; and Doberman pinschers scare the bejesus out of people. What's left are friendly working breeds like retrievers and pointers: animals both social and independent, whose bloodlines have been better maintained than those of most show dogs.

If patrol dogs are the Swiss Army knives of the canine world, detection dogs are the shivs. They don't have to chase down felons, disarm robbers, or respond to the slightest cue. They just have to find bombs. Even so, until recently, only one in four dogs made it through the program. Like *Schutzhund* and guide-dog schools, Auburn sent its puppies to families for basic training, then brought them back for detection work after a year. But the dogs had to contend with so many environments—when I visited, they ran drills in a school, a shopping mall, along a highway, and in a mega-church—that any phobia was eventually found out. Rothschild's dog, for instance, was afraid of slippery floors as a puppy, and he needed weeks of practice to get used to jumping fences.

Four years ago, Auburn decided to try a more rigorous approach. The puppies now go to prisons in Florida and Georgia, where they're trained and cared for by convicts in their cells. The companionship seems to have done the men good: some have been able to reduce their medications, and a few have gone on to become professional trainers. But the effect on the dogs has been even more dramatic. "You have startling noises and startling sights 24/7," one of the trainers told me. "You have crowds, stairs, slick floors, grated floors. If a dog can get used to those, you know he's not going to be fearful." Eighty per cent of Auburn's puppies now go on to become detection dogs.

I went to see the Vapor Wakes the next morning. They were being trained in an abandoned building near the woods, where the Army once taught officers to interrogate prisoners. Its dingy halls were lined with doors marked "Do Not Disturb: Interview in Progress," each one with an identical office behind it. To find a person carrying a bomb in here, an ordinary dog would have had to search the building systematically, sniffing its way from room to room. The Vapor Wakes didn't bother. They'd been taught to track explosives like living prey, following the trail of scent particles left suspended in the air.

"I'll hide in one of these rooms, then you bring her in," Tim Baird, the head trainer, told his assistant. He took a vest filled with TNT and wrapped it around his waist. Then he walked down the hall, turned the corner, and ducked into an office along the next corridor. The assistant brought in a small black Lab named Faye, her tail wagging furiously. She'd had thirty-nine days of detection training and twenty of Vapor Wake, and she knew that every drill was another chance at a reward. She scampered in a circle for a while, flaring the air, then took off in the wrong direction. Nothing there. She doubled back, sniffed at my pants—I'd stood next to Baird while he was stuffing the vest with dynamite—then shook me off and ran down the hall, catching a scent.

A dog sniffs the air like a wine taster, Waggoner had told me. It takes short, sharp breaths—as many as ten per second—drawing the scent deep into the nasal cavity to the olfactory epithelium. The receptors there are a hundred times denser than in a human, and can detect a wide array of molecules. When I followed Faye down the hall, I found her in the office, sitting on her haunches—the signal for "the bomb is here"—watching Baird with barely contained excitement. He reached into his pocket and pulled out a well-chewed tennis ball, then threw it down the hall with a whoop. Faye caught it on the first bounce.

The whole sequence had taken about thirty seconds. In one study, in Michigan in 2000, police dogs managed to track down suspects ninety-three per cent of the time, compared with fifty-nine per cent for teams of two to four police officers. And the dogs did it five to ten times faster. Vapor Wakes focus on explosives—in an adjacent room, Baird taught the dogs to find more than a dozen kinds of chemical by hiding them in a wall fitted with small compartments—but other dogs have been taught to find everything from bedbugs to termites, lung cancer, diabetes, and the lithium in cell phones. At Auburn, a dog that can't cut it as a bomb detector could find work as a fungus hound, sniffing out growths that attack and kill the roots of pine trees in the Southeast.

Its esteem for dogs notwithstanding, the university hasn't given up on mechanizing them. When I was in Waggoner's office, later that day, he played me a video from a project called Autonomous Canine Navigation. It showed a yellow Labrador moving through a bomb site wearing an elaborate headset and a harness. The harness contained a computer, a video camera, a G.P.S., and an accelerometer, all remotely controlled. As we watched, a man on a rooftop transmitted some coordinates to the computer below, which directed the dog to the target by playing tones for "Left," "Right," and "Stop" over the headset. "The computer can get within three metres," Waggoner said. "That's more accurate than under human control." When the dog came to a doorway, it sniffed at the threshold and lay down. By then, a sensor had detected its rapid-fire breathing, which meant an explosive had been found. Lying down set off a switch on its belly, confirming the discovery.

The video ended with a tennis ball flying down from the roof and the dog jumping up to snatch it. Even cyborgs, it seems, can use a little positive reinforcement.

New York City is now experimenting with a simpler version of canine navigation. In October, it acquired an infrared video camera that mounts on a dog's back and can be remotely monitored by police. "We can see what the dog is seeing," John Pappas, the head of the transit squad, told me. "So we can use it in a building search. If there's a suspicious box, instead of sending a human being down there, I'll send in the dog, then call him back if things look suspicious." The purchase was approved after the raid on Osama bin Laden, in which a Belgian Malinois named Cairo played an important role. "The real technology here is the dog," Pappas said, "and a lot of it is centered on the nose. That's the most useful tool we have."

On my last day with the squad, Rothschild and Brenner took the dogs for a sweep of Grand Central Terminal. It was nine o'clock on a Friday morning and a final wave of commuters was rushing from the trains. Police in riot gear stood guard by the tunnels to the tracks, machine guns at the ready, while voices blared overhead. When two of the squad's Vapor Wakes ambled in from the street, they stopped at the entrance and stared. The mess hall in a Georgia prison had nothing on this scene: a thousand New Yorkers late for their appointments. "It's an extreme situation," Rothschild said. "But we try to put the dogs in the hardest scenarios possible. We don't know how the next explosive is going to go through." The dogs didn't seem to mind. They just lifted their noses and sniffed the air.

Earlier that morning, Rothschild had arranged for two decoys to make runs through the subway and the train terminal. One would be carrying seven pounds of ammonium nitrate, wrapped in black panty hose and stuffed in a backpack; the other would have twenty pounds of dynamite in a baby stroller. Vapor Wakes can track a scent in the air for up to half an hour, I was told, but the trail wouldn't last long in Grand Central. "You have the trains pulling in air over here," Rothschild said. "You've got the mass of people pulling the air down under these arches. You've got vents bringing it around, and the smells from all the restaurants." He shook his head. "It's like when a boat passes. You can see the wave right afterward, but eventually it dissipates."

Horacio Maldonado, one of the new recruits, positioned himself under an arched entrance on the west side of the station. His black Lab, Ray, could smell most of the passersby from there—she had a range of about thirty feet—but a crowd like this was full of false leads. The chemicals found in explosives can also be found in drugs, cosmetics, fertilizer, construction supplies, and other mundanities. I'd heard of a police dog driven wild by a table patched with plastic wood filler, and a dog tearing down a wall with nail-gun cartridges hidden inside it. "I remember one time, we stopped a guy in Columbus Circle, he had two hundred nitrogen pills in his pocket," Maldonado told me. "Turned out he was going to Europe and had just come from his doctor. So you've got to use your common sense. The guy's sixty, seventy years old. He isn't sweating. Does he look like a suicide bomber?"

False positives are the bugbears of canine detection, but the bigger problem is miscommunication. A leash can be like a faulty phone line. The handler thinks the dog is telling him something; the dog thinks it's the handler's idea. ("Dogs are pretty easy," one trainer told me. "The problem is usually at the other end of the leash.") At Auburn one afternoon, I'd watched Waggoner put a Labrador into an fMRI scanner, to see which part of its brain lit up when detecting a scent. Some day, he said, detection dogs may carry EEGs that set off an alarm when a bomb is found. For now, though, cops and dogs have no choice but to try to talk to one another.

When the explosives went by, they were about twenty feet from Maldonado. The decoy, a young man in a blue sweatshirt with a Mets cap underneath the hood, was buried so deep in the crowd that I almost missed him. The Vapor Wake didn't. She lunged forward on her leash, Maldonado stumbling behind. The decoy walked beneath the arch and down the corridor, heading toward a set of stairs that led to the subway. Ray cut zigzags across his trail, zeroing in on the scent. Soon, she was only about ten feet away, pulling so hard on the leash that her legs were splayed like a lizard's, claws scrabbling on the tile. She was about to catch up when a middle-aged woman sauntered by with three toy dogs on a leash beside her. Ray stopped and glanced at them—a little hungrily, I thought—then shook her head and continued. But by then the trail had drifted, and the decoy was down the stairs.

It was a rare mistake. I'd seen the Vapor Wakes catch half a dozen decoys that week, and even Ray found her man eventually, when he doubled back through the subway. But would she have caught him in real life? "Yeah, she was in odor," Rothschild said. "She was just eliminating the possibilities. She would have gotten him."

Afterward, when Ray was chasing her tennis ball around, some commuters stopped to watch. They were standing in one of the world's prime targets for terrorism, surrounded by a bomb squad with a suspect in custody, but that didn't seem to concern them. They smiled and watched the nice dog play with its ball, then hurried on their way.

Detection-dog stories almost always have happy endings. If they don't, they aren't about dogs anymore. When the training session was over, Rothschild went to get Danz, who was waiting in a mobile kennel, nearby. His cage was brand new and luxurious by most standards—custom-built and climate-controlled, with sensors that would sound an alarm and open the windows if the air got too hot—but Danz was glad to be free of it. He leaped to the ground when the gate opened, and shook his fur as if casting off a rope. Then he ran to Rothschild's side and waited, as always, for a signal.

It was a cold, clear morning, with sunlight streaming through the treetops, and the last patches of green were aglow in Bryant Park. Rothschild waited a beat, just to remind the dog who was in charge, then quietly said "Empty." Danz jumped into the ivy and lifted his leg to a lamppost, glancing back to make sure this was O.K. A police dog's life is all about delayed gratification. *You know that ball? You can' t have it. Not right now. That treat? Maybe later, if you do exactly what I say.* Danz had an alpha male's domineering drive—it wasn't hard to imagine him howling at the head of a pack—but he'd long since learned to tamp it down. And who was to say he wasn't happier this way: always cared for, always needed, always knowing exactly what was expected of him?

Some police keep their dogs in a crate at night, when the family is around. "My husband doesn't put his gun on the kitchen table," Kurt Dumond's wife, Helen, told me. "And he doesn't let his police dog loose in the house." But Rothschild, who had two young children, let his dog roam free at home. Danz was named for Vincent Danz, a New York cop and family friend, who died in the attacks on September 11th, and Rothschild never forgot that the dog was also looking after him. He let Danz wander through the park a while longer. "This is his time," he said. "His time to play. When he empties, I just let him be a dog."

Critical Thinking

1. What qualities do dogs have that make them suited for police work?
2. How does operant conditioning work?
3. What are some risks in using dogs for police work?
4. What have been the results from having puppies trained by convicts in prisons? For the dogs? For the convicts?

Forensic Techniques Are Subject to Human Bias, Lack Standards, Panel Found

SPENCER S. HSU

In Hollywood, the moment the good guys trace a hair, a bullet fragment or a fingerprint, it's game over. The bad guy is locked up.

But the glamorized portrait is not so simple in real life.

Far from infallible, expert comparisons of hair, handwriting, marks made by firearms on bullets, and patterns such as bite marks and shoe and tire prints are in some ways unscientific and subject to human bias, a National Academy of Sciences panel chartered by Congress found. Other techniques, such as in bullet-lead analysis and arson investigation, survived for decades despite poorly regulated practices and a lack of scientific method.

Even fingerprint identification is partly a subjective exercise that lacks research into the role of unconscious bias or even its error rate, the panel's 328-page report said.

"The forensic science system, encompassing both research and practice, has serious problems that can only be addressed by a national commitment to overhaul the current structure," the panel concluded in 2009.

Now, Congress and the Obama administration are trying to regulate forensic science to help establish standards. Senate Judiciary Committee Chairman Patrick J. Leahy (D-Vt.) and Commerce, Science and Transportation Committee Chairman John D. Rockefeller IV (D-W.Va.) are weighing legislation that could subject techniques to greater scientific scrutiny and help establish their ranges of accuracy.

A Leahy bill would create a new office of forensic science in the Justice Department. Rockefeller is preparing legislation to expand the role of the National Science Foundation and the National Institute of Standards and Technology in setting scientific standards and research goals.

The Obama administration is also looking to "strengthen the linkage between cutting-edge science . . . and the forensic tests used by law enforcement," said Rick Weiss, spokesman for the White House Office of Science and Technology Policy.

Police and law enforcement agencies have rebuffed recommendations to remove crime labs from their control.

Since 2002, failures have been reported at about 30 federal, state and local crime labs serving the FBI, the Army and eight of the nation's 20 largest cities.

Advances in DNA testing are exposing errors at unexpected rates. In November, researchers with the Urban Institute reported that new DNA testing appeared to clear convicted defendants in 16 percent of Virginia criminal convictions between 1973 and 1988 in which evidence was available for retesting.

A 2009 study of post-conviction DNA exonerations—now up to 289 nationwide—found invalid testimony in more than half the cases.

"There are just too many related problems for this to be dealt with ad hoc," said Brandon L. Garrett, a professor at the University of Virginia School of Law.

More DNA testing alone is not the answer, experts say. Biological evidence historically is collected in fewer than 20 percent of criminal cases. Other questioned forensic techniques are used far more often, with mistakes harming defendants and crime victims whose true assailants remain at large.

The National Academy of Sciences report cited the lack of effective standards for examiners, laboratories and court testimony. It also criticized Justice Department agencies for a dearth of research into problems and for being "too wedded" to the status quo to be trusted to lead reforms.

"This is our generation's sole opportunity" to get arguments out of the adversarial system and resolved through science, said Thomas L. Bohan, who was president of the American Academy of Forensic Sciences in 2010. "It's a shame they couldn't have done a good job 10 or 20 years ago."

Research Aids Process

Arson investigation is an example of how research has dramatically improved practices.

Since 1990, the number of U.S. structure fires attributed to arson has dropped by half. One reason is that scientific test burnings have disproved the notion that some burn marks could be caused only by liquid accelerants.

Meanwhile, scientific doubts have festered for decades with fingerprint examination. While fingerprint analysis is one of the most valuable and frequently applied investigative tools, its accuracy has not been scientifically defined.

FBI examiners claimed until recently that they can match fingerprints to the exclusion of any other person in the world with 100 percent certainty using a method with an error rate essentially of zero. The academy report found that assertion was "not scientifically plausible" and had chilled research into error rates.

In 1999, a Justice Department official, Richard Rau, told a federal court that the department delayed such a study because of the legal ramifications. As recently as last year, Pennsylvania State University researcher Cedric Neumann was denied a department grant to determine potential fingerprint error rates using closed cases.

Neumann declined to comment for this article.

A person familiar with the episode blamed a polarized climate in the adversarial legal system, saying, "Few agencies in the forensic-science community want to be the first ones associated with an error rate." The person spoke on the condition of anonymity to discuss sensitive federal research funding decisions.

Meanwhile, errors occur. In 2004, DNA for the first time exonerated a person convicted with a fingerprint match and, separately, the FBI made its first publicly acknowledged fingerprint misidentification. Brandon Mayfield, a Portland, Ore., lawyer, mistakenly was arrested in connection with the terrorist train bombings in Madrid that killed 191 people. The FBI apologized.

Since then, the Justice Department has begun research to try to quantify how complete a fingerprint must be to properly declare a match; how different conditions may affect the reliability of examinations; whether computers can do such work; and how to present forensic testimony about probabilities to judges and juries. The FBI has also required "blind verification" of results by agents unfamiliar with initial examinations.

Measuring Accuracy

The bureau said that skilled analysts are extraordinarily accurate, at least when they know they are being tested. An FBI study with Noblis Corp. last year found that when 169 examiners compared thousands of fingerprints and decided there was enough information to declare a match or not, they were correct 99.8 percent of the time.

Still, the Mayfield case highlighted the need for research into real-world conditions. A 2006 study by a London-based scientist, Itiel E. Dror, asked experts to analyze fingerprints that, unbeknownst to them, they had analyzed earlier in their careers. This time, however, examiners were given biasing statements, such as that a suspect had confessed or that a suspect was locked up at the time of the offense. In 16.6 percent of cases, examiners reversed earlier judgments.

Crime lab directors and prosecutors welcome calls for more money for research and to improve examiners and facilities. But with budgets tight at all levels, Washington has few other tools to prompt 350 state and local labs across the country to improve.

Because techniques have not been scientifically proved does not mean they do not work, defenders say, and mistakes can be handled traditionally through case-by-case appeals.

"In the real life of the criminal justice system, we need more resources for those who are on the front lines," said Scott D. Burns, executive director of the National District Attorneys Association. Noting that prosecutors handle 20 million non-traffic cases a year, Burns said, "The sky isn't falling, and we usually get it right."

Pete M. Marone, director of the Virginia Department of Forensic Science and chairman of the Consortium of Forensic Science Organizations, urged Congress not to "reinvent the wheel" by abandoning all existing accreditation standards or groups such as the one he represents.

"Don't judge forensic science today based on errors from 30 years ago," Marone said. "What we need is someone setting a research agenda and direction. . . . We need leadership."

Critical Thinking

1. What are some of the problems brought to light by the National Academy of Sciences panel?
2. Is more DNA testing the answer to most evidence problems?
3. What's wrong with the FBI claim that their examiners can match fingerprints with 100 percent accuracy?

Understanding the Psychology of Police Misconduct

BRIAN D. FITCH, PHD

Law enforcement is a unique profession, with officers experiencing a host of freedoms not available to the general public, including the application of deadly force, high-speed driving, and seizing personal property. While these liberties may be necessary, they also can create opportunities for wrongdoing, especially if such behavior is likely to go undetected because of poor supervision. The embarrassment caused by misconduct can damage the public trust, undermine officer morale, and expose agencies to unnecessary—and, in many cases, costly—litigation.[1] Consequently, a clear understanding of the psychology underlying unethical behavior is critical to every law enforcement supervisor and manager at every level of an organization, regardless of one's agency or mission.

Law enforcement agencies go to great lengths to recruit hire, and train only the most qualified applicants—candidates who have already demonstrated a track record of good moral values and ethical conduct. Similarly, most officers support the agency, its values, and its mission, performing their duties ethically while avoiding any misconduct or abuse of authority. Yet despite the best efforts of organizations everywhere, it seems that one does not have to look very far these days to find examples of police misconduct particularly in the popular press.[2] Even more disturbing, however, is that many of the officers engaged in immoral or unethical behavior previously demonstrated good service records, absent any of the "evil" typically associated with corruption or abuse.

While it is probably true that at least some of the officers who engage in illicit activities managed somehow to slip through the cracks in the hiring process and simply continued their unethical ways, this account fails to explain how otherwise good officers become involved in misconduct. The purpose of this article is to familiarize law enforcement managers and supervisors with the cognitive rationalizations that can contribute to unethical behavior. The article also offers strategies and suggestions intended to mitigate misconduct, before it actually occurs, by developing a culture of ethics.

Moral Responsibility and Disengagement

Most law enforcement professionals are, at their core, good, ethical, and caring people. Despite the overuse of a popular cliché, many officers do in fact enter law enforcement because they want to make a positive difference in their communities. Officers frequently espouse strong, positive moral values while working diligently—in many cases, at great personal risk—to bring dangerous criminals to justice. Doing so provides officers with a strong sense of personal satisfaction and self-worth. As a result, most officers do not—and in many cases cannot—engage in unethical conduct unless they can somehow justify to themselves the morality of their actions.[3]

Decades of empirical research have supported the idea that whenever a person's behaviors are inconsistent with their attitudes or beliefs, the individual will experience a state of psychological tension—a phenomenon referred to as cognitive dissonance.[4] Because this tension is uncomfortable, people will modify any contradictory beliefs or behaviors in ways intended to reduce or eliminate discomfort. Officers can reduce psychological tension by changing one or more of their cognitions—that is, by modifying how they think about their actions and the consequences of those behaviors—or by adjusting their activities, attitudes, or beliefs in ways that are consistent with their values and self-image. Generally speaking, an officer will modify the cognition that is least resistant to change, which, in most cases, tends to be the officer's attitudes, not behaviors.

One of the simplest ways that officers can reduce the psychological discomfort that accompanies misconduct is to cognitively restructure unethical behaviors in ways that make them seem personally and socially acceptable, thereby allowing officers to behave immorally while preserving their self-image as ethically good people. The following is a partial list of common rationalizations that officers can use to neutralize or excuse unethical conduct.[5]

Denial of victim. Officers who rely on this tactic argue that because no victim exists, no real harm has been done. It is probably safe to suggest that officers do not generally regard drug dealers, thieves, and sexual predators as bona fide victims, regardless of the nature of an officer's conduct. An officer, for instance, who takes money from a suspected drug dealer during the service of a search warrant might argue that because the dealer acquired the currency illegally, the dealer was never actually entitled to the proceeds. Rather, the money belongs to whoever possesses it at the time.

Victim of circumstance. Officers who utilize this method convince themselves that they behaved improperly only because they had no other choice. Officers may claim that they were the victims of peer pressure, an unethical supervisor, or an environment where "everyone else is doing it," so what else could they possibly have done? Regardless of the context, these officers excuse their conduct by alleging that they had no alternative but to act unethically.

Denial of injury. Using this form of rationalization, officers persuade themselves that because nobody was actually hurt by their actions, their behavior was not really immoral. This explanation is especially common in cases involving drugs, stolen property, or large amounts of untraceable cash where it can be difficult, if not impossible, to identify an injured party. Officers who use this tactic may further neutralize their deviant conduct by comparing it to the harm being done by the drug dealer from whom the money was stolen.

Advantageous comparisons. Officers who depend on this explanation rely on selective social comparisons to defend their conduct. Officers who falsify a police report to convict a suspected drug dealer, for example, might defend their actions by minimizing their participation or the frequency of their unethical behavior, while at the same time vilifying a coworker as someone who "lies all the time on reports." In comparison to an officer who routinely falsifies reports, the first officer's conduct can seem less egregious.

Higher cause. Officers who practice this type of cognitive restructuring argue that sometimes, it may be necessary to break certain rules to serve a higher calling or to achieve a more important goal. An officer who conducts an unlawful search to uncover evidence against a suspected pedophile might reason that the nature of the crime justifies breaking the rules. "The ends justify the means," officers might assert—suggesting that they did what was necessary, regardless of the legality or morality of their conduct, to put a dangerous criminal behind bars. This form of rationalization can be especially disturbing because it goes beyond merely excusing or justifying deviant behavior to the point of actually glorifying certain forms of wrongdoing in the name of "justice" or "the greater good."

Blame the victim. An officer who uses this form of justification blames the victim for any misconduct or abuse. If, for instance, officers use unreasonable force on a suspected drug dealer, they can simply argue that the victim brought on this suffering by violating the law. "If the dealer doesn't want to get beat up, the dealer should obey the law," the officer might reason. "I'm not using force on law-abiding citizens, only on drug dealers; they give up their rights when they break the rules." By assigning blame to the victim, the officer not only finds a way to excuse any wrongdoing, but also a way to feel sanctimonious about doing so.

Dehumanization. The amount of guilt or shame officers feel for behaving unethically depends, at least in part, on how they regard the person being abused. To avoid the feelings of self-censorship or guilt that often accompany misconduct, officers can employ euphemistic language to strip victims of their humanity. Using terms like "dirtbag" to describe law violators has the effect of dehumanizing intended targets, generally making it easier for officers to justify, ignore, or minimize the harmful effects of their actions, while at the same time reducing their personal responsibility for behaving in ways that they know are wrong.

Table 1 Rationalizing Misconduct

Strategy	Description
Denial of Victim	Alleging that because there is no legitimate victim, there is no misconduct.
Victim of Circumstance	Behaving improperly because the officer had no other choice, either because of peer pressure or unethical supervision.
Denial of Injury	Because nobody was hurt by the officer's action, no misconduct actually occurred.
Advantageous Comparisons	Minimizing or excusing one's own wrongdoing by comparing it to the more egregious behavior of others.
Higher Cause	Breaking the rules because of some higher calling—that is, removing a known felon from the streets.
Blame the Victim	The victim invited any suffering or misconduct by breaking the law in the first place.
Dehumanization	Using euphemistic language to dehumanize people, thereby making them easier to victimize.
Diffusion of Responsibility	Relying on the diffusion of responsibility among the involved parties to excuse misconduct.

Diffusion of responsibility. An officer who uses this excuse relies on the shared participation—and, by extension, the shared guilt—of everyone involved in an incident of misconduct to excuse or reduce any personal culpability. With each additional accomplice, every individual officer is seen as that much less responsible for any wrongdoing that might have ocurred. If, for instance, money is stolen from an arrestee, officers might assert that there were many officers at the crime scene who could have done this, so an individual cannot be blamed. Similarly, if ten officers were involved in the service of a search warrant, then each officer is only one-tenth responsible for any misconduct that occurs.

Misconduct's Slippery Slope

It is important to note that most officers do not jump headfirst into large-scale misconduct—instead, they weigh in gradually in a process referred to as incrementalism.[6] The strength and ease with which officers can rationalize unethical behavior also depends, at least in part, on how they view their conduct, the people harmed by their actions, and the consequences that flow from their actions. An officer's initial slide down the slippery slope of misconduct can begin with nothing more than simple policy violations that, if left unchecked, generate a mild feeling of psychological tension or discomfort. However, by learning to rationalize wrongdoing in ways that make it psychologically and morally acceptable, officers are able to relieve any feelings of distress or discomfort, effectively disengaging their moral compasses.

Officers can employ cognitive rationalizations prospectively (before the corrupt act) to forestall guilt and resistance, or retrospectively (after the misconduct) to erase any regrets. In either case, the more frequently an officer rationalizes deviant behavior, the easier each subsequent instance of misconduct becomes.[7] This is because the more frequently officers employ rationalizations, the easier it becomes to activate similar thought patterns in the future. With time and repeated experience, rationalizations can eventually become part of the habitual, automatic, effortless ways that officers think about themselves, their duties, and the consequences of their actions, eventually allowing officers to engage in increasingly egregious acts of misconduct with little, if any, of the guilt or shame commonly associated with wrongdoing.

As officers learn to pay less attention to the morality of their actions, the ways they think about misconduct—that is, their attitudes, beliefs, and values—may begin to change as well. Officers can begin defining behaviors that were once seen as unethical or immoral as necessary parts of completing their assigned duties. Even more troubling, however, is that once rationalizations become part of an agency's dominant culture, they can alter the ways officers define misconduct, particularly if wrongdoings are rewarded either informally by an officer's peer group or formally by the organization.

Ethics Education

Law enforcement agencies throughout the United States, as well as abroad, have begun to recognize the importance of ethics training. While such attention represents a significant step in the right direction, ethical instruction is often limited to little more than the discussion and development of proper moral values—an approach commonly referred to as character education.[8] Proponents of this method suggest that officers who possess the right values—and, by extension, the right character—will always do the right thing, regardless of the circumstances. Although few people would argue with the importance of good moral values and character, ethical decisions are not always simple.

Before officers can act ethically, they must recognize the moral nature of a situation; decide on a specific and, hopefully, ethical course of action; possess the requisite moral motivation to take action; and demonstrate the character necessary to follow through with their decisions.[9] To further complicate matters, even the best of intentions can be thwarted by peer pressure or fear of retaliation. For example, the 2003 National Business Ethics Survey found that approximately 40 percent of those surveyed would not report misconduct if they observed it because of fear of reprisal from management.[10]

This cloud does, however, contain a silver lining. Research has demonstrated that ethics education can assist officers in better navigating moral challenges by increasing ethical awareness and moral reasoning—two critical aspects of ethical decision making.[11] However, conducting meaningful ethics education requires more than lengthy philosophical lectures on the importance of character. Rather, instructors should focus on facilitating a dialogue that challenges officers on key moral issues and assumptions; tests their reasoning and decision-making skills; and allows them to share their experiences in a safe, supportive environment.[12]

For ethics education to be truly effective, organizations must make moral discussions a regular part of the agency's training program. In the same way that officers routinely train in defensive tactics, firearms, and law to better prime them for field duties, officers should prepare equally well for any ethical issues they might encounter.[13] Supervisors can stimulate ethical discussions with a video documentary, news clip, or fictional story. Regardless of the stimulus, however, the more frequently officers discuss ethics, the better able they will be to recognize a moral dilemma, make the appropriate ethical decision, and demonstrate the moral courage necessary to behave honorably.

Next, law enforcement agencies must establish a clear code of ethical conduct, including a set of core values and a mission statement. Merely establishing a code of ethical conduct is not enough, however; the department's top management must lead by example. It is important to remember that a code of conduct applies equally to employees at all levels of an organization.[14] As most leaders can confirm from experience, officers can be surprisingly quick to point out any inconsistencies between the organization's stated values and the conduct of senior management. If leaders expect officers to behave ethically, leaders must model the way.

Departments must also work to create systems that reward ethical conduct and punish unethical behavior.[15] Core values and codes of conduct are of little value if they are not supported by wider agency objectives that reward ethical actions. Not only should law enforcement organizations reward officers for behaving ethically, they must also seriously address officers' ethical concerns by thoroughly investigating any allegations, while protecting the confidentiality of those reporting such incidents. And, finally, agencies should strive to create an open environment where ethical issues can be discussed without fear of punishment or reprisal.

In the end, mitigating and, hopefully, eliminating misconduct require regular ethics training, high ethical standards, appropriate reward systems, and a culture in which ethical issues are discussed freely. While the responsibility for creating a culture of ethics rests with leadership, individual officers must do their part to behave ethically, support the moral conduct of others, and challenge misconduct in all its forms. Only by remaining vigilant to the psychology of misconduct can law enforcement professionals focus attention back on the positive aspects of their profession, while enjoying the high levels of public trust necessary to do their jobs.

Notes

1. For a more complete discussion on the impact of police misconduct see Adam Dunn and Patrick J. Caceres, "Constructing a Better Estimate of Police Misconduct," *Policy Matters Journal* (Spring 2010): 10–16.
2. For a more complete description of police misconduct, media coverage, and public attitudes toward law enforcement see Joel

Miller and Robert C. Davis, "Unpacking Public Attitudes to the Police: Contrasting Perceptions of Misconduct with Traditional Measures of Satisfaction," *International Journal of Police Science and Management* 10, no. 1 (2008): 9–22.

3. For a more complete report on the frequency of police misconduct see Mathew R. Durose, Erica L. Smith, and Patrick A. Lanan, *Contacts Between Police and the Public, 2005,* NCJ 215243, Bureau of Justice Statistics, Office of Justice Programs, Special Report (April 2007), http://bjs.ojp.usdoj.gov/content/pub/pdf/cppOS.pdf (accessed November 22, 2010).
4. For a discussion of research on cognitive dissonance, see Joel Cooper, Robert Mirabile, and Steven J. Scher, "Actions and Attitudes: The Theory of Cognitive Dissonance," in *Persuasion: Psychological Insights and Perspectives,* ed. Timothy C. Brock and Melaine C. Green (Thousand Oaks, California: Sage Publications Inc., 2005), 63–80.
5. For a more complete list of cognitive rationalizations, see Albert Bandura et al., "Mechanisms of Moral Disengagement in the Exercise of Moral Agency," *Journal of Personality and Social Psychology* 71, no. 2 (1996): 364–374; John F. Veiga, Timothy D. Golden, and Kathleen Dechant, "A Survey of the Executive's Advisory Panel: Why Managers Bend Company Rules," *Academy of Management Executive* 18, no. 2 (May 2004): 84–90; and Celia Moore, "Moral Disengagement in Processes of Organizational Corruption," *Journal of Business Ethics* 80 (June 2008): 129–139.
6. For a complete discussion of incrementalism, see Ehud Sprinzak, "The Psychopolitical Formation of the Extreme Left in Democracy: The Case of the Weathermen," in *Origins of Terrorism: Psychologies, Ideologies, Theologies, States of Mind,* ed. Walter Reich and Walter Laqueur (Cambridge, England: Cambridge University Press, 1990), 65–85.
7. For a discussion of implicit decision making, see Daniel Kahneman and Shane Frederick, "Representativeness Revisited: Attribute Substitution in Intuitive Judgment" in *Heuristics and Biases: The Psychology of Intuitive Judgment,* ed. Thomas Gilovich, Dale Griffin, and Daniel Kahneman (New York: Cambridge University Press), 20(G), 49–81.
8. See for example, Michael Josephson, *Becoming an Examplary Peace Officer. The Guide to Ethical Decision Making* (Los Angeles: Josephson Institute, 2009).
9. For further discussion on ethical decision making, see Russell Haines, Marc D. Street, and Douglas Haines, "The Influence of Perceived Importance of an Ethical Issue on Moral Judgment, Moral Obligation, and Moral Intent" *Journal of Business Ethics* 81 (2008): 387–399.
10. Ethics Resource Center, *2003 National Business Ethics Survey (NBES)* (May 21, 2003), www.ethics.org/resource/2003-national-business-ethics-survey-nbes (accessed November 24, 2010).
11. See, for example, Cubie L. L. Lau, "A Step Forward: Ethics Education Matters," *Journal of Business Ethics* 92 (2010): 565–584.
12. For a more complete discussion on facilitation, see Peter Renner, *The Art of Teaching Adults: How to Become an Exceptional Instructor and Facilitator* (Vancouver, Canada: Training Associates, 2005).
13. For a more complete discussion of ethics training, see Brian Fitch, "Principle-Based Decision Making," *Law and Order* 56 (September 2008): 64–70.
14. See, for example, Simon Webley and Andrea Werner, "Corporate Codes of Ethics: Necessary but Not Sufficient," *Business Ethics: A European Review* 17, no. 4 (October 2008): 405–415.
15. For further discussion on ethics and supervisory influence, see James C. Wimbush and Jon M. Shepard, "Toward an Understanding of Ethical Climate: Its Relationship to Ethical Behavior and Supervisory Influence," *Journal of Business Ethics* 3, no. 8 (1994): 637–647.

Critical Thinking

1. How can a police officer reduce the psychological discomfort that accompanies misconduct?
2. Explain the slippery slope theory regarding misconduct.
3. What can law enforcement agencies do to make ethics education truly effective?

The Art of the Police Report

A Los Angeles cop writes "just the facts" and still tells one helluva story.

ELLEN COLLETT

Monday through Friday, I'm enthralled by a man I've never met. His name is Martinez and he's a cop with the Los Angeles Police Department.

Martinez works in crime suppression in South Central L.A. He and his partner, Brown, patrol the streets and respond to scenes-of-crimes. Every incident they investigate generates a written account.

I know Martinez only through his incident reports, as a five-digit number on a sheet of paper. In our precinct's Crime Analysis Division, I read and code hundreds of these reports each day. They are written by every serving officer on roster, and by design most of them sound exactly alike.

Surprisingly, writing is the one constant in a cop's daily life. Whether he's assigned to vice or patrol, working bunco or undercover, every day he'll write. Most precincts have specially designated writing rooms, where the average cop hates spending time—worse than on shoot-outs, stakeouts, and court appearances put together. As with everything in the department, strict rules govern report writing, and as with any dangerous undertaking, the department will train you to do it properly. The most despised class at the police academy is the one that teaches writing. A cadet can't be sworn as a police officer without passing it.

The incident report he'll learn to write is the factual narrative account of a crime—of a rape, robbery, murder, criminal threat, lewd act, vandalism, burglary, sexual molestation, kidnapping, or assault. Every event a cop responds to generates a report.

Crime reports are written in neutral diction, and in the dispassionate uni-voice that's testament to the academy's ability to standardize writing. They feel generated rather than authored, the work of a single law enforcement consciousness rather than a specific human being.

So how can I identify Martinez from a single sentence? Why do his reports make me feel pity, terror, or despair? Make me want to put a bullet in someone's brain—preferably a wife beater's or a pedophile's, but occasionally my own? How does he use words on paper to hammer at my heart? Like all great cops, Sergeant Martinez is a sneaky fucker. He's also a master of inflection and narrative voice.

An incident report tells only what happened: where, when, and to whom. It offers multiple perspectives of the same event from often contradictory points of view of cop, victim, suspect, and witnesses. Even when these accounts agree, no two people see things identically or invest their attention in the same details. Each person's agenda is inherently personal.

An incident report lists the inventory of all physical evidence collected and booked. Anything from shell casings and rape-kit underwear to a three-legged dog in a custody dispute.

In structure, an incident report is a strict chronological narrative. It begins with a Source of Activity section, which tees up the story. It's where the narrator introduces himself and offers his credentials for telling this tale: "On 4-6-10 at approx. 1922 hours, my partner Ofcr. Brown (badge #13312) and I (Ofcr. Martinez badge #14231) were in full uniform traveling westbound on Gage Avenue when we received the radio call of an LUAC in progress at 82nd St./Central Ave."

In the investigation section that follows, the narrator tells briefly what his investigation revealed. He lists the actions taken by himself and his partner, and the facts of the case as discovered. The strict emphasis is on verifiable information.

If versions of the event differ from his, these are recorded as witness statements. These can be summaries, but quotes are often included. The narrative voice at the center of an incident report is always emotionally neutral. He's the ultimate reliable narrator. His sole job is to convince us that everything he tells us is the absolute truth. It all begins with diction.

Cadets are taught to write with care and deliberation, to choose each word for maximum accuracy. Precision, not firepower, is the goal; you don't use a semiautomatic at close range when you're packing a Smith & Wesson. Good cop diction means checking each word in a sentence to verify that it can mean only one thing. The officer must avoid words that carry associations, subtext, or bias.

Officers are encouraged to use action verbs in preference to *is* and *has*. *Is* and *has* speak abstractions—existence and possession, respectively—and where they go, descriptors follow. Action verbs, on the other hand, move us through time and space. "The Subject removed a hammer from the kitchen drawer and struck the Victim three times in the head and neck" is a good sentence. It tells what physically happened without embellishment.

"The Subject removed a hammer from the kitchen drawer and struck the Victim three times in the head and neck" is a good sentence.

Avoid modifiers, says the academy. Adverbs—words ending in *ly*—are slippery and subjective; they shade reality and opine. Any adverb can be eliminated by choosing a better verb. "The Suspect snatched the Victim's chain and fled" is a sentence without speculation. To know the manner in which the snatching or fleeing transpired would be interpretive.

The academy dislikes adjectives unless they pertain to direction, color, or amount. These are "empirical adjectives." Because they speak to precision of detail, they resist interpretation. "The black Escalade fired 12 shots into the dwelling on 865 Inglewood Avenue" can mean only one thing.

Parenthetically, the two exceptions to the "no adjectives" rule are the words *bloody* and *suspicious,* invoked to justify officer initiative in field investigations. If a suspect "fled while holding his waistband in a *suspicious* manner," it's presumptive of a concealed weapon. If an officer investigates a neighbor complaint and the victim "opened the door wearing *bloody* clothing," there's a pretext to enter and reconnoiter the premises.

These guidelines about diction and story efficiency serve a deeper purpose, which is the legitimizing of the narrative "voice." The police narrator uses neutral language and uninflected storytelling to assure us of his credibility and to win the reader's trust. He never judges.

The perpetrator in a crime report is always the "Suspect," even when 15 witnesses, half of them preachers, see him exit his car and shoot his cousin at point-blank range in a church parking lot. Until a jury reviews the evidence and pronounces, under the law, no crime took place. The police narrator is careful not to imply that he thinks otherwise.

The police narrator further proves his lack of bias by presenting everyone's version of the same event, giving equal space to the "truth" as reported by victim, suspect, and witness. While he might state that DeWayne "aka Baby Insane" Johnson of the Rolling '60s Crips shot and killed J'Marcus "aka L'il Monster" Faye of Florencia Trece, he'll include Baby's explanation that he was merely examining the gun with an eye toward purchase when that muthafucker up and went off. The narrator's job isn't to judge but to relay facts to the best of his ability, and let the reader decide the truth of it.

Words committed to paper have an agenda. The purpose of a police report is to be cited in court as proof of who did what to whom. Its ultimate agenda is justice. It seeks to protect the weak and punish the guilty. Because the stakes are high—freedom, death, or life without parole—it's written with special care. Above all else, it aims to be truthful. At the same time, to do its job, it needs to be convincing. The story it tells should persuade 12 people in a jury box of something.

On the face of it, these two goals—truthful and persuasive—seem uncomfortably at odds. Shouldn't facts alone persuade? Should truth need composing? And assuming that it's possible to write toward this goal—to be truthful and persuasive at once—shouldn't all fiction writers want to learn how?

Which brings us back to that sneaky fucker, Martinez. Martinez writes incident reports that technically follow the academy's guidelines. He avoids modifiers and descriptors. He traces the physical action of an event without opining or speculating. He offers accounts that contradict his own findings. He's succinct and factual. He tells the literal and empirical truth. He writes in the dispassionate narrative uni-voice that conveys objectivity and distance. So why is Martinez instantly discernable on the page from a hundred other cops?

Despite the neutrality of his diction, Martinez's choices are idiosyncratic. Everything he sees reveals him. And syntactically, though he bends every rule to the breaking point, you can't bust him.

Officer Martinez's choices are idiosyncratic. Everything he sees reveals him. And syntactically, though he bends every rule to the breaking point, you can't bust him.

At a Lewd Acts on Child crime scene, Martinez's partner, Brown, writes, "The Victim sustained multiple injuries." Martinez would tell us, "The baby was bleeding from three orifices." There's a world of difference here. Brown gives us a victim; Martinez gives us a baby. Brown offers a fact; Martinez paints a picture.

Brown's statement moves us forward; Martinez makes us stop dead and envision the horrific crime that caused such injuries. Both statements are neutral on the surface, but the specificity of Martinez's language makes the reader see and feel.

At the same crime scene, Brown says, "We placed the Suspect in a felony prone position and took him into custody without incident." Martinez would write, "We cuffed the father." Martinez's version reminds us of the unnatural aspect of the crime, that a father (presumably) committed it. He edges near the academy no-fly zone with *father* in place of *suspect,* but gets away with it because the sentence describes police action—the cuffing—rather than any actions of the suspect. Also, nobody disputes the fact that the suspect *is* the father; it's the type of father he is that's at issue.

At the same crime scene, Martinez might note that there's "no food in the apartment." This is an empirical fact, so technically admissible. It doesn't speak to the specific crime of Lewd Acts on Child, but it does subtly add to the moral charges against the parents. Martinez inflects the barren apartment and makes it speak. Details bring scenes to life. Sometimes the image can tell everything.

In the witness section of the report, Brown might say, "Victim's mother gave no statement." Martinez would tell us, "Mother refused to cooperate." This carries a totally different emphasis and meaning. Martinez doesn't speculate if she's protecting her husband at the expense of her child. He doesn't need to. What kind of mother refuses to speak when her baby is bleeding from three orifices?

Examine these two versions of the same incident, side by side. They admit the same facts. They're both truthful. But one—Martinez's—is also persuasive. Why? It's subtly inflected in every line to signal its agenda. Though it labors under the constraints of the report format, it uses emphasis and diction to suggest how we interpret what it tells us. It may look impartial, but it's aimed like a weapon.

From a strict moral perspective or the police academy vantage point, Martinez's incident reports are flawed. They're failures of objective reportage. Though everything in them is literally true, they're technically "suspicious"; if Martinez saw a baby-raper, he's making damn sure we do too.

From a reader's perspective, Martinez's incident reports are deeply satisfying. They engage us emotionally; they vest us in the events he describes, and in the teller. They're narratives that hint at larger truths—about Martinez himself and the South Central universe he polices. They reverberate beyond the time it takes to read them. They offer a way to understand the world.

My Sergeant Martinez may be writing reports, but he's also using the alchemy of inflection to turn them into stories—narratives that believe themselves and make us believe them, too.

Martinez succeeds—or fails, if you're his supervisors—because of his commitment to what his stories mean. He continues to protect and serve because inflection isn't illegal, and you won't catch him. It's not a story, it's "just the facts, ma'am."

Like Martinez, a good story always has an agenda.

Like Martinez, a good story is a sneaky fucker.

Critical Thinking

1. What is the purpose of an incident report?
2. Do Martinez's reports fulfill the purpose of an incident report?

As Mental Health Resources Shrink Police Become Front Line with Lives at Stake

HENRI E. CAUVIN

The call came in at the height of the evening rush hour: A man was threatening to jump off an old railroad bridge on Route 1 in Fort Belvoir. Moments later, racing down Richmond Highway, was his best hope for coming down alive.

Leanna Wilson isn't a doctor or a nurse or a social worker. She's a Fairfax County police officer, and, like officers across the country, she has ended up on the front line of the American public mental health system, doing a job she didn't sign up for, trying to fill holes she didn't create.

In her 12 years on the job, Wilson, 36, had encountered suicidal people. But she'd never confronted anyone on the verge of carrying out the threat.

"All I thought . . . was, 'I got 30 seconds to think about what I'm going to talk to this guy about,' " said Wilson, who had no idea whether he was armed.

She had a .40 caliber semiautomatic sitting on her right hip and a black Taser strapped to her left leg, but she wasn't counting on using either. This, she thought, was going to take talking.

Six months earlier, Wilson had been back at the county police academy for a weeklong class on dealing with people in mental crises. Patience, she'd been told, is essential. So is taking the time to connect.

Now, as dusk fell on Fort Belvoir, she was going to find out whether the training would make a difference for this one man.

"Game on," Wilson said to herself as she prepared to scale a dirt hill leading up to the dilapidated track bed.

Volatile and sometimes deadly confrontations between the police and the mentally ill have been more common since state psychiatric hospitals began to discharge large numbers of patients in the 1960s and 1970s.

In response, police departments throughout the United States, including those in Montgomery, Arlington and Fairfax counties and the District and Alexandria, have launched "crisis intervention" training to create cadres of officers with more than just an hour or two of mental health training.

Now, with financially strapped state and local governments cutting community-based mental health programs, the pressures on police could mount as more people become untethered from treatment.

Perhaps more than any other police force in Virginia, Fairfax's has seen up-close the fallout from a shrinking mental health system.

It was along Route 1 that an unarmed 52-year-old man with mental illness was shot and killed by police in 2009 after he had ripped flowers out of a planter. And it was outside the county police station in Chantilly that two officers were killed almost five years ago, shot by a disturbed 18-year-old whose family had struggled to obtain care for their son.

Never before had a Fairfax officer been slain in the line duty.

Wilson was working that day and remembers the harrowing transmissions that came over the radio after gunfire erupted outside the Sully station May 8, 2006.

Detective Vicky O. Armel and Officer Michael E. Garbarino were mortally wounded. So was the shooter, Michael W. Kennedy, who was felled by other officers.

As Wilson was describing her encounter with the suicidal man on Route 1, her mind drifted to Armel and Garbarino, and to Kennedy.

Did any of them have to die, Wilson wondered? "What if somebody had sat down and changed his meds," she asked of Kennedy, "or somebody had convinced him to get help?"

"We wouldn't have those two names on the wall."

Taking Time to Talk

At first, the man refused to let Wilson join him on the bridge. But after she explained that she couldn't hear him well enough from the road, he agreed to let her come up.

"Just you," the man warned.

Built as a supply conduit for the Army base, the nearly 16-foot-high crossing had been out of use since at least the 1980s. The iron rails are still intact across much of the 195-foot-long span, but the wooden beams below are pocked with holes big enough to swallow someone's step.

"I am deathly afraid of heights," Wilson said. "I stepped out on the bridge, and I almost fainted."

The man was about 30 feet away, she said, far enough that he could leap before she would ever have a chance to grab him. If this was going to end well, the man would have to be talked down.

In a job that rewards and even relishes action, taking the time to talk to a troubled soul is no small matter. An officer who lingers at a call can be razzed by colleagues, Wilson said.

"It's just so much easier to put the handcuffs on, take them to jail and you're done with them," said Wilson, a former Army reservist who double-majored in criminology and sociology at Roanoke College. "But you're not solving anything."

During the county's crisis intervention training, which is coordinated by the Fairfax-Falls Church Community Services Board and has been completed by about 150 Fairfax officers, one boss after another hammered home the importance of listening to those in crisis.

It came naturally to Wilson, who'd set her sights on becoming a police officer the day a K-9 unit visited her Prince George's County elementary school. "Yeah, that's what I want to do," she remembers thinking.

She was 24 when she graduated from the academy and started patrolling the Route 1 corridor. The job gave her exactly what she was looking for: career security and the chance to help people such as the desperate man on the bridge.

So, with traffic backed up in both directions on Route 1, she tried to initiate a conversation with him.

In fitful snippets, she learned fragments of his story: He had lost his house and then his job, and he had spent time in the psychiatric ward at Inova Mount Vernon Hospital.

Later, she would learn more. That he was 31 and college educated. That he had been a federal contractor, working overseas at U.S. embassies. But when his home here was mistakenly placed into foreclosure while he was on assignment in Madagascar, the man's security clearance was jeopardized, and his company cut him loose.

"His world," Wilson recalled later, "had just gone right into the sinkhole."

As they talked, he kept one foot planted on the edge of the bridge.

'This Is Not Our Job'

On a rainy morning last month, about a dozen Fairfax officers were on the roof of the county police academy learning what it's like to confront someone on the edge.

A man in black pants, black windbreaker and black sunglasses was talking about the voices he was hearing.

"I'm following orders, but I don't want to die," he told officers Brian Bowers and Sabrina Gonzalez.

The man was a few feet from a plunge that could kill him.

"I don't want you to die, either," Bowers responded. "I want you to talk to me."

"The being is always sending me messages telling me I'm bad," the jumper said.

"I don't think you're bad," Bowers said.

"You're not bad," Gonzalez said.

It was the sort of role-playing that Wilson had gone through six months earlier. Now, other officers were listening to lectures on bipolar disorder, drug addiction, hoarding and autism, and taking turns wrestling with when to act and when to listen.

"I would have handcuffed you in 90 seconds," Officer Joseph Thompson later told David Florence, the retired mental health worker who played the role of the suicidal schizophrenic on the roof.

Sure, Thompson had engaged in the kind of back-and-forth that the exercise encouraged. But the four-year veteran never would have done that in a real-life situation, he said.

With his hands in his pockets and refusing to retreat from the edge, the schizophrenic was a potential threat—perhaps to himself, perhaps to the officers, Thompson said. "I'm not going to talk to you for 20 minutes when you could have two guns in your pockets."

It was one of many efforts that week by Thompson and other officers to make sense of their evolving roles. More than one asked why they were doing what they saw as other people's work and what had happened to the state's mental health system.

"This is not our job," one officer said during a discussion of Virginia's commitment laws.

Like almost a dozen other states, Virginia has been cutting back inpatient and community care for the mentally ill, according to a recent report by the National Alliance on Mental Illness.

And even in Fairfax, where the county's wealth helps supplement state mental health funding, the mental health mobile crisis unit hasn't grown since it was created three decades ago. Since then, Fairfax's population—and the police force—have each nearly doubled in size.

So, much as in 1981, a single mobile team of two mental health workers is available at any given time, which often means that police are on their own.

A Hand to Clasp

The mobile crisis unit, headquartered in Annandale 13 traffic-choked miles from Fort Belvoir, never made it to the bridge. One of the police department's crisis negotiators, Officer Tommy Thompson, arrived about a half-hour into the standoff.

He knew Wilson, and he was encouraged that she was the one on the bridge. "He hasn't jumped," Thompson remembers thinking, "so she's doing something right."

Now he needed a way to join her. It was getting cold, so he took Wilson her coat.

Once he delivered it, the jumper was adamant that Thompson retreat, which he did, but not before whispering a message to Wilson.

"You have to convince this guy to allow me to come back," he said.

Wilson did what she could to talk up Thompson, telling the man what a good guy he was. About 10 minutes later, she nodded to Thompson, who walked out "nice and slow," he recalled.

The man still was standing at the edge and wasn't saying much.

For a moment, he opened up. He had checked himself out of Mount Vernon Hospital after a conflict with the staff, and he had lost his spot at the county-run homeless shelter just south of the bridge.

But even as he talked, the man continued to flirt with the edge. "Please don't do that!" the officers shouted again and again.

At one point, he stepped away from the edge. Then, without warning, he returned to the precipice. Wilson imagined the nightmares she would have if he jumped. "You don't ever want that to be an image in your head," she said.

Finally, the man began to take a couple of steps toward them. It was dark. Nearly an hour had passed since the call first came in.

"Grab my hand. Grab my hand," Wilson said as she and Thompson stepped slowly backward, leading the way off the bridge.

Officers converged, but no one moved to tackle or handcuff the man. Instead, Wilson took his hand.

"That was my handcuff, holding him," she said. "It was also saying, 'Thank you, that you allowed us to come into your life, that you allowed us to help you.' "

Critical Thinking

1. Why do the police and the mentally ill often come in contact with each other?
2. What has lately increased pressures on the mentally ill?

UNIT 4
The Judicial System

Unit Selections

Learning Outcomes

After reading this unit, you will be able to:

- Explain what could motivate an innocent person to plead guilty.
- Argue that a criminal suspect should not agree to be interviewed by police.
- Be skeptical about reports of eye-witness identification of a suspect.
- State why brain scans might be valuable in a criminal case.
- Recognize that while DNA evidence can be a forceful tool for justice, it can also be the cause of serious injustice.
- Show that many innocent people who were wrongly convicted may receive no compensation at all.
- Discuss the death penalty as it relates to wrongful convictions.

Student Website

www.mhhe.com/cls

Internet References

Center for Rational Correctional Policy
www.correctionalpolicy.com

Justice Information Center (JIC)
www.justiceinformationcenter.us

National Center for Policy Analysis (NCPA)
www.public-policy.org

U.S. Department of Justice (DOJ)
www.usdoj.gov

The courts are an equal partner in the American justice system. Just as the police have the responsibility of guarding our liberties by enforcing the law, the courts play an important role in defending these liberties by applying and interpreting the law. The courts are the battlegrounds where civilized "wars" are fought without bloodshed, to protect individual rights and to settle disputes.

The articles in this unit discuss several issues concerning the judicial process. Ours is an adversary system of justice, and the protagonists—the state and the defendant—are usually represented by counsel.

In the opening article of this section, "The Prosecution's Case Against DNA," Andrew Martin reports on prosecutors who refuse to accept that they may have obtained a wrongful conviction after DNA evidence later seems to exonerate the person who was charged. These prosecutors may legitimately believe the new evidence is not exonerating, but some of them may be more concerned with their political futures than with justice.

Next, Robert Kolker tells the story of an innocent man who confessed to committing a horrible murder and was convicted on little more than his false confession—something that happens all too often, in "'I Did It': Why Do People Confess to Crimes They Didn't Commit?"

Because scientists know that eye witness accounts are often unreliable, courts increasingly are facing questions about whether such testimony should be allowed into evidence at trials. Laura Beil describes research findings about memory in "The Certainty of Memory Has Its Day in Court." Following that, Larry Laudan presents some arguments for not preventing such testimony, despite the possibility of false convictions, in his article, "Eyewitness Identifications: One More Lesson on the Costs of Excluding Relevant Evidence."

In the ensuing account, "DOJ Review of Flawed FBI Forensics Processes Lacked Transparency," Spencer S. Hsu, Jennifer Jenkins, and Ted Mellnik report about the investigation of problems in the FBI's crime lab that may have led to false convictions. The investigating task force never publicly released its findings, including the names of defendants who were convicted as a result of suspect lab work. The next article by Spencer S. Hsu, "Convicted Defendants Left Uninformed of Forensic flaws Found by Justice Dept.," details the consequences of flawed forensic work from the FBI lab.

Then, Michael S. Gazzaniga reports that brain scans and other types of neurological evidence could someday be used to assess the character and overall honesty of defendants in "Neuroscience in the Courtroom."

This unit concludes with a discussion by Radley Balko of the impact DNA testing has had on wrongful convictions, and the difficulty exonerees have getting compensated, in "Wrongful Convictions: How Many Innocent Americans Are Behind Bars?"

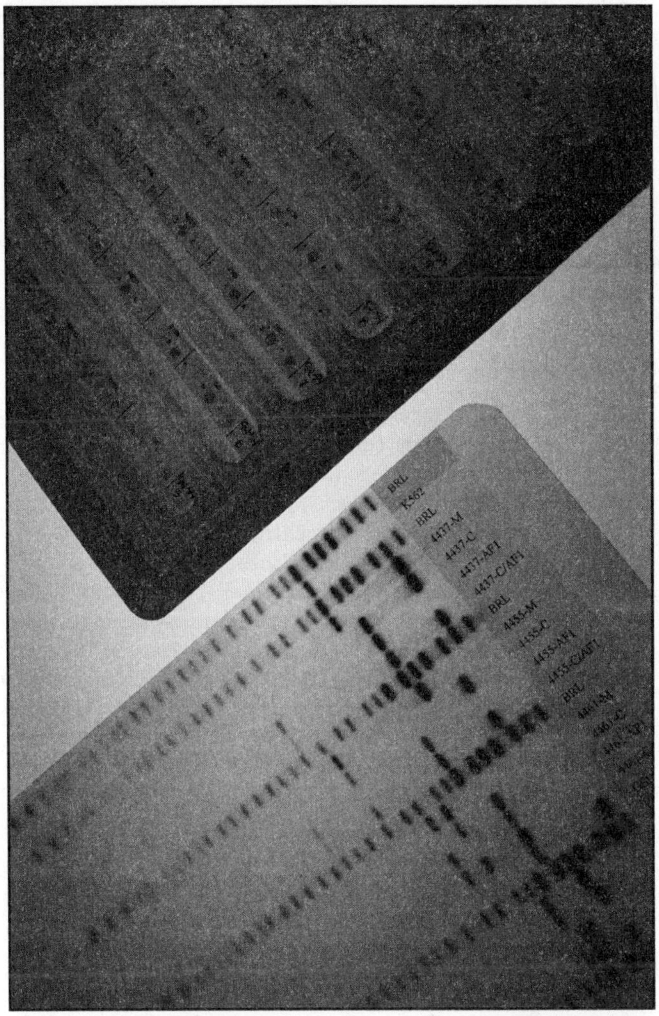

The Prosecution's Case Against DNA

ANDREW MARTIN

By the time Juan Rivera was taken to Lake County for questioning on Oct. 27, 1992, the search for Holly Staker's killer had gone cold. Two and a half months had passed since the 11-year-old girl was raped and stabbed while baby-sitting for two little children, and with the killer still at large, neighborhood-watch groups had formed and wary parents kept their children indoors. The Lake County police had pursued nearly 600 leads and interviewed about 200 people but were not close to making an arrest when they hooked Rivera up to a polygraph machine and began questioning him about his whereabouts on the night of the murder.

A 19-year-old with a ninth-grade education and a history of psychological problems, Rivera was interviewed by the police a few weeks earlier and told them that he was at a party near the crime scene and that he noticed another partygoer there acting strange. This time around, he repeated the same story for two days before finally admitting it was a lie. Still, he denied murdering the girl.

What followed was 24 hours of near constant interrogation, and around 11:30 on the morning of Oct. 30, after banging his head on a cell wall, pulling out a clump of his hair and being handcuffed behind his back and placed in leg shackles, Rivera finally provided investigators with a detailed confession.

In his sworn statement, Rivera detailed how, on Aug. 17, the morning of the killing, he bought two joints and a half gram of cocaine, snorted the cocaine and smoked one of the joints and then headed across town, at which point he came upon Holly standing in front of a two-story apartment building on Hickory Street, just north of downtown Waukegan.

"Ain't you Rebecca's brother?" Holly asked him. His younger sister once introduced him to Holly, and he couldn't believe this girl, a striking blonde with an identical twin sister, was only 11. She was baby-sitting a 5-year-old boy and a 2-year-old girl, and Rivera said she told him that she was lonely and invited him up to the second-floor apartment to keep her company.

"I played with a little boy and little girl, because I really like kids," Rivera told police. When the 2-year-old got tired, he took her to the bedroom to rest, and the boy left the apartment to play. Soon, Rivera said, he was naked and trying to have sex with Holly, but he was unable to get an erection, and she began making fun of him. When the 2-year-old started crying and he went to the bedroom to comfort her, Holly followed him and grabbed his crotch and insulted him again. "Is that all you got?" she said.

"This is when I got really mad, and she kept making fun of how small I was and that I could not get hard," he said. He ran to the kitchen, grabbed a knife from a dish rack and returned to the bedroom. Holly grabbed his wrists and tried to fight him off.

"If she would have stopped yelling and fighting me, I would have stopped cutting her, and she would not have gotten hurt anymore," he said. Rivera described how he pushed her onto a bed and had intercourse with the bleeding girl, whom he stabbed 27 times. He did not remember if he ejaculated. When he was finished, he washed the knife and his hands in the kitchen sink and ran out the back door. On the way out, he grabbed a mop and bashed the door to make it look like a robbery, then wiped the mop with a towel to remove his fingerprints. Once outside, he broke the knife, tossed it in the backyard and ran home.

Rivera's grisly, three-page confession became the key piece of evidence against him in his murder trial in 1993—and again in two subsequent retrials, the latest in 2009. Each time, Rivera was convicted, and he is now serving a life sentence at Stateville Correctional Center near Joliet, Ill. His lawyers are seeking an outright reversal or a fourth trial before the Illinois Appellate Court, arguing that there is no physical evidence and no witnesses linking Rivera to the crime; that his confession was coerced; and, perhaps most significant, that DNA testing in 2005 definitively ruled him out as the source of the semen found inside Holly Staker's body. (At the time this article went to print, a decision from the appellate court was imminent.)

"This is a rape and murder of an 11-year-old child, and the semen found inside the girl excludes Juan Rivera," Jeffrey Urdangen, one of Rivera's lawyers, said. "According to the state's perverse theory, the girl, the unfortunate victim, was having sex with another man who was not the murderer. It's ludicrous."

In the years before DNA evidence was introduced to the legal system, little was known about the extent of wrongful convictions and the situations in which they occurred. That changed in 1986, when an English scientist used DNA testing to help exonerate a man accused of raping and killing two teenage girls (the evidence also led the police to the real killer). Since then, DNA testing has helped exonerate 280 convicted felons in the United States and has exposed deep flaws in our legal system, including misconduct by the police and prosecutors and egregious mistakes made by witnesses and forensic scientists. In his 2011 book, "Convicting the Innocent," Brandon Garrett, a law professor at the University of Virginia, examined most of the case files for the first 250 DNA exonerations. Garrett found that 76 percent of wrongly convicted prisoners were misidentified by a witness and half the cases involved flawed forensic evidence. The testimony of an informant, often a jailhouse cellmate of the accused, was pivotal in 21 percent of the cases. Perhaps most surprising, 16 percent—virtually all of whom were subjected to interrogations lasting several hours and, in many cases, days—confessed to crimes they didn't commit. Garrett pointed out another, striking detail in the false confessions: in 38 of 40 false confessions, the authorities said defendants provided details that could be known only by the actual criminal or the investigators, thus corroborating their own admissions of guilt by revealing secret information about the crime that could only have been provided by them.

The issues raised by DNA exonerations have led to an overhaul of the criminal-justice system. Some states now require that evidence be preserved; others require mandatory videotaping of interrogations. Several states, including Illinois, New Jersey and New York, abolished the death penalty largely because of concerns about executing an innocent person. North Carolina, meanwhile, has created an independent commission to review innocence claims. And some prosecutors' offices, including those in New York and Dallas, have created conviction-integrity units.

More often, though, the fate of an inmate with powerful new evidence of innocence still rests with local prosecutors, some of whom have spun creative theories to explain away the exculpatory findings. In Nassau County on Long Island, after DNA evidence showed that the sperm in a 16-year-old murder victim did not come from the man convicted of the crime, prosecutors argued that it must have come from a consensual lover, even though her mother and best friend insisted she was a virgin. (The unnamed-lover theory has been floated so often that defense lawyers have a derisive term for it: "the unindicted co-ejaculator.") In Florida, after DNA showed that the pubic hairs at the scene of a rape did not belong to the convicted rapist, prosecutors argued that the hairs found on the victim's bed could have come from movers who brought furniture to the bedroom a week or so earlier.

"They essentially argued that there were naked movers," said Nina Morrison, a senior staff lawyer at the Innocence Project, a New York–based group that seeks to exonerate wrongfully convicted inmates.

Why prosecutors sometimes fight post-conviction evidence so adamantly depends on each case. Some legitimately believe the new evidence is not exonerating. But legal scholars looking at the issue suggest that prosecutors' concerns about their political future and a culture that values winning over justice also come into play. "They are attached to their convictions," Garrett says, "and they don't want to see their work called into question."

Few offices have fought post-conviction evidence with as much gusto as the Lake County state's attorney's office, which is coming under increased scrutiny for what defense lawyers and law professors suspect is an alarming number of wrongful convictions. One murder case has unraveled, and several other rape and murder convictions are now being challenged. "They can never admit a mistake," said Kathleen Zellner, a lawyer who is suing Lake County on behalf of a man named Jerry Hobbs, who spent five years in jail for killing his daughter and her friend; he was released last year after sperm found inside one of the girls was linked to a convicted rapist and accused murderer. "They have to solve cases quickly, and if a problem develops or doubt develops about a person's culpability, they feel like they have to press on," she said. "It's a self-defeating philosophy."

Lake County encompasses some of Chicago's wealthiest suburbs, like Lake Forest and Mettawa, but Waukegan, which sits along Lake Michigan on the eastern edge of the county, is a world apart from those communities. It is a once-thriving factory town that in recent years became known for its noxious Superfund sites: remnants of an asbestos plant and an outboard-motor manufacturer. The county legal system is controlled by a relatively small group, almost all Republicans. The state's attorney is Michael Waller, who has held the job since 1990, when he was appointed to fill out the term of his predecessor. Until recently, Waller's wife, Jane, was a long-serving Lake County judge. (Waller declined to be interviewed for this article.) Of the three dozen sitting judges in Lake County, three are Democrats. Two-thirds are former prosecutors, mostly from the office of the Lake County state's attorney. The current sheriff is a Republican and also a former Lake County prosecutor.

In 2009, when the former head of the county's Republican Party, Tom Adams, was sentenced for the possession of child pornography, he received 30 days in jail and 30 months' probation as part of a plea agreement, prompting complaints that he received light punishment. "There is no challenge to the orthodoxy," said David Rutter, who was editor of the local paper, *The Lake County News-Sun*, from 2006 to 2008. "No one is going to run and challenge a judge or prosecutor on reform grounds."

Jed Stone, a local defense lawyer, described the legal community as "an echo chamber." "The problem with everyone coming from the same background, from the same state's attorney's office, from the same narrow political spectrum, is there is a failure to see the other side," he said. "You begin to view people as others. And when you begin to see people as other than you, they begin to become expendable."

Lake County certainly isn't the only county in the United States dominated by one party and an insular political and legal culture. (Neighboring Cook County, for instance, has long been controlled by Democrats and has its own ignoble history of wrongful convictions.) It may be the only place, however, with a prosecutor as obstinate and as gifted as Mike Mermel. A 60-year-old widower, Mermel joined the state's attorney's office in 1990, after a stint as a prosecutor in Cook County. The first time I contacted him and said that I was from *The New York Times*, Mermel immediately announced that he was conservative. He agreed to speak with me on the phone, and later in the lobby of the state's attorney's office, but he refused requests for subsequent interviews and sought to retract all statements from our previous conversation.

Defense lawyers described Mermel's office to me, with a photo of Charlton Heston and a book by Ann Coulter on display. "The first time I was in his office, he played me a videotape of Rush Limbaugh," Stone said. "It was a diatribe on Bill Clinton."

While some of Mermel's tactics have drawn the ire of defense lawyers, others give him grudging respect for his skill in the courtroom. "He's a very effective trial lawyer," Stone said. "But his view of the world is very narrow." In the case of Juan Rivera, Lake County prosecutors have been able to convince juries, not once but three times, that he was the murderer, despite DNA evidence in the last trial that powerfully suggested otherwise. (Mermel was the lead lawyer on the third trial and assisted in the second.)

"We don't fold our tents and run," Mermel told me when we spoke this spring. "We don't quaver because somebody holds up three letters: DNA."

When I asked him specifically about the Rivera case, Mermel said that sometimes post-conviction evidence is irrelevant. "The example I like to give people is next time you go to a motel room, bring a plastic bag, because the dirtiest thing in that room is the remote control. Everybody has sex and then rolls over and goes, 'I wonder what's on?' " he said. "O.K., so you can find DNA in the form of sperm from 10 different people in that room from that remote control or even on a person who has touched it. And that woman gets murdered in that room tonight, and you are going to have a lot of DNA. Is it all going to be forensically significant?"

His theory for why there was sperm that did not come from Juan Rivera inside 11-year-old Holly Staker on the day she was murdered is, to his mind, simple and straightforward. She and her twin sister, Heather, were sexually active, Mermel argues, and Holly must have had sex with someone else before Rivera came along and raped (but didn't ejaculate) and murdered her. There was scant evidence to support this sexual-activity theory, but Mermel dismissed that objection. "Nobody is going to admit to having sex with an 11-year-old girl, even if the statute of limitations has run out," he told me. "But there was a lot of evidence that came to our office that these two girls were sexually active."

It was not the first time prosecutors in Lake County offered such a theory. In one case, Mermel is fighting efforts by a convicted rapist to clear his name after DNA testing excluded him as the source of sperm found inside the victim. Though Lake County prosecutors initially argued that the sperm came from the rapist, Mermel is now arguing just the opposite: that it came from an unnamed lover. In another case, Mermel opposed a new trial for a man convicted of killing an unidentified woman. When her identity became known years later, it turned out that her former husband once admitted that he killed her. Mermel dismissed statements from the husband, who is mentally disturbed, as the rants of a "one-armed Cuban feces-covered masturbator." When asked about the case last year, he told *The Chicago Tribune*: "The taxpayers don't pay us for intellectual curiosity. They pay us to get convictions."

But few cases have damaged Lake County's credibility as much as the one against Jerry Hobbs. In the spring of 2005, Hobbs arrived in Lake County after a two-year stint in a Texas prison for chasing a rival for his girlfriend's affections with a chain saw. His plan was to reconcile with the girlfriend, who was now living in Zion, Ill., and to become reacquainted with their three children.

A few weeks after he arrived, his daughter, Laura, went outside to play with a friend, Krystal Tobias, who was 9. The girls never returned, and that evening the family began looking for them and eventually called the police. After a frantic night of searching, Hobbs said he came across the girls' bodies in a remote wooded area around 6 A.M. They were lying on their backs, fully clothed, with multiple stab wounds and bruises, particularly around their necks and faces.

Hobbs was brought back to the Zion police station by 7:30 that morning, and the questioning began. Investigators thought it was suspicious that an ex-convict who was new to the area discovered the bodies before local residents and the police, and they thought his reaction to finding the bodies was also odd. According to police reports: "Hobbs referred to his daughter Laura and Krystal Tobias as 'them girls' and didn't use Laura's name. Hobbs also didn't show any emotion and avoided looking at us when we talked about Laura." After maintaining his innocence for about 20 hours, Hobbs finally relented and signed a confession stating that when he went to get Laura to come home, the girls resisted, then Krystal pulled out a small knife, and the two girls attacked him. Hobbs said he hit them both and eventually got the knife from Krystal and began stabbing her, then stabbed Laura. "Things just got out of hand, and I lost it," he said.

He was charged with the murders, and prosecutors vowed to seek the death penalty.

An initial examination found no evidence of sexual assault in the case, and Hobbs never mentioned it in his confession. Two years after his arrest, though, a private laboratory hired by his lawyers discovered that there had been sperm in Laura's vagina, anus and mouth, and they tested a sample. The defense lawyers immediately announced that DNA analysis showed the DNA did not match Hobbs's.

When Mermel heard about the findings, he dismissed them and suggested that Laura could have got the sperm on her while playing in the woods, where couples might have sex.

Hobbs remained in jail, awaiting trial, for more than two years before the DNA was found to match a friend of Krystal's older brother named Jorge Torrez, who was already serving a sentence in a Virginia jail for attacking three women, one of whom he raped, choked and left for dead. (He was eventually sentenced to life in prison for those crimes; currently he is also being charged for the 2009 murder of a 20-year-old naval officer.)

In August 2010, Michael Waller, the state's attorney, told reporters he was releasing Hobbs because they could no longer prove his guilt beyond a reasonable doubt.

Lake County has yet to charge Torrez for the murders of Laura and Krystal, and Mermel said he still suspected that Hobbs was the killer and that the sperm was not related to the crime. One plausible scenario, he says, is that Torrez masturbated while visiting Krystal's brother, and then Laura got it on her hands and unknowingly transferred it elsewhere.

"They have popcorn-movie night, and the little girl is in the same bed where this guy did it," Mermel said by way of explanation. "How do we get colds? We touch our mouths, we touch our nose. What does a woman do after she urinates?" We were in the lobby of the prosecutor's office, and Mermel answered his own question by standing and pulling his hand between his legs, as if wiping himself. "Front to back, O.K.?"

Hobbs, who is now 41 and lives in Texas and trims trees for a living, told me he confessed to the crime because he hadn't slept in days and figured the truth would come out. "I found my daughter," he said. "She didn't even have eyes in her head. I was already broken. They didn't have to break me."

He said that he didn't understand why Lake County wasn't pursuing Torrez for the crime, and that he had filed a lawsuit against the county for wrongful prosecution.

"Why haven't they charged him as fast as they railroaded me?" he said.

I met Juan Rivera this spring in a stark conference room at the Stateville Correctional Center near Joliet. He wore dark blue prison pants, a light blue work shirt and white unlaced high-top sneakers. His black hair was slicked straight back, and he had a trim goatee.

He was bigger than he was the last time I saw him, 18 years ago. He's 39 now, 6-foot-3 and 200 pounds, his arms decorated with menacing prison tattoos. Once we started talking, though, Rivera smiled easily and became relaxed, almost serene, a fact that he attributes to a religious conversion in prison. "The only thing that is incarcerated is my body," he said. "My mind is free here."

The first time I met Rivera was in April 1993, when I interviewed him at the Lake County Jail. At the time, I was the police reporter for the newly opened Lake County bureau of *The Chicago Tribune.* Holly's murder came to dominate much of my reporting over the next year, and as the story unfolded, I began to have doubts about the case against Rivera.

For one thing, a prosecution witness, who claimed Rivera confessed to him in jail, tried to sell me case documents at a local McDonald's.

"I never touched that girl," Rivera told me when I first interviewed him. Despite the claim in his statement that he had met her through his sister, he now said: "I don't even know her or her family. I'll keep saying I'm innocent, because I am."

Seven months later, on Nov. 19, 1993, Rivera was convicted of murder. While I was hardly convinced of his guilt, I moved on to other jobs and largely forgot about him. Occasionally, though, his incarceration would nag at me, and last fall, after reading stories about Jerry Hobbs, I began checking in with lawyers again and asked Rivera if I could speak with him in prison.

In the small concrete-block conference room, behind two sets of locked gates, Rivera sat across from me as a prison official hovered nearby. When I asked him why he confessed, Rivera said he blacked out and doesn't remember the specifics. "Coercion is just not physical, but it's also mental," he said. "There's different ways to actually break a person down." He added: "I know that it is easy to overbear a person's mind if you continuously barrage them with questions and accuse them. And that's exactly what they did with me."

Rivera moved to Waukegan about a year before Holly's murder, and while he worked a few jobs, he mostly hung around on the streets and got high. He had a minor criminal record and twice tried to commit suicide. On the night of the murder, he was confined to his home by an electronic leg monitor for stealing a car stereo. The monitoring system was supposed to alert authorities if Rivera left his house, though the system was prone to malfunction. He said he routinely violated his home confinement, infractions that were noted by Lake County authorities, who eventually sent him to prison for them. On the evening of Aug. 17, however, records for his monitor show he was at home.

Rivera said he learned about the murder from a friend who was at a party that night near the crime scene. She was the one who noticed one of the partygoers leave and then return later, acting strange. When he was sent to jail that September for violating his home confinement, Rivera repeated his friend's story, putting himself at the party to protect her, because she had an outstanding warrant. His cellmate contacted police, and Lake County detectives arrived to question him in prison on Oct. 2. Later that month, on Oct. 27, with all their leads turning into dead ends, they took Rivera to Lake County and began questioning him intensively.

Three days later, on Oct. 29, investigators directly accused Rivera of Holly's rape and murder. He became agitated and swore and tried to leave the room. Over the course of that night, detectives continued to press him about inconsistencies in his story. Just after midnight, Sgt. Charles Fagan asked Rivera, "Juan, you were in that apartment with Holly Staker, weren't you?" Rivera nodded and began sobbing. He then told detectives that he killed Holly, but only after she attacked him with a knife because he refused to have sex with her. (Fagan did not respond to requests for comment.)

Shortly after detectives left the room at 3 A.M., Rivera began banging his head against the wall. One jail official later testified that he was unresponsive and stared straight ahead afterward. He was moved to a padded cell, and a nurse who went to check on Rivera later said he was pacing back and forth, speaking incoherently. The nurse testified that he was in a psychotic state and was "not in touch with the reality of what was going on around him."

Around 5 A.M., investigators called Holly's mother and woke her up with news that they had caught the killer. The rest of the Lake County task force was informed of the confession and told to report to work. When Fagan returned to talk to Rivera shortly after 8 A.M., he described the suspect as handcuffed and shackled but nonetheless coherent and cooperative. The detectives read back the confession that Rivera had made earlier, and he signed it.

But there were problems. Even though Rivera admitted to killing Holly, many of the details in his confession didn't match the crime scene, and investigators thought it was implausible that Holly was the aggressor. They gathered in Waller's office at 9 A.M. on Oct. 30, four days before his election as state's attorney, to figure out what to do next. They decided a fresh team of detectives was needed to interview Rivera again to resolve the discrepancies in his statement.

When Lou Tessmann retired from the Waukegan police in 2005, the Illinois House of Representatives passed a resolution praising his two decades of service. The resolution noted that Tessmann, a former Marine, is "well known for his interrogation techniques on suspects of crimes."

Since then, Tessmann has traveled the country offering seminars to police officers on how to investigate homicides and interrogate potential suspects. "Mr. Tessmann has obtained over 80 homicide confessions during his career with only three instances where he was unable to obtain a confession from a homicide suspect"—a 96 percent success rate—according to the Web site of his employer, Wicklander-Zulawski & Associates.

It was Tessmann who was sent in to interrogate Rivera around 11:30 A.M. on Oct. 30, along with Sgt. Michael Maley of the Illinois State Police. In the hour or two before the interview began, Rivera was hitting his head against a glass window and was then on the floor with his wrists and ankles cuffed behind him. Tessmann, however, described Rivera as "very comfortable, very relaxed" during the interview.

Though Tessmann arrived at the police station roughly seven hours before the interview, he testified that he wasn't aware of Rivera's previous confession. (One of his colleagues testified that he gave Tessmann the statement that morning.) He said that Rivera willingly recounted the crime, which then cleared up many of the issues that prosecutors considered problematic. He described how Rivera borrowed a pen to show how he stabbed Holly, and in what was portrayed as a smoking gun, Rivera confessed that he used a mop to bash in the back door to make it look like a burglary. Tessmann said this was the first he had heard of the mop, but a polygrapher testified that Tessmann told him about it prior to Rivera's confession.

The confession was not recorded, but investigators typed it up and presented it to Rivera, who, according to police, corrected several typos before affixing his signature.

In his closing argument in the third trial, Mermel told jurors that the case basically came down to whom they believed: the police or the DNA evidence? "Is there anything in the makeup of any of those men that would lead you to believe that they were the kind of people who had dedicated their lives to this profession, yet just decided to just frame this poor innocent Juan Rivera because they were tired of investigating and wanted to go home?" he said.

What the jury didn't know was that Mermel had already successfully argued against the admissibility of any evidence that might cast doubt on Tessmann's credibility. For instance, Tessmann said in a 1990 deposition and in an official biography that he earned an English degree from the University of Wisconsin. But the school's 13 four-year colleges have no record of him ever attending. (In fact, he graduated from Northeastern Illinois University.) In 1989, Tessmann and four other police officers were sued for allegedly breaking into the wrong home during a police raid and injuring a woman who was seven months pregnant. The woman's lawyer accused the police of writing reports to cover up their conduct and charged that Tessmann "took the lead in creative drama."

According to documents provided by defense lawyers, a judgment was entered against Tessmann and the other officers for $48,500 in that case, and two years later, another judgment of $71,500 was entered against Tessmann in a case brought against him by a man who was wrongfully arrested for robbery.

A decade later, in 2001, a woman named Colleen Blue was charged with murder after she confessed to killing her newborn. Tessmann, then a commander, said to a reporter for *The Chicago Daily Herald,* "She told us she had six kids already and just did not want to deal with another one." He added: "She said she gave birth to the baby when she was all alone, put him in the bag and walked off. She told us she could hear the baby crying until she got close enough to the street that the passing cars drowned out the sound."

Charges against Blue were dropped when DNA testing revealed it wasn't her baby.

When I called to speak with him about the Rivera case, Tessmann said that three different juries found Rivera guilty. "The guy is guilty as the day is long," he said, before abruptly hanging up. He did not respond to a written request to answer subsequent questions. Sergeant Maley, Tessmann's fellow interrogator, agreed with Tessmann's assessment. "I can tell you 100 percent that Juan Rivera did the murder," he said. "He told us things that we later investigated that were found to be true that only the killer would have known."

In the spring I went twice to visit Heather Staker, Holly's twin sister. In the first visit, in her apartment on the second-floor above some offices in downtown Waukegan, Staker, a slight blonde, now 30, wore a bright pink sleeveless shirt, a pink headband and pink pajama bottoms covered with images of Tinkerbell. It was, of course, like looking at a grown-up version of Holly, a fact that Heather knows all too well. "I've never been known as Heather Staker," she said. "I'm known as Holly Staker's twin." She described how she and Holly were best friends when they were kids, that they slept on a bunk bed and shared everything. "We always played games on people because they could never tell us apart unless they saw the mole on my back," she said. "April Fool's, we'd switch classes."

By her own admission, Heather has led a troubled life. She left home at 15, has been arrested multiple times, spent time in prison and battled heroin addiction. Recently, she suffered a stroke, which she says may have been brought on by her unhealthful lifestyle. Her two children are being raised by her mother. She told me that she was the one who was supposed to baby-sit on the evening her sister was murdered, but Holly volunteered to take her place. "I've been a screw-up my whole life because of it," she said. "I just try to live day by day."

Heather was an important witness in Rivera's 2009 trial, testifying that she and Holly were forced to perform oral sex on a friend's brother when they were 8. She also told jurors that they had shown each other how to masturbate. Prosecutors did not present other evidence that Holly was sexually active.

When we talked, though, Heather said it was simply not true. "We were not sexually active," she told me, although she did not deny that they were abused earlier. Still, she made it clear that she had no doubt that Rivera killed her sister. When I asked about the sperm that doesn't match Rivera's, she suggested that maybe someone else was involved along with him, or maybe her sister was raped by another man before the murder.

"Why would you confess?" she said. "If I am getting charged with murder, I am not going to fess to something I did not do and then explain the whole night and how I did it and why I did it and everything like that if I didn't do it."

Earlier this year, Heather got a tattoo on the back of her neck, next to the mole that distinguished her from her sister. It says, "My Missing Half" and "Holly," with wings on the side and a halo above it.

"I think about her a lot," she told me the last time I saw her. She had dyed her hair pink since my previous visit. "I wonder how it would have been if she were here. You know, right now. The two of us running around, you know what I mean?"

On a chilly May morning, on a street not far from where Holly was murdered, Jennifer Linzer, from the Center on Wrongful Convictions at Northwestern University, and Cynthia Estes, a private investigator, visited the home of a man who was arrested for sexually assaulting a boy shortly before Holly was killed. They began by asking what he remembered about the evening of Holly's murder, which wasn't much. They talked about his criminal record, and he pointed out that he liked boys, not girls. Then they asked him if they could get a saliva sample in order to eliminate him as a possible suspect through DNA testing.

"I said, 'This case is probably coming around again, and we are going to give a list to the cops of people who they should look at and test,'" Linzer said. "He said: 'Great. I'll do it.'"

Rivera's lawyers would like to obtain a new trial with a different judge. They believe the judge who presided over the previous three trials unfairly favored the prosecution and should not have allowed prosecutors to introduce evidence about Holly's alleged sexual past, among other supposed judicial errors. But even if Rivera is granted a new trial, with a new judge, there is a realization among his supporters that he could once again be convicted. The crime is simply too heinous, the confession too powerful.

Perhaps the only way to win Rivera's freedom is to prove that someone other than Rivera killed Holly Staker. Which is where Linzer comes in. The wife of Northwestern's provost, Linzer began working as a volunteer at the center a decade ago, after she grew restless as a stay-at-home mom. Before the end of the year, she was working full time, organizing files, directing student volunteers and reviewing innocence claims from inmates. She heard about Rivera's case and eventually began speaking regularly to him on the telephone.

When Rivera lost his third trial, Linzer compiled a spreadsheet of potential suspects and, along with Estes, set about trying to find a killer by asking potential subjects for DNA samples. There are plenty of leads within blocks of the murder. Police reports show that at least two other men told friends that they killed Holly, one of them saying he stabbed her so many times he got tired. There were also at least three convicted sex offenders in the neighborhood, one of whom was convicted of molesting his 11-year-old stepdaughter, and around the corner was a boarding house full of transients. An elderly man a few blocks away supposedly drove around the neighborhood naked and masturbating. When police arrived to interview him, there was a picture of Holly and an envelope with her name on it in his house. A high-school senior had a picture of Holly, too, tucked in his wallet.

"Either this crime touched a lot of people, or there is an inordinate number of perverts in town," Linzer said.

Typically, she and Estes show up at a suspect's home and simply ask them for a saliva sample. If that doesn't work, they resort to other measures. In one instance, they retrieved a cigar butt that a suspect discarded in an alley. In another, they saved a plate of discarded chicken wings that someone had eaten.

Even if Rivera's defenders don't find the killer, Rivera told me he remains optimistic that he will ultimately be freed. "I believe in God," he said. "I believe that everything comes around. . . . Things should come correct. I don't know when it will happen, but I do have faith that one day I will go home."

If Mermel is worried about Rivera's walking free, he doesn't show it. He says that Holly Staker's killer is already in prison, that the sperm found inside her is a red herring. "People love to link the murder and the sex," he said. "It's like peanut butter and jelly." It was his job, though, to separate sex and death, to "look at the evidence," as he put it, "and go, 'What does this add up to?'"

Critical Thinking

1. Do you think police should continue to question a suspect after he denies involvement in the crime? How long?
2. Can we be confident that a statement made by a suspect after many hours of interrogation is reliable?
3. What do you think Jed Stone meant when he said that people begin to become expendable?
4. What did Stone mean by the "echo chamber"?
5. Is prosecutor Mermel correct in his statement about what the taxpayers pay him to do?

Andrew Martin is a reporter for the Business Day section of *The Times*. This is his first article for the magazine.

"I Did It"

Why Do People Confess to Crimes They Didn't Commit?

Robert Kolker

The woman was naked from the waist down, her pants and underwear tossed into the weeds. Her down jacket was pulled to her chest, exposing her left breast to the autumn chill. Her head and face had been pummeled, and embedded in the blows were pellets from a BB gun; smashed shards of the gun were found nearby in the brush. Her hair was so gummed with blood that the hunter who stumbled on her body couldn't tell that it had once been all white.

By nightfall on November 29, 1988, the whole upstate village of Hilton was talking about Viola Manville—74 years old and a grandmother, a free spirit, outspoken, and now a homicide victim. Hilton is a small, blue-collar farm town on the edge of Lake Ontario west of Rochester where a good number of people once worked on the assembly lines at Kodak. The town can be rough—one neighbor from a wealthier suburb calls it "a little Appalachia here in New York"—but Hilton had never seen a murder like this. The Monroe County Sheriff's Office interviewed dozens of people: neighbors, family members, an ex-boyfriend, troubled teenagers. They learned that Manville often had been seen walking along the same set of abandoned railroad tracks where her body was found, even after having been the victim of an attempted rape there three years earlier. The man arrested in that attack, Glen Sterling, was still in prison.

Glen Sterling had a brother named Frank. He was tall but hunched and painfully shy. Frank Sterling grew up just 100 yards from the abandoned railroad tracks, a mile from the spot where the victim's body was found. Both his parents were janitors, and Frank was the middle child, a chain-smoker so lonely that as a teenager he'd do almost anything to make a friend. His classmates at Hilton Central High called him Bug Chower, after a story got around that he ate insects to get attention. The name stuck. "He was the kid in school that everybody berated," says a former classmate, Rob Cusenz. "An easy mark."

At the time of the murder, Frank was 25 and still living at home, working as a school-bus monitor. He had a clean criminal record, but to the police, he had the makings of a motive. What if Frank had been angry that his brother Glen was in jail? What if he'd been nursing a grudge against Manville ever since she accused his brother of trying to rape her? What if this wasn't a sex-related murder but revenge? It was all just speculation, and indeed when the police questioned Sterling, they found his alibi was solid—he'd been seen working on the school bus all morning, and he recited the plots of the *Smurfs* and *Chipmunks* episodes he'd watched that afternoon. There was no physical evidence linking him to the crime, and Sterling was not arrested. Within a few months, other leads also dried up, and the Manville murder went unsolved.

Almost three years later, on July 10, 1991, an unmarked police car with two plainclothes detectives pulled up to the Sterling family's house. This was the third time in four years that the police had come to see him. He was now almost 28. He had become a truck driver and moved to Alabama for a year, then came back when work dried up. That afternoon, he was tired; he'd just finished a job that took him through a half-dozen states over two days. The detectives said they'd been assigned to reinterview people of interest in the case, and they realized Sterling had never been polygraphed. They asked him to come with them to a Rochester police station. He agreed.

At 7 P.M., Sterling followed a polygraph technician, Mark Sennett, into a small room on the fourth floor, where he sat at a table and waited. Before hooking up Sterling to the lie detector, Sennett spent more than two hours asking him questions: Did he know why he was there? Why would the police think he might have killed Vi Manville? Early on, Sennett told him that Glen had told his fellow inmates that one of his brothers had killed Manville—a lie he'd made up on the spot to see how the suspect might react. Sterling was startled; he said (maybe a little too defensively, Sennett thought) that there was no way his brother would have said that. Sennett told Sterling he was in for a long night. When the polygraph man left the room at 10:45 P.M., Sterling began to panic. If he stayed, he feared, the police wouldn't stop—but asking to leave or for a lawyer, he thought, would be as good as admitting he was a murderer.

At 11:20 P.M., another interrogator came to see Sterling. Patrick Crough, a young, confident detective, had worked just two homicide cases before the Manville murder, but he had already shown a natural talent for bonding with suspects. Crough spoke softly and leaned in close to Sterling, taking his time explaining his theory of the case. He talked about the love Sterling must have had for his brother and the anger he must have felt about his not being home for Thanksgiving. He told

Sterling he thought he might have bottled up his anger about Glen being in jail. Maybe, Crough said, it was the reason for his upset stomach, his bad teeth.

Sterling admitted to Crough that he was angry enough to have "killed the bitch"—and threw his lighter across the room, saying, "I didn't kill her, but I sure as hell could have." Still, as midnight approached, Sterling maintained his innocence—and even asked to be hypnotized to prove he wasn't hiding anything. At about 12:45 A.M., Sennett returned and suggested what he called a "relaxation technique." He had Sterling lie down on the floor and keep his feet elevated on his chair. He told him to take four deep breaths, then slid his own chair up to Sterling and held his hand. He asked Sterling if he could picture himself on those railroad tracks, running into a lady with white hair, arguing with her, seeing her lying naked in the bushes. He asked him how he felt about seeing her this way. "Happy," Sterling said.

Seconds later, Sterling jumped to his feet and snapped, "This is a bunch of bullshit! I didn't do nothing!"

"You're right, this is bullshit," Sennett said before walking out of the room. "I think you killed this lady, and I'm going to prove it."

Sterling was trembling now, verging on hysteria. He had been in the small room for close to eight hours. Crough came in again at 2:40 A.M. and started rubbing Sterling's back. "I was whispering," Crough said later, "simply that we would not dislike him, that we were here for him, we understood—we felt he should tell the truth to get it off his chest." Crough's partner, Thomas Vasile, held Sterling's other hand, and the two detectives huddled around him for a long time, gently reassuring him. Finally, according to the police report, Sterling blurted out, "I did it . . . I need help."

Just before dawn, at 5:22, Sterling made a videotaped statement. Onscreen for just over twenty minutes, Sterling can be seen speaking in a slow, defeated monotone, the ash of his cigarette burning to the nub. With Sennett working the camera, Sterling nods and agrees to every detail Crough and Vasile ask about—the BB gun, the naked body—breaking into sobs now and then as the two officers console him. He mentions the purple color of Manville's jacket—a crime-scene detail police said no one else could have known. Sterling's motive, he explains on the videotape, is exactly what Crough had said: "I was already upset about not having my brother home for Thanksgiving. Turned out later she was that one my brother was in prison for. She said the wrong thing at the wrong time. Things transpired . . . After she said, 'Your brother got what he deserved,' I hit her."

Without witnesses or physical evidence linking him to the crime scene, prosecutors made the videotaped confession the centerpiece of their case. On September 29, 1992, Frank Sterling was convicted of murder and later sentenced to 25 years to life in prison, and sent to the state prison in Elmira. And several days after the trial, when a number of people in Hilton came forward saying that a 19-year-old man named Mark Christie was telling everyone he knew that he'd just gotten away with murder, the police didn't pay them much attention. The killer, after all, had confessed.

In the criminal-justice system, nothing is more powerful than a confession. Decades of research on jury verdicts have demonstrated that no other form of evidence—not eyewitnesses, not a video record of the crime, not even DNA—is as convincing to a jury as a defendant who says "I did it." The police, of course, understand the power of confessions and rely on interrogation techniques to produce them quickly so they can clear their cases. This is the stuff of countless TV procedurals—the small interrogation room with a bare table and two-way mirror; the good-cop–bad-cop routine; the deployment of outright lies like "You failed the polygraph" or "Your prints are on the knife." As a society, we have come to view these as acceptable, if blunt, tools of justice. We count on the integrity of police and safeguards like Miranda rights to prevent abuses, and we take it on faith that innocent people would never confess to crimes they haven't committed.

But, of course, they do. In recent years, the use of DNA evidence has allowed experts to identify false confessions in unprecedented and disturbing numbers. In the past two decades, researchers have documented some 250 instances of false confessions, many resulting in life sentences and at least four in wrongful executions. Of the 259 DNA exonerations tracked by a major advocacy group, 63 of them—or one out of every four—was found to have involved a false confession. Counting just the homicide cases, the proportion shoots up to 58 percent of all exonerations. Even this number could be an underestimate. "Most of the documented false confessions have been in highly publicized murder cases," says Steven Drizin, of Northwestern Law School's Center on Wrongful Convictions. "There is no reason not to think the same tactics would be as effective if not more effective in lesser cases, where the punishment that could flow from a confession would be less." False confessions appear to be particularly common in New York State, in which twelve of the 27 DNA-based exonerations have turned out to be based on bogus admissions of guilt.

Researchers who study false confessions say the roots of the problem lie in the interrogation tactics themselves. The most influential such method is the Reid technique, a decades-old, nine-step procedure designed to isolate and persuade a suspect to reveal his deceptions. Virtually every police department in the country has been influenced, directly or indirectly, by the Reid technique. Its defenders see it as the cornerstone of good police work, but its detractors say it places too much power in the hands of interrogating officers. In light of the new research documenting the scope of the problem, reformers in New York and elsewhere are calling for a wholesale reevaluation of the way the police question suspects. Frank Sterling's story should help their cause; it demonstrates just what can go wrong with the science of interrogation.

In 1940, a burly, clean-cut, Irish Catholic cop named John E. Reid was thinking of quitting the Chicago police force. Reid was tough, a former guard on the DePaul University football team, but was never comfortable carrying a gun. At the last minute, he applied for a transfer to a desk job at the Chicago crime lab. He arrived in the midst of a technological revolution in police work. In 1931, a presidential panel known as the Wickersham Commission had exposed abuses brought by the "third degree," the use of force by police to extract confessions. Police across the country had held suspects' heads underwater, hung them out of windows, and beaten them. In 1936, the Supreme Court decision *Brown v. Mississippi*—the brutal case of three black men who were beaten and whipped until they confessed—effectively outlawed confessions brought by brute force. Crime labs like Chicago's began developing new, more scientific means to solve cases: ballistics, document examination, and lie detection.

As much as anyone, John Reid can be credited with leading American law enforcement into the modern age. Reid's advances began with the lie detector. In 1945, he designed a chair that used inflated rubber bladders to detect a subject's jitters. In 1947, he essentially created the modern polygraph procedure with the "control-question technique," a way of measuring a suspect's reaction to provocative questions. That same year, Reid left the crime lab and founded John E. Reid & Associates, which went on to train scores of polygraph analysts, including members of the CIA and the Mossad.

Reid's most influential work focused on the art of the interrogation. Soft-spoken and sincere, he had a knack for gently persuading suspects to confess. "It was almost a priestlike approach," says George Lindberg, who worked for Reid for thirteen years. "He'd hold your hand and say, 'You should really get this off your chest.'" Reid played an important role in a number of high-profile Chicago murder trials, and other cities shuttled him in as a closer for their most sensitive cases. He was credited with personally helping to solve some 300 murders and coaxing 5,000 thieves to confess. Some in law-enforcement circles called him the most famous name next to J. Edgar Hoover. Reid's aim wasn't always true—in 1955, he got a Nebraska man named Darrel Parker to admit to killing his wife, and the real killer confessed 33 years later—but his faith in his own ability, and in the professionalization of his craft, led him to believe interrogations could be systematized to the point of being foolproof. "It's almost as if every crook reads the same book on what to do and say to give themselves away," he liked to say.

In 1962, Reid and his mentor, a Northwestern Law professor named Fred Inbau, co-wrote the first edition of *Criminal Interrogation and Confessions*. Criminologists and law historians credit their method with defining the culture of police-interrogation training for the past half-century. The procedure basically involves three stages meant to break down a suspect's defenses and rebuild him as a confessor. First, the suspect is brought into custody and isolated from his familiar surroundings. This was the birth of the modern interrogation room. Next the interrogator lets the suspect know he's guilty—that he knows it, the cops know it, and the interrogator doesn't want to hear any lies. The interrogator then floats a theory of the case, which the manual calls a "theme." The theme can be supported by evidence or testimony the investigator doesn't really have. In the final stage, the interrogator cozies up to the subject and provides a way out. This is when the interrogator uses the technique known as "minimization": telling the suspect he understands why he must have done it; that anyone else would understand, too; and that he will feel better if only he would confess. The interrogator is instructed to cut off all denials and instead float a menu of themes that explain why the suspect committed the crime—one bad, and one not so bad, but both incriminating, as in "Did you mean to do it, or was it an accident?"

Reid was hailed in his time as the man who made the third degree obsolete. But if his method wasn't physically coercive, it was certainly psychologically so. The Supreme Court's 1966 Miranda decision singled out the Reid method for creating a potentially coercive environment, citing it as one reason suspects needed to be informed of their right to remain silent. Reid and Inbau made minor modifications to the program, adding some language about Miranda to the 1967 edition of their manual, but they remained true believers. *Criminal Interrogation and Confessions* asserts that Reid investigators could judge truth and deception with 85 percent accuracy, a higher rate than anyone else has ever claimed to have achieved—or, as Reid once put it, "better results than a priest."

In Elmira, Frank Sterling kept to himself, spending most of his time in what was called the college block, where inmates can study toward degrees. His family visited for a time, but his father died in 1995, and his mother stopped coming to see him after she developed heart problems and moved to Texas to live with her son Gary. Sterling had his own health issues. The dust at Elmira made it difficult for him to breathe, and some of the prisoners referred to him as Shaky because he trembled. "Each time I'd see Frank upon coming back from being at another prison, I'd see he had aged more—his face, his eyes," says fellow inmate Jeff Deskovic.

Sterling had tried to recant his confession almost immediately after he gave it. He told his lawyer he was so worn down by the police that he didn't even remember what had happened that night. But the authorities weren't moved by that claim. Right after Sterling's trial, Sterling's lawyer filed to vacate the conviction on other grounds: He argued that the rumors surrounding Mark Christie, the man who had been heard bragging about killing Vi Manville after Sterling was convicted, provided sufficient justification to investigate whether he was the real killer. Christie, whose alibi fell apart under new scrutiny, was asked to take a polygraph and agreed. He fidgeted too much for the first test to be considered conclusive but took it again the next day and passed. On December 23, 1992, a judge refused to overturn Sterling's conviction. Christie, the judge said, was simply a young man who liked to brag.

In 1996, four years into Sterling's sentence, Mark Christie reentered the picture. If Sterling had been the weird kid in Hilton, Christie had a creepier reputation: He wore combat fatigues every day and took an eighteen-inch Bowie knife with him wherever he went. Now Christie had confessed to another murder, the brutal killing of a 4-year-old Rochester-area girl named Kali Ann Poulton. His confession prompted Sterling's appeals lawyer, Don Thompson, to file a new motion to overturn Sterling's conviction. If Christie were capable of killing Poulton, couldn't he have killed Vi Manville? A State Supreme Court judge rejected the motion. "Only Sterling confessed to authorities," read the decision. "Only Sterling had a motive to kill Manville. Only Sterling knew facts that had not been publicized."

Sterling and Thompson filed a total of four motions to vacate Sterling's conviction over the next eight years, but all of them failed. Then, in 2004, Thompson sought the help of the Innocence Project—the Benjamin Cardozo School of Law–based group led by Barry Scheck and Peter Neufeld that has won wide acclaim for its work in freeing the wrongly convicted. The first time Neufeld watched Sterling's confession, even he thought he was guilty. But he soon came to see how everything pointed toward Christie. In 2005, Monroe County District Attorney Michael Green agreed to let the Innocence Project conduct DNA tests on some of Manville's clothing from the crime scene. In the fall of 2008, after three years of testing and legal maneuvering, word came back with what seemed like a match. The samples contained so-called touch DNA—a few skin cells—instead of the more definitive evidence found in blood and semen samples. Still, Neufeld says, "the profile had a very rare type. And Christie has that type."

In spite of the apparent match, a year passed, and the Monroe County D.A. still didn't take action. Last fall, an Innocence Project staff attorney named Vanessa Potkin personally visited Christie in prison to try to persuade him to own up to the murder. She spent part of two days talking to Christie, and while he almost seemed to acknowledge his role, and perhaps even to taunt her a bit, he admitted nothing. "His attitude was he's not responsible for Frank being there in prison," Potkin says. "Frank's the one who talked."

Sterling's team decided on a new tactic. On January 22, Potkin visited Christie again, this time with a polygraph and interrogation expert named Richard Byington who worked for the leading company in the field: John E. Reid & Associates. Neufeld had been waiting for the right case to ask the Reid people for pro bono help—a sort of Nixon-in-China move—and the company's president, Joseph Buckley, had agreed. The hope was that Byington, an experienced and highly regarded interrogator, could persuade Christie to confess.

At first, Christie appeared to relish the visit. He boasted to Byington that he had stolen a copy of the Reid-Inbau manual from the Hilton library to try and beat the polygraph he'd been asked to take after the Manville verdict. Of course, he'd aced it. Byington spent several hours trying to get Christie to warm up to him. Eventually, Christie seemed to grow impatient. "What do you want?" Byington remembers Christie saying.

Byington turned more aggressive. "I said, 'Listen, here's the deal. There's no doubt that you committed the Manville murder. The physical evidence says it, and the DNA basically says it. Now you need to do the right thing so Frank, who hasn't done anything, can go home.' " But Christie, who still harbored thoughts of getting out one day, still wasn't inclined to talk. "Why should I say anything?" he told Byington.

Then Byington played another card. In a strange coincidence, the detective who had procured Christie's confession in the Kali Ann Poulton case was Patrick Crough, the same man who had gotten Frank Sterling to confess. Byington pulled out a copy of a newly published memoir Crough had written about child-abduction cases called *The Serpents Among Us* and pointed to the page where Crough calls Christie not just a child-killer but, he believed, a child molester. Christie became furious. After thirteen years in prison, he had no real sense of how well he was remembered in the outside world, and he had hoped Kali Ann's murder, and his role in it, might have been forgotten. Now he saw that Crough was working to keep the case alive—and accusing him of raping the young victim as well. He knew he'd never lead a normal life outside of prison now.

"You know more about this than you're telling me," Byington said to Christie. And shortly after, Christie's confession began.

Earlier this year, on April 28, Frank Sterling was set free. He wept at the courthouse, hugged Don Thompson, and expressed disbelief. Peter Neufeld took a shot at the cops who interrogated Sterling eighteen years earlier. "There's no question that in this case," Neufeld said, "the police officers had tunnel vision."

In the early days of DNA exoneration, even the lawyers working the cases didn't know what to make of the surprising number of false confessions they came across. "It wasn't until the late nineties that we began to see patterns emerge," says Neufeld. "But still, it was running against 25 years of my own experience. Why would an innocent person confess?"

That question was eventually taken up by a handful of researchers, including the University of San Francisco School of Law's Richard Leo, Berkeley sociologist Richard Ofshe, John Jay College's Saul Kassin, and Northwestern Law School's Steven Drizin. False confessions now are generally understood to break down into three categories. There are voluntary false confessions, in which innocent people come forward on their own. Some, like John Mark Karr in the JonBenet Ramsey case, do it for the attention—others to self-punish or because they've lost touch with reality. Then there are what Leo calls "persuaded false confessions," in which people are convinced by the interrogator that they actually committed the crime. In New York, 17-year-old Marty Tankleff famously falsely confessed to killing his parents in 1988 after being convinced he must have blocked it out. Finally, there are compliant false confessions, in which the suspect is psychologically coerced to confess even while believing he's innocent. They do it, Kassin writes, "to escape a stressful situation, avoid punishment, or gain a promised or implied reward . . . often coming to believe that the short-term benefits of confession relative to denial outweigh the long-term costs." This appears to be what happened in the infamous Central Park jogger case. It also seems to explain Frank Sterling's confession.

Critics say the Reid technique is a major source of the problem. What was once seen as the vanguard of criminal science, they argue, is nothing more than a psychological version of the third degree. Even beyond the Reid method, the courts have given police "carte blanche in the interrogation room for any tactics shy of physical abuse," says Drizin. Others believe police shouldn't be able to mislead suspects with lies or manipulate them by suggesting that what they did isn't so bad. Great Britain's police aren't allowed to employ those tactics, and Kassin says the best available data suggest the efficacy with which they arrest and convict criminals isn't diminished by that.

Reid detractors also say that police often feed evidence to suspects, which accounts for why false confessors sometimes know details about a crime that they wouldn't otherwise know. In a recently published study, University of Virginia law professor Brandon Garrett found that in 97 percent of the false-confession cases he studied from the DNA era, the wrongly accused suspects were said to have supplied such telling details—facts either picked up elsewhere or provided by police. Interrogators also tend to be overconfident of their abilities to spot guilty suspects. No study so far (aside from Reid's own research) has shown the police to be any better than average at picking out liars. In fact, they're sometimes worse. In one 1987 study, police officers watched videotaped statements of witnesses, and their record at identifying deceptive testimony was no better than the average person's. Over confidence can blind investigators to evidence suggesting that the suspect is innocent. The pressure to resolve cases quickly and tidily can have a similar effect, especially in high-profile cases. Simply wearing suspects down is another issue: At some point, a given suspect will say anything just to make the immediate discomfort stop. "Why don't they beat people anymore?" asks Don Thompson. "It's not because they're particularly enlightened now. It's because the psychological coercion is so much more effective."

Frank Sterling's confession, Thompson believes, was marked by a number of these problems. After Sterling says he hit Vi Manville, Patrick Crough asks Sterling what he hit her with. Sterling says, "My hand." A moment later, Crough says, "Frank, as best as you can remember, and I know this is difficult for you, did something happen with that BB gun?" Only after being prompted that way does Sterling say, "Yeah, I started hitting her with it." Mark Sennett, the polygraph examiner, lied to Sterling about his brother Glen. Crough teased out the motive and alternately pressured and consoled Sterling. Sterling knew about the supposedly telling crime-scene detail of Manville's purple jacket, but Thompson says many people in Hilton would have seen her on her daily walks in that jacket. Finally, there was Sterling's state of mind. Having been held alone, without counsel, in a small interrogation room and questioned for twelve hours, he became isolated, exhausted, and vulnerable to manipulation. Over the years, Thompson and Crough had crossed paths in Rochester, running into each other around town or at the supermarket. "I'm never really comfortable when I'm talking to him," Thompson says. "He's an accomplished interrogator, which translates to being an accomplished manipulator."

Shortly after Sterling's release, I had dinner with Crough in Rochester. Calm and self-assured, he did what he could to sound gracious about Sterling's ordeal. But he couldn't help but also be defensive. He insisted he did good work that night in 1991. "His responses kept the interview going," he told me. "As a homicide detective, you don't walk out on an interview when the person's giving you a little something." Crough pointed out that he was the one who visited Christie in prison—he volunteered to do it and talked him into giving his DNA sample when Christie didn't have to do that—and it was his book that helped persuade Christie to confess. After a while, though, some contrition bled through. "Like that hasn't haunted me?" he told me. "I've been doing interrogations in major crimes for twenty years. This is the first time I've ever had one go bad on me. That's not a bad statistic, you know."

The law-enforcement community insists current interrogation techniques are sound. The courts have upheld tactics like deceit and minimization, Reid president Joseph Buckley notes, and without such methods police would have a far more difficult time eliciting confessions from suspects who are, in fact, guilty. When false confessions do happen, Byington says it's not the Reid technique that's to blame but the misapplication of it. The police's main mistake with Frank Sterling, he says, was starting in on their suspect before they were reasonably sure he was guilty. Then, when Sterling gave Crough and the others questionable information, they blindly barreled ahead. "When they ask Frank what he was wearing, he says he thinks he was wearing a T-shirt and jeans," Byington says. "Well, if Frank was wearing a T-shirt and jeans, he'd have frozen to death." In Byington's opinion, Sterling had essentially been fed information over twelve long hours, then encouraged to spout it back over twenty minutes of video. In a good confession, Byington says, the suspect should do about 80 percent of the talking, narrating their experience for the benefit of the police, not saying yes and no to a series of prompts.

To prevent false confessions, interrogation critics say there's a solution so simple that it's remarkable it hasn't happened already: videotaping every minute of every police interrogation. Where the idea was once impractical, they note, the digital era changed that. Some law-enforcement officials fear that if juries see how the sausage is made, they might blanch at convicting even guilty suspects. In fact, Kassin's recent research indicates that when people see two versions of a false confession—one with just the confession and another that includes the entire interrogation—they become more effective jurors, correctly acquitting the innocent and convicting the guilty. Still, eighteen states and more than 800 jurisdictions have already started taping interrogations. New York has moved slowly—when they videotape at all, police tend to tape only confessions, not whole interrogations—but the New York State Bar Association has called for taping the full questioning session.

Earlier this year, the NYPD announced with some fanfare that it would test recording interrogations in two precincts. Last week, spokesman Paul Browne told me the bids have been selected, and that the 67th Precinct in Brooklyn and 48th Precinct in the Bronx will soon be outfitted with interrogation rooms ready for digital recording. Tests should start after the first of the year. Commissioner Ray Kelly "is open to seeing what we learn," Browne says, though in the spring, Kelly told me deploying such a system throughout the NYPD was a complicated endeavor, and that it wasn't clear to him yet that the effort would be worth the results.

One group solidly against tape-recording in New York is the Detectives' Endowment Association, whose president, Michael Palladino, holds on to the belief that what happens in an interrogation room is too messy for some jurors to tolerate. He also worries that juries won't be the only ones influenced. "Every taped interrogation can be used as a training film for criminals on what to expect from the police during an interrogation," he says. "Certainly, the element of surprise is gone."

Curiously enough, however, research shows that police and prosecutors forced to tape their interrogations often wind up supporting the practice. One Minnesota prosecutor famously called it "the best thing we've ever had rammed down our throats." A taped record can mean fewer motions to suppress and fewer claims that suspects were unduly deceived or abused. Joseph Buckley says the Reid method and taping can go hand in hand. "When somebody claims there was coercion, the record speaks for itself," he says. Even Patrick Crough says he believes in it, calling it "a tool to let the jury see what we see."

Don Thompson has thought a great deal about what would have happened in 1992 if the jury had been able to see the whole Sterling interrogation and not just the final twenty minutes. "You can't describe to a jury the effects of isolation over a twelve-hour period," he says. "I'd make them sit through the whole twelve hours. Because at that point, even for the jurors sitting in the jury box, it begins to feel like a hostage crisis."

Frank Sterling is standing on the railroad tracks in Hilton behind his old house—a small ranch-style building on a two-lane road, about a quarter-mile from the high school. "When we first moved here, the trains were still running through," he says, pointing at the tracks. "Then they disbanded it."

As we walk down the gravel path, Sterling points in the direction of the Big M supermarket he walked to on the afternoon Vi Manville was killed. To get to the store, he had to cross a train trestle over a creek and then leave the tracks, walking along the opposite creek bed. To get to where Manville was killed, Sterling would have had to continue on the tracks away from the market—"another mile and a half down the road," he says, laughing.

Sterling is heavier now than he was when he was sent to prison. His teeth were neglected for so long that a week before his release, he had nine of them pulled. At the time, he joked to his lawyers that he put them under his pillow for the Exoneration Fairy. He can't drive a truck because of medical issues, but he hopes to find computer work. For now, he is living with friends one town over from Hilton. He drives to Rochester when he needs to see his lawyers about finding health benefits, job training, and donated clothes. Sterling says he's angry, but he tries not to dwell on it. "I don't want it to tear me up." He hasn't decided whether to file a civil suit for wrongful conviction. The first night he was out, he says, he woke up in the middle of the night to the sound of rain on a windowpane. "It was something I couldn't hear for eighteen years," he says. "It's amazing. Something so simple that happens every day. Something everyone complains about."

Is it difficult being back here? "No," Sterling says. "I enjoyed growing up here." The creek is where he liked to fish for salmon. The train trestle is where kids liked to drink and where Frank walked his dogs Outlaw and Shebia. For a time, he says, he considered Vi Manville a friendly presence on the tracks. "She'd reach into her pocket and give the dogs a cookie."

When Crough and his partner first came to Sterling's house in 1991, he says, "they claimed they were looking at others. But I have a feeling they were focused on, 'Okay, we'll make it look like we're looking into others but he's the one who probably did it for revenge.'" He agreed to the polygraph he says "because I didn't do it. I thought, *Okay, well, I've got nothing to hide, so I should pass with flying colors.*"

So why did he confess? "They just wore me down," he says, shaking his head. "I was just so tired. Remember, I hadn't had any sleep since about 2:30 Tuesday night."

He tries to explain what it was like to spar with the police for twelve hours.

"It's like, 'Come on, guys, I'm tired—what do you want me to do, just confess to it?'

'No, we want the truth.'

'Well you're not fucking listening to the truth, I'm telling you. What more do you want me to say?'

'We want to know what happened.'"

Sterling says the police never asked him to say in his own words what happened. "'Yes' and grunts—that's basically what the whole confession is about." Regarding the color of Manville's coat, he says, "I knew in the fall she always wore her purple jacket."

I ask him what he thinks when he watches the twenty-minute confession video now. "When you look, you'll notice I shake a little bit," he says. "But to hold on to the whole cigarette and let the whole cigarette go to ash and never take a drag off of it? I'm a smoker. Normally, I would be sitting there dragging on it, not letting the whole cigarette just sit there burning down. Yeah, I was not in the right mind, looking back at it now."

He knows some people will never understand why he admitted to a crime he didn't commit. "They say, 'Why confess if you didn't do it?' But they don't have the whole understanding of what I was going through at the time. It's like, yeah—I wanted to get it over with, get home, and get some sleep."

He laughs softly. "Eighteen years and nine months later, I finally get to go home."

Critical Thinking

1. What is the Reid technique of interviewing?
2. What did the Supreme Court say about the Reid technique in *Miranda v. Arizona*?
3. What could be done to prevent false confessions?
4. Do you believe it is advisable for a criminal suspect to agree to speak to police?

Article 24

The Certainty of Memory Has Its Day in Court

LAURA BEIL

Witness testimony has been the gold standard of the criminal justice system, revered in courtrooms and crime dramas as the evidence that clinches a case.

Yet scientists have long cautioned that the brain is not a filing cabinet, storing memories in a way that they can be pulled out, consulted and returned intact. Memory is not so much a record of the past as a rough sketch that can be modified even by the simple act of telling the story.

For scientists, memory has been on trial for decades, and courts and public opinion are only now catching up with the verdict. It has come as little surprise to researchers that about 75 percent of DNA-based exonerations have come in cases where witnesses got it wrong.

This month, the Supreme Court heard its first oral arguments in more than three decades that question the validity of using witness testimony, in a case involving a New Hampshire man convicted of theft, accused by a woman who saw him from a distance in the dead of night.

And in August the New Jersey Supreme Court set new rules to cope with failings in witness accounts, during an appeal by a man picked from a photo lineup, and convicted of manslaughter and weapons possession in a 2003 fatal shooting.

Rather than the centerpiece of prosecution, witness testimony should be viewed more like trace evidence, scientists say, with the same fragility and vulnerability to contamination.

Why is a witness's account so often unreliable? Partly because the brain does not have a knack for retaining many specifics and is highly susceptible to suggestion. "Memory is weak in eyewitness situations because it's overloaded," said Barbara Tversky, a psychology professor at Columbia University's Teachers College in New York. "An event happens so fast, and when the police question you, you probably weren't concentrating on the details they're asking about."

Hundreds of studies have cataloged a long list of circumstances that can affect how memories are recorded and replayed, including the emotion at the time of the event, the social pressures that taint its reconstruction, even flourishes unknowingly added after the fact.

While most of us tend to think memory works like a video recorder, it is actually more like a grainy slide show. Lost details, including imaginary ones, often are added later. One of the earliest and more famous experiments to demonstrate that memories are malleable was conducted by Elizabeth Loftus, a psychology professor at the University of California, Irvine, and an early pioneer of witness memory research.

In a 1974 study published in *The Journal of Verbal Learning and Verbal Behavior*, she asked participants to view films of fender-benders in which no car windows or headlights were broken. Later, the subjects who were asked how fast the cars were going when they "smashed" into each other—as opposed to "hit"—were more likely to report speeding and describe shattered glass they never actually saw.

In another experiment, conducted in Scotland, participants were four times as likely to report a memory of a nonexistent event—in this case, a nurse removing a skin sample from their little finger—if they had been asked to imagine it just one week before. Others in the experiment read a description, but were not asked to picture it happening.

Even the process of police questioning and prepping for trial can crystallize a person's own faulty reconstruction. In 2000, Dr. Tversky published a series of experiments conducted at Stanford University in the journal *Cognitive Psychology*. In one, volunteers read profiles of fictitious roommates with both charming and annoying habits; they were then asked to write either a letter of recommendation or letter making a case for a replacement.

When later asked to repeat the original description, the volunteers' recollections were skewed by the type of letter they had written. Their minds had shed qualities that didn't match the first draft of their own recall and had embellished those that did.

"When we don't remember, we make inferences," Dr. Tversky said.

Sometimes we miss details because we weren't paying attention, but sometimes we are concentrating too hard on something else. Nothing is as obvious as it seems.

Few experiments have demonstrated this more notably than one published in 1999 by researchers at Harvard. Participants watched a video of people dressed in either black or white passing a basketball. The subjects were told to count the number of passes made by players in white.

During the test, a woman in a gorilla suit strolled through the players. She was unnoticed by about half the people who took the test, the researchers found. Distraction is not unique to the eyes. During a meeting of the Psychonomic Society this month, Polly Dalton and colleagues at the University of London presented the audio version of the gorilla test, a 69-second recording of two men and two women preparing for a party. Almost all of the study participants instructed to listen to the women did not hear a third man repeating "I'm a gorilla" for 19 seconds midway through the conversation.

The editing of the past occurs without a person's realizing what has been forgotten. In court, witnesses are asked to tell the truth and nothing but the truth. They think they do. Whether in a story told in a courtroom or at a dinner table, the mind is sometimes prone to blur the distinction between reality and fantasy. Brain scans taken as people "recall" something they did not actually see have many similarities to the brain dwelling on an actual memory.

"That's one of the striking findings of the studies," said Daniel Schacter, a psychology professor at Harvard. Whether an event is real or imagined, "many structures involved in the coding and retrieving are the same."

All this makes sense, he said, when you consider the purpose of memory. He and his colleagues believe that memory is designed not just to keep track of what has happened, but to offer a script for something that might.

Evidence for this also comes from brain scans. Just as the "recall" of a bogus event lights up the brain's memory centers, so does thinking about something that might occur.

Because the brain uses memories for mental dress rehearsal, we are not wired to retain every facet of an event, scientists say. We don't have to. A general framework is all that's necessary to keep from getting lost, or find food, or know what to do when a storm is coming.

One 1979 study asked a small group of people to pick out a penny from a series of 15 similar drawings. Less than half chose correctly, because no one needs to know whether Lincoln faces left or right to pay the cashier. Yet witnesses often are asked to remember with similar levels of precision, often about scenes and faces spotted fleetingly.

When selective attention combines with fear, "you have a very strong memory for a few details," said Elizabeth Phelps, a psychology professor at New York University. "Emotion gives us confidence more than it gives us accuracy."

The problem comes when witnesses bring that certainty to the entire memory. In crimes that involve a weapon, Dr. Loftus and other scientists have found that witnesses will fixate on the gun barrel or knife blade but will fail to notice other details as clearly. Yet because they so starkly remember particulars of the weapon and may have the accuracy of parts of their memory affirmed by police officers and prosecutors, witnesses carry an air of assurance into the courtroom.

"Many people think if someone is confident, they must be right," said Dr. Loftus.

Rather than discount witnesses, researchers are trying to use their findings to make trials fairer and testimony more reliable, particularly in the case of suspect lineups, a police staple at the heart of many wrong convictions. In September, Gary Wells, a psychology professor at Iowa State University, released a new report comparing whether the accuracy of lineups improves when the possible suspects are presented to witnesses in sequence, rather than all at once in the traditional lineup.

In studies involving actual cases, Dr. Wells's team found that the likelihood of choosing a stand-in "filler" instead of the suspect fell to 12 percent, from 18 percent, when faces were presented sequentially. The downfall of side-by-side lineups, Dr. Wells said, is that "if the real perpetrator is not in there, there is still someone who looks more like him than the others."

Lineups also may improve when some uncertainties are made clear to witnesses and jurors. Dr. Wells and others recommend changes like making sure a witness knows the perpetrator may not be in the group, and having lineups administered by someone who does not know which photograph is the suspect.

Dr. Wells also believes witnesses should give a statement at the time of the lineup documenting how confident they are in their choice—because once the trial comes around, the witnesses will believe they were always sure.

It may be that witnesses in police stations and courtrooms are being asked the wrong question to begin with—that telling witnesses to pick out a perpetrator, or state exactly what they saw or heard, implies they really can when science suggests that they may well be unable to do so.

"My view is that people should be asked to pick out someone who looks similar to who you saw, or sounds similar to what you heard, and leave it to the jury to decide," said Donald Thomson, a psychology professor at Deakin University in Melbourne, Australia.

Pressing witnesses with questions that appear to have precise answers enhances the likelihood that the innocent will be prosecuted and the guilty will escape, Dr. Thomson said. "It forces people to pick someone and say, 'This is the person,' " he said. "Two months down the track, they go into the witness box and say they are absolutely sure."

Critical Thinking

1. Is there a risk in following Prof. Thompson's suggestion about what witnesses should be asked?
2. What do Schacter and his colleagues believe about memory?
3. Is a person who is robbed, face to face with his attacker, at gunpoint, likely to be a good witness as to the perpetrator's identity?
4. What suggestions does Dr. Wells make about lineups?

Eyewitness Identifications: One More Lesson on the Costs of Excluding Relevant Evidence

LARRY LAUDAN

> Due process does not require that every conceivable step be taken, at whatever cost, to eliminate the possibility of convicting an innocent person. Punishment of those found guilty by a jury, for example, is not forbidden merely because there is a remote possibility in some instances that an innocent person might go to jail. —Justice White[1]

Steven Clark's (2012) article is a nuanced analysis of the data underlying and motivating various fashionable proposals for the reform of eyewitness identification procedures. It exhibits vividly some of the weaknesses and dangers associated with the widespread tendency to suppose that, where certain existing mechanisms for the acquisition of evidence have been shown to be responsible for occasionally producing false convictions of innocent persons, then a modification of those mechanisms is intrinsically desirable, whatever the costs in additional false acquittals might be.

The Dilemmas of Error Distribution

The concern motivating most such reforms is the discovery that certain forms of evidence currently in use sometimes finger innocent persons, occasionally leading to their conviction. Because wrongful convictions are otiose, the next move is usually to insist that we must take measures to minimize such wrongful convictions, even if such measures produce an abundant harvest of false acquittals. Clark rightly stresses that policy choices in such situations require a hard-headed appraisal of the respective costs of false convictions and false acquittals, something that the proponents of such reforms are often loathe to undertake, either because they believe that such reforms can be implemented without increasing the frequency of false acquittals (what Clark calls the "no cost view") or because they hold with Blackstone et al. that false convictions are so much more egregious than false acquittals that one should be prepared to discount the costs of additional false acquittals without hesitation so long as the reforms in question reduce the rate of false conviction.

Such a strategy fails to reckon with the fact that there is no rule of admissibility that will not occasionally lead to the conviction of an innocent defendant. Confessions are sometimes false. Should we exclude them? Expert testimony is occasionally mistaken. Should it be excluded? Innocent defendants sometimes choose not to testify. Do we need a Carter-like rule blocking adverse inferences from silence to protect the innocent, silent defendant from wrongful conviction?[2] Such knee-jerk reactions ignore the fact that confessions are usually true, that expert testimony is generally reliable, and that most non-testifying defendants are guilty. If confessions and expert testimony were routinely excluded from trial, and if jurors followed judges' instructions to ignore defendants' silence, vast numbers of true convictions would be replaced by false acquittals. That is why the quest for evidence that infallibly indicates guilt (or innocence) is a snark hunt. It is provable in principle that there is no rule of evidence or procedure that will not occasionally lead to a false conviction (or a false acquittal). The fact that relevant evidence leads to fallible inferences is no argument for the former's exclusion. It is, however, an argument for telling juries how reliable the evidence is likely to be when we have the pertinent information.

Given that there are few free lunches, almost every exclusion of nonredundant relevant evidence alters both the conviction–acquittal ratio and the ratio of false acquittals to false convictions. The idea that one can reduce the frequency of false convictions by excluding relevant inculpatory evidence without paying a price in terms of increasing the frequency of false acquittals fails to reckon with the meaning of "relevance." So long as a type of evidence increases the probability of guilt (thereby meeting the relevance condition), then a policy of excluding such evidence will lead to cases of guilty defendants who will be acquitted and who would probably not have been let off the hook had the evidence been admitted.

Classically and logically, the standard of proof is the instrument we use for distributing errors; the other rules of evidence are—or should be—designed principally to reduce errors, not to distribute them. Most of the reforms that Clark criticizes have the de facto effect of altering the distribution of errors while increasing, sometimes drastically, their aggregate frequency. This is simultaneously to assign a role to rules of evidence that they should not have, while thwarting their capacity to discharge the error-minimization role that they should have.[3]

Taking Base Rates Seriously

Without doubt, one of the most innovative aspects of Clark's analysis is the attention he pays (rarely found elsewhere in the literature) to the issue of the proportions of suspects submitted to lineups or showups who are guilty and those who are innocent. Clearly, if most such suspects are in fact guilty, then the adoption of a new procedure that significantly lowers the rate of false identification, but also significantly lowers the rate of correct identifications, is ill advised. This is because the (presumed) high frequency of guilt among the suspects means that the absolute numbers of the falsely identified are already low and that our principal interest should be in not lowering significantly the number of truly identified. By contrast, if most suspects are innocent, precisely the opposite conclusion applies. The proposed reforms should be adopted forthwith.

For obvious reasons, settling this empirical question (what proportion of suspects subjected to line ups and showups are guilty) is absolutely essential to making a reasonable decision about whether the proposed reforms to existing procedures for handling eyewitness identification would be progressive or retrograde. Determining the answer to this question obviously requires us to leave the psychological literature in limbo until and unless we can assemble reliable data about the distribution of guilt and innocence among those suspects who are put through lineup-style or showup-style machinations. Clark's hypothetical projections of error rates for several different patterns of distribution of guilt and innocence show just how sensitive this decision about identification techniques is to such variables.

Consider, briefly, a pair of examples from Clark's Table 1. Many reformers hold that the present system of biased instructions should be replaced by unbiased instructions indicating to the eyewitness that the guilty person may not be in the lineup. Suppose that we have a sample of 200 lineups and that exactly half involve the perpetrator ("perp-present") and the other half fail to include the perpetrator ("perp-absent"). There would be a net increase of three errors in the unbiased lineup (nine lost correct identifications and six lost false identifications) in comparison with a biased lineup. An alternative reform—a switch from simultaneous lineups to sequential ones—would produce five additional errors per 200 lineups (assuming, again, that the perpetrator is absent half the time) in comparison with a simultaneous lineup.

Were we to suppose, more realistically, that the proportion of lineups with truly guilty persons is more like 70 percent or 80 percent than a mere 50 percent, these error estimates linked to various proposed reforms would go up steeply. Under such circumstances, the arguments for reforming the system come unstuck with the realization that such reforms would dramatically increase the frequency of errors at trial. What sort of Orwellian twist are we giving to the language when we propose "reforms" that we have every reason to expect will significantly increase the rate of false verdicts? That hardly squares with the oft-repeated view of the Supreme Court that the principal function of a criminal trial is to discover the truth.

Lineups Versus Showups: A False Choice

If I have any bone to pick with Clark's analysis, it is his partial acquiescence in the view that the often proposed reform involving the replacement of showups with lineups is obvious and desirable. His reasons for that conclusion are clear: It is the only prominent reform proposal that existing data suggest might simultaneously reduce false identifications and false nonidentifications. That combination of features would be compelling if it were necessary to choose between showups and lineups. I think Clark pays insufficient attention to the fact that these two forms of eyewitness identification are not necessarily rivals. Almost invariably, a showup occurs immediately or very shortly after the crime (often at the crime scene itself). By contrast, lineups usually occur only after a suspect has been interrogated and they require rather elaborate staging. The fact that these two forms of identification occur at different phases of a police investigation means that it can be appropriate to utilize them both rather than choosing only one or the other. It is particularly useful to use both if there is more than one eyewitness, as this will produce a more probative test of identification than either would produce on its own. Moreover, the showup—occurring much earlier in the investigative process than the lineup—can produce relevant inculpatory evidence much more quickly than a lineup will, thereby preventing the escape of a suspect who might otherwise elude a lineup altogether.[4]

Eyewitness Identification Errors and the Role of the Jury

Unfortunately, and with only a few notable exceptions, the reforms that many researchers propose suffer from two distinct errors, as Clark correctly observes. First, they either ignore whether the remedies they offer will increase the rate of false acquittals or blithely suppose that the remedies will not affect the frequency of such mistakes at all. Secondly, and more egregiously, they ignore the question of the likely distribution of guilty and innocent defendants among those who go to trial. This second mistake is even more serious than the first—if most defendants are truly guilty (as one might infer from existing conviction rates), the scope for false convictions is decidedly limited and most errors that occur will be errors of false acquittal. By contrast, if a substantial proportion of defendants are innocent, then false convictions can become a serious worry. The trouble is that if one pays no heed whatever to the actual distribution of innocence and guilt among those charged with or suspected of a crime, then one has no clue about whether reducing the ratio of false convictions to false acquittals should be the top priority or not.

It is not clear to me that there is any one or any set of eyewitness identification procedures that is unambiguously superior to others in all respects—a kind of lineup for all seasons. Some are more prone to false identifications or false misidentifications than others but until we know more than we now do about the distribution of guilt among suspects submitted to lineups, it is dicey to suppose that one is superior in any given context to another. What is clear, however, is that we now have enough empirical evidence about the error profiles of several different lineup procedures that we are in a position to insist that jurors should be informed about the proneness to error of whatever procedure is used in the case in hand. Armed with that information, the triers of fact can decide for themselves what the probatory power of any given eyewitness identification should be. The sharing of that information with jurors appears to me vastly more important than trying to arrive at the one, unique and definitive format for conducting identifications.

This is another way of saying that the real key to protecting innocent defendants is not the exclusive use of gold-standard, error-distributing identification procedures, but clear communication to jurors that eyewitness identifications, whatever their structure, are fallible. More specifically, jurors need to be informed about the known error profiles of the eyewitness identification(s) used in the case that they are trying. The demands of due process can be met not by limiting lineups to those forms that offer the greatest protection against false identification but by aggressively emphasizing what we now know empirically about the pitfalls of various forms of eyewitness identification.

Declaration of Conflicting Interests

The author declared that he had no conflicts of interest with respect to his authorship or the publication of this article.

Notes

1. *Patterson v. New York* (1977).
2. *Carter v. Kentucky* (1981) established the right of a silent defendant to request that the judge give a limiting instruction to jurors, informing them that the defendant has a right not to testify and that no adverse inferences should be drawn from his exercise of that right. Here is the model federal instruction crafted to satisfy Carter: "The defendant chose not to testify in this case. Under our Constitution, a defendant has no obligation to testify or to present any evidence, because it is the Government's burden to prove a defendant guilty beyond a reasonable doubt. A defendant is never required to prove that he or she is innocent. Therefore, you must not attach any significance to the fact that a given defendant did not testify. No adverse inference against a defendant may be drawn by you because he did not take the witness stand, and you may not consider it in any way in your deliberations in the jury room." (Instruction 5-21, 1-5 Modern Federal Jury Instructions-Criminal §5.07).
3. The case that the rules of evidence and procedure should be error minimizing and party neutral, whereas error distribution is provided for by the standard of proof, is laid out in detail in my book *Truth, Error and Criminal Law* (Laudan, 2006).
4. Clark (2012) acknowledges these differences (see p. 244) but still seems to believe that the replacement of showups with lineups would be an improvement.

References

Carter v. Kentucky, 450 U.S. 288 (1981).

Clark, S. (2012). Costs and benefits of eyewitness identification reform: Psychological science and public policy. *Perspectives on Psychological Science, 7,* 238–259.

Laudan, L. (2006). *Truth, error and criminal law.* Cambridge, UK: Cambridge University Press.

Patterson v. New York, 432 U.S. 197 (1977).

Critical Thinking

1. Should evidence ever be excluded from trial?
2. Do you agree with Blackstone that false convictions are much more egregious than false acquittals?
3. How would Laudan solve the problem of protecting innocent defendants?
4. If most defendants are truly guilty, should we be concerned about the few false convictions that may occur?

Corresponding Author—LARRY LAUDAN, University of Texas School of Law, University of Texas at Austin, Austin, TX 78712 E-mail: ll@larrylaudan.com.

DOJ Review of Flawed FBI Forensics Processes Lacked Transparency

SPENCER S. HSU, JENNIFER JENKINS, AND TED MELLNIK

The bombshell came at the most inopportune time.

An FBI special agent was testifying in the government's high-profile terrorism trial against Omar Abdel Rahman, the "blind sheik" suspected of plotting the first attack on the World Trade Center.

Frederic Whitehurst, a chemist and lawyer who worked in the FBI's crime lab, testified that he was told by his superiors to ignore findings that did not support the prosecution's theory of the bombing.

"There was a great deal of pressure put upon me to bias my interpretation," Whitehurst said in U.S. District Court in New York in 1995.

Even before the Internet, Whitehurst's extraordinary claim went viral. It turned out he had written or passed along scores of memos over the years warning of a lack of impartiality and scientific standards at the famed lab that did the forensic work after the World Trade Center attack and in other cases.

With the FBI under fire for its handling of the 1993 trade center attack, the Oklahoma City bombing and the O.J. Simpson murder case, officials had to act.

After the Justice Department's inspector general began a review of Whitehurst's claims, Attorney General Janet Reno and FBI Director Louis J. Freeh decided to launch a task force to dig through thousands of cases involving discredited agents, to ensure that "no defendant's right to a fair trial was jeopardized," as one FBI official promised at a congressional hearing.

The task force took nine years to complete its work and never publicly released its findings. Not the results of its case reviews of suspect lab work. Not the names of the defendants who were convicted as a result. And not the nature or scope of the forensic problems it found.

Those decisions more than a decade ago remain relevant today for hundreds of people still in the U.S. court system, because officials never notified many defendants of the forensic flaws in their cases and never expanded their review to catch similar mistakes.

A review of more than 10,000 pages of task force documents and dozens of interviews demonstrate that the panel operated in secret and with close oversight by FBI and Justice Department brass—including Reno and Freeh's top deputy—who took steps to control the information uncovered by the group.

"It was not open," said a person who worked closely with the task force and who spoke on the condition of anonymity because the bureau and Justice Department maintain a strong influence in forensic science. "Maybe [a coverup] wasn't the intent, but it did seem to look that way. . . . It was too controlled by the FBI."

The documents and interviews tell a story of how the Justice Department's promise to protect the rights of defendants became in large part an exercise in damage control that left some prisoners locked away or in the dark for years longer than necessary. The Justice Department continues to decline to release the names of defendants in the affected cases.

A *Washington Post* review of the department's actions shows an agency struggling to balance its goal of defending convictions in court with its responsibility to protect the innocent. The Justice Department's decision to allow prosecutors to decide what to disclose to defendants was criticized at the time and allowed most of the process to remain secret. But by cloaking cases in anonymity, failing to ensure that defendants were notified of troubles with their cases and neglecting to publicly report problems or recommend solutions, the task force obscured problems from further study.

Justice Department spokeswoman Laura Sweeney said the federal review met constitutional requirements by allowing prosecutors in the affected cases to make the final decision whether to disclose potentially exculpatory information to the defendants.

"In January 1996 the Department established a Task Force to advise prosecutors of the Office of Inspector General investigation of the FBI lab," Sweeney said in a statement. The task force worked with prosecutors and the FBI "to notify the relevant prosecutors [local, state and federal] so that they could determine what information needed to be disclosed to defense counsel."

Scathing Report

If the Justice Department was secretive, the agency's independent inspector general was not. Michael R. Bromwich's probe culminated in a devastating 517-page report in April 1997 on misconduct at the FBI lab.

His findings stopped short of accusing agents of perjury or of fabricating results, but he concluded that FBI managers failed—in some cases for years—to respond to warnings about the scientific integrity and competence of agents.

The chief of the lab's explosives unit, for example, "repeatedly reached conclusions that incriminated the defendants without a scientific basis" in the 1995 Oklahoma City bombing, Bromwich wrote. The head of toxicology lacked judgment and credibility and overstated results in the 1994 Simpson investigation. After the 1993 World Trade Center attack, the key FBI witness "worked backward," tailoring his testimony to reach the result he wanted. Other agents "spruced up" notes for trial, altered reports without the author's permission or failed to document or confirm their findings.

The investigation led to wide-ranging changes, including higher laboratory standards and requirements for examiners.

Meanwhile, the Justice Department set out to evaluate discredited agents' work in thousands of cases that had gone to trial.

Jim Maddock, the FBI's assistant general counsel, told reporters that the goal of the new task force was to identify any potentially exculpatory information that had arisen in any criminal case involving agents criticized in the report.

"We are undertaking that review," Maddock said at an April 15, 1997, news conference. "And when it is done, we will give a full accounting of our findings."

Interviews and documents show that key decisions about the task force's work were made at the highest levels, including the decisions to exclude defense lawyers from the review and not publicly release the findings.

Task force participants said Reno signed off on the decision allowing prosecutors to decide what to disclose, because normal legal and constitutional requirements give prosecutors that discretion.

Justice Department officials also believed that the public release of the 1997 inspector general report generated enough publicity to give defense attorneys and their clients opportunities to appeal, task force participants said.

"Our job was to do the scientific reviews and then to send the results to the prosecutors, and they were responsible for determining whether they were going to disclose or not," Lucy L. Thomson, the chief of the task force, said in an interview. "That was just the way Janet Reno decided to do it."

Reno is physically ailing and was unable to comment for this article.

Her deputy attorney general until April 1997, Jamie Gorelick, said Reno "was very, very interested in assuring that we weren't keeping in prison people who deserved to have their convictions reviewed."

"I am sure she tried as hard as she could to keep the pressure on the bureau and on the criminal division," Gorelick said.

Delays, Omissions

Documents show that the FBI and Justice Department set strict rules about what information would be disclosed as they prepared to battle defendants who challenged convictions.

The department planned to "monitor all decisions" by federal prosecutors over whether to disclose information, the head of the criminal division, John C. Keeney, wrote in a memo to all U.S. attorneys on Jan. 4, 1996. The division stood ready, if necessary, to "evaluate the allegations and, if appropriate, rebut them," he wrote.

In addition, the Justice Department and the FBI negotiated over the limit and scope of the task force review, the documents show.

For example, in a June 1997 memo, Keeney told federal prosecutors that the criminal division and the FBI would "arrange for an independent, complete review of the Laboratory's findings and any related testimony" in all convictions in which they found there was a "reasonable probability" that work by discredited agents had affected the conviction or sentence.

But two months later, the senior attorney in charge of the task force told Keeney's deputy that the FBI indicated that it planned to require "a cursory paper review" only and generally did not plan to reexamine evidence.

That attorney in charge, Thomson, told Deputy Assistant Attorney General Kevin V. DiGregory in an Aug. 19, 1997, memo that the FBI also wanted to keep the focus off the most vulnerable cases by not conducting reviews if a case was still in litigation or on appeal—even though the panel's work would have been most relevant to a judge at those times.

There were other hitches. One year later, in August 1998, Thomson complained to DiGregory that "no scientists have been retained to date" by the FBI to conduct reviews of cases in which defendants may have been wrongly convicted.

Reviews were "needed as soon as possible in order to avoid possibly undercutting prosecutors' arguments . . . and to ensure that defendants will not exhaust opportunities to file post-conviction relief motions," Thomson said.

As it turned out, reviews would continue for six years, leaving defendants in jail after having been convicted in cases with faulty forensics.

Keeney died last year after retiring in 2010 as the longest-serving federal prosecutor in U.S. history. DiGregory did not return messages left at his home and passed through an associate.

Thomson, now a privacy expert, said that the reviews were not cursory and that she did not know whether any defendants had lost opportunities to appeal their convictions.

Reduced Paper Trail

As the cases became known to state and local prosecutors, many moved swiftly and made full disclosures. Others stymied the effort, whether intentionally or not.

Because of the sheer passage of time, files, trial transcripts or other records often were lost or destroyed. Personnel turnover in prosecutors' offices often left behind no living memory of cases. Many state and local prosecutors worked in small offices with enormous active caseloads and had little stake in the Justice Department process.

As a result, reviewers dropped plans to require that state and local prosecutors sign statements when they determined a discredited agent's work was pivotal to a case, or to explain in writing if they determined it was not, records show.

That reduced the paper trail. As long as the task force got the information, a participant said, it did not matter whether it was written down.

The task force did order reviews for multiple cases in which prosecutors refused to cooperate. For example, Tampa prosecutor Harry Lee Coe III, now deceased, told the department that his lawyers were too overworked to review questioned death penalty cases, documents show.

In South Carolina, the task force completed a scientific review in late 2002 in the case of Roy David Brooks, who had been convicted of murder. But the review came after the state had destroyed records. And the destruction of records came days after the task force wrote to prosecutors for the third time in four years seeking such records.

Even when cases were disclosed to defense counsel, it was not clear what was disclosed.

In some cases, one-sentence notifications were sent to defendants, many of whom were indigent, still in prison or without attorneys.

"Please find enclosed a copy of the Attachment to Independent Case Review Report for CDRU#6480 Case File #95-253567, which we received, from the U.S. Department of Justice," stated the entirety of a letter from prosecutors in Tampa to one defendant in April 2001. That letter came 18 years after the offense.

The attached three-page report did not contain the defendant's name—only strings of four- and eight-digit FBI and Justice Department code numbers. It had nothing to indicate that it involved the particular defendant's case or the meaning of bland statements of scientific results.

In other cases, records indicate that prosecutors told defendants or their attorneys early on about the inspector general's report but never mentioned that the task force found more-specific problems.

The task force gradually wound down when Thomson and DiGregory departed. A new administration arrived months before the Sept. 11, 2001, terrorist attacks, which transformed priorities. In 2002, Michael Chertoff, then assistant attorney general for the criminal division, narrowed the review to speed its completion, dropping unspecified "small cases."

Through a spokesman, Chertoff declined to comment.

In addition, the criminal division stopped asking prosecutors to notify it if they turned over review results to defense attorneys.

Research director Madonna Lebling and researcher Aaron Carter contributed to this report.

Critical Thinking

1. If the failure to publicly release the findings of the 9-year study involving discredited FBI agents was not intended as a cover-up, why does it matter that it looked that way?
2. What effect did the passage of time have on the cases being evaluated?
3. Do you see any problem with asking the Justice Department to review convictions obtained by its prosecutors with evidence from FBI agents?
4. What were some problems listed in the inspector general's report?

Convicted Defendants Left Uninformed of Forensic Flaws Found by Justice Dept.

SPENCER S. HSU

Justice Department officials have known for years that flawed forensic work might have led to the convictions of potentially innocent people, but prosecutors failed to notify defendants or their attorneys even in many cases they knew were troubled.

Officials started reviewing the cases in the 1990s after reports that sloppy work by examiners at the FBI lab was producing unreliable forensic evidence in court trials. Instead of releasing those findings, they made them available only to the prosecutors in the affected cases, according to documents and interviews with dozens of officials.

In addition, the Justice Department reviewed only a limited number of cases and focused on the work of one scientist at the FBI lab, despite warnings that problems were far more widespread and could affect potentially thousands of cases in federal, state and local courts.

As a result, hundreds of defendants nationwide remain in prison or on parole for crimes that might merit exoneration, a retrial or a retesting of evidence using DNA because FBI hair and fiber experts may have misidentified them as suspects.

In one Texas case, Benjamin Herbert Boyle was executed in 1997, more than a year after the Justice Department began its review. Boyle would not have been eligible for the death penalty without the FBI's flawed work, according to a prosecutor's memo.

The case of a Maryland man serving a life sentence for a 1981 double killing is another in which federal and local law enforcement officials knew of forensic problems but never told the defendant. Attorneys for the man, John Norman Huffington, say they learned of potentially exculpatory Justice Department findings from *The Washington Post*. They are seeking a new trial.

Justice Department officials said that they met their legal and constitutional obligations when they learned of specific errors, that they alerted prosecutors and were not required to inform defendants directly.

The review was performed by a task force created during an inspector general's investigation of misconduct at the FBI crime lab in the 1990s. The inquiry took nine years, ending in 2004, records show, but the findings were never made public.

In the discipline of hair and fiber analysis, only the work of FBI Special Agent Michael P. Malone was questioned. Even though Justice Department and FBI officials knew that the discipline had weaknesses and that the lab lacked protocols—and learned that examiners' "matches" were often wrong—they kept their reviews limited to Malone.

But two cases in D.C. Superior Court show the inadequacy of the government's response.

Santae A. Tribble, now 51, was convicted of killing a taxi driver in 1978, and Kirk L. Odom, now 49, was convicted of a sexual assault in 1981.

Key evidence at each of their trials came from separate FBI experts—not Malone—who swore that their scientific analysis proved with near certainty that Tribble's and Odom's hair was at the respective crime scenes.

But DNA testing this year on the hair and on other old evidence virtually eliminates Tribble as a suspect and completely clears Odom. Both men have completed their sentences and are on lifelong parole. They are now seeking exoneration in the courts in the hopes of getting on with their lives.

Neither case was part of the Justice Department task force's review.

A third D.C. case shows how the lack of Justice Department notification has forced people to stay in prison longer than they should have.

Donald E. Gates, 60, served 28 years for the rape and murder of a Georgetown University student based on Malone's testimony that his hair was found on the victim's body. He was exonerated by DNA testing in 2009. But for 12 years before that, prosecutors never told him about the inspector general's report about Malone, that Malone's work was key to his conviction or that Malone's findings were flawed, leaving him in prison the entire time.

After *The Post* contacted him about the forensic issues, U.S. Attorney Ronald C. Machen Jr. of the District said his office would try to review all convictions that used hair analysis.

Seeking to learn whether others shared Gates's fate, *The Post* worked with the nonprofit National Whistleblowers Center, which had obtained dozens of boxes of task force documents through a years-long Freedom of Information Act fight.

Task force documents identifying the scientific reviews of problem cases generally did not contain the names of the defendants. Piecing together case numbers and other bits of information from more than 10,000 pages of documents, *The Post* found more than 250 cases in which a scientific review was completed. Available records did not allow the identification of defendants in roughly 100 of those cases. Records of an unknown number of other questioned cases handled by federal prosecutors have yet to be released by the government.

The Post found that while many prosecutors made swift and full disclosures, many others did so incompletely, years late or not at all. The effort was stymied at times by lack of cooperation from some prosecutors and declining interest and resources as time went on.

Overall, calls to defense lawyers indicate and records documented that prosecutors disclosed the reviews' results to defendants in fewer than half of the 250-plus questioned cases.

Michael R. Bromwich, a former federal prosecutor and the inspector general who investigated the FBI lab, said in a statement that even if more defense lawyers were notified of the initial review, "that doesn't absolve the task force from ensuring that every single defense lawyer in one of these cases was notified."

He added: "It is deeply troubling that after going to so much time and trouble to identify problematic conduct by FBI forensic analysts the DOJ Task Force apparently failed to follow through and ensure that defense counsel were notified in every single case."

Justice Department spokeswoman Laura Sweeney said the federal review was an "exhaustive effort" and met legal requirements, and she referred questions about hair analysis to the FBI. The FBI said it would evaluate whether a nationwide review is needed.

"In cases where microscopic hair exams conducted by the FBI resulted in a conviction, the FBI is evaluating whether additional review is warranted," spokeswoman Ann Todd said in a statement. "The FBI has undertaken comprehensive reviews in the past, and will not hesitate to do so again if necessary."

Santae Tribble and Kirk Odom

John McCormick had just finished the night shift driving a taxi for Diamond Cab on July 26, 1978. McCormick, 63, reached the doorstep of his home in Southeast Washington about 3 A.M., when he was robbed and fatally shot by a man in a stocking mask, according to his widow, who caught a glimpse of the attack from inside the house.

Police soon focused on Santae Tribble as a suspect. A police informant said Tribble told her he was with his childhood friend, Cleveland Wright, when Wright shot McCormick.

After a three-day trial, jurors deliberated two hours before asking about a stocking found a block away at the end of an alley on 28th Street SE. It had been recovered by a police dog, and it contained a single hair that the FBI traced to Tribble. Forty minutes later, the jury found Tribble guilty of murder. He was sentenced in January 1980 to 20 years to life in prison.

Tribble, 17 at the time, his brother, his girlfriend and a houseguest all testified that they were together preparing to celebrate the guest's birthday the night McCormick was killed. All four said Tribble and his girlfriend were asleep between 2 and 4:30 A.M. in Seat Pleasant.

Tribble took the stand in his own defense, saying what he had said all along—that he had nothing to do with McCormick's killing.

The prosecution began its closing argument by citing the FBI's testimony about the hair from the stocking.

This January, after a year-long effort to have DNA evidence retested, Tribble's public defender succeeded and turned over the results from a private lab to prosecutors. None of the 13 hairs recovered from the stocking—including the one that the FBI said matched Tribble's—shared Tribble's or Wright's genetic profile, conclusively ruling them out as sources, according to mitochondrial DNA analyst Terry Melton of the private lab.

"The government's entire theory of prosecution—that Mr. Tribble and Mr. Wright acted together to kill Mr. McCormick—is demolished," wrote Sandra K. Levick, chief of special litigation for the D.C. Public Defender Service and the lawyer who represents Gates, Tribble and Odom. In a motion to D.C. Superior Court Judge Laura Cordero seeking Tribble's exoneration, Levick wrote: "He has waited thirty-three years for the truth to set him free. He should have to wait no longer."

In an interview, Tribble, who served 28 years in prison, said that whether the court grants his request or not, he sees it as a final chance to assert his innocence.

"Ms. Levick has been like an angel," Tribble added, ". . . and I thank God for DNA."

Details of the new round of hair testing illustrate how hair analysis is highly subjective. The FBI scientist who originally testified at Tribble's trial, Special Agent James A. Hilverda, said all the hairs he retrieved from the stocking were human head hairs, including the one suitable for comparison that he declared in court matched Tribble's "in all microscopic characteristics."

In August, Harold Deadman, a senior hair analyst with the D.C. police who spent 15 years with the FBI lab, forwarded the evidence to the private lab and reported that the 13 hairs he found included head and limb hairs. One exhibited Caucasian characteristics, Deadman added. Tribble is black.

But the private lab's DNA tests irrefutably showed that the 13 hairs came from three human sources, each of African origin, except for one—which came from a dog.

"Such is the true state of hair microscopy," Levick wrote. "Two FBI-trained analysts, James Hilverda and Harold Deadman, could not even distinguish human hairs from canine hairs."

Hilverda declined to comment. Deadman said his role was limited to describing characteristics of hairs he found.

Kirk Odom's case shares similarities with Tribble's. Odom was convicted of raping, sodomizing and robbing a 27-year-old woman before dawn in her Capitol Hill apartment in 1981.

The victim said she spoke with her assailant and observed him for up to two minutes in the "dim light" of street lamps through her windows before she was gagged, bound and blindfolded in an hour-long assault.

Police put together a composite sketch of the attacker, based on the victim's description. About five weeks after the assault, a police officer was talking to Odom about an unrelated matter. He thought Odom looked like the sketch. So he retrieved a two-year-old photograph of Odom, from when he was 16, and put it in a photo array for the victim. The victim picked the image out of the array that April and identified Odom at a lineup in May. She identified Odom again at his trial, telling jurors her assailant "had left her with an image of his face etched in her mind."

At trial, FBI Special Agent Myron T. Scholberg testified that a hair found on the victim's nightgown was "microscopically like" Odom's, meaning the samples were indistinguishable. Prosecutors explained that Scholberg had not been able to distinguish between hair samples only "eight or 10 times in the past 10 years, while performing thousands of analyses."

But on Jan. 18 of this year, Melton, of the same lab used in the Tribble case, Mitotyping Technologies of State College, Pa., reported its court-ordered DNA test results: The hair in the case could not have come from Odom.

On Feb. 27, a second laboratory selected by prosecutors, Bode Technology of Lorton, turned over the results of court-ordered nuclear DNA testing of stains left by the perpetrator on a pillowcase and robe.

Only one man left all four partial DNA profiles developed by the lab, and that man could not have been Odom.

The victim "was tragically mistaken in her identification of Mr. Odom as her assailant," Levick wrote in a motion filed March 14 seeking his exoneration. "One man committed these heinous crimes; that man was not Kirk L. Odom."

Scholberg, who retired in 1985 as head of hair and fiber analysis after 18 years at the FBI lab, said side-by-side hair comparison "was the best method we had at the time."

Odom, who was imprisoned for 20 years, had to register as a sex offender and remains on lifelong parole. He says court-ordered therapists still berate him for saying he is not guilty. Over the years, his conviction has kept him from possible jobs, he said.

"There was always the thought in the back of my mind . . . 'One day will my name be cleared?' " Odom said at his home in Southeast Washington, where he lives with his wife, Harriet, a medical counselor.

Federal prosecutors declined to comment on Tribble's and Odom's specific claims, citing pending litigation.

One government official noted that Odom served an additional 16 months after his release for an unrelated simple assault that violated his parole.

However, in a statement released after being contacted by *The Post*, Machen, the U.S. attorney in the District, acknowledged that DNA results "raise serious questions in my mind about these convictions."

"If our comprehensive review shows that either man was wrongfully convicted, we will promptly join him in a motion to vacate his conviction, as we did with Donald Gates in 2009," Machen said.

The Trouble with Hair Analysis

Popularized in fiction by Sherlock Holmes, hair comparison became an established forensic science by the 1950s. Before modern-day DNA testing, hair analysis could, at its best, accurately narrow the pool of criminal suspects to a class or group or definitively rule out a person as a possible source.

But in practice, even before the " 'CSI' effect" led jurors to expect scientific evidence at every trial, a claim of a hair match packed a powerful, dramatic punch in court. The testimony, usually by a respected scientist working at a respected federal agency, allowed prosecutors to boil down ambiguous cases for jurors to a single, incriminating piece of human evidence left at the scene.

Forensic experts typically assessed the varying characteristics of a hair to determine whether the defendant might be a source. Some factors were visible to the naked eye, such as the length of the hair, its color and whether it was straight, kinky or curly. Others were visible under a microscope, such as the size, type and distribution of pigmentation, the alignment of scales or the thickness of layers in a given hair, or its diameter at various points.

Other judgments could be made. Was the hair animal or human? From the scalp, limbs or pubic area? Of a discernible race? Dyed, bleached or otherwise treated? Cut, forcibly removed or shed naturally?

But there is no consensus among hair examiners about how many of these characteristics were needed to declare a match. So some agents relied on six or seven traits, while others needed 20 or 30. Hilverda, the FBI scientist in Tribble's case, told jurors that he had performed "probably tens of thousands of examinations" and relied on "about 15 characteristics."

Despite his testimony, Hilverda recorded in his lab notes that he had measured only three characteristics of the hair from the stocking—it was black, it was a human head hair, and it was from an African American. Similarly, Scholberg's notes describe the nightgown hair in Odom's case in the barest terms, as a black, human head hair fragment, like a sample taken from Odom.

Hilverda acknowledged that results could rule out a person or be inconclusive. However, he told jurors that a "match" reflected a high likelihood that two hairs came from the same person. Hilverda added, "Only on very rare occasions have I seen hairs of two individuals that show the same characteristics."

In Tribble's case, federal prosecutor David Stanley went further as he summed up the evidence. "There is one chance, perhaps for all we know, in 10 million that it could [be] someone else's hair," he said in his closing arguments, sounding the final word for the government.

Stanley declined to comment.

Flaws Known for Decades

The Tribble and Odom cases demonstrate problems in hair analysis that have been known for nearly 40 years.

In 1974, researchers acknowledged that visual comparisons are so subjective that different analysts can reach different conclusions about the same hair. The FBI acknowledged in 1984 that such analysis cannot positively determine that a hair found at a crime scene belongs to one particular person.

In 1996, the Justice Department studied the nation's first 28 DNA exonerations and found that 20 percent of the cases involved hair comparison. That same year, the FBI lab stopped declaring matches based on visual comparisons alone and began requiring DNA testing as well.

Yet examples of FBI experts violating scientific standards and making exaggerated or erroneous claims emerged in 1997 at the heart of the FBI lab's worst modern scandal, when Bromwich's investigation found systematic problems involving 13 agents. The lab's lack of written protocols and examiners' weak scientific qualifications allowed bias to influence some of the nation's highest-profile criminal investigations, the inspector general said.

From 1996 through 2004, a Justice Department task force set out to review about 6,000 cases handled by the 13 discredited agents for any potential exculpatory information that should be disclosed to defendants. The task force identified more than 250 convictions in which the agents' work was determined to be either critical to the conviction or so problematic—for example, because a prosecutor refused to cooperate or records had been lost—that it completed a fresh scientific assessment of the agent's work. The task force was directed to notify prosecutors of the results.

The only real notice of what the task force found came in a 2003 Associated Press account in which unnamed government officials said they had turned over results to prosecutors and were aware that defendants had been notified in 100 to 150 cases. The officials left the impression that anybody whose case had been affected had been notified and that, in any case, no convictions had been overturned, the officials said.

But since 2003, in the District alone, two of six convictions identified by *The Post* in which forensic work was reassessed by the task force have been vacated. That includes Gates's case, but not those of Tribble and Odom, who are awaiting court action and were not part of the task force review.

The Gates exoneration also shows that prosecutors failed to turn over information uncovered by the task force.

In addition to Gates, the murder cases in Texas and Maryland and a third in Alaska reveal examples of shortcomings.

All three cases, in addition to the District cases, were handled by FBI agent Malone, whose cases made up more than 90 percent of scientific reviews found by *The Post.*

In Texas, the review of Benjamin Herbert Boyle's case got underway only after the defendant was executed, 16 months after the task force was formed, despite pledges to prioritize death penalty cases.

Boyle was executed six days after the Bromwich investigation publicly criticized Malone, the FBI agent who worked on his case, but the FBI had acknowledged two months earlier that it was investigating complaints about him.

The task force asked the Justice Department's capital-case review unit to look over its work, but the fact that it failed to prevent the execution was never publicized.

In Maryland, John Norman Huffington's attorneys say they were never notified of the findings of the review in his case, leaving them in a battle over the law's unsettled requirements for prosecutors to turn over potentially exculpatory evidence and over whether lawyers and courts can properly interpret scientific findings.

In Alaska, Newton P. Lambert's defenders have been left to seek DNA testing of remaining biological evidence, if any exists, while he serves a life sentence for a 1982 murder. Prosecutors for both Huffington and Lambert claim they disclosed findings at some point to other lawyers but failed to document doing so. In Lambert's case, *The Post* found that the purported notification went to a lawyer who had died.

Senior public defenders in both states say they received no such word, which they say would be highly unlikely if it in fact came.

Malone, 66, said he was simply using the best science available at the time. "We did the best we could with what we had," he said.

Even the harshest critics acknowledge that the Justice Department worked hard to identify potentially tainted convictions. Many of the cases identified by the task force involved serious crimes, and several defendants confessed or were guilty of related charges. Courts also have upheld several convictions even after agents' roles were discovered.

Flawed Agents or a Flawed System?

Because of the focus on Malone, many questionable cases were never reviewed.

But as in the Tribble and Odom cases, thousands of defendants nationwide have been implicated by other FBI agents, as well as state and local hair examiners, who relied on the same flawed techniques.

In 2002, the FBI found after it analyzed DNA in 80 selected hair cases that its agents had reported false matches more than 11 percent of the time. "I don't believe forensic science truly understood the significance of microscopic hair comparison, and it wasn't until [DNA] that we learned that 11 percent of the time, two hairs can be microscopically similar yet come from different people," said Dwight E. Adams, who directed the FBI lab from 2002 to 2006.

Yet a *Post* review of the small fraction of cases in which an appeals court opinion describes FBI hair testimony shows that several FBI agents gave improper testimony, asserting the remote odds of a false match or invoking bogus statistics in the absence of data.

For example, in testimony in a Minnesota bank robbery case, also in 1978, Hilverda, the agent who worked on Tribble's case, reiterated that he had been unable to distinguish among different people's hair "only on a couple of occasions" out of more than 2,000 cases he had analyzed.

In a 1980 Indiana robbery case, an agent told jurors that he had failed to tell different people's hair apart just once in 1,500 cases. After a slaying in Tennessee that year, another agent testified in a capital case that there was only one chance out of 4,500 or 5,000 that a hair came from someone other than the suspect.

"Those statements are chilling to read," Bromwich said of the exaggerated FBI claims at trial.

Todd, the FBI spokeswoman, said bureau lab reports for more than 30 years have qualified their findings by saying that hair comparisons are not a means of absolute positive identification. She requested a list of cases in which agents departed from guidelines in court. *The Post* provided nine cases.

Todd declined to say whether the bureau considered taking steps to determine whether other agents intentionally or unintentionally misled jurors. "Only Michael Malone's conduct was questioned in the area of hair comparisons," Todd said. "The [inspector general] did not question the merits of microscopic hair comparisons as a scientific discipline."

Experts say the difference between laboratory standards and examiners' testimony in court can be important, especially if no one is reading or watching what agents say.

"It seemingly has never been routine for crime labs to do supervision based on trial testimony," said University of Virginia School of Law professor Brandon L. Garrett. "You can have cautious standards, but if no one is supervising their implementation, it's predictable that analysts may cross the line."

'Veil of Secrecy'

A review of the task force documents, as well as *Post* interviews, found that the Justice Department struggled to balance its roles as a law enforcer defending convictions, a minister of justice protecting the innocent, and a patron and practitioner of forensic science.

By excluding defense lawyers from the process and leaving it to prosecutors to decide case by case what to disclose, authorities waded into a legal and ethical morass that left some prisoners locked away for years longer than necessary. By adopting a secret process that limited accountability, documents show, the task force left the scope and nature of scientific problems unreported, obscuring issues from further study and permitting similar breakdowns.

"The government has hidden behind the veil of secrecy to shield these abuses despite official assurances that justice would be done," said David Colapinto, general counsel of the National Whistleblowers Center.

The American Bar Association and others have proposed stronger ethics rules for prosecutors to act on information that casts doubt on convictions; opening laboratory and other files to the defense; clearer reporting and evidence retention; greater involvement by scientists in setting rules for testimony at criminal trials; and more scientific training for lawyers and judges.

Other experts propose more oversight by standing state forensic-science commissions and funding for research into forensic techniques and experts for indigent defendants.

A common theme among reform-minded lawyers and experts is taking the oversight of the forensic labs away from police and prosecutors.

"It's human to make mistakes," said Steven D. Benjamin, president-elect of the National Association of Criminal Defense Lawyers. "It's wrong not to learn from them."

More specifically, the D.C. Public Defender Service, Benjamin's group and others said justice would be served by retesting hair evidence in convictions nationwide from 1996 and earlier. "If microscopic hair analysis was a key piece of evidence in a conviction, and it was one of only a limited amount of evidence in a case, would it be worthwhile to retest that using mitochondrial DNA? I would say absolutely," said Adams, the former FBI lab director.

The promised review by federal prosecutors of hair convictions in the District would not include cases before 1985, when FBI records were computerized, and would not disclose any defendant's name. That approach would have missed Gates, Odom and Tribble, who were convicted earlier.

Representatives for Machen, the FBI and the Justice Department also declined to say why the review should be limited to D.C. cases. *The Post* found that 95 percent of the troubled cases identified by the task force were outside the District.

Avis E. Buchanan, director of the D.C. Public Defender Service, said her agency must be "a full participant" in the review, which it has sought for two years, and that it should extend nationwide. "Surely the District of Columbia is not the only place where such flawed evidence was used to convict the innocent," she said.

Staff researcher Jennifer Jenkins and database editor Ted Mellnik contributed to this report.

Critical Thinking

1. In addition to not releasing the findings of the review of cases involving flawed forensic work, what other problem does the article mention?
2. Do you believe the DOJ fulfilled its obligation to do justice?
3. What is the problem with hair analysis?
4. How long have the problems with hair analysis been known to the FBI?
5. Should FBI agents' testimony about forensics claims be monitored?
6. Do you believe forensics labs should be under the control of police and prosecutors?

Neuroscience in the Courtroom

Brain scans and other types of neurological evidence are rarely a factor in trials today. Someday, however, they could transform judicial views of personal credibility and responsibility.

MICHAEL S. GAZZANIGA

By a strange coincidence, I was called to jury duty for my very first time shortly after I started as director of a new MacArthur Foundation project exploring the issues that neuroscience raises for the criminal justice system. Eighty of us showed up for selection in a case that involved a young woman charged with driving under the influence, but most of my fellow citizens were excused for various reasons, primarily their own DUI experiences. Finally, I was called to the judge. "Tell me what you do," he said.

"I am a neuroscientist," I answered, "and I have actually done work relevant to what goes on in a courtroom. For example, I have studied how false memories form, the nature of addiction, and how the brain regulates behavior."

The judge looked at me carefully and asked, "Do you think you could suspend all that you know about such matters for the course of this trial?" I said I could try. And with that, he said I was excused.

I was dismayed but should not have been. In the interest of fairness, judges and attorneys are supposed to seek jurors who will be guided solely by what they hear in the courtroom and to steer clear of those whose real or imagined outside expertise might unduly influence fellow jurors. Yet, in a way, the judge's dismissal of me also paralleled the legal system's wariness today of the tools and insights of neuroscience. Aided by sophisticated imaging techniques, neuroscientists can now peer into the living brain and are beginning to tease out patterns of brain activity that underlie behaviors or ways of thinking. Already attorneys are attempting to use brain scans as evidence in trials, and the courts are grappling with how to decide when such scans should be admissible. Down the road, an ability to link patterns of brain activity with mental states could upend old rules for deciding whether a defendant had control over his or her actions and gauging to what extent that defendant should be punished. No one yet has a clear idea of how to guide the changes, but the legal system, the public and neuroscientists need to understand the issues to ensure that our society remains a just one, even as new insights rock old ideas of human nature.

Unacceptable Evidence (For Now)

With the growing availability of images that can describe the state of someone's brain, attorneys are increasingly asking judges to admit these scans into evidence, to demonstrate, say, that a defendant is not guilty by reason of insanity or that a witness is telling the truth. Judges might approve the request if they think the jury will consider the scans as one piece of data supporting an attorney's or a witness's assertion or if they think that seeing the images will give jurors a better understanding of some relevant issue. But judges will reject the request if they conclude that the scans will be too persuasive for the wrong reasons or will be given too much weight simply because they look so impressively scientific. In legal terms, judges need to decide whether the use of the scans will be "probative" (tending to support a proposition) or, alternatively, "prejudicial" (tending to favor preconceived ideas) and likely to confuse or mislead the jury. So far judges—in agreement with the conventional wisdom of most neuroscientists and legal scholars—have usually decided that brain scans will unfairly prejudice juries and provide little or no probative value.

Judges also routinely exclude brain scans on the grounds that the science does not support their use as evidence of any condition other than physical brain injury. Criminal defense attorneys may wish to introduce the scans to establish that defendants have a particular cognitive or emotional disorder (such as flawed judgment, morality or impulse control), but—for now at least—most judges and researchers agree that science is not yet advanced enough to allow those uses.

Functional magnetic resonance imaging (fMRI) offers an example of a process that can provide good scientific information, of which fairly little is legally admissible. This technology is a favorite of researchers who explore which parts of the brain are active during different processes, such as reading, speaking or day-dreaming. It does not, however, measure the firing of brain cells directly; it measures blood flow, which is thought to correlate to some extent with neuronal activity. Further, to define the imaging signal associated with a particular pattern of brain activity, researchers must usually average many scans from a group of test subjects, whose individual brain patterns may diverge widely. A defendants fMRI scan may appear to differ greatly from an average value presented in court but could still be within the statistical boundaries of the data set that defined that average.

Moreover, scientists simply do not always know the prevalence of normal variations in brain anatomy and activity in the population (or groups within it). Showing a defendant's brain scan without data from an appropriate comparison group might profoundly mislead a jury. Judges have already had a hard time evaluating whether to admit physical brain-scan evidence of neurological or psychiatric problems that might bear on a defendant's culpability; they may face more difficulty in the years ahead when deciding whether to allow brain images to serve as indicators for more complex mental states, such as a witness's credibility or truthfulness.

Since the early 20th century, when psychologist and inventor William Moulton Marston first claimed that a polygraph measuring blood pressure, pulse, skin conductivity and other physiological signs could determine whether someone is lying, lie detection has been a hot topic in legal circles. U.S. courts have largely dismissed polygraph results as inadmissible, but other technologies are being developed, and courts will surely be forced eventually to evaluate their admissibility as well. These tools include brain-imaging methods that aim to detect mental states reflective of truthful behavior.

Detecting Lies and Determining Credibility

Recent work by Anthony D. Wagner and his colleagues at Stanford University, for instance, has revealed that under controlled experimental conditions fMRI, combined with complex analytical algorithms called pattern classifiers, can accurately determine that a person is remembering something but not whether the content of the detected memory is real or imagined. In other words, we might be able to use fMRI to detect whether individuals believe that they are recalling something, but we cannot tell whether their beliefs are accurate. Wagner concludes that fMRI methods may eventually be effective in detecting lies but that additional studies are needed.

Other experiments help to expose the nature of honesty: Does honesty result from the absence of temptation or from the exercise of extra willpower to resist it? In 2009 Joshua D. Greene and Joseph M. Paxton of Harvard University gave test subjects placed in a scanner a financial incentive to overstate their accuracy in a coin toss; the researchers were able to obtain fMRI images of individuals deciding whether or not to lie. Dishonest behavior correlated with extra activity in certain brain regions involved in impulse control and decision making. Yet Greene and Paxton noted that some subjects who told the truth also exhibited that same brain activity, so the fMRI images may capture only their extra struggle to resist temptation, not their ultimate truthfulness. The researchers therefore urge judges to be cautious about allowing these kinds of data in today's courtroom.

Their view is not universal, however. Frederick Schauer, professor of law at the University of Virginia and an expert on legal evidence, points out that courts now routinely admit many types of evidence that are far more dubious than the lie-detection science that is being excluded. The current approach to assessing whether witnesses or others are telling the truth is inaccurate and based on misconceptions about dishonest behavior: demeanor, for example, does not always provide reliable clues to honesty. The law has its own standards for determining admissibility into a court, and those standards are more lenient than scientific standards. Schauer argues that jurors should be allowed to consider the result of a lie-detection test that has a 60 percent accuracy rate because it could provide reasonable doubt as to guilt or innocence.

One of the first cases to tackle the use of brain-scanning technology for lie detection recently ended in a federal district court in Tennessee. In *United States v. Semrau,* a magistrate judge found that the evidence offered by a commercial fMRI lie-detection company should be excluded in part because of Federal Rule of Evidence 403, which holds that evidence must be probative and not prejudicial.

Furthermore, the judge explained why he found that the unfair prejudicial influence of the technology in the case substantially outweighed its probative value. The magistrate's main objection was that the defense expert conducting the lie-detection test could not tell the court whether the answer to any particular question was true or false. In fact, the expert testified that he could tell only whether the defendant was answering the set of questions about the case truthfully overall.

The use of neuroscience to assess the character and overall honesty of defendants may eventually trump its use for probing their truthfulness on any one matter.

One must wonder: In future cases, might the results be admissible with the more limited goal of simply determining whether or not the defendant was being deceptive in general? The use of neuroscience to assess the character and overall honesty of defendants may eventually trump its use for probing their truthfulness on any one matter in the courtroom. Federal Rule 608(b) provides that once the character of a witness has been attacked, counsel can introduce as evidence opinions about the witness's "character for truthfulness or untruthfulness." Today this type of evidence consists simply of testimony by others about the character of the witness. But what about tomorrow? Will juries want to know how a witness scores on a test of probable dishonesty? Will the evidence that someone tends toward dishonesty be more prejudicial if it comes out of a fancy machine? My guess is that such evidence will eventually be used and that it will initially tend to be prejudicial but that as society acquires more experience with the technology, the prejudicial effect will diminish.

Scanning for Psychopaths

Judges and attorneys are already being forced to work out the role of brain scans in the courtroom. In the long run, however, the greatest impact of neuroscience on the legal system will surely come from deeper insights into how our brain shapes our behavior. Even in infancy humans manifest innate senses of fairness and reciprocity, as well as desires to comfort the mistreated and punish transgressors. We are judge and jury from birth. On top of these instincts we have built our enlightened view of how culture should regard and punish antisocial behavior. Someday neuroscience could well force the legal system to revise its rules for determining culpability and for meting out sentences. It could also shake up society's understanding of what it means to have "free will" and how best to decide when to hold someone accountable for antisocial actions.

Consider the psychiatric and legal standing of psychopaths, who constitute less than 1 percent of the general population but roughly 25 percent of those in prison. That label, though used popularly as a catchall for many violent and nonviolent criminals, is properly reserved for those with a well-defined psychiatric condition diagnosed through a test called the Hare Psychopathy Checklist—Revised (PCL-R).

Psychopaths often display superficial charm, egocentricity, grandiosity, deceitfulness, manipulativeness, and an absence of guilt or empathy, all of which the PCL-R can assess. Yet psychometric tests such as the PCL-R are only proxies for measuring the neurological dysfunctions underlying these people's disturbed mental lives. Neuroimaging measurements of brain processes should therefore, at least in theory, provide a much better way to identify psychopaths.

To date, numerous studies have associated psychopathy with unusual brain activity. Psychopaths seem to exhibit, for example, abnormal neurological responses to stimuli that demand close attention and to words with emotional, concrete or abstract meanings. But such responses may also be found in people who have suffered damage to an area known as the medial temporal lobe—meaning they cannot be used as definitive signs of psychopathy. Other studies suggest psychopaths may have damage to the deep-brain structures of the limbic system, which helps to give rise to emotions, but the finding is preliminary.

Scientists are also beginning to look for abnormal connections in psychopaths' brains. Marcus E. Raichle, Benjamin Shannon and their colleagues at Washington University in St. Louis, along with Kent Kiehl of the University of New Mexico, analyzed fMRI data from scans of adult inmates and of juvenile offenders, all of whom were also assessed for psychopathy with the PCL-R. The adults, they found, had a variety of unusual connections between regions in their brains, although no one alteration predominated. Striking differences appeared more consistently and exclusively in the young offenders—and the degree of those changes increased along with their individual levels of impulsivity. One interpretation is that the impulsive juveniles lack some of the normal neural constraints on their choices of actions. Perhaps among juveniles who go untreated a brain abnormality that promotes impulsiveness eventually becomes more widespread, resulting in the diverse neural abnormalities seen in adults. Such a difference may also help explain why psychiatric treatments for psychopathy in juveniles are more successful than in adults, who are largely unresponsive.

Controversially, psychopathy is not now a recognized basis for an insanity defense. Instead psychopaths are seen as more dangerous than offenders without the pathology, and they receive longer or harsher sentences. A neuroimaging tool or method that could reliably identify psychopaths would be useful at the sentencing phase of a trial because it could help determine whether the defendant might deserve medical confinement and treatment rather than punitive incarceration. Getting the public to accept that people identified in this way should be committed to a mental hospital instead of a prison may be a tough sell, but with enough evidence the practice could eventually become legal doctrine. By then, one hopes, neuroscience will also have come up with better ways to help rehabilitate or cure them.

Neuroscience and Criminal Defenses

Criminal law currently accepts only a short list of possible defenses—will modern neuroscience begin to add to it? For example, the courts have consistently refused to accept a formal "battered woman defense" from defendants who retaliated with lethal force against spouses who regularly and violently beat them. Nevertheless, in some states the courts do allow experts to testify that battered-woman syndrome is a type of post-traumatic stress disorder, which judges and juries can take into consideration when assessing the credibility of a woman's claim that she acted to protect herself. Such precedents open a door to wider judicial uses of neuroscience.

How one defines a defendant's *mens rea,* or mental state, in a given context has a major effect on how much responsibility to ascribe to him or her. In ongoing fMRI-based research, Read Montague of Baylor College of Medicine and Gideon Yaffe, a law professor at the University of Southern California, study whether certain addicted individuals suffer from a subtle form of "risk blindness." Reasonable people learn not to rob stores by realizing that committing the crime would jeopardize their ability to enjoy a life with friends and family, pursue rewarding careers, and so on. Montague and Yaffe see indications, however, that at least some addicts cannot think through the benefits of those alternative courses of action. Potentially their findings could justify modifying the "reasonable person" standard in criminal law so addicts could be judged against what a reasonable addict, rather than a reasonable nonaddict, would have done in a given situation; such a finding might then lead to acquittal or reduction in punishment for an addicted defendant.

When the foregoing examples are taken together, profound questions emerge about how our culture and the courts will manage antisocial behavior. As neuroscientist William T. Newsome of Stanford University has asked, Will each of us have a personalized "responsibility" ranking that may be called on should we break the law? If we soon all carry our personal medical histories on a memory stick for reference, as some experts predict, will we also perhaps include a profile derived from knowledge of our brain and behavior that captures our reasonableness and irresponsibility? Would this development be good for society and advance justice, or would it be counterproductive? Would it erode notions of free will and personal responsibility more broadly if all antisocial decisions could seemingly be attributed to some kind of neurological deviation?

Would it erode notions of free will and personal responsibility if all antisocial decisions could seemingly be attributed to some kind of neurological deviation?

I feel it is important to keep scientific advances on how the brain enables mind separate from discussions of personal responsibility. People, not brains, commit crimes. As I have spelled out elsewhere, the concept of personal responsibility is something that arises out of social interactions. It is a part of the rules of social exchange, not a part of the brain.

Proceed with Caution

In spite of the many insights pouring forth from neuroscience, recent findings from research into the juvenile mind highlight the need to be cautious when incorporating such science into the law. In 2005 in the case *Roper v. Simmons,* the U.S. Supreme Court held that the execution of a defendant who committed a murder at age 17 or younger was cruel and unusual punishment. It based its opinion on three differences between juveniles and adults: juveniles suffer from an impetuous lack of maturity and responsibility; juveniles are more susceptible to negative influences and lack the independence to remove themselves from bad situations; and a juvenile's character is less formed than an adult's. Although the court realized it was drawing an arbitrary line, it ruled that no person who was younger than 18 at the time of a crime could receive the death penalty.

In May 2010 the court expanded that limitation. In *Graham v. Florida,* it held that for crimes other than homicide, a sentence of life without the possibility of parole for a person under the age of 18 violated the Constitution's prohibition of cruel and unusual punishment. Citing information provided by the American Medical Association, the court stated that "psychology and brain science continue to show fundamental differences between juvenile and adult minds."

But how consistently do neuroscience and psychology support that opinion? A study by Gregory S. Berns, Sara Moore and C. Monica Capra of Emory University explored whether the irrefutable tendency of juveniles to engage in risky behavior resulted from immaturity in the cognitive systems that regulate emotional responses. This team tested the theory using a technology called diffusion tensor imaging (DTI) to examine the tracts of white matter that connect different control regions of the cortex in 91 teenage subjects. Surprisingly, the juveniles who engaged in risky behavior had tracts that looked *more adult* than did those of their more risk-averse peers.

Advanced neuroimaging has thus presented a finding directly contrary to the conventional scientific and legal perspectives on the capacity of juveniles. If further research supports those conclusions, then the law, by its own logic, might need to hold juvenile delinquents to adult criminal standards. Alternatively, justice might require that convicted juveniles undergo DTI or a successor technology to determine whether their white matter structure is adultlike. The results of such a test could then provide guidance to the court on sentencing. The scope of these consequences highlights why the courts should not incorporate insights from neuroscience into the law until a substantial body of studies have confirmed them.

Exciting as the advances that neuroscience is making every day are, all of us should look with caution at how they may gradually come to be incorporated into our culture. The legal relevance of neuroscientific discoveries is only part of the picture. Might we someday want brain scans of our fiancées, business partners or politicians, even if the results could not stand up in court? As the scientific understanding of human nature continues to evolve, our moral stance on how we wish to manage a just society will shift as well. No one I know wants to rush into a new framework without extreme care being given to each new finding. Yet no one can ignore the changes on the horizon.

More to Explore

Patterns of Neural Activity Associated with Honest and Dishonest Moral Decisions. Joshua D. Greene and Joseph M. Paxton in *Proceedings of the National Academy of Sciences USA,* vol. 106, no. 30, pages 12,506–12,511; July 28, 2009.

Adolescent Engagement in Dangerous Behaviors Is Associated with Increased White Matter Maturity of Frontal Cortex. Gregory S. Berns, Sara Moore and C. Monica Capra in *PLoS ONE,* vol. 4, no. 8, e6773; August 26, 2009.

Altered Functional Connectivity in Adult and Juvenile Psychopathy: A Rest-State fMRI Analysis. Benjamin Shannon et al. Abstract from the 16th Annual Meeting of the Organization for Human Brain Mapping. Barcelona, 2010.

Detecting Individual Memories through the Neural Decoding of Memory States and Past Experience. Jesse Rissman, Henry T. Greely and Anthony D. Wagner in *Proceedings of the National Academy of Sciences USA* vol. 107, no. 21, pages 9,849–9,854; May 25, 2010.

Who's in Charge? Free Will and the Science of the Brain. Michael S. Gazzaniga. Ecco HarperColins, 2011.

The Law and Neuroscience Project: www.lawandneuroscience project.org.

Critical Thinking

1. How could brain scans assist criminal defendants?
2. Should courts allow brain scans into evidence?

Article 29

Wrongful Convictions

How Many Innocent Americans Are behind Bars?

RADLEY BALKO

When Paul House was finally released from prison in 2008, he was a specter of the man who had been sentenced to death more than 22 years earlier. When I visit his home in Crossville, Tennessee, in March, House's mother Joyce, who has cared for him since his release, points to a photo of House taken the day he was finally allowed to come home. In that photo and others from his last days in prison, House is all of 150 pounds, ashen and drawn, his fragile frame nearly consumed by his wheelchair. In most of the images he looks days away from death, although in one he wears the broad smile of a man finally escaping a long confinement.

When House's aunt called to congratulate him on his first day back, his mother handed him her cell phone so he could chat. He inspected the phone, gave her a frustrated look, and asked her to find him one that worked. That kind of Rip Van Winkle moment is common among people freed after a long stint in prison. Dennis Fritz, one of the two wrongly convicted men profiled in John Grisham's 2006 book *The Innocent Man,* talks about nearly calling the police upon seeing someone use an electronic key card the first time he found himself in a hotel after his release. He thought he'd witnessed a burglar use a credit card to jimmy open a door.

"Paul's first meal when he got home was chili verde," Joyce House says. "It's his favorite. And I had been waiting a long time to make it for him." And apparently quite a few meals after that. House, now 49, has put on 75 pounds since his release. More important, he has been getting proper treatment for his advanced-stage multiple sclerosis, treatment the Tennessee prison system hadn't given him.

The years of inadequate care have taken a toll. House can't walk, and he needs help with such basic tasks as bathing, feeding himself, and maneuvering around in his wheelchair. His once distinctively deep voice (which had allegedly been heard by a witness at the crime scene) is now wispy and high-pitched. He spends his time playing computer games and watching game shows.

In the hour or so that I visit with House, his mental facilities fade in and out. Communicating with him can be like trying to listen to a baseball game broadcast by a distant radio station. He will give a slurred but lucid answer to one question, then answer the next one with silence, or with the answer to a previous question, or just with a random assortment of words. He frequently falls back on the resigned refrain, "Oh, well," delivered with a shrug. The gesture and phrasing are identical every time he uses them. It's what House says to kill the expectation that he will be able to deliver the words others in the room are waiting for. It's his signal to stop waiting for him and move on.

In 1986 House was convicted of murdering Carolyn Muncey in Union County, Tennessee, a rural part of the state that shoulders Appalachia. He was sentenced to death. His case is a textbook study in wrongful conviction. It includes mishandled evidence, prosecutorial misconduct, bad science, cops with tunnel vision, DNA testing, the near-execution of an innocent man, and an appellate court reluctant to reopen old cases even in the face of new evidence that strongly suggests the jury got it wrong.

House also embodies the tribulations and frustrations that the wrongly convicted encounter once they get out. According to the doctors treating him, his current condition is the direct result of the inadequate care he received in prison. If he is ever granted a formal exoneration—a process that can be as much political as it is judicial—he will be eligible for compensation for his years behind bars, but even then the money comes with vexing conditions and limitations.

Since 1989, DNA testing has freed 268 people who were convicted of crimes they did not commit. There are dozens of other cases, like House's, where DNA strongly suggests innocence but does not conclusively prove it. Convicting and imprisoning an innocent person is arguably the worst thing a government can do to one of its citizens, short of mistakenly executing him. (There's increasing evidence that this has happened too.) Just about everyone agrees that these are unfathomable tragedies. What is far less clear, and still hotly debated, is what these cases say about the way we administer justice in America, what we owe the wrongly convicted, and how the officials who send innocent people to prison should be held accountable.

Since 1989, DNA testing has freed 268 people who were convicted of crimes they did not commit. Seventeen had been sentenced to death. The average exoneree served 13 years in prison before he or she was freed.

How Many Are Innocent?

According to the Innocence Project, an advocacy group that provides legal aid to the wrongly convicted, the average DNA exoneree served 13 years in prison before he or she was freed. Seventeen had been sentenced to death. Remarkably, 67 percent of the exonerated were convicted after 2000, the year that marked the onset of modern DNA testing. Each new exoneration adds more urgency to the question that has hovered over these cases since the first convict was cleared by DNA in 1989: How many more innocent people are waiting to be freed?

Given the soundness of DNA testing, we can be nearly certain that the 268 cleared so far didn't commit the crimes for which they were convicted. There are hundreds of other cases where no DNA evidence exists to definitively establish guilt or innocence, but a prisoner has been freed due to lack of evidence, recantation of eyewitness testimony, or police or prosecutorial misconduct. Those convictions were overturned because there was insufficient evidence to overcome reasonable doubt; it does not necessarily mean the defendant didn't commit the crime. It's unclear whether and how those cases should be factored into any attempt to estimate the number of innocent people in prison.

In a country where there are 15,000 to 20,000 homicides each year, 268 exonerations over two decades may seem like an acceptable margin of error. But reform advocates point out that DNA testing is conclusive only in a small percentage of criminal cases. Testing is helpful only in solving crimes where exchange of DNA is common and significant, mostly rape and murder. (And most murder exonerations have come about because the murder was preceded by a rape that produced testable DNA.) Even within this subset of cases, DNA evidence is not always preserved, nor is it always dispositive to the identity of the perpetrator.

Death penalty cases add urgency to this debate. In a 2007 study published in the *Journal of Criminal Law and Criminology,* the Seton Hall law professor Michael Risinger looked at cases of exoneration for capital murder-rapes between 1982 and 1989, compared them to the total number of murder-rape cases over that period for which DNA would be a factor, and estimated from that data that 3 percent to 5 percent of the people convicted of capital crimes probably are innocent. If Risinger is right, it's still unclear how to extrapolate figures for the larger prison population. Some criminologists argue that there is more pressure on prosecutors and jurors to convict someone, *anyone,* in high-profile murder cases. That would suggest a higher wrongful conviction rate in death penalty cases. But defendants also tend to have better representation in capital cases, and media interest can also mean more scrutiny for police and prosecutors. That could lead to fewer wrongful convictions.

In a study published in the *Journal of Criminal Law and Criminology* in 2005, a team led by University of Michigan law professor Samuel Gross looked at 328 exonerations of people who had been convicted of rape, murder, and other felonies between 1989 and 2003. They found that while those who have been condemned to die make up just 1 percent of the prison population, they account for 22 percent of the exonerated. But does that mean capital cases are more likely to bring a wrongful conviction? Or does it mean the attention and scrutiny that death penalty cases get after conviction—particularly as an execution date nears—make it more likely that wrongful convictions in capital cases will be discovered?

Many states have special public defender offices that take over death penalty cases after a defendant has exhausted his appeals. These offices tend to be well-staffed, with enough funding to hire their own investigators and forensic specialists. That sometimes stands in stark contrast to the public defender offices that handled the same cases at trial. Perversely, this means that in some jurisdictions, a defendant wrongly convicted of murder may be better off with a death sentence than with life in prison.

Even if we were to drop below the floor set in the Risinger study and assume that 2 percent of the 2008 prison population was innocent, that would still mean about 46,000 people have been convicted and incarcerated for crimes they didn't commit. But some skeptics say even that figure is way too high.

Joshua Marquis, the district attorney for Clatsop County, Oregon, is an outspoken critic of the Innocence Project and of academics like Risinger and Gross. He is skeptical of the belief that wrongful convictions are common. "If I thought that 3 to 5 percent of people in prison right now were innocent, I'd quit my job," Marquis says. "I'd become a public defender or something. Maybe an activist. Look, nobody but a fool would say that wrongful convictions don't happen. As a prosecutor, my worst nightmare is not losing a case—I've lost cases; I'll lose cases in the future. My worst nightmare is convicting an innocent person, and I tell my staff that. But the question here is whether wrongful convictions are epidemic or episodic. And I just don't think it's possible that the number could be anywhere near 3 to 5 percent."

"If I thought that 3 to 5 percent of people in prison right now were innocent, I'd quit my job," says Clatsop County, Oregon, District Attorney Joshua Marquis. "I'd become a public defender or something."

Marquis and Gross have been butting heads for several years. In a 2006 *New York Times* op-ed piece, Marquis took the 328 exonerations Gross and his colleagues found between 1989 and 2003, rounded it up to 340, then multiplied it by 10—a charitable act, he wrote, to "give the professor the benefit of the doubt." He then divided that number by 15 million, the total number of felony convictions during the same period, and came up with what he said was an error rate of just 0.027 percent. His column was later quoted in a concurring opinion by U.S. Supreme Court Justice Antonin Scalia in the 2006 case *Kansas v. Marsh,* the same opinion where Scalia made the notorious claim that nothing in the U.S. Constitution prevents the government from executing an innocent person.

Gross responded with a 2008 article in the *Annual Review of Law and Social Science,* pointing out that his original number was by no means comprehensive. Those were merely the cases in which a judicial or political process had exonerated someone. The figure suggested only that wrongful convictions *happen.* "By [Marquis'] logic we could estimate the proportion of baseball players who've used steroids by dividing the number of major league players who've been caught by the total of all baseball players at all levels: major league, minor league, semipro, college and Little League," Gross wrote, "and maybe throw in football and basketball players as well."

Whatever the total number of innocent convicts, there is good reason to believe that the 268 cases in which DNA evidence has proven innocence don't begin to scratch the surface. For one thing, the pace of these exonerations hasn't slowed down: There were 22 in 2009, making it the second busiest name-clearing year to date. Furthermore, exonerations are expensive in both time and resources. Merely discovering a possible case and requesting testing often isn't enough. With some commendable exceptions, prosecutors tend to fight requests for post-conviction DNA testing. (The U.S. Supreme Court held in 2009 that there is no constitutional right to such tests.) So for now, the pace of genetic exonerations appears to be limited primarily by the amount of money and staff that legal advocacy groups have to uncover these cases and argue them in court, the amount of evidence available for testing, and the willingness of courts to allow the process to happen, not by a lack of cases in need of further investigation.

It's notable that one of the few places in America where a district attorney has specifically dedicated staff and resources to seeking out bad convictions—Dallas County, Texas—has produced more exonerations than all but a handful of *states*. That's partly because Dallas County District Attorney Craig Watkins is more interested in reopening old cases than his counterparts elsewhere, and partly because of a historical quirk: Since the early 1980s the county has been sending biological crime scene evidence to a private crime lab for testing, and that lab has kept the evidence well preserved. Few states require such evidence be preserved once a defendant has exhausted his appeals, and in some jurisdictions the evidence is routinely destroyed at that point.

"I don't think there was anything unique about the way Dallas was prosecuting crimes," Watkins told me in 2008. "It's unfortunate that other places didn't preserve evidence too. We're just in a unique position where I can look at a case, test DNA evidence from that period, and say without a doubt that a person is innocent. . . . But that doesn't mean other places don't have the same problems Dallas had."

If the rest of the country has an actual (but undetected) wrongful conviction rate as high as Dallas County's, the number of innocents in prison for felony crimes could be in the tens of thousands.

If the rest of the country has an actual (but undetected) wrongful conviction rate as high as Dallas County's, the number of innocents in prison for felony crimes could be in the tens of thousands.

The Trial and Conviction of Paul House

As with many wrongful convictions, the case against Paul House once seemed watertight. House was an outsider, having only recently moved to Union County when Carolyn Muncey was murdered in 1985, and he was an ex-con, having served five years in a Utah prison for sexual assault. He got into scuffles with locals, although he considered Muncey and her husband, Hubert, friends. When Muncey turned up dead, House was a natural suspect.

House has claimed he was innocent of the Utah charge. His mother, Joyce, says it was a he said/she said case in which her son pleaded guilty on the advice of his attorney. "He could have been paroled earlier if he had shown some remorse," she says. "But he said, 'I pled guilty the one time, because that's what the lawyer told me I should do. I'm not going to say again that I did something I didn't do.' He said he'd rather serve more time than admit to the rape again." Joyce House and Mike Pemberton, Paul House's attorney, are hesitant to go into much detail about the Utah case, and public records aren't available due to the plea bargain. But while what happened in Utah certainly makes House less sympathetic, it has no bearing on whether House is the man who killed Carolyn Muncey.

House also didn't do himself any favors during the Muncey investigation. In initial questioning, he lied to the police about where he was the night of the murder, saying he was with his girlfriend all night. But he later admitted he had gone for a walk at one point and had come back without his shoes and with scratches on his arms. He initially lied to police about the scratches too, saying they were inflicted by his girlfriend's cats. House later said he'd been accosted by some locals while on his walk, scuffled with them, then fled through a field, where he lost his shoes. (House would learn years later that his shoes were found by police before his trial. There was no blood or other biological evidence on them, potentially exculpatory information that was never turned over to House's lawyers.)

"I think it was a situation where you're on parole, you're an outsider, and this woman has just been killed near where you live," says Pemberton, House's attorney. "It wasn't smart of him to lie to the police. But it was understandable."

Carolyn Muncey's husband, who House's attorneys would later suspect was her killer, also lied about where he was when she was killed. He would additionally claim, falsely, that he had never physically abused her. Still, House was clearly the early suspect.

The strongest evidence against House was semen found on Muncey's clothing, which an FBI agent testified at trial "could have" belonged to House. DNA testing didn't exist in 1986, but the agent said House was a secretor, meaning he produced blood type secretions in other body fluids, including semen, and that the type secreted in semen found on Muncey's nightgown was a match to House's type A blood. About 80 percent of people are secretors, and about 36 percent of Americans have type A blood. The agent also said the semen found on Muncey's panties included secretions that *didn't* match House's blood type, but added, inaccurately, that House's secretion could have "degraded" into a match. Muncey's husband was never tested.

The other strong evidence against House was some blood stains on his jeans that matched Muncey's blood type, but not his own. Those stains on House's jeans did turn out to have been Muncey's blood; the question is how they got there.

House was never charged with rape; there were no physical indications that Muncey had been sexually assaulted. But the semen was used to put him at the crime scene, and the state used the possibility of rape as an aggravating circumstance in arguing that House should receive the death penalty.

House was convicted in February 1986. The morning after his conviction, just hours before the sentencing portion of his trial, House slashed his wrists with a disposable razor. He left behind a suicide note in which he professed his innocence. Jail officials rushed him to a hospital in Knoxville, where doctors saved his life and stitched up his wounds. He was then sent back to the courthouse, where a jury sentenced him to death.

It wasn't until more than a decade later, in 1999, that the case against House began to erode. New witnesses came forward with accusations against Hubert Muncey, Carolyn's husband. Several said he was an alcoholic who frequently beat her. At an ensuing evidentiary hearing, two other women said Hubert had drunkenly confessed to killing his wife several months after the murder. When one went to the police with the information the next day, she said at the hearing, the sheriff brushed her off. Another witness testified that Hubert Muncey had asked her to lie to back up his alibi.

But it was the forensic evidence presented at that 1999 hearing that really unraveled the state's case. When House's attorneys were finally able to get DNA testing for the semen found on Carolyn Muncey's clothes, it showed that the semen was a match to Muncey's husband, not House. The state responded that rape was never part of their case against House (though it is why he was initially a suspect, it was the only conceivable motive, and it was presented as evidence in the sentencing portion of his trial). Besides, prosecutors argued, there was still the blood on House's jeans.

Except there were problems with that too. Cleland Blake, an assistant chief medical examiner for the state of Tennessee, testified that while the blood did belong to Muncey, its chemical composition indicated it was blood that had been taken *after* she had been autopsied. Worse still, three-quarters of a test tube of the blood taken during Muncey's autopsy went missing between the time of the autopsy and the time House's jeans arrived at the FBI crime lab for testing. The test tubes with Muncey's blood and House's jeans were transported in the same Styrofoam box. The blood on House's jeans, his attorneys argued, must have either been planted or spilled because of sloppy handling of the evidence.

It is extraordinarily difficult to win a new trial in a felony case, even in light of new evidence, and House's case was no exception. A federal circuit court judge denied his request for post-conviction relief, and the U.S. Court of Appeals for the 6th Circuit affirmed that decision. Somewhat surprisingly, the U.S. Supreme Court agreed to hear House's case, and in 2006 issued a rare, bitterly divided 5-to-3 ruling granting House a new trial.

The Supreme Court has occasionally thrown out death penalty convictions because of procedural errors or constitutional violations, but it's rare for the Court to methodically review the evidence in a capital case. Writing for the majority, Justice Anthony Kennedy did exactly that, finding in the end that "although the issue is close, we conclude that this is the rare case where—had the jury heard all the conflicting testimony—it is more likely than not that no reasonable juror viewing the record as a whole would lack reasonable doubt."

It was a surprising and significant victory for House. But it would be another three years before he would be released from prison.

How Do Wrongful Convictions Happen?

The most significant consequence of the spate of DNA exonerations has been a much-needed reassessment of what we thought we knew about how justice is administered in America. Consider the chief causes of wrongful convictions:

Bad forensic evidence. DNA technology was developed by scientists, and it has been thoroughly peer-reviewed by other scientists. Most of the forensic science used in the courtroom, on the other hand, was either invented in police stations and crime labs or has been refined and revised there to fight crime and obtain convictions. Most forensic evidence isn't peer-reviewed, isn't subject to blind testing, and is susceptible to corrupting bias, both intentional and unintentional. The most careful analysts can fall victim to cognitive bias creeping into their work, particularly when their lab falls under the auspices of a law enforcement agency. Even fingerprint analysis isn't as sound as is commonly believed.

A congressionally commissioned 2009 report by the National Academy of Sciences found that many other forensic specialties that are often presented in court with the gloss of science—hair and carpet fiber analysis, blood spatter analysis, shoe print identification, and especially bite mark analysis—lack the standards, peer review, and testing procedures of genuinely scientific research and analysis. Some are not supported by any scientific literature at all. Moreover, the report found, even the forensic specialties with some scientific support are often portrayed in court in ways that play down error rates and cognitive bias.

According to an Innocence Project analysis of the first 225 DNA exonerations, flawed or fraudulent forensic evidence factored into about half of the faulty convictions.

Eyewitness testimony. Social scientists have known about the inherent weakness of eyewitness testimony for decades. Yet it continues to be the leading cause of wrongful convictions in America; it was a factor in 77 percent of those first 225 cases. Simple steps, such as making sure police who administer lineups have no knowledge of the case (since they can give subtle clues to witnesses, even unintentionally) and that witnesses are told that the actual perpetrator may not be among the photos included in a lineup, can go a long way toward improving accuracy. But such reforms also make it more difficult to win convictions, so many jurisdictions, under pressure from police and prosecutor groups, have been hesitant to embrace them.

False confessions. Difficult as it may be to comprehend, people do confess to crimes they didn't commit. It happened in about one-quarter of the first 225 DNA exonerations. Confessions are more common among suspects who are minors or are mentally handicapped, but they can happen in other contexts as well, particularly after intense or abusive police interrogations.

In a candid 2008 op-ed piece for the *Los Angeles Times,* D.C. Police Detective Jim Trainum detailed how he unwittingly coaxed a false confession out of a 34-year-old woman he suspected of murder. She even revealed details about the crime that could only have been known to police investigators and the killer. But Trainum later discovered that the woman couldn't possibly have committed the crime. When he reviewed video of his interrogation, he realized that he had inadvertently provided the woman with those very specific details, which she then repeated back to him when she was ready to confess.

Trainum concluded that all police interrogations should be videotaped, a policy that would not just discourage abusive questioning but also provide an incontrovertible record of how a suspect's confession was obtained. Here too, however, there has been push-back from some police agencies, out of fear that jurors may be turned off even by legitimate forms of questioning.

Jailhouse informants. If you were to take every jailhouse informant at his word, you'd find that a remarkably high percentage of the people accused of felonies boast about their crimes to the complete strangers they meet in jail and prison cells. Informants are particularly valuable in federal drug cases, where helping a prosecutor obtain more convictions is often the only way to get time cut from a mandatory minimum sentence. That gives them a pretty good incentive to lie.

There is some disagreement over a prosecutor's duty to verify the testimony he solicits from jailhouse informants. In the 2006, Church Point, Louisiana, case of Ann Colomb, for example, Brett Grayson, an assistant U.S. attorney in Louisiana, put on a parade of jailhouse informants whose claims about buying drugs from Colomb and her sons were rather improbable, especially when the sum of their testimony was considered as a whole. According to defense attorneys I spoke with, when one attorney asked him if he actually believed what his informants were telling the jury, Grayson replied that it doesn't matter if he believes his witnesses; it only matters if the jury does. He expressed a similar sentiment in his closing argument.

After indicating that he isn't familiar with the Colomb case and isn't commenting on Grayson specifically, Josh Marquis says that sentiment is wrong. "A prosecutor absolutely has a duty to only put on evidence he believes is truthful," Marquis says. "And that includes the testimony you put on from informants."

In a 2005 study, the Center on Wrongful Convictions in Chicago found that false or misleading informant testimony was responsible for 38 wrongful convictions in death penalty cases.

The professional culture of the criminal justice system. In addition to the more specific causes of wrongful convictions listed above, there is a problem with the institutional culture among prosecutors, police officers, forensic analysts, and other officials. Misplaced incentives value high conviction rates more than a fair and equal administration of justice.

Prosecutors in particular enjoy absolute immunity from civil liability, even in cases where they manufacture evidence that leads to a wrongful conviction. The only time prosecutors can be sued is when they commit misconduct while acting as investigators—that is, while doing something police normally do. At that point they're subject to qualified immunity, which provides less protection than absolute immunity but still makes it difficult to recover damages.

Marquis says this isn't a problem. "Prosecutors are still subject to criminal liability," he says. "In fact, my predecessor here in Oregon was prosecuted for misconduct in criminal cases. State bars will also hold prosecutors accountable."

But criminal charges are few and far between, and prosecutors can make egregious mistakes that still don't rise to the level of criminal misconduct. Professional sanctions are also rare. A 2010 study by the Northern California Innocence Project found more than 700 examples between 1997 and 2009 in which a court had found misconduct on the part of a prosecutor in the state. Only six of those cases resulted in any disciplinary action by the state bar. A 2010 investigation of federal prosecutorial misconduct by *USA Today* produced similar results: Of 201 cases in which federal judges found that prosecutors had committed misconduct, just one resulted in discipline by a state bar association. Prosecutorial misconduct was a factor in about one-quarter of the first 225 DNA exonerations, but none of the prosecutors in those cases faced any significant discipline from the courts or the bar.

There is also a common misconception that appeals courts serve as a check on criminal justice abuse. It is actually rare for an appeals court to review the evidence in a criminal case. Appeals courts make sure trials abide by the state and federal constitutions and by state or federal rules of criminal procedure, but they almost never second-guess the conclusions of juries.

In a 2008 article published in the *Columbia Law Review,* the University of Virginia law professor Brandon L. Garrett looked at the procedural history of the first 200 cases of DNA exoneration. Of those, just 18 convictions were reversed by appellate courts. Another 67 defendants had their appeals denied with no written ruling at all. In 63 cases, the appellate court opinion described the defendant as guilty, and in 12 cases it referred to the "overwhelming" evidence of guilt. Keep in mind these were all cases in which DNA testing later proved actual innocence. In the remaining cases, the appeals courts either found the defendant's appeal without merit or found that the errors in the case were "harmless"—that is, there were problems with the case, but those problems were unlikely to have affected the jury's verdict due to the other overwhelming evidence of guilt.

"We've seen a lot of exoneration cases where, for example, the defendant raised a claim of ineffective assistance of counsel," says Peter Neufeld, co-founder of the Innocence Project of New York. "And in those cases, the appellate courts often found that the defense lawyer provided sub standard representation. But they would then say that the poor lawyering didn't prejudice the case because the evidence of guilt was so overwhelming. Well, these people were later proven innocent! If you have a test that is frequently producing erroneous results, there's either something wrong with the test, or there's something wrong with the way it's being implemented."

Life on the Outside

Paul House was diagnosed with multiple sclerosis in 2000, a year after the evidentiary hearing that would eventually lead to his release. But while House was convicted of Carolyn Muncey's murder less than a year after it happened, it took a decade after his conviction was called into serious question for House to get back home to Crossville. During those 10 years, the state's case continued to fall apart. So did House's body.

After the U.S. Supreme Court overturned House's conviction in 2006, Paul Phillips, the district attorney for Tennessee's 8th Judicial District and the man who prosecuted House in 1986, pushed ahead with plans to retry him. In December 2007, after a series of delays, Harry S. Mattice Jr., a U.S. district court judge in Knoxville, finally ordered the state to try House within 180 days or set him free. Those 180 days then came and went without House being freed, thanks to an extension granted by the 6th Circuit.

In another hearing held in May 2008, Phillips argued that House—who by that point couldn't walk or move his wheelchair without assistance—presented a flight risk. Later, Tennessee Associate Deputy Attorney General Jennifer Smith attempted to show that House presented a danger to the public because he was still capable of feeding himself with a fork, which apparently meant he was also capable of stabbing someone with one. House's bail was set at $500,000, later reduced to $100,000. In July 2008, an anonymous donor paid the bail, allowing House to finally leave prison.

That same month, Phillips told the Associated Press that he would send two additional pieces of biological evidence off for DNA testing: a hair found at the crime scene, and blood found under Carolyn Muncey's fingernails. House's defense team had asked to conduct its own testing of any untested biological evidence for years, but had been told that either there was no such evidence or, if there was, the state didn't know where it was. Philips told the A.P. that if the new tests didn't implicate House, he would drop the murder charge and allow House to go home. In February 2009 the results came back. They didn't implicate House, and in fact pointed to a third, unidentified man. In May of that year, Phillips finally dropped the charge. But he still wouldn't clear House's name, telling Knoxville's local TV station WATE, "There is very adequate proof that Mr. House was involved in this crime. We just don't know the degree of culpability beyond a reasonable doubt." (Phillips' office did not respond to my requests for comment.)

By the time House was diagnosed with M.S. in 2000, his symptoms were already severe, although it took his mother, and not a prison doctor, to notice something was wrong. "I was visiting him, and I brought along some microwave popcorn," Joyce House recalls. "He asked me to heat it up, and I said, 'No, you heat it up.' When he got up, he had to prop himself up and drag along the wall to get to the microwave. He couldn't even stand up straight." According to Joyce House, her son's doctors today say that the Tennessee prison system's failure to diagnose House's M.S. earlier—then treat it properly after it was diagnosed—may have taken years off his life. (M.S. is also exacerbated by stress.) The disease has also significantly diminished the quality of the life House has left.

Under Tennessee's compensation law for the wrongly convicted, if House is formally exonerated—and that's still a big *if*—he will be eligible for $50,000 for each year he was in prison, up to $1 million. But there's a catch. The compensation is given in annual $50,000 installments over 20 years. If House dies before then, the payments stop.

Most of the 27 states with compensation laws similarly pay the money off in installments. Last October, A.P. ran a story about Victor Burnette, a 57-year-old Virginia man who served eight years for a 1979 rape before he was exonerated by DNA testing in 2006. Burnette actually turned down the $226,500 the state offered in compensation in 2010 because he was offended by the stipulation that it be paid out over 25 years. Even after the DNA test confirmed his innocence, it took another three years for Burnette to officially be pardoned, which finally made him eligible for the money. The installment plans make it unlikely that many exonerees—especially long-timers, who are arguably the most deserving—will ever see full compensation for their years in prison.

Only about half the people exonerated by DNA testing so far have been compensated at all. Most compensation laws require official findings of actual innocence, which eliminates just about any case that doesn't involve DNA. Some states also exclude anyone who played some role in their own conviction, which would disqualify a defendant who falsely confessed, even if the confession was coerced or beaten out of them.

Only about half the people exonerated by DNA testing so far have been compensated at all.

Paul House has yet another predicament ahead of him. Even if he does win an official exoneration, and even if he somehow lives long enough to receive all of his compensation, he'll have to lose his health insurance to accept it. House's medical care is currently covered by TennCare, Tennessee's Medicare program. If he accepts compensation for his conviction, he will be ineligible. His $50,000 per year in compensation for nearly a quarter century on death row will then be offset by a steep increase in what he'll have to pay for his medical care.

These odd, sometimes absurd predicaments aren't intentionally cruel. They just work out that way. Paul House's attorney Mike Pemberton points out that the prosecutors in these cases aren't necessarily evil, either. "Paul Phillips is an honorable man, and an outstanding trial attorney," Pemberton says. "But on this case he was wrong." Pemberton, who was once a prosecutor himself, says the job can lend itself to tunnel vision, especially once a prosecutor has won a conviction. It can be hard to let go. We have a system with misplaced incentives and very little accountability for state actors who make mistakes. That's a system ripe for bad outcomes.

When I ask Paul House why he thinks it has taken so long to clear his name, he starts to answer, then stammers, looks away, and retreats again to *Oh well,* his cue to move on because he has no answer.

That may be an understandable response from a guy with advanced M.S. who just spent two decades on death row. But for too long our national response to the increasing evidence that our justice system is flawed has been the same sort of resignation. DNA has only begun to show us where some of those flaws lie. It will take a strong public will to see that policymakers address them.

Critical Thinking

1. When innocent people who were wrongly convicted are exonerated, how are they compensated?
2. Should states that have the death penalty reconsider it?
3. Do you agree with Marquis' analysis of the incidence of wrongful convictions?
4. Do you believe Dallas County is unique regarding bad convictions?
5. What do you think of the prosecutor's reaction to House's conviction being overturned?

Radley Balko (rbalko@reason.com) is a senior editor at *Reason*.

UNIT 5

Juvenile Justice

Unit Selections

Learning Outcomes

After reading this unit, you will be able to:

- State risk factors for adolescent dating.
- Discuss what the various studies show about teenage dating violence.
- Distinguish between a juvenile offender whose life is now crime-free and one who is leading a successful life.
- State the risk factors for bringing children into the court system for minor infractions.
- Discuss the consequences of mental health problems for some children.
- Describe some of the problems facing politicians regarding young offenders in California.
- Define cognitive behavioral therapy and show how it can be applied to criminal offenders.
- Discuss why Americans should be concerned about the way teenagers who commit crimes are treated by the criminal justice system.

Student Website

www.mhhe.com/cls

Internet References

Gang Land: The Jerry Capeci Page
www.ganglandnews.com

Institute for Intergovernmental Research (IIR)
www.iir.com

National Criminal Justice Reference Service (NCJRS)
www.ncjrs.gov

Partnership Against Violence Network
www.padv.org

Although there were variations within specific offense categories, the overall arrest rate for juvenile violent crime remained relatively constant for several decades. Then, in the late 1980s, something changed; more and more juveniles charged with a violent offense were brought into the justice system. The juvenile justice system is a twentieth-century response to the problems of dealing with children in trouble with the law, or children who need society's protection.

Juvenile court procedure differs from the procedure in adult courts because juvenile courts are based on the philosophy that their function is to treat and to help, not to punish and abandon, the offender. Recently, operations of the juvenile court have received criticism, and a number of significant Supreme Court decisions have changed the way that the courts must approach the rights of children. Despite these changes, however, the major thrust of the juvenile justice system remains one of diversion and treatment, rather than adjudication and incarceration, although there is a trend toward dealing more punitively with serious juvenile offenders.

In this unit's opening article, "Violence in Adolescent Dating Relationships," the authors cover the violent side of dating relationships and why this continues to be a problem. Next, in "Misbehavior," Donna St. George reports that some states are examining discipline practices in schools, including law enforcement referrals and school ticketing. In Texas, police issue tickets to students for misconduct in school, such as schoolyard fights, offensive language, and class disruption, and thousands of students end up in court with fines of up to $500.

In the next article, Colette S. Peters and Shannon Myrick look at the issue of recidivism and argue that it should be connected to positive youth outcomes, not just staying out of trouble, in "Juvenile Recidivism—Measuring Success or Failure: Is There a Difference?" Following is "Whither Young Offenders? The Debate Has Begun," an article in which Trey Bundy reports that California's juvenile prison system, in the opinion of one former inmate, was no better than the streets he came from.

"At D.C. Superior Court Program, a Focus on Helping Minors with Mental Health Problems," is an article in which Justin Moyer writes about a new program in D.C. Superior Court that recognizes that kids who get in trouble may have undiagnosed mental health problems. A juvenile court has been established there to help minors with mental health problems avoid the harsh consequences and limited rehabilitation opportunities in the juvenile system.

© Brand X Picture

The next article deals with a youth who committed murder and was prosecuted as an adult. Rachael Aviv, in "No Remorse," describes someone who was 14 when he killed his grandfather, and who showed no remorse about it. The expectation that defendants will display remorse, either shortly after their crimes or else never, is generally accepted as common sense. But a study of juveniles charged with violent crimes found a more complicated reality. Then, according to Patrick Clark in "Preventing Future Crime with Cognitive Behavioral Therapy," reduction in future criminal behavior can be accomplished by therapeutic approaches based on counseling, skill building, and other services.

This section ends with "Opinion Recap: Narrow Ruling on Young Murderers' Sentences," in which Lyle Denniston reports on the Supreme Court's decision barring a mandatory life sentence for minors who commit murder. The article considers the application of this decision to other situations for minors.

Violence in Adolescent Dating Relationships

"The early- to mid-teenage years mark a time in which romantic relationships begin to emerge. From a developmental perspective, these relationships can serve a number of positive functions. However, for many adolescents, there is a darker side: dating violence."

ERNEST N. JOURILES, CORA PLATT, AND RENEE MCDONALD

For many, the early- to mid-teenage years mark a time in which romantic relationships begin to emerge. From a developmental perspective, these relationships can serve a number of positive functions. However, for many adolescents, there is a darker side: dating violence. In this article, we discuss the definition and measurement of adolescent dating violence, review epidemiological findings regarding victimization, and describe correlates of victimization experiences. We end with a discussion of prevention and intervention programs designed to address adolescent dating violence and highlight important gaps in our knowledge.

Defining and Measuring Adolescent Dating and Dating Violence

"Dating" among adolescents is complicated to define and measure, in part because the nature of dating changes dramatically over the course of adolescence (Connolly et al., 1999; Feiring, 1996). In early adolescence, dating involves getting together with small groups of friends of both sexes to do things together as a group. From these group experiences, adolescents progress to going out with or dating a single individual. Initial single-dating relationships are typically casual and short-term; more serious, exclusive, and longer-lasting relationships emerge in mid- to late-adolescence.

"Dating" among adolescents is complicated to define and measure.

In research on adolescent dating violence, adolescents are often asked to respond to questions about a "boyfriend" or "girlfriend" or someone with whom they have "been on a date with or gone out with." However, what constitutes a boyfriend or girlfriend or a dating partner is not clear, and these judgments are likely to vary tremendously across adolescents. These judgments are probably also influenced by a number of factors including the amount of time spent with each other, the degree of emotional attachment, and the activities engaged in together (Allen, 2004). They are also likely to change over the course of adolescence, as youth mature and become more experienced with dating.

Most everyone has a general idea about what constitutes "violence" in adolescent dating relationships, but not everyone conceptualizes and defines it the same way. In the empirical literature, multiple types of dating violence have been studied, including physical, sexual, and psychological violence. Definitions for these different types of violence vary from study to study, but each is typically based on adolescents' reports of the occurrence of specific acts. For example, physical violence often refers to adolescents' reports of hits, slaps, or beatings; sexual violence refers to forced kissing, touching, or intercourse; and psychological violence to reports of insults, threats, or the use of control tactics. These different types of violence are sometimes further subdivided. For example, indirect aggression (also referred to as relational or social aggression), which includes spreading hurtful rumors or telling cruel stories about a dating partner, has recently begun to be conceptualized as a form of dating violence that may be distinct from more overt forms of psychological or emotional abuse (Wolfe, Scott, Reitzel-Jaffe et al., 2001). As another example, in a recent prevalence study, sexual assault was distinguished from drug- or alcohol-facilitated rape, with the latter defined as sexual assault that occurred while the victim was "high, drunk, or passed out from drinking or taking drugs" (Wolitzky-Taylor et al., 2008).

In the bulk of studies on adolescent dating violence, the youth are surveyed about the occurrence of specific acts of violence within a particular time period, for example, during the previous 12 months. These surveys are typically administered on a single occasion, in either a questionnaire or interview format. Some include only one or two questions about violence; others include comprehensive scales of relationship violence with excellent psychometric properties (e.g., Wolfe et al., 2001). A handful of investigators have attempted to study adolescent dating violence using other methods, such as laboratory observations (e.g., Capaldi, Kimm, & Shortt, 2007), and repeated interviews over a short, circumscribed period of time (e.g., Jouriles et al., 2005). However, studies using alternatives to one-time, self-report survey assessments are few and far between.

This first section highlights some of the complexities involved in conceptualizing adolescent dating violence and describes how different types of dating violence are often defined and measured, providing a backdrop for understanding and interpreting empirical findings in the literature. As illustrated in the section below, different conceptualizations and definitions of dating violence lead to different research findings and conclusions. Similarly, various data collection methods (such as using more questions and/or repeated questioning) also yield different results. At the present time, there is no gold standard with respect to defining or measuring adolescent dating violence; the field is still developing in this regard.

Prevalence of Adolescent Dating Violence

Over the past decade, data from several different national surveys have been used to estimate the prevalence of the various forms of adolescent dating violence. Surveys conducted by the Centers for Disease Control suggest that 9–10% of students in grades 9–12 indicate that a boyfriend or girlfriend has hit, slapped, or physically hurt them on purpose during the previous 12 months, and approximately 8% report having been physically forced to have sexual intercourse against their wishes (Howard, Wang, & Yan, 2007a, 2007b). The 2005 National Survey of Adolescents (NSA) indicates that 1.6% of adolescents between 12 and 17 years of age have experienced "serious dating violence" (Wolitzky-Taylor et al., 2008). Serious dating violence was defined as experiencing one or more of the following forms of violence from a dating partner: physical violence (badly injured, beaten up, or threatened with a knife or gun), sexual violence (forced anal, vaginal, or oral sex; forced penetration with a digit or an object; forced touching of genitalia), or drug/alcohol-facilitated rape.

Most studies in this area ask about male-to-female and female-to-male violence or include gender-neutral questions without assessing whether a respondent is in an opposite-sex or same-sex relationship. The National Longitudinal Study of Adolescent Health is unique in that it reports data on violence in opposite-sex as well as same-sex romantic relationships. As can be seen in Table 1, prevalence rates for both physical and psychological violence are similar in opposite-sex and same-sex romantic relationships among adolescents in grades 7–12.

Table 1 Prevalence of Dating Violence in Same-Sex and Opposite-Sex Romantic Relationships

Data from National Longitudinal Study of Adolescent Health

In the previous 18 months partner had been:	Opposite-sex relationship	Same-sex relationship
Physically violent	12%	11%
Psychologically violent	29%	21%

Halpern, Oslak, Young, Martin, & Kupper, 2001; Halpern, Young, Waller, Martin, & Kupper, 2004.

Prevalence rates for both physical and psychological violence are similar in opposite-sex and same-sex romantic relationships among adolescents in grades 7–12.

The prevalence of physical dating violence appears to be fairly similar across studies of national samples. Variation across estimates most likely reflects differences in how violence is defined, and perhaps differences in the samples from which the estimates were derived (e.g., different age ranges sampled). It should be noted that prevalence estimates based on smaller, less representative, localized samples tend to be higher than those based on national samples. In fact, a number of researchers have reported prevalence estimates for physical dating violence among adolescents (over a one-year period or less) to be over 40% (Hickman, Jaycox, & Aronoff, 2004). These elevated estimates might stem directly from sampling differences, but also perhaps from differences in the conceptualization and measurement of dating violence. For example, in many of the smaller samples, investigators assessed dating violence more extensively (such as using more questions and/or through repeated questioning), which might contribute to higher prevalence estimates.

Taken together, the results across studies yield some general conclusions about the nature and scope of adolescent dating violence. Regardless of how it is defined, it appears that a substantial number of United States youth are affected by dating violence. Even with very conservative definitions, such as the one used in the NSA, it was projected that approximately 400,000 adolescents have been victims, at some point in their lives, of serious dating violence (Wolitzky-Taylor et al., 2008).

Psychological violence appears to be much more common than either physical or sexual violence. Data are mixed on the relative prevalence of physical and sexual violence, but some of the national surveys suggest that they are approximately equal in prevalence.

Onset and Course

Dating violence appears to emerge well before high school. For example, cross-sex teasing and harassment, which involve behaviors often construed as either psychological or sexual violence, is evident among 6th graders and increases in prevalence over time (McMaster et al., 2002). One-third of a sample of 7th graders who indicated that they had started dating also reported that they had committed acts of aggression (physical, sexual, or psychological) toward a dating partner; in over half of these cases, physical or sexual aggression was involved (Sears et al., 2007). In the NSA, serious dating violence victimization was not reported by 12-year-olds, but it was by 13-year-olds (Wolitzky-Taylor et al., 2008).

Longitudinal data on the course of adolescent dating violence are scarce, but there is evidence that psychological aggression predicts subsequent physical aggression (O'Leary & Slep, 2003). In fact, different types of dating violence commonly co-occur within adolescent relationships, with the occurrence of one type of violence (physical, psychological, or sexual) associated with an increased likelihood of other types of violence (Sears, Byers, & Price, 2007). In research on interpersonal victimization in general, victims of violence are known to be at increased risk for subsequent victimization. This appears to be true for victims of adolescent dating violence as well (Smith, White, & Holland, 2003).

Demographics of Adolescent Dating Violence

Certain demographic variables including age, race and ethnicity, geographic location, and sex are associated with increased risk for victimization. Specifically, the risk for dating violence victimization increases with age, at least through the middle and high school years. This trend appears to be true for physical, psychological, and sexual violence (e.g., Halpern et al., 2001; Howard et al., 2007a, 2007b; Wolitzky-Taylor et al., 2008). This might be attributable to a number of things, including the changing nature of dating over the course of adolescence. Some evidence has emerged pointing to racial and ethnic differences in adolescents' experiences of dating violence, but other recent, large-scale studies call these findings into question. For example, a number of investigators have found Black adolescents to be more likely than their White counterparts to experience physical and sexual dating violence (e.g., Howard et al., 2007a, 2007b). However, these differences have sometimes disappeared when other variables, such as prior exposures to violence, are considered (Malik, Sorenson, & Aneshensel, 1997). Moreover, recent, well-designed studies of very large samples have found no evidence of racial or ethnic differences in adolescent victimization (e.g., O'Leary et al., 2008; Wolitzky-Taylor et al., 2008). There do appear to be regional differences in dating violence, with adolescents in southern states at substantially greater risk for experiencing dating violence than adolescents in other regions of the U.S. (Marquart, et al., 2007). Although the reasons for regional differences are not known, it is interesting to note that the South has a higher prevalence rate of overall violence than other regions in the U.S. In short, there may be factors in the Southern U.S. that facilitate the promotion, acceptance, or tolerance of violent behavior.

When violence is defined broadly, prevalence rates for male and female victimization tend to be similar (e.g., Halpern et al., 2001). However, narrower definitions of violence point to some sex differences in the experience of violence. For example, female adolescents are more likely than males to experience severe physical violence (violent acts that are likely to result, or actually have resulted, in physical injuries) and sexual violence (e.g., Molidor & Tolman, 1998; Wolitzky-Taylor et al., 2008). Females are also more likely than males to experience fear, hurt, and the desire to leave the situation for self-protection (Molidor & Tolman, 1998; Jackson, Cram, & Seymour, 2000). In addition, females are more likely to report physical injuries and more harmful and persistent psychological distress after being victimized (O'Keefe, 1997).

Correlates of Adolescent Dating Violence

Most of the findings on the correlates of adolescent dating violence come from studies in which data were collected at a single point in time. Thus, it is difficult to discern if observed correlates are precursors or consequences of the violence, or if they are simply related to experiencing violence, but not in a cause-and-effect manner. Although it is tempting to interpret some of these associations in a causal, unidirectional manner, more often than not, alternative explanations can also be offered. For example, the documented association between dating violence and psychological distress is typically interpreted to mean that experiencing dating violence causes psychological distress (e.g., Howard et al., 2007a, 2007b; Molidor & Tolman, 1998). However, it is not too difficult to imagine how feelings of psychological distress might influence an adolescent's decision about whom to go out with (i.e., adolescents who are psychologically distressed, compared with those who are not, may make different choices about whom to date) and, perhaps, lead an adolescent to an abusive relationship.

Many adolescents engage in antisocial or illegal activities, but those who do so consistently and frequently are at increased risk of dating violence victimization (e.g., Howard et al., 2007a, 2007b). In addition, simply having antisocial friends increases risk for victimization. For example, females who associate with violent or victimized peers appear to be at increased risk for dating violence victimization (Gagne, Lavoie, & Hebert, 2005). Similarly, male and female adolescents exposed to peer-drinking activities within the past 30 days (e.g., "Hanging out with friends who drank") were victimized more often than their counterparts who were not exposed to such activities (Howard, Qiu, & Boekeloo, 2003).

Many other adolescent experiences have also been associated with dating violence victimization. For example, earlier exposures to violence, both within and outside of the family, are associated with victimization (e.g., Gagne et al., 2005; Malik et al., 1997). Negative parent-child interactions and parent-child boundary violations at age 13 predict victimization at age 21 (Linder & Collins, 2005). Trauma symptoms, which may result from violence exposure and untoward parent-child interactions, are posited to interfere with emotional and cognitive processes important in interpreting abusive behavior, and possibly to heighten tolerance for abuse (Capaldi & Gorman-Smith, 2003). Having had prior sexual relationships with peers increases adolescent females' risk for experiencing relationship violence (e.g., Howard et al., 2007a, 2007b). Also, the likelihood of victimization increases as the number of dating partners increases (Halpern et al., 2001).

Several different dimensions of adolescent relationships have been examined in relation to dating violence. For example, physical violence is often reciprocated within relationships, meaning that when dating violence is reported, both partners are typically violent toward one another (e.g., O'Leary, Slep, Avery-Leaf, Cascardi, 2008). Relationship violence is more likely to happen in serious or special romantic relationships, rather than more casual ones (O'Leary et al., 2008; Roberts, Auinger, & Klein, 2006). It is also more likely to occur in relationships with problems, conflict, and power struggles (Bentley et al., 2007; O'Keefe, 1997).

Relationship violence is more likely to happen in serious or special romantic relationships, rather than more casual ones.

Although there are many risk factors for adolescent dating violence, some protective factors have emerged as well. For instance, having high-quality friendships at age 16 is associated with reduced likelihood of experiencing dating violence in romantic relationships at age 21 (Linder & Collins, 2005). High-quality friendships are characterized by security, disclosure, closeness, low levels of conflict, and the effective resolution of conflict that does occur. Also, adolescents who do well in school and those who attend religious services are at decreased risk for experiencing dating violence (Halpern et al., 2001; Howard et al., 2003).

Prevention and Intervention

Much of the prevention research in this area is directed at an entire population (e.g., 9th grade at a school) with the goal of preventing violence from occurring. However, the prevalence data indicate that a sizable number of adolescents in high school, and even middle school, have already perpetrated and/or experienced dating violence. Thus, in most cases the research is not technically universal prevention, from the standpoint of preventing violence before it ever occurs. Rather, it is an attempt to reduce dating violence, by preventing its initial occurrence as well as preventing its re-occurrence among those who have already experienced it.

A sizable number of adolescents in high school, and even middle school, have already perpetrated and/or experienced dating violence.

Many of the school-based prevention programs share a number of commonalities, in addition to the joint focus on prevention and intervention (Whitaker et al., 2006). Most are designed to address perpetration and victimization simultaneously. Many are incorporated into mandatory health classes in middle or high school. Most are based on a combination of feminist and social learning principles, and involve didactic methods to increase knowledge and change attitudes regarding dating violence. Despite these similarities, there are potentially important differences in the structure (e.g., duration) and content of these various programs. Unfortunately, most of these school-based programs have not undergone rigorous empirical evaluation to determine whether they actually reduce occurrences of violence.

A notable exception is Safe Dates, a program developed for 8th and 9th grade students (Foshee, Bauman, Arriaga et al., 1998) that has undergone a fairly rigorous evaluation. Safe Dates includes: (a) ten interactive classroom sessions covering topics such as dating violence norms, gender stereotyping, and conflict management skills, (b) group activities such as peer-performed theater productions and a poster contest, and (c) information about community resources for adolescents in abusive relationships. Evaluation results indicate that Safe Dates reduces psychological and physical violence perpetration, but not victimization, among the students who participated in the program. At first glance, this result might be puzzling: How can the perpetration of violence go down, without a commensurate reduction in victimization? This might be explained, in part, by the fact that not all individuals who participated in Safe Dates dated other Safe Date participants. Although the Safe Dates participants were less likely to commit acts of dating violence after completing the program, they were not necessarily less likely to date individuals who commit violent acts.

Evaluations of other school-based programs using techniques similar to those employed in Safe Dates have not had demonstrable effects on violence perpetration or victimization. Some of these evaluations simply did not include measures of perpetration or victimization as outcomes. Others, however, have attempted to measure intervention effects on violent behavior and victimization, but have found no effects (e.g., Avery-Leaf et al., 1997; Hilton et al., 1998). Many of these school-based programs, however, *have* achieved changes in knowledge or attitudes regarding dating violence (e.g., Avery-Leaf et al., 1997; Hilton et al., 1998; Krajewski et al., 1996; Weisz & Black, 2001).

Another program with demonstrated results is The Youth Relationships Project (YRP) (Wolfe et al., 2003). YRP is a community-based intervention designed for 14–16 year olds who were maltreated as children and were thus at increased risk of being in abusive relationships in the future. YRP is an 18-session, group-based program with three primary components: (a) education about abusive relationships and power dynamics within these relationships, (b) skills development, and (c) social action. The skills targeted in this program include communication skills and conflict resolution. The social action portion of the program includes, among other things, allowing program participants the opportunity to become familiar with and to practice utilizing resources for individuals in violent relationships, as well as the chance to develop a project to raise awareness of dating violence within the community. Sessions include skills practice, guest speakers, videos, and visits to relevant community agencies. Evaluation results indicate that YRP reduces physical dating violence perpetration and physical, emotional, and threatening abuse victimization.

It is encouraging that Safe Dates and the YRP have yielded promising results in reducing dating violence among adolescents. However, given the current state of the prevention literature in this area, it would be erroneous to suggest that we know how to prevent adolescent dating violence. Systematic reviews of this literature indicate that the vast majority of studies attempting to evaluate a dating violence prevention program have *not* found intervention effects on behavioral measures, and even though changes in knowledge and attitudes are often documented, it is not really clear if such changes lead to changes in either perpetration or victimization (Hickman et al., 2004; Whitaker et al., 2006). The promising findings of the Safe Dates and YRP programs require replication, and more information is needed on how these programs accomplished their positive effects. Researchers and practitioners can use these programs as a starting point in their own efforts at preventing relationship violence, but it is still important to continue exploring new ideas about prevention in this area.

Concluding Remarks

It is clear that violence in adolescent dating relationships is a prevalent problem with potentially devastating consequences. We also know a great deal about correlates of such violence. On the other hand, there are still important gaps in our knowledge. For example, longitudinal research on this topic is extremely scarce; thus, we know little about the emergence and unfolding of dating violence and victimization over time. This is particularly true for high-risk groups, such as children from violent homes and other groups potentially at risk. In addition, we know very little about how to address the problem of adolescent dating violence effectively. This might be due, in part, to the dearth of well-designed longitudinal studies on this topic, which are necessary to develop a solid knowledge base on the causes of relationship violence and targets for intervention. Although there are promising and notable efforts in the area of understanding and preventing violence in adolescent dating relationships, we still have much to learn.

Longitudinal research on this topic is extremely scarce; thus, we know little about the emergence and unfolding of dating violence and victimization over time.

References

Allen, L. (2004). "Getting off" and "going out": Young people's conceptions of (hetero) sexual relationships. *Health & Sexuality, 6,* 463–481.

Avery-Leaf, S., Cascardi, M., O'Leary, K.D., & Cano, A. (1997). Efficacy of a dating violence prevention program on attitudes justifying aggression. *Journal of Adolescent Health, 21,* 11–17.

Bentley, C.G., Galliher, R.V., & Ferguson, T.J. (2007). Associations among aspects of interpersonal power and relationship functioning in adolescent romantic couples. *Sex Roles, 57,* 483–495.

Capaldi, D.M., & Gorman-Smith, D. (2003). The development of aggression in young male/female couples. In P. Florsheim (Ed.), *Adolescent Romantic Relations and Sexual Behavior: Theory, Research, and Practical implications* (pp. 243–278). Lawrence Erlbaum Associates, Publishers.

Capaldi, D.M., Kim, H.K., & Shortt, J.W. (2007). Observed initiation and reciprocity of physical aggression in young, at risk couples. *Journal of Family Violence, 22,* 101–111.

Connolly, J., Craig, W., Goldberg, A., & Pepler, D. (1999). Conceptions of cross-sex friendships and romantic relationships in early adolescence. *Journal of Youth and Adolescence, 28,* 481–494.

Feiring, C. (1996). Concept of romance in 15-year-old adolescents. *Journal of Research on Adolescence, 6,* 181–200.

Foshee, V., Bauman, K.E., Arriaga, X.B., Helms, R.W., Koch, G.G., & Linder, G.F. (1998). An evaluation of safe dates, an adolescent dating violence prevention program. *American Journal of Public Health, 88,* 45–50.

Gagne, M., Lavoie, F., & Hebert, M. (2005). Victimization during childhood and revictimization in dating relationships in adolescent girls. *Child Abuse & Neglect, 29,* 1,155–1,172.

Halpern, C.T., Oslak, S.G., Young, M.L., Martin, S.L., & Kupper, L.L. (2001). Partner violence among adolescents in opposite-sex romantic relationships: Findings from the national longitudinal study of adolescent health. *American Journal of Public Health, 91,* 1,679–1,685.

Halpern, C.T., Young, M.L., Wallet, M.W., Martin S.L., & Kupper, L.L. (2004). Prevalence of partner violence in same-sex romantic and sexual relationships in a national sample of adolescents. *Journal of Adolescent Health, 35,* 131.

Hickman, L.J., Jaycox, L.H., & Aranoff, J. (2004). Dating violence among adolescents: Prevalence, gender distribution, and prevention program effectiveness. *Trauma, Violence, and Abuse, 5,* 123–142.

Hilton, N.Z., Harris, G.T., Rice, M.E., Krans, T.S., & Lavigne, S.E. (1998). Antiviolence education in high schools: Implementation and evaluation. *Journal of Interpersonal Violence, 13,* 726–742.

Howard, D.E., Qiu, Y., & Boekeloo, B. (2003). Personal and social contextual correlates of adolescent dating violence. *Journal of Adolescent Health, 33,* 9–17.

Howard, D.E., Wang, M.Q., & Yan, F. (2007a). Psychosocial factors associated with reports of physical dating violence among U.S. adolescent females. *Adolescence, 42,* 311–324.

Howard, D.E., Wang, M.Q., & Yan, F. (2007b). Prevalence and psychosocial correlates of forced sexual intercourse among U.S. high school adolescents. *Adolescence, 42,* 629–643.

Jackson, S.M., Cram, F., & Seymour, F.W. (2000). Violence and sexual coercion in high school students' dating relationships. *Journal of Family Violence, 15,* 23–36.

Jouriles, E.N., McDonald, R., Garrido, E., Rosenfield, D., & Brown, A.S. (2005). Assessing aggression in adolescent romantic relationships: Can we do it better? *Psychological Assessment, 17,* 469–475.

Krajewsky, S.S., Rybarik, M.F., Dosch, M.F., & Gilmore, G.D. (1996). Results of a curriculum intervention with seventh graders regarding violence in relationships. *Journal of Family Violence, 11,* 93–112.

Linder, J.R., & Collins, W.A. (2005). Parent and peer predictors of physical aggression and conflict management in romantic relationships in early adulthood. *Journal of Family Psychology, 19,* 252–262.

Malik, S., Sorenson, S.B., & Aneshensel, C.S. (1997). Community and dating violence among adolescents: Perpetration and victimization. *Journal of Adolescent Health, 21,* 291–302.

Marquart, B.S., Nannini, D.K., Edwards, R.W., Stanley, L.R., & Wayman, J.C. (2007). Prevalence of dating violence and victimization: Regional and gender differences. *Adolescence, 42,* 645–657.

McMaster, L.E., Connolly, J., Pepler, D., & Craig, W.M. (2002). Peer to peer sexual harassment in early adolescence: A developmental perspective. *Development and Psychopathology, 14,* 91–105.

Molidor, C., & Tolman, R.M. (1998). Gender and contextual factors in adolescent dating violence. *Violence Against Women, 4,* 180–194.

O'Keefe, M. (1997). Predictors of dating violence among high school students. *Journal of Interpersonal Violence, 12,* 546–568.

O'Leary, K.D., & Slep, A.M.S. (2003). A dyadic longitudinal model of adolescent dating aggression. *Journal of Clinical Child and Adolescent Psychology, 32,* 314–327.

O'Leary, K.D., Slep, A.M., Avery-Leaf, S., & Cascardi, M. (2008). Gender differences in dating aggression among multiethnic high school students. *Journal of Adolescent Health, 42,* 473–479.

Roberts, T.A., Auinger, M.S., & Klein, J.D. (2006). Predictors of partner abuse in a nationally representative sample of adolescents involved in heterosexual dating relationships. *Violence and Victims, 21,* 81–89.

Sears, H.A., Byers, E.S., & Price, E.L. (2007). The co-occurrence of adolescent boys' and girls' use of psychologically, physically, and sexually abusive behaviours in their dating relationships. *Journal of Adolescence, 30,* 487–504.

Smith, P.H., White, J.W., & Holland, L.J. (2003). A longitudinal perspective on dating violence among adolescent and college-age women. *American Journal of Public Health, 93,* 1,104–1,109.

Weisz, A.N., & Black, B.M. (2001). Evaluating a sexual assault and dating violence prevention program for urban youths. *Social Work Research, 25,* 89–102.

Whitaker, D.J., Morrison, S., Lindquist, C., Hawkins, S.R., O'Neil, J.A., Nesius, A.M., Mathew, A., & Reese, L. (2006). A critical review of interventions for the primary prevention of perpetration of partner violence. *Aggression and Violent Behavior, 11,* 151–166.

Wolfe, D.A., Scott, K., Reitzel-Jaffe, D., Wekerle, C., Grasley, C., & Straatman, A.-L. (2001). Development and validation of the conflict in adolescent dating relationships inventory. *Psychological Assessment, 13,* 277–293.

Wolfe, D.A., Wekerle, C., Scott, K., Straatman, A.L., Grasley, C., & Reitzel-Jaffe, D. (2003). Dating violence prevention with at-risk youth: A controlled outcome evaluation. *Journal of Consulting and Clinical Psychology, 71,* 279–291.

Wolitzky-Taylor, M.A., Ruggiero, K.J., Danielson, C.K., Resnick, H.S., Hanson, R.F., Smith, D.W., Saunders, B.E., & Kilpatrick, D.G. (2008). Prevalence and correlates of dating violence in a national sample of adolescents. *Journal of the American Academy of Child and Adolescent Psychiatry, 47,* 755–762.

Critical Thinking

1. How would you define violence in dating?
2. Why do you think it is difficult to reduce the number of violent dating incidents?
3. What would you do if a friend of yours was victimized by a violent dating partner?

Ernest N. Jouriles, PhD is Professor in the Department of Psychology and Co-Director of the Family Research Center at Southern Methodist University. **Cora Platt** is a doctoral student in the Department of Psychology at Southern Methodist University. **Renee McDonald, PhD** is Associate Professor in the Department of Psychology and Co-Director of the Family Research Center at Southern Methodist University.

Misbehavior

DONNA ST. GEORGE

In a small courtroom north of Houston, a fourth-grader walked up to the bench with his mother. Too short to see the judge, he stood on a stool. He was dressed in a polo shirt and dark slacks on a sweltering summer morning.

"Guilty," the boy's mother heard him say.

He had been part of a scuffle on a school bus.

In another generation, he might have received only a scolding from the principal or a period of detention. But an array of get-tough policies in U.S. schools in the past two decades has brought many students into contact with police and courts—part of a trend some experts call the criminalization of student discipline.

Now, such practices are under scrutiny nationally. Federal officials want to limit punishments that push students from the classroom to courtroom, and a growing number of state and local leaders are raising similar concerns.

In Texas, the specter of harsh discipline has been especially clear.

Here, police issue tickets: Class C misdemeanor citations for offensive language, class disruption, schoolyard fights. Thousands of students land in court, with fines of up to $500. Students with outstanding tickets may be arrested after age 17.

Texas also stands out for opening up millions of student records to a landmark study of discipline, released in July. The study shows that 6 in 10 students were suspended or expelled at least once from seventh grade on. After their first suspension, they were nearly three times more likely to be involved in the juvenile justice system the next year, compared with students with no such disciplinary referrals.

Citing the Texas research, federal officials announced last month an initiative to break what many call the "school-to-prison pipeline." Suspensions, expulsions and arrests are used too often to enforce school order, officials said.

"That is something that clearly has to stop," U.S. Attorney General Eric Holder said in Washington alongside Education Secretary Arne Duncan.

This month, Duncan recounted that in his old job as Chicago schools chief, he was stunned to learn that so many arrests occurred in schools. The first response to student misbehavior, he said, "can't be to pick up the phone and call 911."

The federal focus comes amid other change. In Colorado, a legislative task force is examining discipline practices including law enforcement referrals and school ticketing. Los Angeles police recently agreed to cut back on ticketing tardy students en route to school.

Connecticut officials have begun screening cases after students wound up in court on violations such as for having soda, running in the hall and dressing improperly. "It's not that we don't think these things should be handled," said William Carbone, the state's executive director of court support services. "We just think they should be handled in the school rather than the court."

Research shows that students who have been arrested or appeared in court are more likely to drop out of high school, said Gary Sweeten, an Arizona State University criminologist. Dropouts, in turn, are more likely than graduates to be incarcerated or unemployed.

'Defied Common Sense'

The suburban Houston courtroom was packed with students, parents and siblings. Justice of the Peace Judge J. Kent Adams spoke of the importance of consequences, the duties of parents and the reality of being ticketed.

The fourth-grader who tussled on the bus was 10. After his appearance, his mother, Kimberly Smith, questioned whether her son belonged in court.

"I'm all for consequences, but I think it could have been handled another way," she said. She had no chance to mention her son's attention-deficit hyperactivity disorder and bipolar disorder, she said.

The child was ordered to do eight hours of community service and take classes in anger management and decision-making, at a cost of $370, Smith said. "I'm a single parent," she said. "Four hundred dollars? I have two other boys."

It is hard to pinpoint the beginning of ticketing in Texas, but advocates say it expanded during the 1990s as many school systems started police forces and as zero-tolerance policies proliferated.

Texas is not alone in school-based ticketing, which occurs in several other states. In the Washington area, where Fairfax County has reexamined discipline policies in the aftermath of a student athlete's suicide, school and police officials report no such ticketing practices.

In Texas, many question whether ticketing went too far.

In one highly publicized case, a middle school student in Austin was ticketed for class disruption after she sprayed herself with perfume when classmates said she smelled.

In Houston one recent day, a 17-year-old was in court after he and his girlfriend poured milk on each other. "She was mad at me because I broke up with her," he said.

Student Precilla Sanchez, 15, said most of her friends "have one ticket or more."

"You got to a point where police were writing tickets for things that were not appropriate," said Brock Gregg of the Association of Texas Professional Educators. He said the association supports police in schools but wants more emphasis on helping students rather than sending them to court.

Debate over ticketing heated up in January after a 200-page report from Texas Appleseed, a public interest law center, documented 275,000 juvenile tickets in fiscal 2009, including 120,000 for truancy. The statewide data did not separate school tickets from those issued in other settings.

But the report's data from 22 Texas school districts showed ticketing rates that ranged from less than 1 percent of students in Pasadena to 11 percent in Galveston.

"It really defied common sense," said Deborah Fowler, the report's lead author, who found tickets issued to students as young as 5.

The study also found that as school police staff grew, often so did ticketing. In Austin, for example, district police staff rose 31 percent over six years as ticketing climbed 50 percent.

"More misbehaving students are being bumped into the court system nationally, and the main reason is the increasing presence of police in schools," said Paul Hirschfield, a Rutgers University sociologist.

Parents in Texas complain that tickets are written up too easily and that authorities overlook whether students have disabilities or are acting in self-defense.

Lawyer Yvonne Q. Taylor, who works for a juvenile justice project at Texas Southern University's Earl Carl Institute for Legal and Social Policy, said her experience bears out a finding of the ticketing report: Racial disparities are common.

In Dallas, where 30 percent of students are African American, 62 percent of those ticketed are black, the report said. In the Houston area, Taylor said, "I rarely see a white face in the courtroom."

One of her recent cases involved Yiovani Williams, the son of a police detective. The 15-year-old said he talked back to an English teacher after she repeatedly said he could not use the restroom. The teacher accused him of cursing, which he denied. He was ticketed for disorderly conduct and suspended for a day.

His parents, Racquel and Willie Williams, said they were stunned such an incident could be considered criminal. Earlier, their older son had been ticketed after a classroom incident.

"We have worked so hard to keep our children out of the same court system they put them into so easily," Willie Williams said. "For something as minor as this, he has to be criminalized?"

Still, ticketing has supporters.

Ken Knippel, an assistant superintendent of the Aldine Independent School District, with 62,000 students and 39 police officers, said a ticket is one of many responses to an infraction. "Should it be used to modify all behavior? No," he said. "Are there times when it is appropriate? Yes, there are."

Gregg Anderson, president of the Texas Association of School Resource Officers, said that tickets don't get written every day or for every offense but that when a problem is repeated or severe, "it's another tool in our belt." Some police officers ticket more than others, he said, noting that he supervised a middle school with perhaps 10 tickets all year.

Ticketed students can't just mail in a fine, as drivers could with a traffic ticket. In Texas, they must appear with a parent in an adult court—in a municipal court, or before a justice of the peace.

At a recent court date, parent Avril Jenkins was leaning toward paying a $165 fine rather than higher costs for a deferred disposition program that included classes.

"I'd still get into college with that, right?" asked her worried 16-year-old daughter.

The question of criminal records is complex. A new law seals court records once misdemeanor judgments are satisfied. Paperwork also can be filed to expunge records at age 18 for one-time offenders.

How much such issues matter in college applications depends on the offense and a student's overall record and explanation, admissions officers said.

Alienating Students

In downtown Houston, Municipal Court Judge David Fraga sees perhaps 150 juvenile ticketing cases a day during the school year, about half of them school-related. In his court, punishments include community service and behavior-related workshops, and many offenders are able to avoid fines. The idea is, he said, "to learn to make good choices."

But others ask: Why are minor offenses here at all?

"It's oftentimes dumb teenage behavior, which most of us did at one time or another," said state Sen. John Whitmire (D-Houston). In the spring, Texas lawmakers passed legislation to scale back ticketing for younger children and truancy cases.

Janell Blackburn, who was in Fraga's court after her teen daughter and an ex-boyfriend had argued and bumped each other, said ticketing should be ended for all but the most severe offenses.

"It's almost like when they gave the school districts the right to have the police officers there," she said, "and they gave them the tablets of tickets, they started writing it all up."

For the students, she said, "it's turning them against the school itself. They don't want to go back there."

Critical Thinking

1. What does research show about sending kids to court for misbehaving in school?
2. Do you think giving students tickets is a good way to teach them that there are consequences for their actions?

Shaken-Baby Syndrome Faces New Questions in Court

EMILY BAZELON

At 4 months, Noah Whitmer was an easy baby. *Super tranquilo,* remembers Trudy Eliana Muñoz Rueda, who took care of Noah at her home day care center in Fairfax County, Va. Rueda and Noah's mother, Erin Whitmer, both noticed when he stopped taking his bottle well and napping as usual in the middle of his fifth month, in April 2009. Whitmer thought this was because Noah had just started eating solid food. She and Rueda talked about it early on April 20, both of them hunched over Noah in his car seat when Whitmer dropped him off.

That afternoon, after a morning in which Noah didn't nap and drank only a couple of ounces of formula, Rueda says she prepared a bottle for him while he lay on a mat. In her native Peru, Rueda, who is 46, ran a travel agency and taught college courses for prospective tour guides. Her husband was trained as a lawyer. After they moved to the United States in 2001, the couple had a second child, and three years later Rueda converted her basement into a home day care center so she could work while spending time with her two kids. When Rueda sat down to feed Noah, her 13-year-old daughter was at school, her 5-year-old was upstairs watching TV and the four other children in her care were taking naps. Rueda's sister-in-law, who spent the morning with the children while Rueda was at a doctor's appointment, had just left the house. "Everything was calm and quiet," Rueda, who has soft features and dark hair, told me in Spanish while her lawyer translated.

There are two irreconcilable versions of how that calm shattered. Rueda says that Noah was crying, and she picked him up, sat on the couch and gave him the bottle to help put him to sleep. While she was feeding him, she felt Noah's arm go limp, and when she moved to take the bottle out of his mouth, he made a sound that she didn't recognize. "I could tell something was happening," she says. She stood up and put Noah on her shoulder, patting him on the back. "As I did this, his body tensed up in a ball. It was as if he was looking for air, and he couldn't breathe." Rueda put Noah on the floor and started C.P.R., at the same time reaching for her phone to call 911. She put the dispatcher on speakerphone so she could keep tending to Noah. "I said, 'Please, please get someone here,'" she said. "I knew it could hurt him if there wasn't enough oxygen going to his brain."

Erin Whitmer's account of the moments before Noah lost consciousness is entirely different. "Around 2:30 on April 20, 2009, Noah was shaken," she wrote on her blog Noah's Road, on the one-year anniversary of the incident. "He'd been crying. He needed something that his day care provider wasn't providing him. Maybe he was tired of lying on the mat where she'd had him. Maybe he needed a hug, a laugh, a kind touch. Instead, she picked him up, her fingers gripping him tightly, feeling the softness of his velour pants and his cotton onesie under her fingers, and she shook him."

Whitmer's account of what Rueda must have done to Noah was based on evidence presented at Rueda's trial and information from the doctors who treated him after he was rushed to Inova Fairfax Hospital. The doctors gave Noah a CT scan, which showed subdural hemorrhaging (bleeding in a space between the skull and the brain) and an ophthalmological exam revealed retinal hemorrhaging (bleeding at the back of the eyes). Also, his brain was swelling. For decades, these have been the three telltale signs linked to the kind of child abuse commonly called shaken-baby syndrome.

Noah had no external marks on his body—no bruises or cuts or fractures, no sign that he was forcefully gripped and no evident neck injury that would seem to result from vigorous shaking. But an M.R.I. confirmed the CT scan findings and showed that the subdural bleeding was extensive. The doctors at Inova Fairfax tested Noah for clotting disorders that can cause these kinds of hemorrhages. The tests came back negative. The doctors told Erin and Michael Whitmer, who are both 32, that they strongly suspected Noah was violently shaken in the moments before he stopped breathing. While Noah lapsed into a coma, police went to question Trudy Rueda. A day later, Rueda was arrested. She was charged with two felony counts: abuse of a child causing serious injury and cruelty to a child.

Before April 20, 2009, Noah was a healthy baby. Trudy Rueda also had nothing suspect in her past. In five years as a day care provider, she had a pristine record with state regulators—she had taken the classes required for her license and extra ones as well. She cared for a boy with autism and a girl with one arm, reportedly with calm and assurance. "She was more patient than all of us," one mother testified at Rueda's trial. A second said, "What she's accused of now I could not begin to imagine Trudy doing." And yet Noah emerged from her home with terrible and permanent injuries.

Between 1,200 and 1,400 children in the United States sustain head injuries attributed to abuse each year. Most of them are less than a year old. Usually, there's not much dispute that these children were abused, because doctors discover other signs of mistreatment—cuts, bruises, burns, fractures—or a history of such injuries. There is no exact count of shaken-baby prosecutions, but law-enforcement authorities think that there are about 200 a year. In an estimated 50 percent to 75 percent of them, the only medical evidence of shaken-baby syndrome is the triad of internal symptoms: subdural and retinal hemorrhage and brain swelling.

For a year after Noah came out of his coma, he had as many as 32 seizures a day. Now he is 2, and his parents watch as his 1-year-old brother surpasses him developmentally. Noah sometimes nods his head "yes" and gives high fives, but he is not yet talking; doctors are not sure of his cognitive prognosis. Erin Whitmer, a slender woman with large brown eyes who chose Rueda for part-time day care after a careful search, cried when she found out that Rueda had been arrested. Now she says, "It will never completely leave me, the horror that I trusted my son with someone and she did this to him."

At Rueda's trial in January 2010, the prosecutor presented six doctors who testified that Noah's brain scans showed he had been abused. The doctors' reading of the scans were the main evidence that a crime had taken place, of its timing and even of Rueda's state of mind, since they agreed that only an act of great violence could inflict such injuries. Two doctors who treated Noah in the hospital said that the baby's scans showed that he had an acute subdural hemorrhage—the bleeding had begun suddenly—which was, as one doctor stated, "inconsistent with accidental trauma." Another witness, Craig Futterman, a doctor at Inova Fairfax and president of the board of the Shaken Baby Alliance, put it more bluntly, "This child was shaken, or shaken and slammed against something."

The usual explanation for how a caregiver can become an abuser is that in a moment of intense frustration, she snaps. The prosecutor, Gregory Holt, imagined for the jury a scenario in which Rueda was aggravated that she could not get Noah to stop crying: "Put him on the mat, put him on the chair, he's not drinking his milk. Getting a little bit frustrated?" And he claimed that Rueda confessed to shaking Noah.

On the day of Noah's injuries, Rueda spoke to the police without a lawyer and denied hurting him. The next day, Joslyn Waldron, a social worker for Virginia's Child Protective Services, visited Rueda at home. Waldron knew that Noah's doctors at Inova Fairfax suspected that he had been abused because of his symptoms. She and Rueda spoke together in Spanish while a detective, who did not speak Spanish, was present. At the trial, Waldron testified that Rueda confessed to shaking Noah when he was crying and before she gave him a bottle. The social worker said she wrote in her notes, "Might have shaken him about three times, but not sure" (using a standard Spanish word, *sacudir,* for shake).

As is protocol in her department, Waldron offered to tape the interview; Waldron says Rueda declined. Rueda has denied telling Waldron that she shook Noah. At the trial, she testified in heavily accented, halting English, frequently interrupting herself because she didn't understand the questions. Rueda said that she told Waldron, "I probably moved kind of rough with Noah," at the moment that she lifted him to give him the bottle, but that she had not gotten frustrated with the baby or harmed him.

When her lawyer asked her what she thought happened to Noah, Rueda answered: "I imagine the parents, we all want to know what happened. But I cannot give you an explanation about what I don't know."

The Whitmers dismissed Rueda's denials of guilt. "It's a complicated thing to look at someone who always smiled at you, to know that your baby loved her, and to know that because of her, you struggle each day to adapt to a new sense of reality," Erin Whitmer wrote on her blog, which has had more than a million visits, after Rueda's first criminal hearing. Michael Whitmer expressed his rage at Rueda's next hearing by wearing a T-shirt he made. On the back is a picture of Noah taken in the hospital, with tubes coming out of his mouth and the words: "Ask me what happens when you shake a baby."

At the trial, the prosecution presented one more piece of testimony against Rueda. The pediatrician who saw Noah in the I.C.U. told the jury that given the severity of the baby's injuries, their "onset would have been very rapid, so it would have been within minutes of when the injury occurred." This meant that the person with the baby right before he stopped breathing—Rueda—was necessarily the guilty party.

Rueda's lawyer didn't challenge this assumption directly. Medical experts, however, have begun to point out that clinical observations show that it's possible for a child to have a brain injury and still remain conscious. The child may be lethargic or fussy or may not eat or sleep normally for hours or days, while the subdural hemorrhage and other injuries become more serious, ending in acute crisis. This has made some doctors wary of pinpointing the timing of a child's injury—even when they are sure that abuse occurred—lest the wrong adult take the blame. "The police want us to time it within one to three hours," says John Leventhal, a Yale pediatrics professor and medical director of the child-abuse programs at Yale-New Haven Children's Hospital. "But sometimes we can only time it to within days."

In this case, because Rueda had been at the doctor that morning and her sister-in-law stayed to help with lunch, she spent only about an hour alone with the children in the day care center before calling 911. Arguing that another adult had harmed Noah would have meant implicating Rueda's sister-in-law, whom Rueda says she has never suspected, or the Whitmers, whom no one has accused. Rueda, her husband and their lawyers decided not to take this tack. The defense relied primarily on Ronald Uscinski, a neurosurgeon on the faculty of the medical schools of George Washington University and Georgetown. When he took the stand, Uscinski refuted all the prosecution experts who said that Noah's hemorrhaging was acute—the sudden result of a new injury. Uscinski testified that he saw chronic subdural bleeding on the scans, which he said was the result of trauma at birth. "Rebleeds" like Noah's, he testified, "can occur with minimal or no trauma. They can occur spontaneously." On cross-examination, Uscinski said that he earned approximately $200,000, which was about 30 percent of his income, as an expert witness in 2009.

For the prosecution, Cindy Christian, a pediatrics professor at the University of Pennsylvania, who has published extensively about shaken-baby syndrome, rejected Uscinski's reading of Noah's brain scans. "That's false, he did not have a rebleed from a chronic hematoma from birth," she said. "There was no evidence of that."

After five days of testimony, the jury deliberated for five hours and voted to convict. Virginia's sentencing guidelines called for a minimum sentence of 3 years and a maximum of 15. The jury recommended 10½ years and Erin and Michael Whitmer took the stand in support of that punishment. "This is a life sentence for my son, for my wife, for me, and for our family," Michael Whitmer told the jury.

"Really still, now, I can't comprehend it," Rueda told me, looking wan and bereft when I visited her at the Fluvanna Correctional Center for Women in Virginia. Rueda's daughters have gone to live with her older sister in Peru while her husband works extra hours to support the family and pay for her appeal. Rueda can rarely speak to her children."It is so hard to talk about this separation," she said, and started to cry.

A dozen years ago, the medical profession held that if the triad of subdural and retinal bleeding and brain swelling was present without a fracture or bruise that would indicate, for example, that a baby had accidently fallen, abuse must have occurred through shaking. In the past decade, that consensus has begun to come undone. In 2008, the Wisconsin Court of Appeals, after reviewing a shaken-baby case, wrote that there is "fierce disagreement" among doctors about the shaken-baby diagnosis, signaling "a shift in mainstream medical opinion." In the same year, at the urging of the province's chief forensic pathologist, the Ontario government began a review of 142 shaken-baby cases, because of "the scientific uncertainty that has come to characterize that diagnosis." In Britain, after one mother's shaken-baby conviction was overturned, Peter Goldsmith, then attorney general, reviewed 88 more cases. In 2006, he announced doubts about three of the convictions because they were based solely on the triad; in the other cases, Goldsmith said, there was additional evidence pointing to the defendant's guilt.

A small but growing number of doctors warn that there can be alternate explanations—infections or bleeding disorders, for example—for the triad of symptoms associated with shaken-baby syndrome. Across the country, the group of lawyers that has succeeded in exonerating hundreds of people based on DNA evidence is now mounting 20 to 25 appeals of shaken-baby convictions. "No one wants child abuse," says Keith Findley, a lawyer for the Wisconsin Innocence Project. "But we should not be prosecuting and convicting people in shaken-baby cases right now, based on the triad of symptoms, without other evidence of abuse. If the medical community can't agree about all the conflicting data and research, how is a jury supposed to reach a conclusion that's beyond a reasonable doubt?"

Much of the science of shaken-baby syndrome dates from the late 1960s, when a neurosurgeon named Ayub Ommaya conducted a brutal animal experiment to figure out how much acceleration it took to cause a head injury. Ommaya took more than 50 rhesus monkeys and strapped each one into a chair mounted on wheels, leaving their heads unsupported. He placed the chair on a 20-foot-long track, and an air-powered piston sent the monkeys zooming into a wall. Fifteen emerged with some kind of cerebral hemorrhage. Eight of those also had injuries to the brain stem or cervical cord.

Ommaya's experiment involved neither shaking nor infants. Still, two pediatric specialists, John Caffey and A. Norman Guthkelch, each wrote a paper that pointed to the work as evidence that unexplained subdural bleeding in babies could occur without direct impact to the head and with or without a visible neck injury. In the 1980s, the term "shaken-baby syndrome" came into broad use, and a national prevention and awareness campaign was set in motion.

As the diagnosis of shaken-baby syndrome took hold in medicine, and prosecutors began to bring charges based on it, doctors testified that shaking could generate the same terrible force as throwing a child from a second-story window. It turned out they were wrong. In 1987, a neurosurgeon named Ann-Christine Duhaime published a paper that included the autopsy results of 13 babies with symptoms associated with shaken-baby syndrome. In all of them she found evidence of trauma that was actually caused by impact. She teamed up with biomechanical engineers to create infant-sized dummies equipped with sensors to measure acceleration."We shook them as hard as we could, and we thought something was wrong, because the accelerations we measured were unexpectedly low," Duhaime says. Instead, the force level shot up when the testers released the dummies after shaking them, even if they hit a soft surface like a bed or a couch.

Later experiments confirmed this finding and have made some doctors and biomechanical engineers skeptical that shaking alone can cause severe brain damage or death. At the same time, the experiments have not ruled this out, Duhaime says. Among other things, the dummies are not live children, and while their heads and necks can exhibit the effects of acceleration, impact on brain tissue is still hard to model.

Many doctors who treat child abuse say that decades of clinical observation, as well as confessions, show that it's possible for shaking alone to cause the triad of subdural and retinal bleeding and brain swelling. A 2009 position paper from the American Academy of Pediatrics, written by Cindy Christian, recommends that doctors use the more general term "abusive head trauma" but also calls shaking an "important mechanism" of such trauma. Many doctors who testify for the defense agree that shaking could in theory cause the triad of symptoms but only if there is an injury to the neck or spinal cord, "where the breathing center is," as one doctor puts it. It's the absence of signs of this kind of an injury that makes some shaken-baby cases particularly fraught.

In 1993, Audrey Edmunds left her job as a secretary and started caring for children in her home near Madison, Wis. Like Trudy Rueda, Edmunds says that a baby she was taking care of, 7-month-old Natalie Beard, suddenly collapsed while drinking a bottle of milk; Natalie was propped up with the bottle in a car seat while Edmunds was out of the room getting her two daughters and another child ready for preschool. In the hospital, a CT scan showed that Natalie had the triad of shaken-baby symptoms but no spinal-cord injury. The baby died, and the doctors agreed that Edmunds, who was pregnant with her third child, had to be responsible. She was charged with first-degree reckless homicide.

At Edmunds's trial, a librarian testified that she once heard a thump and then the cries of a child who was with Edmunds, but she didn't see what had happened. Edmunds denied ever harming a child in her care. Her neighbors testified to her calm around children. Natalie "was a real fussy baby," one said, "but Audrey was very patient with her." Another day care provider in the neighborhood said, "I looked up to Audrey . . . when I started doing my day care."

Still, the prosecution's medical experts said that only Edmunds's violence could explain Natalie's injuries. A forensic pathologist, Robert Huntington, testified that the baby most likely had been abused at some point during the two hours before her collapse—which was when she was with Edmunds. The jury convicted Edmunds, and she was sentenced to 18 years; she went to prison two days after her youngest daughter's first birthday.

A decade later, Edmunds had a hearing to determine whether she should have a new trial. Huntington this time took the stand on her behalf. When Keith Findley, her lawyer, asked whether Huntington was comfortable with his 1996 testimony, the pathologist said, "No, sir, no I am not." He explained that in the years since her trial, he observed a child with subdural and retinal bleeding who was lucid for a period between her brain injury and her collapse. After that, he returned to the medical literature and found research to support this possibility. Huntington now believed that a "lucid interval is a distinct, discomforting but real possibility." He said he could no longer precisely time the injury that caused Natalie's death. For how long could Natalie have appeared relatively normal—fussy, but not obviously in crisis? "I'm sorry, I just don't know," Huntington said.

Huntington's change of heart reflects a new explanation for the manifestation of brain injury in babies. In a 2001 study, the British neuropathologist Jennian Geddes found that most babies with the triad of shaken-baby symptoms suffered not from a rupture of the nerve fibers of the brain but rather from a lack of blood caused by oxygen deprivation to the brain's cells.

The rupture of the brain's nerve fibers is immediate and produces instant coma; the effects of oxygen deprivation can be slower and more subtle. This can explain how a child with the triad of shaken-baby symptoms could, for some period of time, seem fussy or lethargic or stop eating or sleeping well. In 2005, Christian co-wrote a study that concluded, "Although infrequent, young victims of fatal head trauma may present as lucid before death."

This possibility introduces questions about whether the last person to care for a child before he or she stops breathing is necessarily guilty of abuse. In most cases of assault or murder, jurors could weigh this doubt in light of other evidence—witness testimony, perhaps, or the motive the defendant would have had to commit the crime. In shaken-baby cases, however, this kind of additional evidence is often absent. Doubts raised about the medical testimony loom large because it's so central to the prosecution.

At Edmunds's hearing for a new trial, five doctors joined Huntington on the side of the defense. Opposing them were four doctors for the prosecution. The Wisconsin Court of Appeals ruled in January 2008 that the disagreement among the physicians represented a shift in medical opinion and warranted a new trial: a jury would have to hear both sides. Edmunds called her daughters to tell them she was coming home. Six months later, prosecutors dropped the charges against her.

Audrey Edmunds's successful appeal was built on a foundation laid by defense lawyers a decade earlier in the first big courtroom fight over shaken-baby syndrome. In that case, prosecutors in Massachusetts charged an English au pair, Louise Woodward, with the murder of 8-month-old Matthew Eappen, who stopped breathing in her care. Matthew had the triad of shaken-baby symptoms, along with a skull fracture. Woodward, who was 19, told the police that she shook Matthew lightly when she couldn't wake him from a nap. Prosecutors decided that the shaking must have been violent. They also said that to cause the skull fracture, Woodward must have smashed Matthew's head on a hard surface at a velocity of more than 25 miles per hour.

Woodward's lead counsel was Barry Scheck, who went on to found the Innocence Project at Cardozo law school with Peter Neufeld. He enlisted seven medical experts, including Ommaya, the neurosurgeon who experimented with the rhesus monkeys, and Ronald Uscinski, a colleague. The defense's theory was that Matthew's skull fracture was three weeks old when he died, and that because of it, a slight jarring could have caused his fatal bleeding. Scheck didn't try to explain how the fracture happened. "We didn't know, so we didn't claim anything," he told me. But the defense experts testified that because tests showed no swelling at the site of the fracture, it had to be old.

The prosecution, for its part, lined up the doctors who treated Matthew at Children's Hospital in Boston. Among them was Patrick Barnes, then a pediatric radiologist at Children's. He had written, with another doctor, a chapter in a textbook that embraced the traditional theory of shaken-baby syndrome and shared the assumptions that pointed to Woodward's guilt.

Barnes testified for the prosecution at the trial, saying Matthew's brain scans showed his injuries were a result of shaking as well as a skull fracture. The prosecutors also asked Barnes to help them prepare for their cross-examination by briefing them on what to expect from the defense's doctors. He spent evenings watching Court TV tapes of their testimony. He heard doctors from fields other than pediatrics—biomechanics, neurosurgery and neuropathology—discuss scientific findings about traumatic brain injury that contradicted his belief in the traditional method for diagnosing shaken-baby syndrome. He started to question his assumptions. "I'd been in lockstep with the child-abuse establishment for 20 years," he told me. "For the first time, I saw that there were well-qualified experts on the other side giving opinions I'd never heard, that I knew nothing about."

Woodward's case ended in a stalemate. After the jury found her guilty of second-degree murder, the judge reduced the conviction to involuntary manslaughter and released her for time served. But a lasting legacy of that case was the eventual conversion of Patrick Barnes from an upholder of the medical orthodoxy surrounding shaken-baby cases to one of its strongest critics.

After Woodward's trial, Barnes continued to think about his newfound doubts. He read widely in the medical literature. He started to look at brain scans brought to him by defense lawyers. In a New York case in which a father was being prosecuted, Barnes says, he found strong support in the medical literature for a diagnosis of infant stroke, which he thought was likely related to an infection like meningitis. Now he says that he sometimes sees other explanations for the triad of symptoms. "There are a number of things you have to look for in these children—infections, bleeding and clotting problems," Barnes says. "Even now, I am most concerned about looking very carefully for predisposing or complicating medical conditions, in particular for infants younger than 6 months."

Trudy Rueda's lawyer asked Barnes to review Noah Whitmer's brain scans before her trial. Barnes wasn't able to testify because of a scheduling conflict, but he says the scans indicate that the baby had a thrombosis—a blood clot within a blood vessel. The prosecution's doctors saw the thrombosis, too, but they claimed it was a result of abuse. To Barnes, the clotting suggested infant stroke, which can be triggered by an infection. He says the fact that Noah was not taking a bottle or napping normally in the days before he was hospitalized suggests that his condition could have been subtly deteriorating during that time. "It's a very striking pattern," Barnes says of the thrombosis. "The baby not eating well may reflect the process that starts this. Usually, it's not a process that happens acutely and the baby crashes. It can start relatively slowly."

Barnes also testified at Audrey Edmunds's hearing challenging her conviction. He said that it was difficult to know for sure what had happened to Natalie Beard based on her scans; at the time of her death, hospitals were using CT scans, rather than also using M.R.I.'s, which provide more detail. But he did say that he saw the possibility of a thrombosis.

To a degree, some of the alternative explanations from defense-side doctors are accepted in the child-abuse field. A 2009 textbook that Cindy Christian co-edited includes a discussion of diseases and accidental injuries that can mimic the effects of abusive head trauma. Leventhal, the Yale pediatrician, told me about an unusual case involving an accidental fall. "A child who was sitting in a highchair and put his feet up on the table in front of him and rocked himself backward," Leventhal said. "When the child was taken to the hospital, the ophthalmologist said, 'This is shaken baby,' because of the massive retinal bleeding. Luckily, there were seven people playing cards in the room when the baby fell." Leventhal continued, "The subdural hematoma continued to bleed, and it turned out he had a previous bleeding disorder, a clotting problem."

Leventhal and others in the child-abuse field emphasize that such hemorrhaging as a result of a fall is very rare. In order for doctors to determine what caused an injury, they begin with a list of alternatives, ruling out the ones that don't match a patient's symptoms until they arrive at a diagnosis, with a reasonable degree of medical certainty. But defense-side doctors like Barnes say that in a criminal case, physicians should be more careful about testing their assumptions, and they should give the possibility of an alternative explanation—a stroke, say, caused by an infection—more weight.

It's on this question of probable causes that the doctors who testify in these cases split. Prosecution-side experts rely on a set of studies that indicate that when children have subdural bleeding and extensive retinal hemorrhaging, they are far more likely to have been abused than injured in any other way. In a 2010 paper in *Pediatrics,* Christian and the pediatric ophthalmologist Alex Levin concluded that the evidence supporting the "diagnostic specificity" of "severe" retinal hemorrhaging has significantly increased. "Some children have such severe retinal hemorrhaging that it is much more likely to be from abusive head trauma," Christian told me. She testified to this at Rueda's trial, because Noah Whitmer had severe retinal hemorrhaging. Levin similarly called Natalie Beard's retinal bleeding "textbook severe" when he testified for the prosecution at Audrey Edmunds's 2007 hearing. When the prosecutor asked him how significant these findings were for diagnosing shaken-baby syndrome, Levin answered: "Very important. We really don't have any other cause for this particular kind of hemorrhaging and retinal findings."

Defense experts, however, criticize the methodology of these studies. And even taken at face value, they say, the studies show that severe retinal hemorrhaging is far more common in abuse cases, not that it's never found in any other circumstance. At the 2010 meeting of the American Academy of Forensic Sciences, the Canadian forensic pathologist Evan Matshes presented the results of a study, under peer review, of 123 autopsies performed on infants in Miami-Dade County who died under natural or accidental circumstances, or from homicides. Of the children with retinal hemorrhages, 53 percent died from accidental or natural causes, and 47 percent died as a result of homicide. Severe retinal hemorrhages were identified in some of the children in the accident group. Although the children in the homicide group were more likely to have severe retinal hemorrhages than the other group, this finding could be explained by factors other than abuse, according to Matshes. The children in the homicide group had isolated head injuries and were more likely to be resuscitated for a period of time, he says. In the aftermath, they were more likely to develop brain swelling and bleeding disorders that may explain the severe retinal hemorrhaging. Matshes puts his conclusions like this, "It is simply incorrect to state that severe retinal hemorrhaging is diagnostic of abuse or shaking." He is now working on a study that looks at whether infants with subdural and retinal hemorrhaging might in fact have neck injuries, which could indicate shaking, that go undetected, because doctors haven't looked in the right place for them. Matshes and his team are conducting autopsies of the entire cervical spinal column, which is not usually dissected in shaken-baby cases. The goal is to determine whether injuries there could explain how shaking can cause brain damage or death—and whether this additional diagnostic tool might one day help distinguish which babies have in fact been abused, and which have subdural and retinal bleeding from other causes.

Underlying the clash over the medical research on shaken-baby syndrome is another one about human nature. How likely is an adult with no history of wrongdoing to do terrible harm to a child by violently shaking it? To pediatricians like Leventhal and Christian, the sad answer, born of experience, is that such a lapse is all too possible. When I described Trudy Rueda's case to Leventhal, he told me about cases in which he had met and liked a parent or caregiver who ended up confessing to harming a child. Was there truly *no* indication that the adult in question was capable of such an act? The doctors who treat abused children insisted that sometimes, there isn't. They described disturbing confessions, like one that made headlines in Florida last year after a 22-year-old mother told the police that she had shaken her 3-month-old baby and perhaps caused him to hit his head, because he wouldn't stop crying while she was playing FarmVille. Leventhal cites a 2010 study that included 29 people who confessed in the French courts to shaking infants and who described the abuse as extremely violent.

Doctors like Barnes, on the other hand, emphasize that confessions are not always reliable. The exonerations of recent years have shown that people sometimes falsely admit to crimes because of police pressure or the promise of a plea bargain. In the first case from Canada's shaken-baby inquiry to reach the Ontario Court of Appeal, the judges overturned the conviction of Dinesh Kumar, a 44-year-old father who pleaded guilty to shaking his 5-week-old son to death. Kumar says now that at the time of his guilty plea, he believed he had no hope of prevailing against the damning testimony of the state's pathologist, who has since been discredited for giving error-riddled testimony based on botched autopsies.

In response to the critics who question the basis for some shaken-baby convictions, many in the child-abuse-treatment field have fired back with a critique of their own. Christian and Leventhal dismiss defense-side experts' alternate explanations, like Uscinski's theory that children suffer spontaneous rebleeds from birth injuries. "Every year they come up with a new alternate theory that we have to refute," Christian says.

Normally, of course, this is how science progresses: One researcher comes up with a hypothesis, which others question and test. But shaken-baby cases are haunted by the enormous repercussions of getting it wrong—the conviction of innocent adults, on the one hand, and on the other, the danger to children of missing serious abuse. In one study, researchers looked into the deaths of five children who had head injuries that initially were misjudged to be accidents and found that four of them could have been prevented if an earlier pattern of abuse had been detected. If parents are the focus of a shaken-baby investigation, doctors must weigh this risk in helping the state determine whether a child should be removed from the home. "When babies are sent home with an injury that's misattributed to an accident, we know that one-quarter to one-third of them will come back with another serious injury or, in some cases, death," Leventhal says.

Barnes, who is now part of a child-abuse-protection team at Stanford, doesn't dispute the need to investigate shaken-baby symptoms. But he says that most of his colleagues don't present the science dispassionately. "They have built their careers, their entire standing on this issue." His opponents, for their part, dismiss the defense experts as hired guns. "They're aggrandizing themselves and making a lot of money testifying," says Robert Block, the president-elect of the American Academy of Pediatrics. While it's true that experts like Uscinski can make six figures a year testifying (he says he testifies free when a defendant cannot afford to pay him), it's also the case that some witnesses for the prosecution are paid. Barnes no longer takes fees to testify in either criminal or custody cases. Neither did four of the other five defense experts who testified for Audrey Edmunds.

Last September, the fight among the doctors broke out in public on the Web, after Deborah Tuerkheimer, a former prosecutor and a law professor at DePaul, wrote a *New York Times* Op-Ed warning of wrongful convictions and calling on the National Academy of Sciences to referee the shaken-baby-syndrome dispute. On the website CommonHealth, about 20 doctors commented, mostly to express outrage. One of them was Block. He wrote that Tuerkheimer had "been beguiled by a group of physicians who are using the courtroom to distort science, facts and reality." And he denounced her for "furthering the cause of the so-called innocence project."

Philipp Baumer was born after a difficult delivery and spent his first week in the newborn-intensive-care unit. His mother, Victoria, who had given up her last baby for adoption, struggled with drug addiction. Her sister Julie, who was 27 and a loan officer for a mortgage company, was helping take care of Victoria's oldest child. She volunteered to adopt Philipp. "I didn't want to see anyone else leave the family," she told me in November when I met her in Ann Arbor, Mich.

When Philipp came home, neither Julie Baumer nor her parents could get him to take a bottle regularly. On Oct. 3, 2003, when he was 6 weeks old, Philipp was not able to keep down food for 12 hours, Baumer says. She called his pediatrician, who sent her to the emergency room at Mount Clemens Regional Medical Center outside of Detroit.

The E.R. doctor who saw Philipp found he was dehydrated and septic, gave him fluids and antibiotics and ordered a CT scan. But the test was canceled when Philipp was scheduled for transfer to the region's specialty facility for pediatrics, Children's Hospital of Michigan in Detroit. At Children's, Philipp went straight to intensive care. But he waited 28 hours for the CT scan. By then, Philipp had been in the hospital for a total of 33 hours. The scan showed subdural bleeding, which was so extensive that his fontanelle (the soft spot on a baby's head) was bulging. An ophthalmologist saw retinal bleeding. Philipp also had a skull fracture, although it was not near the site of the hemorrhage. In an emergency operation, a shunt was placed to relieve the pressure on Philipp's brain, but it was too late to prevent severe damage. Philipp, who is now 7, has cerebral palsy; he cannot walk on his own, talk or see.

Four months after Philipp's injuries occurred, Julie Baumer was charged with child abuse in the first degree. The prosecutor didn't present a theory about why Baumer would have harmed Philipp, saying that it was the state's job to show that Baumer intended to shake the baby, not what motivated her. Two doctors from Children's Hospital testified for the prosecution: Steven Ham, the neurosurgeon who put in the shunt; and Cristie Becker, a radiologist who treated Philipp later. Becker said Philipp's injuries were inflicted by shaking and timed them to "likely within 24 hours" of the CT scan. She said the skull fracture may have been an old birth-related injury. Looking at the scan, Ham said the fracture was new and that Philipp's injuries were the result of blunt-force trauma that occurred "within the previous 12 to 24 hours." He said he could pinpoint the timing based on "how sick the child was, and then the fact that in looking at the scan we could see fresh blood in the scan."

Becker and Ham didn't note in court that their 24-hour time frame meant that Philipp would have started hemorrhaging while he was at Children's—and no longer in Baumer's care. (When I called Becker, she said, "I don't care to revisit that issue, and best of luck trying to find the truth in the midst of that trial." Ham did not return my calls.) Baumer's trial lawyer failed to point out this flaw in the prosecution's case. The lawyer also did not find a defense expert who could read Philipp's brain scans. Baumer had no money to hire one, and her lawyer didn't know that he could have asked for court funds to cover the expense. In 2005, Baumer was convicted and sentenced to 10 to 15 years.

Baumer was raised Catholic, and in 2007, a nun saw her name on a prayer list and came to visit her in prison. When she heard her story, the nun asked Baumer if she needed a new lawyer and wrote on her behalf to Charles Lugosi, then a professor at the Catholic law school Ave Maria. Lugosi agreed to take Baumer's case and enlisted the help of a former prosecutor, Carl Marlinga, who had opened a defense practice. Later, the University of Michigan Innocence Clinic joined the defense.

The defense team sent Philipp's brain scans to Patrick Barnes. At the bottom of the images, Barnes saw a distinctive bright triangle surrounding the major vein that brings blood in and out of the brain. To Barnes, the triangle clearly pointed to a diagnosis unrelated to abuse: Venous sinus thrombosis, or stroke, probably from an infection—an explanation similar to the one Barnes gave for Noah Whitmer's injuries. Another radiologist and a forensic pathologist concurred with Barnes's reading of Philipp's scans. The defense experts also saw suggestions of an earlier smaller stroke, which could have triggered the feeding problems that led Julie to call Philipp's pediatrician. This reading of the scans matched the time frame Becker and Ham had given at trial: Philipp could have started to show some symptoms, and then had a major stroke after he was admitted to the hospital. The defense experts agreed with Becker that the skull fracture was old. They said it was likely the result of Philipp's difficult birth.

This testimony won Baumer a new trial. It also gave the defense team an answer to the question that hovers over every shaken-baby prosecution: What happened to hurt the child? During a trial, solving that mystery isn't supposed to be the defense's responsibility—the burden of proof rests with the prosecution. But a credible response makes it easier to lift the weight of the medical evidence from the shoulders of the defendant.

At Baumer's second trial, which took place in October, the defense called neighbors and friends who testified that she was gentle and loving with children. The prosecution introduced no evidence to the contrary. Baumer has two drunken driving offenses on her record from the late 1990s, but they weren't introduced at the trial.

Back on the stand, Ham and Becker now said they had misspoken about the time frame, and came up with new estimates: Becker said that Philipp's internal bleeding could have begun five days before the CT scan, and Ham said one or two days. They both remained convinced that Philipp's hemorrhages were inflicted. "Before they testified, they both said that it was their opinion from the beginning that the injuries occurred before Philipp came to the E.R.," Richard Goodman, the prosecutor at the second trial, says. And the prosecution's doctors disagreed with Barnes and the other defense-side experts that Philipp's scans showed a thrombosis. On cross-examination, Baumer's lawyer, Marlinga, asked Ham and Becker if they were trying to deflect criticism of the hospital for failing to give Philipp the care he needed because of the delay of his CT scan. The doctors denied that their revised testimony had anything to do with protecting the hospital.

The jurors began their deliberations by taking a poll. Nine out of 12 thought Baumer should be found not guilty. "For me, it came down to this: For the prosecution to be right, I was required to believe that a woman with no history or indication of violent tendencies or instability hit this baby's head so hard that she fractured his skull, and shook him so hard that she caused extensive brain damage, while leaving no marks on him," says Carman Minarik, a juror who is a minister at First United Methodist Church in Mount Clemens. "That just didn't make a lot of sense to me."

Sera Miller, a claims representative for the Social Security Administration, was one of the three jurors who thought at first that Baumer was guilty. She found the medical testimony dense and confusing. "I think we needed 12 doctors on that jury," she said. After an afternoon of deliberations, she went home and couldn't sleep. In the morning she decided that the defense had done enough to introduce reasonable doubt. The jury found Baumer not guilty.

When Philipp was 3 months old and ready to leave the hospital, he was put into foster care with Debi and Phil Zentz, who later adopted him and changed his name to Ben. When the second jury announced that it found Baumer not guilty, the Zentzes were in court. Baumer looked at Debi. "I was hoping for a bridge between the families," Baumer says. Instead, Debi Zentz gave this statement to the press: "The verdict does not change our belief. Reasonable doubt does not equate to innocence." When I called her in January, she said, "I have absolutely no doubt that Julie Baumer shook and horribly injured my son."

The Whitmers also feel certain that Trudy Rueda harmed their son and that she wronged them by putting them through a trial. "We got to a point where we said that if she stands up and admits what she did, we might be able to put this behind us," Michael Whitmer said. "But now, how do you forgive?"

He and his wife were sitting on a couch in their living room, in the Cape Cod-style house in Alexandria, Va., that Michael renovated by hand. Noah, his blue eyes sometimes focused and sometimes vacant, walked a bit unsteadily on the floor in front of us, picking up books and toys and putting them in his mouth. Noah can see now because a few months after his injury, he slept standing up for weeks to drain the blood from behind his eyes. His seizures have stopped, but only thanks to a strict and labor-intensive ketogenic diet. How *could* the Whitmers forgive, given the medical testimony from doctors they trust? Rueda's conviction is now on appeal, with a hearing scheduled for mid-February.

As for Audrey Edmunds, she has been out of prison for about three years. Now 49, she is blond and slim, and when I met her at a mall near her home outside Minneapolis, she talked to me about her three daughters. She wore jeans and open-toed sandals and showed me pictures of her children at a Twins game and talked about the delight she takes in taking snacks to her youngest girl's soccer practice. For a few minutes, her 11 years in prison seemed like a balloon she has let go.

But Edmunds does not live with her children. Her husband divorced her four years into her sentence; she says the separation was just too much for him. He stopped taking the girls to see her every week. When she got out of prison, she moved in with a friend and took a job at a Kwik Trip convenience store. Better work is hard to come by because of the time Edmunds served in prison. She also wants the early shift so she can see her kids in the afternoons. Sometimes, though, they go on a trip with their father and forget to call. "I was gone for so long," she says.

Edmunds said, however, that she had to come to terms with the drive to prosecute her. As we walked through the mall, she pointed out a Dora the Explorer display she thought young kids would like. Then she turned away from it. "A baby has died," she said simply. "They want to blame somebody."

Critical Thinking

1. What are the three tell-tale medical signs of shaken-baby syndrome?
2. When and how did the science of shaken-baby syndrome originate?
3. What is the state of medical thinking today regarding the signs of shaken-baby syndrome?

Emily Bazelon, a contributing writer, is a senior editor at Slate and the Truman Capote law-and-media fellow at Yale Law School.

Juvenile Recidivism—Measuring Success or Failure: Is There a Difference?

COLETTE S. PETERS AND SHANNON MYRICK

Consider the situations of two young offenders, both of whom are real individuals who were released several years ago from a youth correctional facility. They were sentenced to a juvenile correctional facility for felonies involving person-to-person assaults. They both had some strengths on which to build—they had completed treatment while in custody and received high school diplomas. They also both faced some challenges—neither had family or a home to return to after being released.

"Aaron"[1] has made positive connections with community members who are helping him negotiate the paths to independence and reentry. Since the date of his parole, the community has wrapped its arms around this young man. Community members have helped him find housing, helped him enroll in college, and aided him in finding part-time work. He has remained crime-free and continues working toward his undergraduate degree at a local university.

"Brad" has not fared as well. His community did not have the resources available to help him continue to build on his successes while in custody. Despite ongoing attempts to find a job, he remains unemployed. He has ended up homeless, couch-surfing through a series of friends' apartments while receiving federal food assistance. Like Aaron, Brad also has remained crime-free, but he continues to struggle with finances and depression.

By any measure besides recidivism, there is just one success story here. But if the only way a juvenile corrections agency measures performance is through recidivism rates, both young men are equally successful. Both are crime-free. The agency has "done its job."

Pros and Cons of Measuring Recidivism

Measuring and reporting recidivism rates are important responsibilities of juvenile correctional agencies and historically have been the primary measures used to track performance. Recidivism is an easy, cost-effective measure to track, and it resonates with members of the public and legislators who are concerned about crime rates. However, focusing exclusively on recidivism data reflects a deficit-based approach to delinquency intervention and juvenile corrections, rather than a strengths-based approach. When used as the primary indicator of an agency's performance, recidivism does not reflect the full range of the work that juvenile correctional agencies, youths, families, schools and communities perform on a daily basis.

Recidivism reveals whether juvenile offenders who leave custody go on to lead crime-free lives, but not whether they lead productive crime-free lives. Recidivism does not measure whether these young adults demonstrate successful pro-social behavior and contribute in a positive way to their communities. To really understand which programs and treatments are effective in reforming young offenders and placing them on a firm footing in life, juvenile correctional agencies are beginning to track not only what goes wrong, but also what goes right by tracking positive youth outcomes.

Pros and Cons of Measuring Success

Research and experience have suggested that successful transitions from childhood to adolescence and then adolescence to adulthood require positive development in several areas. These areas include education, pro-social family and peer relationships, health and well-being, and work and life skills.[2]

Much of the day-to-day work in correctional agencies and other areas of the juvenile justice system acknowledges and embraces an approach to reducing delinquency through youth development. Although some agencies more explicitly express their youth development goals, every agency conducts assessments to identify risk and protective factors in several domains such as substance abuse history, familial relationships, living arrangements, school or employment history and mental health. Case plans strategize ways to reduce dynamic risk factors and increase protective factors. Youths, families and staff work to build on youths' strengths while reducing risk factors.

Agencies are seeking positive youth outcomes that go beyond just remaining crime-free. What the juvenile justice system lacks, however, is a way to consistently define, monitor and measure those positive outcomes in a manner that resonates with the public and legislators. Agencies are beginning to clearly demonstrate which programs and treatments are effective and merit funding.

By knowing which factors help a youth successfully transition into adulthood and thrive in his or her community, states can make informed, evidence-based funding decisions that involve an appropriate array of services. Given the youth development goals and values reflected in the existing practices of many juvenile corrections agencies, it is important that this well-rounded approach to youth development does not carry through to performance measurement at the agency level. Together, recidivism and other outcomes data can paint a more comprehensive picture and supply much needed information for decision-making. Therefore, recidivism and other outcome measures are complementary.

Building the Foundation

Positive youth outcomes generally refer to indicators of protective factors, competence or strengths. The notion of measuring positive outcomes is rooted in a positive youth development (PYD) philosophy. Butts and colleagues note a basic underpinning of PYD is that even youths from the most challenging of circumstances can achieve optimal development if the right mix of resources are present, including opportunities to engage in positive relationships, activities and prosocial experiences with positive role models.[3] By paying attention to the potential positive youth outcomes that can result from the work juvenile justice agencies perform, corrections professionals can begin to answer questions about effectiveness in a more complete way than simply attending to recidivism.

Before corrections professionals can begin to measure positive youth outcomes, they have to consider the intervention that precedes the outcome. Intervention strategies tend to have a built-in theoretical framework that guides the activities and suggests potential outcomes. Therefore, if corrections professionals seek to increase the capacity to measure positive youth outcomes, they must consider the types of interventions used. Traditionally, juvenile justice agencies have followed a deficit-based model—treatment is focused on reducing anger, eliminating drug and alcohol use, or addressing mental health issues. Although these are important treatment interventions, the inherent focus on the problems a youth presents is somewhat inconsistent with measuring the healthy development of a youth through positive youth outcomes.

Positive youth outcomes should address the development of new skills and competencies, establishing a pro-social identity, and other elements essential to transitioning to adulthood for all youths. Since agencies cannot revolutionize their approach to treatment overnight, they need to get creative in discovering elements of existing interventions that lend themselves to positive youth outcomes. For example, if the program is focused on drug and alcohol abuse, is there a way to promote general physical well-being through exercise and self care? If so, the agency can measure health indicators and survey youths on knowledge gains related to maintaining a healthy lifestyle devoid of drugs and alcohol. In an anger-reduction treatment program, are youths being given the opportunity to find alternative methods of expression, such as art, writing or sports? In addition, is there a way to train youths in mediation skills or conflict management?

Many agencies are already engaged in efforts consistent with the measurement of positive youth outcomes. These activities include assessing youths for risk and protective factors upon admission, completing case-planning to provide treatment and opportunities for youths to develop skills, and engaging families and communities in the process. The next step is to quantify these efforts and identify the most relevant positive youth outcomes agencies should track. Ideally, agencies would provide a number of programs or interventions that support positive youth outcomes. Butts and colleagues suggest focusing on six areas, or practice domains, that may be most important in achieving measurable positive youth outcomes: work, education, relationships, community, health and creativity.[3] Currently, agencies may already have the capability to track such outcomes as the number of youths completing vocational training, the number of resumes or job applications submitted, the number of youths earning a high school diploma or GED certificate, or the number of volunteer hours completed.

The goal of connecting recidivism and positive youth outcomes is to paint a more vivid picture of a juvenile justice agency's impact on the youths it serves.

Connecting Recidivism and Positive Youth Outcomes

Agencies should maintain recidivism as a fundamental outcome measure in determining performance. Reducing future criminality is a principal goal of public service agencies. It is an indicator of performance that legislatures and the public are not only used to hearing but also are expecting. The goal of connecting recidivism and positive youth outcomes is to paint a more vivid picture of a juvenile justice agency's impact on the youths it serves. Youths should be returned to their communities with increased skills, gained competence and tools to help them become productive crime-free citizens of their communities. However, the sustainability of measuring and reporting positive youth outcomes is potentially dependent upon correlating those outcomes to recidivism. Presumably, the positive youth outcomes an agency chooses to measure will be inversely correlated with recidivism; in other words, the greater the educational attainment, the lower the recidivism. In an environment that increasingly expects evidence of treatment effectiveness, it is essential to demonstrate to lawmakers and the public that positive youth outcome measures are inversely correlated to recidivism.

For the past year, the Council of Juvenile Correctional Administrators (CJCA) has been examining the issue of measuring positive youth outcomes in a juvenile justice context. The goal of this effort has been to develop a more consistent and comprehensive set of performance measures that address positive youth outcomes that can be implemented in agencies around the country. A theme of the work of this group has been to maintain a nexus back to recidivism while promoting the measurement of positive youth outcomes. A set of guidelines and strategies will result from this effort and should be a resource for agencies to begin to build the foundation of measuring positive youth outcomes.

Measuring Real Success

As CJCA moves forward with development of proposed measures, agencies will be better able to demonstrate the effectiveness of treatments based on achieving positive youth outcomes, and they will be able to retain legislative and public support for those programs. Those measures also will tell a more useful story about whether youths are served well while in the juvenile justice system. It will be apparent when looking at the outcomes achieved by "Aaron" and "Brad" that only one of those youths is succeeding. Through treatment and services provided both within correctional institutions and in communities, it will be clear how to ensure more youths end up like "Aaron."

Notes

1. Names have been changed.
2. Butts, J.A., G. Bazemore, and S.A. Meroe. 2010. *Positive youth justice—Framing justice interventions using the concepts of positive youth development.* Washington, D.C.: Coalition for Juvenile Justice.

   Catalano, R.F., M.L. Berglund, J.A.M. Ryan, H.S. Lonczak, and J.D. Hawkings. 1998. *Positive youth development in the United States: Research findings on evaluations of positive youth development programs.* Seattle: University of Washington, School of Social Work.
3. Ibid.

Critical Thinking

1. Should taxpayers pay for juvenile delinquents' education while they are in custody?
2. How should juvenile justice agencies measure success?

Collette S. Peters is director of the Oregon Youth Authority and chair of the Council of Juvenile Correctional Administrators Postive Youth Outcomes Committee. **Shannon Myrick, PhD**, is a research analyst for the Oregon Youth Authority.

Whither Young Offenders? The Debate Has Begun

TREY BUNDY

Joaquin E. DiazDeLeon, a former Fresno gang member, spent two years inside California's juvenile prison system. What he found there, he said, was no better than the streets he came from.

Instead of rehabilitating young offenders, he said, correctional officers spent most of their time separating rival gangs. Violence was so pervasive, he said, that he kept his gang affiliation just to protect himself.

"Basically you're being thrown in a box and expected to change," said Mr. DiazDeLeon, 21, now a student at City College of San Francisco.

Gov. Jerry Brown's recent proposal to eliminate California's Division of Juvenile Justice was billed as a way to cut $242 million from the state budget. It was also the culmination of a decade-long effort to shut the state's troubled youth prison system, which for years has been plagued by violence, abuse and decaying facilities.

Much of that effort has been centered in the Bay Area after accusations of abuse and neglect at the institutions surfaced in a 2003 Alameda County lawsuit. In recent years, some local judges often refused to send young offenders to state institutions, preferring to confine them in county facilities regarded as safer and more effective.

Mr. Brown's initiative would take that unofficial policy further. It would scrap the state juvenile justice system and shift responsibility for confining the most violent young offenders to the local level, where they are nearer to family and have more community treatment options. The move would affect the 1,300 youths in state care, down from 10,000 in 1996.

Even among critics of the Division of Juvenile Justice, the proposed shift has set off a new debate over whether counties are equipped to handle an influx of severely troubled young people.

"I'm disgusted with myself to think of defending D.J.J. with all the things that have happened over the years," said Sue Burrell, a lawyer at the Youth Law Center in San Francisco, "but if you ask me right now, I would opt for keeping a very, very small D.J.J. open and not throwing the kids to the wolves."

Ms. Burrell said she was concerned that prosecutors might see counties as unfit to handle serious offenders and thus try many juveniles as adults, forcing teenagers into adult prisons.

Barry Krisberg, a senior fellow at the University of California, Berkeley, School of Law, said that keeping young offenders at the county level might offer them fewer rehabilitation options.

"I would bet that those kids would end up in juvenile hall, in isolation, getting fewer services," Mr. Krisberg said. "I don't think we can shut down the entire state system."

But Dan Macallair, executive director of the Center on Juvenile and Criminal Justice, a nonprofit group in San Francisco, said he believed young offenders could receive better support at the local level. "In county juvenile halls, you don't have the entrenched gang culture and violence you have at the state youth authority," Mr. Macallair said. "The counties can offer a continuum of options—maximum security, minimum security, intensive services in the community—that the state could never come close to matching."

Mr. Macallair, who has called the state institutions "relics of the 19th century," agreed that the proposed state closings presented challenges, but he said too much hand-wringing would keep resources at the state level and prevent needed changes.

"The state system is not set up for major change," he said. "If the money won't be flowing to counties, counties won't get any better, and you'll be left with the status quo."

For years, the Division of Juvenile Justice has been in steady decline. The Preston Youth Correctional Facility, an hour northeast of Stockton, is scheduled to be shut down by June. It will be the ninth state youth detention facility to close since 2002. Only four will remain.

The population of young offenders in state care has plummeted since 1996, to 1,300 from 10,000, because of lower crime rates and laws mandating that only the most serious offenders remain in state custody. The vast majority of young offenders are held at county facilities.

Mr. DiazDeLeon, who was first arrested at 14 on a charge of attempted burglary, agrees with those who say the California youth justice system is obsolete.

"Kids are broken, kids are abused" coming into the state facilities, he said. "I was an abused child growing up into a wounded man."

Mr. DiazDeLeon said the institution's need to constantly quell the threat of violence meant he had essentially been left to rehabilitate himself.

"The correctional officers' job was to keep control of the facility," he said. "When I was there, they were told to do rehabilitation, but they didn't fully engage in that because they didn't really believe rehabilitation was possible for some of the young men there."

If the counties are going to do better than the state, they will need more money and rehabilitation services to deal with young people for whom violence is common, said Donna Hitchens, a retired San Francisco judge who said she was among those who tried to avoid sending young offenders to state institutions.

"On a policy level, it's a great idea," Ms. Hitchens said. "But long-term treatment requires really strong programs in a secure setting, and a campus environment since they're going to be there for so long."

A memo released last week by the Chief Probation Officers of California after the Brown proposal was announced stated that county probation departments were ready to participate in the governor's plan—with one major caveat. "We must be sure we can afford the new responsibilities the state contemplates for local probation," the memo said.

Mr. Brown intends to compensate counties by extending existing sales tax and vehicle license fees, according to the California Department of Finance. The state's 58 county probation departments would split $242 million in state money over the next four years.

In the 2003 Alameda County lawsuit, Judge Jon Tigar of Superior Court found that conditions at state youth institutions were unsafe and not conducive to rehabilitation. The court ordered the Division of Juvenile Justice to provide young offenders with vastly improved facilities, education and treatment programs.

In an interview before the announcement of Mr. Brown's plan, a spokesman for the division, Bill Sessa, said that the state was in 85 percent compliance with the court's mandates and that more changes were in progress.

"What may have been true more than a decade ago totally mischaracterizes the reality of the Division of Juvenile Justice today," Mr. Sessa said.

He said he had no comment on Mr. Brown's proposal to eliminate the Division of Juvenile Justice.

Based on his own experience incarcerated at state and county facilities, Mr. DiazDeLeon said counties should embrace the inevitable.

"I think D.J.J. can be replaced with something better within counties," Mr. DiazDeLeon said. "Their model is outdated. You're already coming from a dysfunctional background and going into dysfunctional system. What do you expect?"

Critical Thinking

1. What are the problems the California juvenile prison faces?
2. How would the state government's proposal to deal with state's youth prison system affect the counties?

At D.C. Superior Court Program, a Focus on Helping Minors with Mental Health Problems

JUSTIN MOYER

JM-4 in D.C. Superior Court isn't your typical courtroom. No one is on trial. Defendants, called "respondents," are surrounded by social workers, psychologists and, often, family members. There's no mention of the criminal charges against them.

But don't be deceived. A lot is at stake in JM-4, home of a 14-month-old juvenile court intended to help minors with mental health problems avoid the harsh consequences and limited rehabilitation opportunities in the juvenile system.

Known formally as the juvenile mental health diversion court, it is the latest stop for Magistrate Judge Joan Goldfrank, who has spent much of her career on the bench navigating the intersection of mental health and criminal justice.

In JM-4, where art by young people who have passed through the courtroom hangs on the walls, Goldfrank dispenses encouragement, wisdom—and snacks.

"The message I want to give them is that they are supported," Goldfrank said. "The whole point of juvenile justice is rehabilitation. How could we not do it on the kids' side?"

In recent years, the District's courts and social services agencies have increased mental health resources for young people, although advocates say the efforts still fall short of the need. Last week, the D.C. Council gave preliminary approval to legislation that would expand mental health services in the city's public schools.

On a couple of days last month, *The Washington Post* was permitted to observe proceedings in juvenile mental health court on the condition that none of the participants or their families be identified.

For the mother of a 17-year-old girl, the court was the latest stop in a frustrating effort to obtain help. After her daughter "got in trouble"—the mother wouldn't go into details—the family had difficulty working with probation officers, coordinating curfews and developing an education plan.

"They were sending me all around the world when it first came out for me trying to seek help for my daughter," the mother said. "They were telling me to sign my parental rights away." For her, Goldfrank's court was different. "I felt that she still listened to me," the mother said.

Goldfrank does listen, but she and the people who work with her also deliver news that families don't want to hear. The young people must not only be held accountable for their behavior but also must come to terms with their mental health diagnoses, which are often rooted in trauma that the juveniles have witnessed or experienced.

Accepting that can be hard. Asked by a reporter about her daughter's problems, the 17-year-old's mother said she wasn't aware that her daughter had been diagnosed with any mental health issue.

Indeed, overcoming family apprehension is one of the challenges the court faces. "Nobody wants to be known as the kid who's suffering from depression or suffering from PTSD," said Superior Court Judge Zoe Bush, who, as head of the family court division, helped design the program. "It's not a weakness if you've lost someone close to you, to get treatment for depression or dealing with that loss."

D.C.'s juvenile mental health diversion court, one of about a dozen similar courts around the country, is part of a broader movement toward "problem-solving" courts that try to tackle social problems such as drug use and prostitution without incarcerating offenders.

D.C. Superior Court's diversion programs have included an adult mental health court and adult drug court as well as a prostitution court, which was discontinued.

When mental health courts work—and some experts say the results are mixed—they reduce the number of offenders behind bars while linking people to services that can help them avoid being arrested again.

In the District, a minor charged with an eligible offense—mostly misdemeanors and nonviolent offenses such as attempting to flee a law enforcement officer or driving while intoxicated—can apply to have a case diverted to Goldfrank's court if he or she has a mental health diagnosis, such as generalized anxiety disorder or social phobia.

Instead of facing incarceration, which can increase the odds that the juvenile will re-offend, juveniles in diversion must deal with their problem behavior. If they're cutting school, they have to go back—or consider getting a GED or a job. If they're doing drugs, they have to get tested and get treatment. If they need therapy, they have to see a psychologist.

If they succeed, they graduate from the program and have their cases dismissed. If they fail, they may find their cases back on the regular juvenile calendar.

"You can't overstate how important it is to have real interventions that are targeted to the real needs of the youth," Bush said. Bush, who used to run D.C.'s juvenile drug court, said there she saw kids who, "80 to 90 percent of the time," were smoking marijuana to self-medicate for undiagnosed mental health problems.

"If you just get the kids to stop smoking, that anxiety and depression and trauma is still untreated," she said. "You really want to get to the underlying problem that they are self-treating and self-medicating. If you do that, you're getting them to adjust better at home, at school and in the community."

Whether the new mental health diversion court is meeting those objectives will be the subject of two internal reviews by D.C. Superior Court.

Early statistics are encouraging. A report from the D.C. Department of Mental Health showed that 56 juveniles were enrolled in diversion in 2011. Eight, or 14 percent, were re-arrested, compared with 40 percent in regular court. Nationally, the re-arrest rate is 60 percent, according to the report.

"I'm saying we're cautiously excited," said Marie Morilus-Black, the mental health agency's director of children and youth services. "The recidivism rate—we're just blown away by it. It's actually showing that it's working."

Juveniles are generally prosecuted by the D.C. attorney general's office, and Assistant Attorney General Rachele Reid is the prosecutor assigned to the juvenile mental health court. In an interview, Reid said that diversion efforts fit into the city's objectives.

"Families and communities are looking for alternatives to detention, but we are there to ensure public safety," said Reid, who sees up to 30 families a week in JM-4. "Believe it or not, the mind set of our section . . . is to be looking to diversion programs." After all, treatment today can prevent future crimes. As Reid puts it: "We don't want them back here."

James L. Nolan, a sociology professor at Williams College who has authored two books on problem-solving courts, said enthusiasm should be tempered. Although the first mental health court was established in Florida, in 1997, it's still not clear how well such programs stop bad behavior.

"It is not uncommon for local court programs to exaggerate success rates," Nolan said. "This clearly happened in the early years of the drug court movement. Many of the locally generated evaluations had serious design flaws. This did not dissuade most problem-solving advocates, nor did it seem to dampen the general enthusiasm for these programs."

But teenagers such as a 17-year old who was referred to diversion last October offer the staff hope that juvenile mental health court will succeed.

The young woman was already attending drug treatment programming at Federal City Recovery Services in Southeast Washington twice a week, and the diversion program offered her the prospect of avoiding traditional prosecution.

After almost six months in the diversion program, the teenager graduated last month with a framed certificate of completion, a letter from the office of the attorney general, a gift-wrapped copy of "Anne Frank: The Diary of a Young Girl" and a handshake from Goldfrank.

"This isn't something I want you to hang in your bathroom," Goldfrank said, stepping from behind the bench—a rare sight in other courtrooms—to hand the young woman her certificate. "When problems come up, don't feel like you have to sort them out yourself."

Critical Thinking

1. Are the juveniles in JM-4 held accountable for their actions?
2. Why do you think a special court is needed for juveniles with mental health problems?
3. What are risks of incarceration for juveniles?

No Remorse

Should a teen-ager be given a life sentence?

RACHEL AVIV

Shortly after midnight on March 6, 2010, Dakotah Eliason sat in a chair in his bedroom with a .38-calibre pistol in his hands, thinking about what the world would be like if he didn't exist. One of his friends had recently killed himself, and his girlfriend had dumped him. Earlier that night, Dakotah, who was fourteen, had taken his grandfather's loaded gun off the coatrack. The breakup felt like a sign that he would always be a failure, and he figured no one would miss him after a few days. He got a pencil and tried to compose a suicide note, but he didn't know what he should say.

Dakotah wondered if he was ready to die, and contemplated taking someone else's life instead. He thought about how people have good and evil sides, and how the good doesn't always win. It was the theme of an adventure story he was writing. He drank a can of Mountain Dew, then went to the bathroom and looked at himself in the mirror. He was pale and lanky, with sandy bangs swept to the side. "What am I doing?" he said to himself. "Why? Why do I have the gun? I know better than this."

He walked into the living room and stared at his grandfather, Jesse Miles, who was sleeping on the couch. A retired machinist and an avid hunter, Jesse often fell asleep while watching the Discovery Channel, and stayed on the couch all night so his smoker's cough wouldn't wake his wife. For forty-five minutes, Dakotah sat on a wooden chair, three feet from his grandfather, and talked to himself quietly, debating what to do next. If he got hand towels from the bathroom, he could gag his grandpa. If he used a steak knife, the whole thing might be quieter. He figured he'd use the cordless phone on his bed to report the crime. He felt as if he were watching a movie about himself. Finally, at just after three in the morning, he raised the handgun, his arms trembling, and shot his grandfather in the head.

"Man, I shot Papa!" he shouted. He put the gun on the floor and rushed into his grandmother Jean's bedroom. She yelled for Dakotah to call 911, and he followed her orders "like a little puppy," she said later. When officers from the police department in Niles, a rural town in southeast Michigan, arrived, seven minutes later, Dakotah was waiting outside next to his grandmother, who was in her pajamas and frantically waving her hands. Jean explained that Dakotah had shot Jesse. "This is my grandson," she said, placing her hand on his shoulder.

A trooper named Brenda Kiefer handcuffed Dakotah, read him his Miranda rights, and told him that she needed to know what had happened but that she "was not here to judge." She asked if he wanted a parent there and heard him say no. (Dakotah insists that he said "Uh-huh," indicating that he did want a parent present, and that he rarely says "yes" or "no," a habit for which his father scolds him.) Dakotah had always admired police officers, and he responded politely to Kiefer's questions, as his grandfather, unconscious and bleeding heavily, was loaded into an ambulance. Dakotah told Kiefer that he had a loving relationship with his grandparents and often spent the weekends at their home, where he had his own room. He didn't know why he'd picked up the gun, but he guessed that it was "sadness and pent-up anger."

After talking to Kiefer for fifteen minutes, Dakotah was put in a patrol car, which was parked at the bottom of the driveway. The officer who sat up front, Eugene Castro, asked Dakotah his name, and then realized he had gone to high school with Dakotah's father, Steve. "So was he good at sports?" Dakotah asked. Castro said that Steve had played hockey and tried to end the conversation cordially, but Dakotah updated him on his father's path since graduation: after losing his job as a construction worker, he'd begun an associate's-degree program in criminal justice. Dakotah added that it would be nice to be on the police force, because of the job security.

Several times, Castro stepped outside the cruiser to answer phone calls. When Dakotah was alone in the car, which had a video camera running, his breathing became heavy and rapid, and he coughed and made retching noises. Then an Avril Lavigne song, "My Happy Ending," came on the radio. "Ugh, why does this song have to play!" he said. He began singing along with the chorus: "So much for my happy ending / Oh oh, oh oh."

Out the window, Dakotah could see the flash of cameras inside his grandparents' home, a two-story farmhouse that the couple had lived in for thirty-five years. "It looks like forensics is doing their thing," Dakotah said when Castro returned. "So what do you predict will happen to me? I mean, murder charge—that's big. I'm still a minor, but . . ." Castro said he didn't know, and explained that a judge, not the police, would decide. "My life just turned into 'Law & Order,'" Dakotah said. "But with no commercials."

When the officer didn't respond, Dakotah began breathing heavily again. "I wish I could take it back, but now I understand the feeling people get when they do that," he said, drawing out his words slowly. "You feel like nothing could ever hurt you—just for that split second, once you realize what you've done."

Steve Eliason had been asleep for only a few hours when a detective knocked at his door and told him that his stepfather, who had raised him, was in the hospital in critical condition and that his son had been arrested. Still groggy from a night of drinking with his wife, Lisa, and out-of-town guests, Steve expected that there would be some reasonable explanation. Dakotah's only previous encounter with the police involved a missing backpack, and he had quickly been absolved of blame. He was an honor-roll student with a close group of friends who called themselves the Randoms, because, unlike the jocks and the preps who occupied the upper tier of their school's social hierarchy, their hobbies were varied: video games, fan fiction, classic rock, anime.

The detective, Fabian Suarez, drove Steve to the police station and, just before five in the morning, led him into a windowless, fluorescent-lit room with a Formica table and three chairs. Dakotah sat alone at the table, and Steve stared at his son, shook his head, and then pulled up a chair next to him. For the second time that morning, Dakotah heard his Miranda rights—Suarez went through the litany rapidly, in a dispassionate monotone.

"Are you angry with me?" Steve asked Dakotah, his voice shaking. "Is it something I did?" He told Suarez that a family doctor had once suggested that Dakotah see a therapist, because Dakotah was upset that nothing he did could ever please his dad. Dakotah didn't play sports—he preferred singing, drawing, and writing stories—which meant that he didn't have to maintain his grade-point average for a team. "So I try to push him," Steve explained.

Detective Suarez asked if he could have a private conversation with Dakotah, whose focus had drifted; he was shaking his wrists, blowing on the skin where the handcuffs had been. Steve agreed and told Dakotah, "We are trying to get to the bottom of this. Please, please answer."

Alone with the detective, Dakotah was initially sluggish, as if humoring a concerned teacher. But when Suarez asked what made him angriest in life he said that he was mad at his mother, Mary, who had abandoned him when he was a baby and dropped in and out of his life, depending on whether or not she was with a new man.

Dakotah said it had never occurred to him to hurt his grandfather, but "something overcame me." It had been a typically boring Saturday: he played racing and fighting games on his PlayStation console for four hours, and watched part of "Terminator 3" and a few shows on Comedy Central. Then he had a brief, pleasant conversation with his grandmother before she went to sleep. Later that night, he started thinking about how his family and friends were too distant; it felt like everyone he loved was drifting away. For about two hours, the "main argument was homicide or suicide," he told Suarez. "You ever hear people talk about having voices in their head? Well, it's not so much that as multiple personalities. One is like the good guy and the other is essentially the bad guy."

"The thing is when you actually do kill somebody, whether you have an emotional attachment or not, you get about five seconds," Dakotah said. "All the tension goes away." He propped his elbows on the table and rested his head in his hands, rubbing his face. "It's just that initial feeling," he continued. "It's an overwhelming feeling—I'm not really sure how to explain it."

After ten minutes, Steve demanded to be let back into the room. He had spoken with his brother, who was at the hospital, and learned that their father had died. By the time he returned, the interview was over. Steve was aggressive and agitated, and told Dakotah he couldn't make sense of what had happened. "Help me understand," he pleaded. "You always seemed happy."

Dakotah looked up at him blankly, his hands folded on the table.

"You're not showing any remorse, Dakotah. I'm not saying it in a bad way, but is something wrong with your head? Do you have problems with thinking? I mean, because you're a very intelligent young man." Steve told him to imagine what would happen "if you weren't my kid, and I was in this room with the person that shot my dad." He raised his voice: "This is the shit they talk about. Kids get into these goddamn video games and they don't pull their head out of the fucking game. They think they can just go"—he pressed his finger into Dakotah's biceps—"hit the re-start button!" He said he couldn't accept "I don't know" as an answer. "Why would you shoot Papa, D.? Papa loved you."

Dakotah's face had turned deep red, and he hung his head a couple of inches from the table. He wiped his eyes with his sleeve.

"Don't hold it in. Let it out," Steve said. He put his arms around Dakotah, who had begun sobbing, and pulled him toward his chest. Dakotah circled his arms around his father, letting his weight collapse into him. "You've got to be strong for me, O.K.?" Steve whispered, rubbing Dakotah's back and staring at the wall with a bewildered expression. "You're my little boy."

Watching the local news the next day, Steve learned that Dakotah would be tried as an adult for first-degree homicide, which in Michigan carries a mandatory sentence of life imprisonment without the possibility of parole. The county's prosecuting attorney, Arthur Cotter, a towering man with white hair who was elected to office in 2008, had reviewed videotapes of Dakotah's statements to the police and concluded that Dakotah didn't belong in the juvenile justice system, which releases offenders from custody when they turn twenty-one. Cotter said that the decision was easy, because Dakotah had shown "an utter lack of remorse." "Even his father noticed it," he told me.

In Michigan, as in many states, prosecutors can try defendants older than fourteen in adult court without a hearing, a statement of reasons, or an investigation into the adolescent's background. The decision cannot be reviewed or appealed. This allows prosecutors to bypass the juvenile justice system, which was built upon the premise that youths are still malleable, in need of the state's protection, and uniquely capable of rehabilitation.

The first juvenile courts, which emerged at the turn of the twentieth century, aimed to treat criminal behavior, not punish it, by intervening in the domestic lives of children whose parents had failed them. The establishment of a separate court system for youths followed other progressive reforms, like compulsory education and child-labor laws, which extended the boundary of childhood. The psychologist G. Stanley Hall lent scientific legitimacy to the concept of adolescence, describing it, in 1904, as a "genetic period of storm and stress," with a "curve of despondency" that rises at the age of eleven and falls by twenty-three. Juvenile hearings were sealed to the public and focussed on the personal history of the offender rather than on the offense. Judges designed individualized treatment plans to address whatever had thwarted the child's development: neglect, abuse, a poor education, an overcrowded home, unrestricted exposure to books about bandits. In 1910, Benjamin Lindsey, one of the first juvenile-court judges in the country, wrote that "our laws against crime are as inapplicable to children as they would be to idiots."

The juvenile justice system quickly became a model for courts throughout the world—the judicial scholar Francis Allen called it the "greatest legal institution invented in the United States"—but the system's paternalistic outlook often led to capricious rulings. In the sixties, a new generation of children's advocates tried to redefine the "best interests of the child," focussing on liberating rather than protecting youths. In 1967, the Supreme Court reviewed the case of a fifteen-year-old who had been committed to a detention home for six years for making a lewd phone call, and ruled that the "condition of being a boy does not justify a Kangaroo Court." The decision established that juveniles deserve many of the same due-process rights as adults, including the right to a lawyer and the right against self-incrimination.

Once hearings became adversarial (resembling "junior varsity criminal trials," as one court decision put it), the system's original mission was gradually obscured. In the eighties, when youth crime rates began to rise, most visibly in gang-related violence, reformers argued that modern adolescents were more sophisticated than the youths of earlier eras. In 1985, Alfred Regnery, the head of the Justice Department's Office of Juvenile Justice and Delinquency Prevention, accused the juvenile courts of naïvely adopting Rousseau's theory that youths are "incapable of evil unless they are corrupted" and of listening to the "psychobabble of social workers." In the following decade, juvenile gun homicides more than tripled, leading to widespread hysteria, promoted by sensational news reports, about a rising generation of juvenile "super-predators." They are "doing homicidal violence in 'wolf packs,'" wrote John DiIulio, then a professor of politics and public affairs at Princeton, who helped popularize the idea of a "demographic crime bomb." (He has since expressed regret, acknowledging that the prediction was never fulfilled.) Juvenile courts became increasingly punitive, and by the late nineties nearly half of committed juveniles were behind bars, rather than in community-supervision or treatment programs, and a quarter of them were locked up because of misdemeanors or probation violations. Forty-six states rewrote their laws to make it easier for minors to be tried as adults.

Although judges have long been attuned to the difficulty of trying mentally ill defendants, there is little recognition that people may be incompetent to stand trial because of their age. Each year, more than two hundred thousand offenders younger than eighteen are tried as adults, yet only about half of them understand the Miranda warning. According to studies of delinquent adolescents, they have trouble grasping that a "right" is an absolute privilege that they may exercise without penalty. Defendants fifteen and younger are particularly impaired, and waive their rights much more frequently than do adults. The vast majority misinterpret at least one of the four statements that make up the Miranda warning, stumbling on terms like "consult," "interrogation," "appoint," and "entitled," which may be above their reading level.

At a hearing to determine whether Dakotah's confessions were made voluntarily and could be used at trial, Dakotah maintained that he didn't realize that he was free to stop talking to the police once he had already started. The prosecutor, Arthur Cotter, broke down the Miranda warning and asked Dakotah which sentences he couldn't comprehend. Dakotah conceded that he understood the language ("Yeah, I know what a lawyer is"), but not its implications. He explained, "I just felt I had no choice but to answer the questions."

The judge, Scott Schofield, was not persuaded and ruled that all Dakotah's statements could be admitted as evidence. He pointed out that Dakotah watched "Law & Order," had proofread one of his father's papers for a criminology class, and used big words. (The trooper, Brenda Kiefer, testified that Dakotah, when describing his grandparents' property, had used the word "elevation" and warned that frozen ruts on the driveway were "treacherous.") Schofield dismissed the claim that Dakotah was in a psychotic or altered state of mind. He interpreted Dakotah's reference to hearing voices as an externalization of his own conscience, "a debate that he was having with himself—should I do the right thing, or should I not do the right thing?"

Dakotah often talked of becoming a writer. Throughout his freshman year, he wrote fantasy stories and shared them with his friends, who critiqued the plots and gave him tips for improvement. Tashawn Reese, who collaborated with him, said that Dakotah's stories were about underdogs who faced emotional challenges—the hero falls in love with an irresistible girl who's unavailable, or his parents die, or his school morphs into a crater—and usually the "theme was the eternal struggle between good and evil." The last story Dakotah brought to school was about two boys, one of whom develops demonic powers while the other acquires angelic ones; at the end, both soar into the sky.

Kelsey Crago, who dated Dakotah briefly, couldn't recall his doing anything unusual in the weeks before the murder. She knew that he was disappointed by his recent breakup—his girlfriend had broken things off by text message—but he didn't talk about it, because he didn't like drama. Kelsey described Dakotah as a "great listener, the main person I trusted if I needed advice," but he rarely shared his own problems. In letters to Dakotah, she repeatedly asked him why he had killed his grandfather, but never felt satisfied by his answers. "I wasn't thinking," he told her, and wrote that maybe he had watched too many crime shows.

At the Berrien County Juvenile Center, fifteen miles from his home, Dakotah complained that every time he closed his eyes he saw his grandfather's death, "like a movie." He told a caseworker that he was still trying to figure out what had happened and that he wished he had killed himself instead. He was forced to wear suicide garb, clothes too stiff to be torn, and was unable to sleep. His grandmother Jean, a petite, well-dressed woman with short white hair, wrote him a letter telling him that she forgave him, and visited him at the center after two weeks. "It was hard for him to look at me, with him knowing what he'd done," she told me. "He'd look up and then look away. Mostly, he just held my hand and rubbed it."

Steve berated himself for acting like a "maniac drill instructor" and losing his temper over anything his son did wrong. He also blamed Dakotah's "bio-mom," as he called her. In her statement to the police, Mary explained that she'd never intended to have a child with Steve. "I had a party at my apt.," she wrote. "We got drunk, we got pregnant." (Mary would not talk to me, explaining, "I have nothing to say.") She was rarely involved in Dakotah's life until he was seven; then she went to court to obtain joint custody. When Dakotah was twelve, she changed her mind and relinquished all her rights as a parent. Steve remembers Dakotah coming home from a visit and "brushing his hands like he'd just had crackers and was getting rid of the crumbs. He said, 'Mom finally washed her hands clean of me.' "

For Steve and his wife, the fact that Dakotah had killed his grandfather, a man he had loved, was proof that he'd been temporarily insane. A week after Dakotah was arrested, Steve hired Lanny Fisher, a local attorney who had gone to the same high school, was "great at sports but humble about it," and had been practicing law for three years. (Fisher offered to charge a fraction of his normal fee, since Steve and Lisa were living on her hourly wages from Subway.) Fisher, assuming that the trial would be a battle between mental-health experts, said he was "devastated" when he received the results of Dakotah's psychiatric report. The examiner, who interviewed Dakotah for a little more than three hours, noted that Dakotah preferred his own fantasies to reality, but he did not think his imaginary life had ever reached psychotic proportions.

Two more psychiatric reports were done, and neither found that Dakotah met the criteria for legal insanity, which would have meant that he could not appreciate the wrongfulness of his crime or conform his behavior to meet the requirements of the law. No history of physical or sexual abuse was uncovered. Fisher and Arthur Cotter had been discussing a possible plea bargain—fourteen years to life for second-degree murder—but after reading the psychiatric reports Cotter chose to go to trial, a decision that several family members endorsed. Jesse Miles's forty-seven-year-old daughter, Vickie Hartz, Steve's stepsister, told me that she was disappointed that Michigan doesn't have the death penalty. "My dad was an easygoing, mellow guy who did everything for that kid," Hartz said. "And Dakotah killed him with as much emotion as if he were moving a chair."

The murder trial began on August 17th, less than six months after Jesse Miles's death. Judge Scott Schofield, who presides over all the criminal trials in Niles, is known for running a "rocket docket" when his cases get local media attention. He set brisk deadlines for motions and hearings, saying, "It's a cliché, I know," but "justice delayed is justice denied." The courtroom was filled to capacity, with reporters from four local TV stations. Schofield referred to the microphone as an ice-cream cone and encouraged jurors to hold it close to their mouths so they wouldn't make a mess.

At the juvenile center, where residents spend six hours a day in school and attend workshops on risk and anger management, Dakotah was "student of the week" three times, and received awards for "social skills," "fabulous achievement and effort," and "making a difference." Still, Cotter requested that Dakotah's legs be shackled during the trial, saying that he might pose a security risk because of "his feelings of power." "When he shot his grandfather, he felt for fifteen seconds that nothing in the world could hurt him," Cotter told the court. Judge Schofield acknowledged that defendants have the right to be free of restraint but concluded that in this case the shackles were warranted, since "the Court has some concerns about Mr. Eliason being psychologically conflicted."

Cotter, in his opening statement, portrayed Dakotah as a sociopath so callous he was capable of "chitchat" and making a "whooey sound" in the patrol car just moments after shooting his grandfather. Dakotah was fascinated by death, he said, and would have killed his grandmother, too, if she hadn't woken up. Cotter cautioned the jury that when they viewed the videotape of Dakotah's interview at the police station they might be moved by the sight of Steve Eliason, "in a true test of the unlimitedness of a parent's love," embracing his son. "Do not confuse the emotions you're going to feel—the empathy that you are going to feel when you watch that point with his father—with any sadness that that young man felt remorse," Cotter said.

Lanny Fisher, unassuming and amiable, opened with a speech that laid bare his own confusion. "Most cases, most stories, they have the who, the what, the where, the when, and the why," he said. "The reason that we're all here today is the why." After months of research, he could find no coherent motive, so he presented the crime's incomprehensibility as proof that it couldn't have been deliberate. Cotter referred to Dakotah as a "young man"; Fisher called him a "boy." He emphasized that in the past year Dakotah had endured a series of losses: his cousin had been in a fatal car crash, his father had told him they were losing their house because he could not pay the mortgage, a friend had committed suicide, and his dog, Bam-Bam, had died of old age.

Fisher's other line of defense was to urge the jury to recall how it felt to be fourteen. "You can't drink," he said. "You have to be twenty-one to do that. You can't smoke, or vote, or join the armed services. You have to be eighteen to do that. Can't even drive a car . . . That's the person that's on trial, ladies and gentlemen."

The trial lasted two and a half days, and much of it focussed on testimony from police officers and forensic technicians who established details about the crime that were not contested by the defense. Fisher chose not to have Dakotah testify, since juveniles tend to make poor witnesses—they are easily misled or intimidated and often give inconsistent, idealized accounts of their own actions. For character witnesses, Fisher called Dakotah's high-school principal, who said that Dakotah was never sent to his office and was "probably not the top student, but pretty good," and a family friend who described him as "very mild-mannered, kind." Since Fisher was not advancing any theory about the crime, his conversations with the witnesses for the defense lacked direction and at times helped the prosecutor's argument as much as his own. When Jean Miles, weeping, took the stand, Fisher helped her paint an image of domestic normalcy:

Fisher: Your house was kind of a getaway for him, wasn't it?

Miles: Yes.

Fisher: It would be you, and Jesse, and Dakotah, and he could kind of play video games, watch movies?

Miles: Yes.

Fisher: And you guys gave him attention?

Miles: Yes.

Fisher: O.K. He had fun over at your house?

Miles: Yes. I hope so.

Cotter concluded the trial by describing Dakotah as a young man incapable of reciprocating his family's love. He argued that the crime exemplified premeditation, since Dakotah "considered the pros and cons of killing" for more than two hours. "It's almost like he was building up the courage to do it," Cotter said, before acting out Dakotah's interior monologue: "Are you going to do it? Do it. Do it! Shoot him." Cotter described Dakotah's reaction to the shooting as "just bizarre": there was "not a tear, not a sob," no "ounce of emotion." He dwelled on Dakotah's remark that the "tension goes away" after murdering someone. "That's when it *starts*, that's when the conscience kicks in," Cotter said. "He's got the emotional curve all wrong."

The expectation that defendants will display remorse either shortly after their crimes or never is generally accepted as common sense. In a *Columbia Law Review* study of cases of juveniles charged with violent crimes, the Emory law professor Martha Grace Duncan found that youths who failed to express their contrition promptly and appropriately, as adults would, were often penalized for showing "less grief than the system demands." In many cases, she writes, the juveniles appeared to be in shock or in a kind of dissociative state and failed to appreciate the permanence of what they had done. "Less under the sway of the reality principle," they were more prone than adults to engage in forms of denial. But prosecutors and judges interpreted their strange reactions—falling asleep after the crime, giggling, rapping—as signs of irreparable depravity. Duncan found that courts looked for remorse in "psychologically naïve ways, without regard for defense mechanisms, developmental stages, or the ambiguity that inheres in human behavior."

One of Dakotah's closest friends, Christina Wardlaw, who sat through the trial, told me that she had to suppress the urge to laugh as she listened to Dakotah's recorded conversations with the police. "He still saw himself as the same old Dakotah, jabbering and singing and making jokes," she said. "He had no idea what he'd become."

Dakotah's reaction, with its apparent remorselessness, less than three hours after shooting his grandfather, was discussed by three witnesses for the prosecution. It also figured in the jurors' deliberations. They asked to view Dakotah's videotaped conversation with the detective again, and an hour after watching the tape, and just three hours after beginning deliberations, they announced that Dakotah was guilty of first-degree homicide.

One juror told me that several people on the jury were troubled by Dakotah's youth, but they'd been instructed that if the evidence indicated that the offense was premeditated and deliberate the crime was first-degree murder. Age had no place in that calculus. As is required under Michigan law, the jury was not informed that the conviction carried the automatic penalty of life imprisonment without the possibility of parole.

Before the sentencing hearing, Lanny Fisher filed a brief asserting that the punishment violated the Eighth Amendment, which prohibits sentences that are cruel and unusual, based on the "evolving standards of decency in our maturing society." Life imprisonment for juveniles is forbidden by the United Nations Convention on the Rights of the Child, a treaty ratified by every country in the world except the United States and Somalia. In his brief, Fisher relied heavily on two recent Supreme Court cases, which, he maintained, suggest that the U.S. is increasingly recognizing the "distinct emotional, psychological and neurological status of youth."

In a 2005 case, *Roper v. Simmons,* the United States became the last Western country to abolish the death penalty for juveniles. The decision drew on a growing body of scientific research that reaffirmed what, a hundred years earlier, passed for common sense: "the personality traits of juveniles are more transitory, less fixed." Anthony Kennedy, in his opinion, pointed out that the *Diagnostic and Statistical Manual of Mental Disorders* explicitly prohibits psychiatrists from giving people under eighteen a diagnosis of antisocial disorder (a euphemism for sociopathy), since many signs of the disorder—egocentricity, failure to accept responsibility, impulsiveness, proneness to boredom—are natural aspects of adolescence. Kennedy noted that "adolescents are overrepresented statistically in virtually every category of reckless behavior."

The Court extended the reasoning it had used three years earlier when it outlawed capital punishment for defendants with I.Q.s below seventy. But the four dissenting Justices in *Roper* rejected the idea that the same claim of diminished culpability could be made for all juveniles, since the Court's analysis had been based on aggregate differences between youths and adults, which may have little bearing on the sophistication of individual defendants, particularly those at the "margins between adolescence and adulthood." Antonin Scalia criticized the American Psychological Association, which submitted a brief in favor of abolition, for taking a conflicting stance on teen maturity in an earlier case regarding the rights of juveniles to get abortions. The large body of research on adolescent cognition, Scalia wrote, had allowed the Court to "look over the heads of the crowd and pick out its friends," finding empirical support for previously held opinions.

Five years later, in *Graham v. Florida,* the Court again pointed to "developments in psychology and brain science [that] continue to show fundamental differences between juvenile and adult minds," and, for the first time in a quarter century, invalidated a sentence other than capital punishment. Now the Court ruled that for juveniles—but only those whose crimes did not result in death—a sentence that offers "no chance for reconciliation with society, no hope" is cruel and unusual. Life-without-parole sentences have tripled since the early nineties, both because the punishment offers an alternative to death and because of crime policies that emphasize retribution and incapacitation rather than rehabilitation. The ruling did not guarantee young prisoners eventual release, only the possibility of it. In the decision, Justice Kennedy alluded to studies, outlined in a brief submitted by the American Medical Association, showing that the prefrontal cortex, which is associated with behavioral control, does not fully develop until people reach their twenties. Kennedy noted that in many states inmates who are ineligible for parole are denied access to educational programs, leading to the "perverse consequence in which the lack of maturity that led to an offender's crime is reinforced by the prison term."

Judge Schofield gave Cotter a week to submit a written response to Fisher's constitutional challenge and scheduled his own ruling and sentencing for the following week. At the hearing, on October 25th, Schofield gave a rhapsodic speech about how the legislative branch of government makes the law, and how the judicial branch has "nothing to do with that. And that's the way it should be." He called the case a "textbook example of our separation of powers" and denied Fisher's motion. He noted that the punishment wasn't unusual; thirty-nine states allow fourteen-year-olds to be sentenced to life without parole. No appellate or trial court has held that *Graham* applies to those convicted of homicide. Currently, there are some twenty-five hundred American inmates who were given life sentences for killing someone before their eighteenth birthday; for more than half of them, it was their first crime.

During the sentencing, Dakotah, who had just turned fifteen, periodically grasped at his chest and bent over, as if struggling to take in air. He wore a green prison jumpsuit, he had a new military buzz cut, and he showed early signs of a weak beard. At the end of the hearing, he was given an opportunity to speak before the court for the first time. He stood up and said that his heart was pounding so hard that he thought he was going to die, and he was trying not to pee in his pants. "If I don't regret this every day, then I truly am less than human," he said. "Then I do deserve to die in prison."

He began crying and apologized to his aunt and his cousins, who were sitting on the prosecutor's side of the courtroom and had publicly expressed their wish that he never reenter society. "No matter how much anyone hates me—it doesn't make a difference—I will still love you all because you're my family," Dakotah said. "I never finished that statement at the courthouse or at the station. The tension, it goes away, but it comes back tenfold. You deal with it on a scale that can never be measured."

Nine days after his sentencing, Dakotah was transferred to Thumb Correctional Facility, a medium-security prison on the eastern edge of the state, two hundred miles from his home and sixty miles from Detroit. The forty-acre prison complex, which is a half mile from Interstate 69, is surrounded by three sets of twelve-foot fences, edged with coils of razor-ribbon wire. Although the law mandates that incarcerated juveniles have no contact with adult prisoners, the same protections do not apply to youths who have been prosecuted as adults. The prison has six squat beige brick units, two of which house four hundred and thirty inmates who are under twenty-one years old. They cross paths with the Old Heads, as they are called, during visits to the library, church, and the segregation unit, where prisoners of all ages are punished with solitary confinement.

The prison rarely permits media visits, and, last January, the warden denied my request, citing Dakotah's age and "health-related" concerns. Journalists are subject to the same admission requirements as the general public, so I waited six months, until Dakotah was eligible to update his list of ten visitors who are not immediate family, and visited him for the first time last June, eight months after he had arrived at the prison.

The prison's visiting room has an atmosphere of casual boredom, like the waiting room of a doctor's office. About fifty upholstered metal chairs are arrayed around coffee tables, and inmates and their visitors pass time by playing Uno or checkers, drifting to the vending machines and back, or holding each other subtly enough to escape the guards' scrutiny. Two kisses are permitted, one at the beginning of the visit and one at the end.

I got a Coke for Dakotah, who had been assigned a seat near the guard's podium, and he quietly thanked me, then took a dramatic swig. "If I drink Coke like I'm drinking beer, it's because I've had a few beers before," he said nervously. He admitted that he didn't consider himself cool in other respects. "I was the smiley wannabe emo kid," he said. The only physical activity he excelled at was dodgeball. He had also taken karate, when he was nine, and was grateful to his dad for enrolling him in the class, because "it could definitely be helpful, if I have to protect myself."

At the juvenile center, Dakotah had developed a close relationship with a pastor and been born again. For several months, his mind had been on the afterlife. Since he'd been in prison, though, the spiritual world seemed less relevant. "No two ways about it, I ain't worth shit religiously," he said tentatively, as if testing the sound of the phrase. When I asked why, he explained that he talked like a sailor and was getting to be racist. Black inmates who didn't even know him would tell him to "shut your white ass up," and refer to him as "white bitch," "snowflake," and "cracker," a term he didn't fully understand until he checked out a book on the Civil War from the prison library.

At the prison's health-care center, Dakotah had received a diagnosis of bipolar disorder, and he now took a heavy daily dose of an antidepressant and a sedative. The drugs had removed "this great weight, this nervous energy pouring off me," but they had also made him less creative. He rarely wrote stories anymore, and even letters to friends felt like an exertion. Though the medications helped, he wasn't convinced that the diagnosis was right; he still wished "someone could pinpoint what's wrong with me." He said that every time he hears a loud noise, like a door slam, "my mind goes right back to the incident, and all I hear is white noise."

Initially, other inmates wanted to know what he was in for (he kept his answer brief: "I shot someone"), but no one asked about his background anymore. Conversations rarely went much deeper than "What's for chow?" He scored well on the G.E.D. exam after taking the prison's prep class, but it was just a review of things he learned freshman year or picked up from the books he used to read secretly when classes were boring. "All I've learned in prison is some better ways to work out," he told me. He earned $1.14 a day mowing the grounds at the prison, and he figured that he would become a professional landscaper. He spoke casually of things he planned to do when he got out of prison, only occasionally catching himself to add "*if* I get out." He cheerily informed me that the prison has a policy whereby "guards will take you cuffed and shackled to your own funeral," before becoming flustered and correcting himself, explaining that he might get to attend the service when his grandmother dies.

Dakotah dreamed of becoming a country or rock singer, though he considered the goal cheesy. His first demo would be called "Generation Millennials." He spent most of his time listening to his MP3 player, purchased from the prison commissary, and singing along in his eight-by-eleven-foot cell. Depending on how much money his dad put into his account, he could buy about a dozen new songs a month, and he tried to memorize the lyrics to each one. The other day, his crew yard boss had referred to him as "the kid who sings," which he liked, since he'd become accustomed to responding to "white boy."

Dakotah quizzed me on the songs I knew, and each time I failed to recognize a hit he laughed and sang it for me in a whispery, high-pitched voice. As soon as he finished one song, he tried to find another, searching for anything I might know. "The only thing I really need is my music," he said, tapping his foot. "If I've got music, I'm straight—I can do my time. You won't hear a peep out of me."

Three months after the trial, Dakotah's case was assigned to the state appellate defender's office, which represents indigent clients who can't afford private counsel. His lawyer, the office's deputy director, has contested his sentence on the ground that Dakotah received ineffective counsel, in part because Lanny Fisher never brought in an expert to explain why Dakotah failed to show "stereotypical signs of adult-like remorse." A new medical evaluation characterized Dakotah as a "traumatized youth without access to his emotions in the moment." An evidentiary hearing will be held in February to determine whether Dakotah deserves a new trial.

Dakotah's sentence may also be affected by two cases that will be argued before the Supreme Court next term. Both cases, which will be heard in tandem, challenge the constitutionality of life-without-parole sentences for juveniles fourteen and younger. The two defendants maintain that early adolescence is a distinct developmental period during which susceptibility to influence reaches its peak. "Relative to the cognition of adults and even older adolescents, young teenage judgment is handicapped in nearly every conceivable way," one petition reads.

But pegging legal protections to age markers also invites the escalating possibility of further dividing populations. It is well documented, for instance, that girls mature faster than boys, both physically and psychologically. (At a teen-ager's recent murder trial, a University of Pennsylvania neuropsychologist testified that "biology would say" that boys should be held accountable for their crimes at a later age than girls.) Terry Maroney, a Vanderbilt law professor, said that legal arguments based on developmental research, which have become more prevalent since *Roper v. Simmons,* could be used to challenge children's autonomy rights and create an "unduly complicated system with different rules for each potential subgroup." Deborah LaBelle, a lawyer and the author of a report on Michigan inmates sentenced to life for crimes they committed before the age of eighteen, said that she doesn't want to redraw a boundary that, for more than a century, has reflected the fact that "society has a different kind of responsibility to youth."

In *Roper,* the dissenting Justices argued that judgments about a defendant's maturity and culpability should be left to juries. But, in the new cases before the Supreme Court, both fourteen-year-olds were tried in states with mandatory sentencing for murder, so jurors couldn't take their age into account. One of the petitioners was physically abused by his alcoholic father, had attempted suicide six times, and was drunk and high on the night of the crime. His lawyer has argued that his mandatory penalty is cruel and unusual and violates the Fourteenth Amendment, which protects defendants' rights to due process. In death-penalty cases, trial procedure requires that juries consider mitigating factors, such as youth, mental health, and prior record, but there are no parallel safeguards in place for the penultimate punishment.

In Michigan, several judges have described their discomfort with sentencing an adolescent to die in prison, but the state's automatic-sentencing laws leave them no choice. In July, a federal district court ruled that the American Civil Liberties Union can proceed with a lawsuit challenging the state's mandatory-sentencing scheme for juveniles. Michigan has the second-highest number of juveniles sentenced to life without parole, and in 2008 the state's House of Representatives voted to abolish the practice, but the bill never passed in the state Senate; the issue is politically unpopular.

Prosecutors, who are elected officials, are also subject to political pressures, yet they have unfettered discretion to set the terms of a juvenile's charge. LaBelle told me, "I can't think of anywhere else in the world where the state can change the legal status of an individual—'Yes, I know you are a child, but now I will make you an adult'—so rapidly and in a factual vacuum." She continued, "We are telling these kids there is no such thing as redemption. They can never make amends."

For many juveniles, it is several years before they grasp the gravity of their crime and the permanence of the penalty. Joshua Miller, a twenty-nine-year-old inmate at the Wilkinson County Correctional Facility, in Mississippi, told me that it wasn't until he reached his mid-twenties that the "'without parole' part of my sentence finally dawned on me." After killing his girlfriend when he was fourteen—she rejected him, and he wanted to stage a "'Romeo and Juliet' kind of thing"—Miller was placed in an adult prison, where older inmates "treated me like the weak coward that I was," he said.

During his first few years of imprisonment, Miller tried to stay abreast of new albums, movies, and fashions, but eventually he realized there was no point in "keeping tabs on a structure I could never be part of." He stopped reading fiction, because it was too painful to "journey into the free world." He said that he has never had sex. He considers his girlfriend, who was thirteen when he murdered her, the love of his life. Although he looks back longingly on his childhood, he doesn't like to hear stories about what became of his peers. "I can't ruin a memory, or I'll lose another attachment to that life," he said. "I refuse to believe that my friends aren't still children."

When I visited the Eliason family in June, Steve, Lisa, and their nine-year-old daughter had moved into Jean Miles's house, in order to save money. They had got a new couch and rearranged the living room, but the rest of the downstairs looked the same as it had in the police photographs. On top of the television was a framed photograph of Dakotah and his family standing in front of a pastoral autumn scene painted on a cinder-block wall in the prison's visiting room. Steve and Jean both told me with pride that Dakotah was learning to be a model inmate. He had called home, upset, the night before because the toilet in his cell had overflowed, and, when the guards wouldn't respond to his calls for help, he stayed composed and mopped up the sewage with his own clothes. "I tell him that if we go through the appeals process and nothing changes, then he can get as wild and crazy as he wants," Steve said. He has noticed Dakotah's language becoming foul, which "eats me up—he was a soft boy."

Steve and I had spoken on the phone several times before, and, in each conversation, he offered new theories about his stepfather's death and the ways it could have been prevented. At the house, he reenacted the crime as his mother sat in a rocking chair beside us. With his thumb and index finger extended like an imaginary handgun, he stood where he assumed Dakotah had been when he pulled the trigger. "If he had just missed by an inch, the bullet would have hit the glass cabinet over there and woken my father, who would have whupped Dakotah's ass," he said. "Then we would have gotten him some help."

Jean cried quietly throughout the demonstration, and added that Dakotah was a "loving grandson up until that moment." "I would bring him home tonight," she said. "I know the person he is." She often thought about what would have happened if she had forced her husband to hide his gun—it was kept by the door in case of intruders—or had sat down with Dakotah for dinner that night. All he ate was three cupcakes. "But I had all kinds of stuff for him in the freezer," she said under her breath.

The family talked about Dakotah's diagnosis of bipolar disorder, though it won't be relevant for the appeal—the legal bar for insanity is higher than simply having a psychiatric diagnosis. Since Dakotah's arrest, Steve had discovered a history of bipolar disorder in his family, and he, too, received a diagnosis of the illness. He often repackages lessons from his own therapy sessions for his son, who calls home every day. The family talks to him on a speakerphone until the prison phone service cuts them off, after fifteen minutes. When Dakotah complains of feeling homesick, Steve jokes with him, "Grow your beard a little thicker, and I'll shave my hair like you. You'll sneak out, and I'll take your place."

By September, Dakotah had spent nearly three months in solitary confinement. In April, 2011, after six months in prison, he got his first ticket for a rule violation, Threatening Behavior, which resulted in the standard punishment: thirty days in segregation. Dakotah had told a boy in his unit that he'd kill him if he kept prying into his case. The boy had been joking around, saying, "Who'd you kill? Who'd you kill?" Two months later, Dakotah received another ticket, for Sexual Misconduct, after a female guard accused him of exposing his penis through the vertical window on his steel door. According to Dakotah, he was sleeping at the time. He told the guard that it must have been his cellmate, but she said the skin she saw looked light, and his cellmate was black. Dakotah confronted his cellmate, a fifteen-year-old convicted of sexual assault, "but he just laughs about it," he said. "He giggles about all sorts of childish shit."

Two weeks after his punishment ended, he and his cellmate got into a fistfight, and, at the end of August, both boys were transferred to the segregation unit. His cinder-block cell had one barred window, a bed, a stainless-steel desk and stool that were attached to the floor, a toilet, a sink, and a mirror. All his meals were delivered to him through a metal flap on his door, starting with breakfast, at 4 A.M. The only time he could leave his cell was to shower, three times a week; he was handcuffed on the way there and locked into the shower stall.

When I visited Dakotah in September, it was the first time in nearly three weeks that he'd had an extended conversation with another person. We sat in a narrow cinder-block room, divided in half by shatterproof glass, and spoke to each other using rotary telephones whose dial pads had been removed.

Dakotah had been animated in our previous conversations, but now he spoke in a dull, listless tone and sat slouched in his chair, his head resting against the wall of the cubicle. His eyes were dilated, and his lips were so chapped they looked bruised.

He told me that he was disgusted with himself for ruining his chance to see his family, who, for more than a month, had planned to visit on the second Sunday in September. It was the second time they'd had to cancel their plans at the last minute because he'd been placed in seclusion. (After a week without calls or letters from Dakotah, Steve had called the prison, and a phone operator told him that Dakotah was in the segregation unit, where visiting hours are restricted to Friday mornings.) Dakotah spent his first few nights in the segregation cell lying underneath his steel-framed bed, on the concrete floor, wearing nothing but shorts. "Oh, man, I was going off the deep end, like, living below the water," he said, jiggling the phone cord. "The little flame lighting my candle of sanity just blew out."

The effects of the sedative he'd been prescribed seemed to have worn off, and he struggled to sleep through the night. He woke up in cold sweats, with such vivid, violent dreams that he examined his body to see if he'd somehow been injured. "I don't understand sleep anymore," he told me. He had developed a theory, adapted from "The Matrix," which he had watched countless times, that maybe life is an illusion, a kind of thought experiment, and dreams are the true reality.

Dakotah began talking to himself in his cell, little comments and reminders at first, and then, as the days passed, full conversations. "I go into this other mode," he said, blowing air out of his mouth. "I can have all these conversations criss-crossing the room; there's a version of me on the bed, at the desk, at the sink."

At the end of my previous visits, Dakotah had chattered rapidly, nearly free-associating, occasionally singing, as if he would lose his visitor as soon as he paused. I had found myself coming to visiting hours later, to avoid prolonging the drama of separating. He would pick lint or stray hairs off my shirt or touch a scab on my hand, assuring me that it would fall off soon—any excuse for physical contact. But this time, our first visit with glass between us, he was the one to end the conversation. "I'm worn out," he told me. "My mind is kind of dead."

His sixteenth birthday was the next week, and I wished him happy birthday. "Yeah, I'm alive," he said, rolling his eyes. "Whoopdefuckingwhoo."

The day before Dakotah's birthday, September 23rd, Steve drove four hours to the prison to surprise him. Dakotah had recently been transferred to the Behavioral Modification Unit, where he had contact with other prisoners, but most of his privileges, including use of the phone, were still suspended. In the partitioned cubicle, Steve and Dakotah pressed their knuckles against the glass, as if they were touching. It had been three months since they'd seen each other. "You look pasty, son," Steve said tenderly. Dakotah, smiling broadly, smoothed the collar of his prison jumpsuit and confessed, "I don't feel like I look so good."

Steve updated Dakotah on developments in the lives of neighbors, relatives, and their pets, and then spoke at length about the mood-stabilizing medication he'd been taking. He said that he no longer acted like a tyrant at home, high-strung and aggressive. "That's one of our traits—not knowing how to express our emotions," he told Dakotah. The more Steve talked about their matching diagnoses, the more he seemed to convince himself that he was complicit in Dakotah's crime. He couldn't forgive himself for yelling at his children, which he now saw as a form of abuse. Dakotah, quiet and deferential, deflected his father's comments with reassuring jokes. (At an earlier visit, he described his dad as his role model, except for his domineering manner: "He was Sgt. Pepper, and I was the Lonely Heart Band.")

Steve wore an oversized tank top, which revealed a tattoo on his right shoulder in memory of his stepfather: "J.E.M., 1940–2010." Dakotah had wept when he first saw the tattoo, more than a year earlier, and now he intended to get one, too. He also wanted the name of his dead dog tattooed on his biceps, his dead cat on his forearm, and his great-grandmother's initials on his chest. At his father's request, he planned to wait until he got to the adult side of the prison, since the Old Heads were more likely to clean their needles.

Both father and son vaguely hoped that other problems, too, would be resolved on the adult side of prison: the units might be less chaotic and noisy, the inmates calmer and more responsible. Steve had reconciled himself to the possibility that Dakotah would eventually get affiliated—with the Aryan Brotherhood, he guessed—because he would need that protection. At the end of the visit, Steve reassured Dakotah that he would find mentors when he moved to the adult population. "Not someone who will take advantage of you but a man who was locked away from his own kids," Steve said. "I want a father in there watching over you."

Critical Thinking

1. Do you think a teenager who commits murder should receive a life sentence?
2. Should a teenager who commits murder be tried as if he were an adult?
3. If Dakotah Eliason should ever be released from prison, do you believe he will be a danger to society?
4. What do you think of the arguments made in the two cases that will soon go to the U.S. Supreme Court?

Preventing Future Crime with Cognitive Behavioral Therapy

One form of psychotherapy stands out in the criminal justice system.

PATRICK CLARK

Cognitive behavioral therapy reduces recidivism in both juveniles and adults.

The therapy assumes that most people can become conscious of their own thoughts and behaviors and then make positive changes to them. A person's thoughts are often the result of experience, and behavior is often influenced and prompted by these thoughts. In addition, thoughts may sometimes become distorted and fail to reflect reality accurately.

Cognitive behavioral therapy has been found to be effective with juvenile and adult offenders; substance abusing and violent offenders; and probationers, prisoners and parolees. It is effective in various criminal justice settings, both in institutions and in the community, and addresses a host of problems associated with criminal behavior. For instance, in most cognitive behavioral therapy programs, offenders improve their social skills, means-ends problem solving, critical reasoning, moral reasoning, cognitive style, self-control, impulse management and self-efficacy.

Recently, Mark Lipsey of Vanderbilt University examined the effectiveness of various approaches to intervention with young offenders.[1] His review analyzed the results of 548 studies from 1958 to 2002 that assessed intervention policies, practices and programs.

Lipsey grouped evaluations into seven categories:

- Counseling
- Deterrence
- Discipline
- Multiple coordinated services
- Restorative programs
- Skill building
- Surveillance

When he combined and compared the effects of these interventions, he found that those based on punishment and deterrence appeared to increase criminal recidivism. On the other hand, therapeutic approaches based on counseling, skill building and multiple services had the greatest impact in reducing further criminal behavior.

Lipsey also examined the effectiveness of various therapeutic interventions. In particular, he compared different counseling and skill-building approaches. He found that cognitive behavioral skill-building approaches were more effective in reducing further criminal behavior than any other intervention.

In a different research review, Nana Landenberger and Lipsey showed that programs based on cognitive behavioral therapy are effective with juvenile and adult criminal offenders in various criminal justice settings, including prison, residential, community probation and parole.[2] They examined research studies published from 1965 through 2005 and found 58 that could be included in their review and analysis. The researchers found that cognitive behavioral therapy significantly reduced recidivism even among high-risk offenders.

Therapeutic approaches based on counseling, skill building and multiple services had the greatest impact in reducing further criminal behavior.

Perceptions Affect Behavior

Beliefs, attitudes and values affect the way people think and how they view problems. These beliefs can distort the way a person views reality, interacts with other people and experiences everyday life.

Cognitive behavioral therapy can help restructure distorted thinking and perception, which in turn changes a person's behavior for the better. Characteristics of distorted thinking may include:

- Immature or developmentally arrested thoughts.
- Poor problem solving and decision making.
- An inability to consider the effects of one's behavior.
- An egocentric viewpoint with a negative view or lack of trust in other people.
- A hampered ability to reason and accept blame for wrongdoing.
- A mistaken belief of entitlement, including an inability to delay gratification, confusing wants and needs, and ignoring the rights of other people.
- A tendency to act on impulse, including a lack of self-control and empathy.
- An inability to manage feelings of anger.
- The use of force and violence as a means to achieve goals.

What is CBT?

Cognitive behavioral therapy is a treatment that focuses on patterns of thinking and the beliefs, attitudes and values that underlie thinking. CBT has only recently come into prominence as one of the few approaches to psychotherapy that has been, broadly validated with research, although it has been used in psychological therapy for more than 40 years. It is reliably effective with a wide variety of personal problems and behaviors, including those important to criminal justice, such as substance abuse and anti-social, aggressive, delinquent and criminal behavior.

Unlike other approaches to psychotherapy, CBT places responsibility in the hands of clients while supplying them with the tools to solve their problems, focusing on the present rather than the past. People taking part in CBT learn specific skills that can be used to solve the problems they confront all the time as well as skills they can use to achieve legitimate goals and objectives. CBT first concentrates on developing skills to recognize distorted or unrealistic thinking when it happens, and then to changing that thinking or belief to mollify or eliminate problematic behavior.

The programs, often offered in small group settings, incorporate lessons and exercises involving role play, modeling or demonstrations. Individual counseling sessions are often part of CBT. Clients are given homework and conduct experiments between sessions. These components are used to gauge the individual's readiness for change and foster engagement in that change. A willingness to change is necessary for CBT or any other treatment to be effective in reducing further criminal behavior.

Brand name programs often limit clients to 20–30 sessions, lasting over a period of up to 20 weeks. The more treatment provided or the more sessions participants attend over time, the greater the impact on and decrease in recidivism.

The typical CBT program is provided by trained professionals or paraprofessionals. Training for non-therapist group facillitators often involves 40 hours or more of specialized lessons and skill building. Licensed and certified therapists are often part of cognitive programs, especially those involving individual counseling.

Characteristics of the counselor are important to a program's effectiveness. Counselor honesty, empathy and sensitivity are helpful traits. Support and encouragement, partnership or alliance, and acceptance are necessary in establishing effective rapport, which is especially important in CBT because counselors often take on the role of coach. It is important that counselors be consistent in modeling and expressing the pro-social attitudes and behaviors, moral values and reasoning that are often part of CBT with criminal offenders.

Positive findings from research on CBT are common. Over the years, studies have shown the therapy is effective with various problems, including mood disorders, anxiety and personality and behavioral disorders. Unlike other traditional and popular therapies, CBT has been the subject of more than 400 clinical trials involving a broad range of conditions and populations. It has successfully addressed many issues experienced by children, including disruptive or noncompliant behavior, aggressiveness, oppositional defiant disorder and attention deficit hyperactivity disorder. For adults, CBT has been shown to help with marital problems, sexual dysfunction, depression, mood disorders and substance abuse. It has also been shown to be as useful as antidepressant medication for individuals with depression and appears to be superior to medication in preventing relapses.

Therapy can help a person address and change these unproductive and detrimental beliefs, views and thoughts.[3]

Cognitive Behavioral Therapy and Criminal Offenders

Landenberger and Lipsey found that even high-risk behavior did not reduce the therapy's effectiveness. For example, some of the greatest effects were among more serious offenders. It may be that the therapy's enabling, self-help approach is more effective in engaging typically resistant clients, that it increases their participation and therefore the benefits of participation. The therapy is more effective in reducing further criminal behavior when clients simultaneously receive other support, such as supervision, employment, education and training, and other mental health counseling.

The cognitive behavioral therapy approach has recently been used in many prepackaged, brand name programs, such as "Reasoning and Rehabilitation," "Aggression Replacement Therapy," "Thinking for Change" and others. The National Institute of Corrections recently published a thorough and comprehensive review of cognitive behavioral therapy, which provides detailed descriptions of these and other programs.[4] Interestingly, although the Landenberger and Lipsey review showed these programs were effective, no single program was superior in reducing recidivism.

More research is needed to determine if it would be effective for offenders to receive cognitive behavioral therapy earlier in their criminal careers or as part of early intervention or parenting training programs.

Notes

1. Lipsey, M.W., "The Primary Factors That Characterize Effective Interventions with Juvenile Offenders: A meta-analytic Overview," *Victims and Offenders* 4 (2009): 124–147.
2. Landenberger, N.A., and M. Lipsey, "The Positive Effects of Cognitive-behavioral Programs for Offenders: A Meta-analysis of Factors Associated with Effective Treatment," *Journal of Experimental Criminology,* 1 (2005): 451–476.
3. Yochelson, S., and S.E. Samenow, *The Criminal Personality, Volume I: A Profile for Change,* New York: Jason Aronson, 1976; and Walters, G., *The Criminal Lifestyle: Patterns of Serious Criminal Conduct,* Newbury Park, Calif.: Sage Publications, 1990.
4. Milkman, H., and K. Wanberg, *Cognitive-Behavioral Treatment: A Review and Discussion for Correction Professionals,* Washington, DC: U.S. Department of Justice, National Institute of Corrections, 2007, http://nicic.gov/Library/021657.

Critical Thinking

1. In what ways can cognitive behavioral therapy reduce recidivism?
2. What do you think about using CBT in parenting programs?
3. Why are counselors' characteristics important?

Patrick Clark is a Social Science Analyst with NIJ's Crime Control and Prevention Division.

From *National Institute of Justice Journal,* issue 265, April 2010, pp. 22–25. Published by U.S. Department of Justice.

Opinion Recap: Narrow Ruling on Young Murderers' Sentences

LYLE DENNISTON

Analysis

States—and the federal government—that allow life prison sentences without a chance of release for minors who commit murder are now on notice, from the Supreme Court, that they may have a hard time justifying any such sentence that is actually imposed. In a 5–4 ruling on Thursday, the Court left open the possibility that such sentences could still be imposed, even as it barred making such a sentence mandatory in all cases of homicides by youths under age 18. At a minimum, any life-without-parole sentence for an adolescent murderer will get very heavy scrutiny if it goes to the Supreme Court. Indeed, the Court said it expects such a sentence to be uncommon from here on.

The new decision, written by the newest Justice, Elena Kagan, continues the trend that started a quarter-century ago of demanding that criminal punishment for children generally must be different—and less harsh—than for adults. The whole premise behind that trend is that children are not adults, but rather are unformed people with the capacity to change, and to grow beyond being a thoroughly corrupted individual beyond redemption.

In earlier rulings in that trend, the Court had flatly barred the death penalty for minors who commit murder and had flatly barred life without parole for minors who commit a crime that does not involve the death of the victim (so-called non-homicide crimes). In the new combined cases of *Miller v. Alabama* (10-9646) and *Jackson v. Hobbs* (10-9647), youths convicted of murders when they were 14 years old asked the Court to extend such a flat ban to life without parole when the victim is murdered. As an alternative, the two youths asked the Court at least to rule out entirely any such sentence if the youth were only 14 when the crime occurred.

The Court chose not to adopt either approach. Instead, it simply struck out any requirement that life without parole be the mandatory penalty for murder by a minor. The Court did not rule on whether that sentence would be invalid in the two cases before it—involving Evan James Miller of Speake, Ala., and Kuntrell Jackson, of Blytheville, Ark. It sent their cases back to state courts to make the kind of "individualized" sentencing decision that the new ruling demands. If, once again, they are sentenced to life without parole, their cases conceivably could return to the Supreme Court.

What sentencing judges now must do, when a youth is convicted of murder that occurred before age 18, is to focus directly and only on that one individual in choosing a sentence. The judge must assess the specific age of that individual, examine that youth's childhood and life experience, weigh the degree of responsibility the youth was capable of exercising, and assess that youth's chances to become rehabilitated. Only if the judge then concludes that life without parole is a "proportional" penalty, given all of the factors that mitigate the youth's guilt, can he impose such a sentence.

The decision provided no specific guidelines, nor any clearly defined list of factors, that are to control that sentencing decision. The opinion noted that, taking into account everything the Court had said in the string of decisions limiting punishment for minors, about children's "diminished culpability and heightened capacity for change," the Court thinks that "appropriate occasions for sentencing juveniles to this harshest possible penalty will be uncommon."

It commented that judges with a youthful murderer before the bench will have "great difficulty" distinguishing between a minor whose crime reflected "unfortunate yet transient immaturity" and "the rare juvenile offender whose crime reflects irreparable corruption." The opinion concluded: "Although we do not foreclose a sentencer's ability to make that judgment in homicide cases, we require it to take into account how children are different, and how those differences counsel against irrevocably sentencing them to a lifetime in prison."

Justice Kagan's opinion was joined by Justice Anthony M. Kennedy, who has been the Court's leader in monitoring the sentencing of youths who commit crimes; as the senior Justice in the majority, Kennedy assigned the opinion in this case to the junior Justice. The opinion also was joined by Justices Stephen G. Breyer and Sonia Sotomayor (who, in a separate opinion written by Breyer, argued that if the state of Arkansas again seeks to impose life without parole on Kentrell Jackson, it should have to prove that Jackson personally killed or intended to kill the robbery victim who was shot to death in that case. Without that finding, those two Justices said, life without parole would be an unconstitutional sentence for Jackson). Justice Ruth Bader Ginsburg also joined the Kagan opinion, and did not write separately; neither did Kennedy.

Three of the four dissenters wrote opinions: Chief Justice John G. Roberts, Jr., joined by Justices Samuel A. Alito, Jr., Antonin Scalia, and Clarence Thomas; Justice Thomas, joined by Scalia, and Justice Alito, also joined by Scalia.

Plain English Summary

In a series of decisions dating back to 1988, the Supreme Court has repeatedly ruled that youths under age 18 who commit crimes must not necessarily get as severe a punishment as adults who committed the same kind of crimes. Among other rulings, the Court has forbidden the death penalty for minors who commit murders, and it has barred a sentence of life in prison without a chance of release for minors who commit crimes in which the victim is not killed. In this new ruling, the Court avoided imposing such a flat ban on life without parole for a minor who commits murder, but it did rule out such a sentence as a mandatory requirement in all such cases. It said, though, that it does not expect very many youths under age 18 to get such a sentence that essentially would require them to stay in prison until they die.

Critical Thinking

1. What was the U.S. Supreme Court's ruling in *Miller v. Alabama*?
2. Should courts consider the immaturity of juveniles who commit crimes when it comes to sentencing them?

UNIT 6

Punishment and Corrections

Unit Selections

Learning Outcomes

After reading this unit, you will be able to:

- Argue that the lash instead of prison might not be so preposterous after all.
- Show the effect of drug laws on the high incarceration rate in the U.S.
- Explain Operation Ceasefire.
- Explain why HOPE and Operation Ceasefire have been effective in helping parolees stay out of trouble.
- Argue that private prisons contribute to the high American incarceration rate.
- Discuss what effect the high American rates of incarceration have had on the "war on drugs."
- Show why inmates should have access to education.
- Indicate the kinds of problems facing women in the workforce.

Student Website

www.mhhe.com/cls

Internet References

American Probation and Parole Association (APPA)
www.appa-net.org

The Corrections Connection
www.corrections.com

Critical Criminology Division of the ASC
www.critcrim.org

David Willshire's Forensic Psychology & Psychiatry Links
http://members.optushome.com.au/dwillsh/index.html

Oregon Department of Corrections
http://egov.oregon.gov/DOC/TRANS/CC/cc_welcome.shtml

In the American system of criminal justice, the term "corrections" has a special meaning. It designates programs and agencies that have legal authority over the custody or supervision of people who have been convicted of a criminal act by the courts. The correctional process begins with the sentencing of the convicted offender. The predominant sentencing pattern in the United States encourages maximum judicial discretion and offers a range of alternatives, from probation (supervised, conditional freedom within the community) through imprisonment, to the death penalty.

Selections in this unit focus on the current condition of the U.S. penal system and the effects that sentencing, probation, imprisonment, and parole have on the rehabilitation of criminals.

This section begins with a provocative article by Peter Moskos, "Bring Back the Lash: Why Flogging Is More Humane than Prison," in which he argues that flogging may seem brutal but only because we are in mass denial about the greater brutality of our supposedly civilized and progressive prisons.

Next is Mary Beth Pfeiffer's article "Drug Reforms Cut Prison Rolls: Fewer Inmates Are Black, Female; More Had Violent Crimes," in which she reports that the decline in drug-convicted inmates in New York State has led to fewer female inmates and more of the type of inmate for which penitentiaries were constructed: violent offenders.

Following is a report on private prisons from the Justice Policy Institute, "Gaming the System: How the Political Strategies of Private Prison Companies Promote Ineffective Incarceration Policies." It shows how campaign donations and lobbying increase the political influence of the two companies that own and/or operate the majority of for-profit private prisons. And growing evidence shows that many people lose in this political game at the individual and community levels.

Cindy Chang, in her piece "Prison Re-entry Programs Help Inmates Leave the Criminal Mindset Behind, but Few Have Access to the classes," reports that all inmates leaving Louisiana state prisons receive some version of a 10-week re-entry program. While behind bars, they can learn trades such as auto mechanics and welding. Even those serving life terms have ample opportunities to better themselves; however, most inmates in local lockups are not even getting the basic re-entry curriculum, let alone new skills that could help them land a decent job.

Jeffrey Rosen, in "Prisoners of Parole," reports on the apparent success of the HOPE program in reducing prison populations through probation and parole reform. In the final article, "Addressing Gender Issues among Staff in Community Corrections," Kelli D. Stevens argues that, while community corrections organizations are actively addressing the needs of female offenders, they are still struggling to meet the needs of female professionals working in the field.

© David R. Frazier Photolibrary, Inc.

Article 39

Bring Back the Lash

Why Flogging Is More Humane than Prison

PETER MOSKOS

You're about to get whipped. Mentally more than physically. It's going to hurt—but it's supposed to.

I write in defense of flogging, something most people consider too radical for debate and even unworthy of intellectual discussion. But please, don't turn the page, upset I dared to broach the subject.

My defense of flogging—whipping, caning, lashing, call it what you will—is meant to be provocative, but only because something extreme is needed to shatter the status quo. There are 2.3 million Americans in our prisons and jails. That is too many. I want to reduce cruelty, and corporal punishment, once common in America and still practiced in places like Singapore, may be the answer.

So first let me begin with a simple question: Given the choice between five years in prison and ten brutal lashes, which would you choose?

Yes, flogging is a severe and even brutal form of punishment. Under the lash, skin is literally ripped from the body. But prison means losing a part of your life and everything you care for. Compared to this, flogging is just a few very painful strokes on the behind. And it's over in a few minutes.

If you had the choice, if you were given the option of staying out of jail, wouldn't you choose to be flogged and released?

Consider your answer to that question. Then consider the fact that the United States now has more prisoners than any other country in the world. Ever. In sheer numbers and as a percentage of the population. Our rate of incarceration is roughly seven times that of Canada or any Western European country. Despite our "land of the free" rhetoric, we deem it necessary to incarcerate more of our people than the world's most draconian regimes. We have more prisoners than China, and they have *a billion* more people than we do. We have more prisoners than soldiers; prison guards outnumber Marines.

It wasn't always this way. In 1970, just 338,000 Americans were behind bars. There was even talk of abolishing prison altogether. That didn't happen. Instead, fear of crime led to "tough-on-crime" politics and the war on drugs. Crime has gone up and down since then, but the incarceration rate has only increased, a whopping 500 percent in the past forty years.

In truth, there is very little correlation between incarceration and the crime rate. From 1970 to 1991 crime rose while we locked up a million more people. Since then we've locked up another million and crime has gone down. Is there something so special about that *second* million? Were they the only ones who were "real criminals"? Did we simply get it wrong with the first 1.3 million people we put behind bars?

Today's prison reformers—and I wish them well—tinker at the edges of a massive failed system. We need much more drastic action. To bring our incarceration back to a civilized level—one we used to have, and one much more befitting a rich, modern nation—we would have to reduce the number of prisoners by 85 percent. Without alternative punishments, this will not happen anytime soon. Even the most optimistically progressive opponent of prison has no plan to release two million prisoners.

Perhaps, as a law-abiding citizen, with all there is to worry about in the world today, you don't have the fate of convicted criminals in our prison system at the top of your list of concerns. But who hasn't, at some point, committed a crime? Perhaps you've taken illegal drugs. Maybe you once got into a fight with a friend, stranger, or lover that came to blows. Or you drove back from a bar drunk. Or you clicked on an online picture of somebody who turned out to be a bit young. Perhaps you accepted a "gift" from a family member and told the IRS it was a loan. Or did you go for the white-collar big leagues and embezzle millions of dollars? If your luck runs out, you can end up in jail for almost anything, big or small. Even if you have done nothing wrong, imagine that in a horrific twist of fate you are convicted of a crime you did not commit. It's not inconceivable; it happens all the time.

As you sit in court on sentencing day, you begin to wonder what prison will be like. Are there drugs, gangs, and long times in solitary? Will you come out stronger—or broken? Will you be raped? Will it be like the brutal TV show *Oz*? God, you hope not. But you don't know. And that's the rub. Prison is a mystery to all but the millions of people forced to live and work in this gigantic government-run system of containment. And as long as we don't look at what happens on the inside, as long as we refuse to consider alternatives, nothing will change.

Is flogging still too cruel to contemplate? If so, given the hypothetical choice between prison and flogging, why did you choose flogging? Perhaps it's not as crazy as you thought. And even if you're adamant that flogging is a barbaric, inhumane form of punishment, how can offering criminals the choice of the lash in lieu of incarceration be so bad? If flogging were really worse than prison, nobody would choose it. Of course most people would choose to be caned over incarceration. And that's my point. Faced with the choice between hard time and the lash, the lash is better. What does that say about prison?

Sometime in the past few decades we seem to have lost the concept of justice in a free society. Now we settle for simple efficiency of process. We tried rehabilitation and ended up with supermax and solitary confinement. Crime, violence, and drug prohibition help explain why so *many* people are behind bars. But they don't explain why so many people are *behind bars.*

I am not proposing to completely end confinement or shut down every prison. Some inmates are, of course, too violent and hazardous to simply flog and release. Pedophiles, terrorists, serial rapists, and murderers, for example, need to remain behind bars—but they are relatively few in number. They are being kept in prison not only to punish them, but also because we don't want them to hurt us. We're afraid of them. But for the millions of other prisoners—particularly those caught up in the war on drugs (which I for one would end tomorrow if I could)—the lash is better than a prison cell. Why not at least offer the choice?

Is flogging still too cruel to contemplate? If so, given the hypothetical choice between prison and flogging, why did you choose flogging? Perhaps it's not as crazy as you thought.

That prisons have failed in such a spectacular manner should matter more than it does. But it should come as no surprise, since prisons were designed not to punish, but to "cure." Just as hospitals were for the physically sick, penitentiaries were created—mostly by Quakers in the late eighteenth century—to heal the criminally ill. A stated goal of the early prison advocates was nothing less than the complete elimination of punishment. The penitentiary would be a kinder and gentler sentence, one geared to personal salvation, less crime, and a better life for all. Like so many utopian fairy tales, the movement to cure criminals failed. Early prison reforms may have had the best of intentions, but today we should know better.

The disastrous consequences of prison became clear as soon as the first one was built, in Philadelphia in 1790: inmates began to go crazy. When Charles Dickens toured this prison, he noted with despair, "I hold this slow and daily tampering with the mysteries of the brain, to be immeasurably worse than any torture of the body."

Today violent offenders are mixed with immigrants who may have committed no crime other than crossing our border. Lifers are thrown in the same cellblock as people who serve twelve months. Kids get raped. The mentally ill are left to fend for themselves in some antipsychotic-medicine haze. And given the impossible task of total control, some guards inevitably abuse their authority.

Because one stint in prison so often leads to another, millions of criminals have come to alternate between incarceration and freedom while their families and communities suffer the economic and social consequences of their absence. When I was a police officer in Baltimore's rough Eastern District, I don't think I ever arrested anybody for the first time. Even the juveniles I arrested all had a record. Because not only does incarceration not "cure" criminality, in many ways in makes it worse. From behind bars a prisoner can't be a parent, hold a job, maintain a relationship, or take care of their elders. Their spouse suffers. Their children suffer. And because of this, in the long run, we all suffer.

But maybe you still have your doubts about flogging. Perhaps you are concerned that the practice is torture. It is not. Torture is meant to achieve a goal, and until that goal is achieved, it continues. Punishment is finite and is prescribed in accordance with clear rules of law. And certainly offering criminals the option of flogging cannot be viewed as more torturous than the status quo.

Indeed it is our current system of imprisonment that most resembles torture. Overwhelming evidence suggests that by locking people in cells and denying them meaningful human contact, as is the case with solitary confinement, we cause irreparable damage; when prisoners are held in group living quarters, they often form criminal associations and reinforce aggressive antisocial norms; and through parole boards' decisions, we hold the power to continue such punishment for extended periods of time. In addition, it's terribly expensive. And for what? What do we gain? Why incapacitate criminals in a non-rehabilitative environment never meant for punishment? It is like being entombed alive, something more torturous than flogging could ever be.

And worse, given that life inside the concertina wire is so well hidden from those of us on the outside, prison is a dishonest way of dealing with the problem of punishment. Flogging, on the other hand, is different. Physical violence has the advantage of being honest, transparent, inexpensive, and easy to understand. What you see is what you get. If you want someone to receive more punishment, you give more lashes. If you want them to receive less punishment, you give fewer.

As ugly as it may seem, corporal punishment would be an effective and comparatively humane way to bring our prison population back in line with world standards. To those in prison (after the approval of some parole board designed to keep the truly dangerous behind bars) we could offer the lash in exchange for sentence years. I propose that each six months of incarceration be exchanged for one lash. As a result, our prison population would plummet. This would not only save money, it would also save prisons for those who truly deserve to be there. And if you think that flogging isn't punishment enough, that prisons are necessary precisely because they torture so cruelly and horribly—then we've entered a truly bizarre world of unparalleled cruelty. Flogging may be too harsh or too lenient, but it can't be both.

As ugly as it may seem, corporal punishment would be an effective and comparatively humane way to bring our prison population back in line with world standards.

Make no mistake: this is punishment, and punishment must by definition hurt. Even under controlled conditions, with doctors present and the convict choosing a lashing over a prison sentence, the details of flogging are enough to make most people queasy. Those receiving lashes have described the cane cutting through layers of flesh and tissue, leaving "furrows that were . . . bloody pulp." Even if these wounds were attended to immediately, a full recovery could take weeks or months. In some cases, the scars would remain as permanent reminders of the ordeal.

The lash, which metes out punishment without falsely promising betterment, is an unequivocal expression of society's condemnation. For better or for worse, flogging would air the dirty laundry of race and punishment in America in a way that prisons—which, by their very design, are removed from society—can never do. To highlight an injustice is in no way to condone it. Quite the opposite.

Without a radical defense of flogging, changes to our current defective system of justice are hard to imagine. The glacial pace of reform promises only the most minor adjustments to the massive machinery of incarceration. Bringing back the lash is one way to destroy it—if not completely, then at least for the millions of Americans for whom the punishment of prison is far, far worse than the crime they have committed. Yes, flogging may seem brutal and retrograde, but only because we are in mass denial about the greater brutality of our supposedly civilized and progressive prisons.

Critical Thinking

1. What were prisons designed to do?
2. Do they accomplish their goals?
3. Are today's American prisons places of torture?
4. Should corporal punishment ever be an option in the American criminal justice system?

Peter Moskos is a sociologist at John Jay College of Criminal Justice and the Graduate Center of the City University of New York. He is a former Baltimore police officer and the author of *Cop in the Hood.* This article is adapted with permission from the author's forthcoming book *In Defense of Flogging,* available in May from Basic Books.

Drug Reforms Cut Prison Rolls: Fewer Inmates Are Black, Female; More Had Violent Crimes

MARY BETH PFEIFFER

Nearly 40 years after tough new drug laws led to an explosion in prison rolls, New York has dramatically reversed course, chalking up a 62 percent drop in people serving time for drug crimes today compared with 2000, according to a *Poughkeepsie Journal* analysis.

The steep decline—driven, experts said, by shifting attitudes toward drug offenders and lower-level crime—means that nearly 16,000 fewer minorities serve state time today than in 2000, groups that were hardest hit by the so-called war on drugs.

Overall, the prison population declined 22 percent.

The rolls of eight state prisons in Dutchess and Ulster counties, which employ nearly 4,400 people, dropped 14 percent since 2000, to 7,600 inmates.

Though noting that Hispanics and blacks are still vastly overrepresented in prisons, incarceration experts said the overall figures were impressive.

"This is very intriguing stuff and encouraging," said Marc Mauer, executive director of the Sentencing Project, a Washington, D.C.–based organization that has criticized sentencing policies as racially biased and counterproductive.

When compared nationwide, New York's figures are especially stunning. Among the 50 states, New York charted the biggest drop in its prison rolls from 2000 to 2010, a decade when 37 state prison systems had double-digit population hikes. Ironically, it was the state's 1973 drug laws, championed by then-Gov. Nelson A. Rockefeller, that helped kick off a massive national prison buildup—and the highest incarceration rate in the industrialized world.

Now, with state prison spending at $3.7 billion in fiscal 2010, or $55,000 per inmate, New York may be leading the way back.

Fewer Minorities

The state's stark prison decline means that thousands of people are not in prison today who would have been there a decade ago.

Nearly 7,700 fewer blacks are incarcerated in state prison in 2011 compared with 2000, the *Journal* study found.

In addition, 35 percent fewer female inmates serve time—and 77 percent fewer women serve drug sentences as their top crime. Inmates also were older, by three years on average, according to the analysis, which used databases of the inmate population on one day each in April 2000 and March 2011.

The trend is an outgrowth, experts said, of an array of factors including the diversion of more drug offenders to treatment, changes in drug laws and lower crime rates, especially in New York City, which currently ranks among the safest big cities in America.

Though the New York City policies are controversial—600,000 people were frisked in 2010, statistics show, 90 percent of them minority—there's little doubt of the city's mighty contribution to the state's prison reversal.

The five boroughs charted a 42 percent decline in sentenced inmates in 2011 compared with 2000; inmates from the rest of the state actually increased 17 percent. Both the city and upstate saw big declines in drug commitments but the city's decline, 76 percent, was three times that of upstate.

Similarly, the rolls of city jails dropped 16 percent since 2000, while county lockups statewide saw a 15 percent hike, statistics show.

The decline in drug-convicted inmates means more of the type of inmate for which penitentiaries were constructed: violent offenders.

Today, the No. 1 top crime of sentenced inmates is second-degree murder, with just over 8,000 convicts—about the same as in 2000.

Mindset Change

In 2000, the most common top crime for which inmates were incarcerated was third-degree criminal sale of a controlled substance, with almost 10,000 people sentenced. That's now down to about 3,000.

"It wasn't in anyone's interest to wholesale incarcerate anyone who committed a drug crime," said Janet DiFiore, a former judge and current Westchester County district attorney. "For those hundreds and hundreds and hundreds of people who were just unfortunately drug-addled people, that wasn't the right view."

DiFiore ties the prison downturn both to drug-law reforms—in 2004, 2005 and 2009—and a recognition in law enforcement that alternatives like drug treatment were needed.

The reforms are an outgrowth of something much larger than a drug-war backlash, prison observers say, among these reasons are ballooning prison budgets, the economic downturn and a realization that punishment isn't always the answer.

"Prosecutors were recognizing that our job was not just about handcuffs and prison," said DiFiore, who is also president of the District Attorneys Association of the State of New York. "It was a mindset change."

When he announced his latest prison-closure plans this year, Gov. Andrew Cuomo called the system "too inefficient and too costly with far more capacity than what is needed."

But he also recognized that prisons were "a major source of employment and economic sustainability," and set up a $50 million economic development fund to help affected communities.

Critical Thinking

1. How has New York State's changing attitude about drug crimes affected its prison population?
2. How do New York State's incarceration rates compare with those nationwide?
3. Why were fewer minorities and women serving time in 2011 compared with 2000?
4. What was the top crime of sentenced inmates in 2000?

Gaming the System: How the Political Strategies of Private Prison Companies Promote Ineffective Incarceration Policies

Introduction

Approximately 129,000 people were held in privately managed correctional facilities in the United States as of December 31, 2009;[1] 16.4 percent of federal and 6.8 percent of state populations were held in private facilities. Since 2000, private prisons have increased their share of the "market" substantially: the number of people held in private federal facilities increased approximately 120 percent, while the number held in private state facilities increased approximately 33 percent. During this same period, the total number of people in prison increased less than 16 percent. Meanwhile, spending on corrections has increased 72 percent since 1997, to $74 billion in 2007.[2] The two largest private prison companies, Corrections Corporation of America (CCA) and GEO Group, combined had over $2.9 billion in revenue in 2010.[3]

As revenues of private prison companies have grown over the past decade, the companies have had more resources with which to build political power, and they have used this power to promote policies that lead to higher rates of incarceration.

The following are some of the main findings in the Justice Policy Institute's June 2011 report, *Gaming the System: How the Political Strategies of Private Prison Companies Promote Ineffective Incarceration Policies.*

The Players

Today, two companies own and/or operate the majority of for-profit private prisons, with a number of smaller companies running facilities across the country.

Corrections Corporation of America

Founded in 1983, the Corrections Corporation of America (CCA) is the first and largest private prison company in the U.S.[4] In 2010, CCA operated 66 correctional and detention facilities, 45 of which they owned with contracts in 19 states, the District of Columbia and with the three federal detention agencies.[5]

In 2010, CCA saw record revenue of $1.67 billion, up $46 million from 2009.[6] The majority of that revenue (50 percent or $838.5 million) came from state contracts, with 13 percent ($214 million) from the state of California;[7] approximately 10,250 people from the state of California are held in prisons run by CCA.[8] The other significant portion of their revenue was from federal contracts, which accounted for 43 percent of revenue in 2010.

The GEO Group (Formerly Wackenhut Corrections Corporation)

Currently, GEO operates 118 correctional, detention, and residential treatment facilities encompassing approximately 80,600 beds around the world.[9] The U.S. Corrections Business Unit is the company's founding operating unit and accounts for over 60 percent of GEO's total annual revenue.[10] Founded in 1984 under the name Wackenhut Corrections Corporation, the company solidified its first contract with the Bureau of Immigration and Custody Enforcement, in 1987.[11]

As of 2010, GEO contracts with 13 states, the Federal Bureau of Prison, the U.S. Marshals Service, and U.S. Immigration and Customs Enforcement.[12] In 2010, 66 percent ($842 million) of GEO's $1.27 billion in revenue was from U.S. corrections contracts.[13] Of the $842 million in revenue, 47 percent came from corrections contracts with 11 states.[14]

On August 12, 2010 the GEO Group acquired Cornell Companies—a for-profit private prison company with revenues of over $400 million in 2009[15]—in a merger estimated at $730 million.[16] With the acquisition of Cornell by GEO, the majority of private prisons are now under the management of either GEO or CCA.

The Stakes

Over the past 15 years, while the incarceration rate in the U.S. has grown, it has been outpaced by the growth in the number of people placed in private prisons. Due to ineffective criminal justice policies that promote incarceration over more effective alternatives, an increasing need for prison beds has resulted in more private prison contracts and subsequently more revenue for private prison companies as states have less money to pay for the construction of their own prison beds.

However, between 2008 and 2009 the number of people in state prisons declined for the first time in 40 years.[17] While the number of people in federal prisons continues to rise, the decline in the state prison population—private prison companies' largest revenue stream—sets the stage for private prison companies to implement an aggressive, multipronged strategy to ensure their growing revenues.

The Strategy: The Triangle of Private Prison Political Influence

Since private prison contracts are written by state and federal policymakers and overseen by state and federal agency administrators, it is in the best interest of private prison companies to build the connections needed to influence policies related to incarceration. For-profit private prison companies primarily use three strategies to influence policy: lobbying, direct campaign contributions, and building relationships, networks, and associations.[18]

Campaign Donations

By maintaining contacts and favorable ties with policymakers, private prison companies can attempt to shape the debate around the privatization of prisons and criminal justice policy. One way to do that is to make direct, monetary contributions to political campaigns for elected officials and specific policies. These updated figures have emerged in the fall of 2011:

- Since 2000, private prison companies have contributed over $7.2 million to state candidates and political parties.[19]
- Between the 2002 and 2012 election cycles, CCA and GEO's Political Action Committees (PACs) have doled out $1,212,889[20] and $1,010,002[21] respectively to federal parties, candidates and committees.
- Since 2000, private prison companies (CCA, GEO and Cornell Corrections) have given $867,010 —to federal candidates alone.[22]

Lobbying

Similar to other industries, private prison companies employ lobbying firms and lobbyists to advocate for their business interests in Congress and state legislatures. Since private prisons make money from putting people behind bars, their lobbying efforts focus on bills that affect incarceration and law enforcement, such as appropriations for corrections and detention.

Over the last decade, CCA, GEO and Cornell Corrections spent, on average, hundreds of thousands of dollars to employ lobbyists to represent their business interests to federal policymakers. Since 2003, CCA has spent upwards of $900,000 annually on federal lobbying.[23]

- Since 2000, private prison companies (CCA, GEO and Cornell Corrections) have spent over $21 million on federal lobbying efforts with the majority,[24] over $17 million being spent by CCA alone.[25]

Relationships and Associations

Organizational theories about relationships and leadership indicate that individual people influence the operations and behavior of an organization through prior relationships, associations, experiences, and networks.[26] In other words, people bring with them the lens of previous affiliations, and a sense of obligation to represent their world view; they may also be subject to pressure from previous professional relations to act in ways that benefit these relations.

Private prison companies have benefited from their relationships with government officials as evidenced by appointments of former employees to key state and federal positions. The pervasiveness of these connections is evidenced with the recent example from the Kasich Administration in Ohio.

After serving 18 years in the U.S. House of Representatives John Kasich retired in 2000 and took a managing director position in Ohio with Lehman Brothers.[27] Lehman Brothers has a long standing history with private prison companies, spending most of the late 1990s and 2000s before their collapse underwriting bonds and managing credit for both CCA and Cornell.[28] After winning the governorship of Ohio in 2010, Kasich laid out his plans for privatizing state prison operations along with appointing a former CCA employee to head the Ohio Department of Rehabilitation and Correction.[29] Rounding out Kasich's connections to CCA is his close friend and former Congressional chief of staff whose lobbying firm was hired to represent CCA in January 2011.[30]

Losing the Game

When private prison companies are successful at the game of political influence, their profits rise, benefitting their stockholders and top management. However, growing evidence shows that many people lose in this political game at the individual and community levels. The policies that private prison companies promote negatively impact communities in terms of costs and public safety. And the increasing use of private prisons due to rising incarceration rates negatively impacts private prison employees. But the biggest losers in this political game are the people who are taken away from their families and communities due to the policies private prison companies promote to increase the number of people going into prisons and the length of time they spend behind bars.

Recommendations

- States and the federal government should look for real solutions to the problem of growing jail and prison populations.
- Invest in front-end treatment and services in the community, whether private or public.
- Additional research is needed to effectively evaluate the cost and recidivism reduction claims of the private prison industry.

Notes

1. Heather C. West, William J. Sabol, and Sarah J. Greenman, *Prisoners in 2009* (Bureau of Justice Statistics, Washington, DC: 2010). http://bjs.ojp.usdoj.gov/content/pub/pdf/p09.pdf.
2. Camille Graham Camp and George M. Camp, *The Corrections Yearbook, 1997* (South Salem, NY: The Criminal Justice Institute, 1997); Tracey Kyckelhahn, *Justice Expenditure and Employment Extracts 2007,* Table 1 (Washington, DC: Bureau of Justice Statistics, 2010).
3. Corrections Corporation of America, *2010 Annual Report,* 2011; The GEO Group, *2010 Annual Report* (Boca Raton, FL: The GEO Group, 2011). www.geogroup.com/AR_2010/images/Geo_Group-AR2010.pdf.
4. Corrections Corporation of America, "About CCA," November 2010. www.cca.com/about.
5. Corrections Corporation of America, *2010 Annual Report,* 2011.
6. Corrections Corporation of America, *2010 Annual Report,* 2011.
7. Corrections Corporation of America, *2010 Annual Report,* 2011.
8. Corrections Corporation of America, *2010 Annual Report,* 2011.
9. The GEO Group, Inc., "Who We Are," December 2010.
10. The GEO Group, Inc., "Who We Are," December 2010; The GEO Group Inc., *2009 Annual Report* (Boca Raton, FL: The GEO Group, 2010). www.geogroup.com/AR_2009_ClientDL/images/GEO_Group-AR2009.pdf.
11. The GEO Group, Inc., "Historic Milestones," December 2010. www.geogroup.com/history.asp.
12. The GEO Group, Inc., "Federal, State, and Local Partnerships," December 2010. www.geogroup.com/federal-state-local.asp.
13. The GEO Group, *2010 Annual Report,* 2011.
14. Alaska, Louisiana, Virginia, Indiana, Texas, Oklahoma, Mississippi, California, Arizona, New Mexico and Florida; The GEO Group, *2010 Annual Report,* 2011.
15. Cornell Companies, Inc., *2009 Annual Report—Form 10-K* (Washington, DC: U.S. Securities and Exchange Commission, 2010). www.sec.gov/Archives/edgar/data/1016152/000110465910010293/a09-36304_110k.htm#Item15_ExhibitsAndFinancialStatem_125526.
16. The GEO Group, Inc., *The GEO Group Completes Transformational Merger with Cornell Companies* (Boca Raton, FL: 2010). www.thegeogroupinc.com/documents/Merger.pdf.
17. Heather C. West and others, *Prisoners in 2009,* 2010.
18. Brigette Sarabi and Edwin Bender, *The Prison Payoff: The Role of Politics and Private Prisons in the Incarceration Boom* (Portland, OR: Western States Center and the Western Prison Project, 2000).
19. National Institute on Money in State Politics, "Correctional facilities construction & management/for-profit Contributions to All Candidates and Committees," accessed September 28, 2011.
20. Center for Responsive Politics, "CCA 2002–2012 Election Cycle PAC Giving — to Parties, Candidates, and Committees," accessed September 28, 2011. www.opensecrets.org/pacs/lookup2.php?cycle=2012&strID=C00366468.
21. Center for Responsive Politics, "The GEO Group 2002–2012 Election Cycle PAC Giving - to Parties, Candidates, and Committees," accessed September 28, 2011. www.opensecrets.org/pacs/lookup2.php?strID=C00382150.
22. Center for Responsive Politics, "Miscellaneous Business: PAC Contributions to Federal Candidates," accessed September 28, 2011. www.opensecrets.org/pacs/industry.php?txt=N12&cycle=2012.
23. Center for Responsive Politics, "Lobbying Corrections Corp of America—Summary 2010," June 2011. www.opensecrets.org/lobby/clientsum.php?lname=Corrections+Corp+of+America&year=2010.
24. Center for Responsive Politics, "Wackenhut Corp 2000–2003 Annual Federal Lobbying," accessed September 28, 2011. www.opensecrets.org/lobby/clientsum.php?id=D000026342&year=2003; Center for Responsive Politics, "The GEO Group 2004–2011 Annual Federal Lobbying," accessed September 28, 2011. www.opensecrets.org/lobby/clientsum.php?id=D000022003&year=2011; Center for Responsive Politics, "CCA 2000–2011 Annual Federal Lobbying," accessed September 28, 2011. www.opensecrets.org/lobby/clientsum.php?id=D000021940&year=2011; Center for Responsive Politics, "Cornell Companies 2000 and 2006–2010 Annual Federal Lobbying," accessed September 28, 2011. www.opensecrets.org/lobby/clientsum.php?id=D000025148&year=2010.
25. Center for Responsive Politics, "CCA 2000–2011 Annual Federal Lobbying," accessed September 28, 2011. www.opensecrets.org/lobby/clientsum.php?id=D000021940&year=2011.
26. Christine Oliver, "Determinants of Interorganizational Relationships: Integration and Future Directions," *The Academy of Management Review* 15, no. 2 (1990): 241–265.
27. *The New York Times,* "Lehman Hires Kasich," January 11, 2001. www.nytimes.com/2001/01/11/business/lehman-hires-kasich.html.
28. Public Services International Research Unit, *Prison Privatization Report International* (London, England: University of Greenwich, 2001). www.psiru.org/justice/ppri44.asp.

29. Mark Niquette, "Private-prison Consultant Chosen to Run ODRC," *Columbus Dispatch,* January 4, 2011. www.dispatch.com/live/content/local_news/stories/2011/01/04/private-prison-consultant-chosen-to-run-ODRC.html.
30. Joe Hallett, "Kasich: Ex-advisers Won't Get Lobbying Favors," *Columbus Dispatch,* February 2, 2011. www.dispatchpolitics.com/live/content/local_news/stories/2011/02/02/copy/kasich-ex-advisers-wont-get-lobbying-favors.html?adsec=politics&sid=101.

Critical Thinking

1. What effect has the increased political influence of private prison companies had on stockholders top management? On communities?
2. Do you believe there are any alternatives to incarcerating lawbreakers?

Prison Re-entry Programs Help Inmates Leave the Criminal Mindset Behind, but Few Have Access to the Classes

CINDY CHANG

The rats, the roaches, the stabbings and the suicides have never stopped J.C. Alford from coming back. Out of prison for a year or two, then back on a drug charge here, a burglary there—it's a cycle he's been repeating since 1977. More than three decades since his first arrest, he is now 52, sitting in a classroom full of other inmates at Orleans Parish Prison, learning how to leave his criminal ways behind.

"What you been doing while locked up?" Leo Hayden, director of the prison's new re-entry program, asked the class one afternoon in December. "Nuttin'," "Sleep all day," came the answers.

So it has gone for Alford during his stints at the prison, notorious for its poor living conditions. Each time his release date arrived, he was let out on the street, no better than when he entered, perhaps worse for the company he kept—until now.

"All these years I've been coming back here, nobody give a damn about nobody back here," said Alford, a gray knit cap pulled over his head, his beaded necklace and tattoo-covered legs distinguishing him in a sea of orange jumpsuits.

"You know what's different now? You're going back out there with me in your corner," Hayden replied, to applause. One inmate, then another, came up to shake Hayden's hand. No more idleness. Their days are now occupied with coursework: anger management, character-building, job interviewing, computer training, money management, resume writing.

Hayden is like a rock star with this audience of convicted felons, singing of the troubles they've known and how to be a better man. A former NFL running back whose drug habit landed him behind bars for five years, he speaks from hard experience. Sheriff Marlin Gusman brought Hayden down from Chicago to run a 10-week curriculum for prisoners nearing release. For the first time, the hundreds of men serving state time at OPP are targets of a concerted effort to prevent them from ever losing their freedom again.

On Family Night, relatives bring their loved ones' favorite foods and listen to guest speakers. If someone needs an outfit for an interview, Hayden has been known to pull a shirt from his own closet. There are the Hayden-invented mantras that some graduates will repeat to themselves over and over as they face the trials and temptations of life on the outside.

Two months at the tail end of their sentences might be too little, too late. Still, it is something, and many of the men are hungry for second chances. Until Gusman launched the re-entry program a year ago with Hayden and a staff of four, an Orleans Parish Prison inmate was simply shown the door on his release date, after months or years of sitting around with nothing to do. Statewide, 50 percent of ex-cons end up back in prison within five years.

"We're helping people reconnect with their humanity," Hayden said. "If we do that, the killings will stop. People will realize that losing their freedom is not a rite of passage but a sentence to death."

Re-entry Programs Scarce

Louisiana's prison system has a unique and damaging wrinkle. Fewer than half of inmates are housed in state prisons like Angola, Dixon or Hunt. The rest serve out their time in the custody of a sheriff, whether in their home parish or somewhere in rural north Louisiana's prison belt—often so the sheriff can make a profit.

These are the very people who will soon be back on the streets because they are serving less time for less serious crimes. Of the 15,000 prisoners released each year, 11,000 come from local prisons.

All inmates leaving state prisons receive a version of the 10-week re-entry program. While behind bars, they can learn trades such as auto mechanics and welding. Lifers at Angola state penitentiary have ample opportunities to better themselves.

But most in local prisons are not even getting the basic re-entry curriculum, let alone new skills that could help them land a decent job. Louisiana's world-leading incarceration rate—one in 86 adults is behind bars—makes the question of re-entry especially crucial. In New Orleans, the nation's murder capital, one in 14 black men is in state custody, with many more having served time at some point in their lives. At any given time, about 6,600 people in the city are on probation or parole.

Jimmy LeBlanc, head of the Department of Corrections, is a believer in re-entry. He started the re-entry program at Dixon Correctional Center when he was the warden there, and he has made re-entry a centerpiece of his systemwide reform efforts.

Under LeBlanc's plan, the pilot program in Orleans Parish, along with a similar one in Shreveport, will eventually develop into regional re-entry centers, hosting all soon-to-be released inmates from those areas. LeBlanc hopes that, someday, all local prison inmates will graduate from re-entry. But with budget cutbacks, as well as the need for buy-in from every sheriff, the goal remains elusive.

Re-entry has also become a buzz word among New Orleans city officials, who are making room for it in their anti-violence initiatives. More business owners are ready to offer ex-cons what they need most: jobs.

The average education level among Louisiana prison inmates is seventh grade, limiting many to menial, low-paying jobs. In addition to whatever got them in trouble in the first place, they now have the stigma of a criminal record. Usually, the path to success requires avoiding old friends and old haunts.

The obstacles are daunting. But there is increasing recognition that turning miscreants into productive citizens could someday make the city safer.

"They're at this place, 60 miles from nowhere, and we're giving them a timeout," said Arthur Hunter, an Orleans Parish Criminal Court judge who co-founded a re-entry program at the Louisiana State Penitentiary at Angola. "Are they just sitting in a chair and looking at the wall, or is something constructive being done so they won't have to get that timeout again? It goes back to not only being tough and giving them punishment but also being smart as well. Re-entry is being smart. Smart is also cheaper for taxpayers."

'You Can Make a Dent'

Almost two years in, the OPP program is too young to have generated hard statistics. Hayden estimates that about half have found jobs, but it is too soon to tell how many will end up back in prison. There are some who can't be helped, like the four graduates who were murdered in their short time back on the streets.

"When we lose one, it's always a gut check, because the work becomes life and death," Hayden said.

Hunter's Angola program, which he started with another Orleans Parish judge, Laurie White, could be described as the Cadillac of re-entry. About 60 young men who would otherwise be doing their time at OPP have been sent to Angola to learn from reformed lifers who serve as mentors. Participants receive instruction in a trade, such as auto mechanics, plumbing or air-conditioning repair, from fellow inmates.

They are also assigned "social mentors" who know the criminal mindset and counsel the younger men on how to leave it behind. The program may eventually expand, but because of the resources required, its reach is limited.

Lafayette Parish Sheriff Mike Neustrom is one of the few Louisiana sheriffs who has made rehabilitating inmates a priority. He devotes about $2.5 million of his annual budget to an array of educational, substance abuse and mental-health services that begin as soon as a person is sentenced. Neustrom said he believes the investment is worth it because it will ultimately result in less crime.

"The bottom line is, most of them are going to come back to Lafayette—it's where they grew up," he said. "If they're better when they come back, that's good. That's the hope. That's the intent."

Gusman, the Orleans Parish sheriff, sees Lafayette as a model, but one that may be out of reach. More than money, he needs space. His annual re-entry budget of $500,000 could accommodate more students, but the makeshift classrooms can only hold so many at a time. The current plan for a new FEMA-funded prison calls for a drastically downsized facility that may not have much space for education programs such as re-entry. A recent move to temporary quarters doubled re-entry from 90 to 200 inmates. Others, such as violent offenders, do not qualify for the program at all, even though they, too, will soon be back on the streets of New Orleans.

"We're doing the right thing. I think we need to do more, offer more and invest more resources," Gusman said. "Real evil people? I don't see them here."

For those who work with parolees and are used to seeing the same names reappear on their rolls, the positive impact of re-entry is a given. After LeBlanc started the Dixon program, parole officers noticed a difference: A person released from Dixon was more likely to beat the odds and turn his life around.

Many of those who end up incarcerated again have not committed new crimes but have merely violated the conditions of their parole. Staying out of trouble also includes keeping appointments, cutting ties with other convicted felons and not going near drugs or alcohol—some of the same "soft skills" emphasized in the reentry curriculum.

"You can make a dent," Frank Palestina, head of probation and parole for the New Orleans district, said of reentry. "Focus on not having anything—like I said, inmate in, inmate out. I'm telling you, my first 10 years, '91 to '01, these people didn't change. . . . How can you change when you're not adding any new ingredients?"

Getting a Chance

"How many of you guys truly think that you are a bad person?" Hayden asked the class.

"In other's eyesight, there's always going to be judgment," one inmate responded. "The things you've done are always going to be there. You this, you that, you going to be there forever. I don't feel like I'm a bad person myself, but the rest of the world is going to feel that way."

It was the perfect lead-in to one of Hayden's favorite maxims: "Living justly in an unjust world." You may have been dealt a bad hand, but you need to stop blaming others and make the best of it.

"When they view us as felons, that's when we need to be our most gracious, our most intelligent, our most committed, to dispel all those myths about us, to be the most human," Hayden said. "They'll give you a chance."

Victor McGill, 42, serving time for forgery, was not content with making do. He seized on Hayden's use of the word "chance." Why aren't there vocational programs in prison, so we can learn a trade and have a better chance of becoming productive members of society? he asked.

The class applauded. Hayden explained that he is doing the best he can with limited resources. He described the bulletin board in his office, which is covered with the business cards he requests from every single person he meets—his doctor, a visiting journalist—on the off chance of procuring a job for an ex-con. Then he laid out the challenges, without sugar coating.

"The problem is, the economy is at rock bottom. I know there are college students looking for the same jobs," Hayden said. "We've got to be real creative. What's going to keep me from hiring the college student? I don't know. We've got to figure it out and make you competitive, gentlemen, make you somebody that somebody wants to hire."

One man asked about work release—with the limited slots in the city, could they be shipped up north to gain a foothold in the workforce there? Hayden noted that most of the guys in the room were not even eligible for work release.

A morale boost arrived a few minutes later. Hayden pulled out a turquoise jumpsuit emblazoned on the back with the word "Re-entry." He had finagled a few hundred dollars so the students could take pride in their uniforms, a cut above the usual prison orange.

"Don't forget us, Mr. Leo!" several called as Hayden left.

'Don't Stop, Don't Give Up'

As Hayden pointed out, it is a tough world for ex-cons, made even tougher by the slow economy. At the Community Service Center in Uptown, tales of woe from former prisoners are common, despite the help with housing and job placement they receive from the small nonprofit. Several said they were homeless.

Elbert Best, 45, served two years for theft and aggravated flight from a police officer, actions he says were brought on by a substance-abuse problem. He started at LaSalle Correctional, a privately run prison near Jena, before being transferred to the custody of the Madison Parish sheriff. He says the move cost him a chance at a work-release job, which could have gotten him back on his feet. He was willing to consider relocating up north if that job had led to a permanent offer.

In seven months living with his mother and young daughter in Gentilly, Best sent out numerous job applications. Despite two decades of experience in the hospitality industry, he did not get a single interview, a failure he attributes in part to his criminal record. Patience and perseverance are a must. In January, he moved to Connecticut to try his luck there, and he is now employed as a restaurant cook.

"Don't stop, don't give up," he said. "Even if you may have several doors closed and you're on the brink of giving up, one of those doors might open."

As part of a growing citywide re-entry initiative, the New Orleans Business Council is recruiting companies willing to employ ex-offenders. But the solution is not as simple as providing jobs, said Dwayne Bernal, president of Royal Engineering, who is coordinating the Business Council effort. The thousands of former prisoners living in New Orleans also need help with housing, transportation and mental health issues, or they will revert to their old ways.

"You can't distance yourself from them. They're not on an island and you can expect them not to exist," Bernal said. "If you don't provide that opportunity, you will see recidivism."

Success Story

Kevin Payton is one success story to come out of Orleans Parish Prison re-entry. At 44, he has racked up six convictions on burglary, theft and drug charges.

His re-entry instructors advised him to make a detailed game plan for his first days on the outside, and he followed it to the letter. Mock job interviews gave him confidence to face real employers. Within days, he had secured a position at a restaurant on the Riverwalk from a manager willing to give him a chance. On weekends, he waited tables. During the week, he loaded a chicken boat. He recently started a new job at a concrete plant in eastern New Orleans.

He is slowly earning back the trust he lost with his relatives, who used to hide their wallets and car keys from him. Now, he shares a car with his mother and mows her lawn in his spare time. He has a steady girlfriend, instead of splitting his time among "three or five" women.

He often recites one of Hayden's mantras: To stay out of trouble, he must change "people, places and things." He still keeps the journal he started while in re-entry. Recently, he returned to the prison on Broad Street, neatly dressed in a button-down shirt and jeans, not as a convict, but as an inspirational speaker for the class.

"Look at me, I'm a big old boy, I'm going to work in the morning and coming back tired," Payton told his former cohorts. "I'm not running from the police. There ain't nobody kicked my momma's door in looking for me."

Critical Thinking

1. Since most people who are incarcerated are eventually released, what purposes should incarceration serve?
2. What makes the question of re-entry especial crucial in Louisiana?

Cindy Chang can be reached at cchang@timespicayune.com or 504.826.3386.

Article 43

Prisoners of Parole

JEFFREY ROSEN

In 2004, Steven Alm, a state trial judge in Hawaii, was frustrated with the cases on his docket. Nearly half of the people appearing before him were convicted offenders with drug problems who had been sentenced to probation rather than prison and then repeatedly violated the terms of that probation by missing appointments or testing positive for drugs. Whether out of neglect or leniency, probation officers would tend to overlook a probationer's first 5 or 10 violations, giving the offender the impression that he could ignore the rules. But eventually, the officers would get fed up and recommend that Alm revoke probation and send the offender to jail to serve out his sentence. That struck Alm as too harsh, but the alternative—winking at probation violations—struck him as too soft. "I thought, This is crazy, this is a crazy way to change people's behavior," he told me recently.

So Alm decided to try something different. He reasoned that if the offenders knew that a probation violation would lead immediately to some certain punishment, they might shape up. "I thought, What did I do when my son was young?" he recalled. "If he misbehaved, I talked to him and warned him, and if he disregarded the warning, I gave him some kind of consequence right away." Working with U.S. marshals and local police, Alm arranged for a new procedure: if offenders tested positive for drugs or missed an appointment, they would be arrested within hours and most would have a hearing within 72 hours. Those who were found to have violated probation would be quickly sentenced to a short jail term proportionate to the severity of the violation—typically a few days.

Alm mentioned his plan to the public defender, who suggested that it was only fair to warn probationers that the rules were going to be strictly enforced for the first time. Alm agreed, and on Oct. 1, 2004, he held a hearing for 18 sex offenders, followed by another one for 16 drug offenders. Brandishing a laminated "Wanted" poster, he told them: "I can guarantee that everyone in this courtroom wants you to succeed on probation, but you have not been cutting it. From now on, you're going to follow all the rules of probation, and if you don't, you're going to be arrested on the spot and spend some time in jail right away." He called the program HOPE, for Hawaii's Opportunity Probation with Enforcement, and prepared himself for a flood of violation hearings.

But they never materialized. There were only three hearings in the first week, two in the second week and none in the third. The HOPE program was so successful that it inspired scholars to evaluate its methods. Within a six-month period, the rate of positive drug tests fell by 93 percent for HOPE probationers, compared with a fall of 14 percent for probationers in a comparison group.

Alm had stumbled onto an effective strategy for keeping people out of prison, one that puts a fresh twist on some venerable ideas about deterrence. Classical deterrence theory has long held that the threat of a mild punishment imposed reliably and immediately has a much greater deterrent effect than the threat of a severe punishment that is delayed and uncertain. Recent work in behavioral economics has helped to explain this phenomenon: people are more sensitive to the immediate than the slightly deferred future and focus more on how likely an outcome is than how bad it is. In the course of implementing HOPE, Alm discovered another reason why the strategy works: people are most likely to obey the law when they're subject to punishments they perceive as legitimate, fair and consistent, rather than arbitrary and capricious. "When the system isn't consistent and predictable, when people are punished randomly, they think, My probation officer doesn't like me, or, Someone's prejudiced against me," Alm told me, "rather than seeing that everyone who breaks a rule is treated equally, in precisely the same way."

Judge Alm's story is an example of a new approach to keeping people out of prison that is being championed by some of the most innovative scholars studying deterrence today. At its core, the approach focuses on establishing the legitimacy of the criminal-justice system in the eyes of those who have run afoul of it or are likely to. Promising less crime and less punishment, this approach includes elements that should appeal to liberals (it doesn't rely on draconian prison sentences) and to conservatives (it stresses individual choice and moral accountability). But at a time when the size of the U.S. prison population is increasingly seen as unsustainable for both budgetary and moral reasons—the United States represents 5 percent of the world's population and nearly 25 percent of the world's prison population—the fact that this approach seems to work may be its biggest draw.

The HOPE program, if widely adopted as a model for probation and parole reform, could make a surprisingly large contribution to reducing the prison population. In many states, the majority of prison admissions come not from arrests for new crimes, as you might think, but from probation and parole violations. Nationwide, roughly two-thirds of parolees fail to complete parole successfully. Todd Clear, a professor at John Jay College of Criminal Justice in New York, estimates that by eliminating imprisonment across the nation for technical parole violations, reducing the length of parole supervision and ratcheting back prison sentences to their 1988 levels, the United States could reduce its prison population by 50 percent.

Some in government are beginning to take notice. In November, invoking the HOPE program as a model, the Democratic congressman Adam Schiff of California and his Republican colleague Ted Poe of Texas introduced legislation in the House that would create federal grants for states to experiment with courts that deliver swift, predictable and moderate punishment for those who violate probation.

There also appears to be a national audience for a broader conversation about new ways to shrink the prison population. Last year, a three-judge panel in California ordered the overcrowded state prison system—the largest in the country, with more than 170,000 prisoners at its peak—to reduce the inmate population by tens of thousands of prisoners within two years in order to comply with constitutional standards for medical and mental health care. Facing a tightening budget crisis in September, California legislators added to the pressure by demanding a reduction in the prison budget of $1.2 billion. In the U.S. Senate, Jim Webb of Virginia is leading a crusade for prison reform, insisting that fewer jail terms for nonviolent offenders can make America safer and more humane, while also saving money. And in the Obama administration, Attorney General Eric Holder is questioning the value of relentlessly expanding prisons. In July, he declared that "high rates of incarceration have tremendous social costs" and "diminishing marginal returns."

The most effective way to shrink the prison population, of course, is not just to reform probation and parole but also to deter groups of potential lawbreakers from committing crimes in the first place. If, in addition to bringing down the numbers of probation and parole revocations, police officers and judges could also address the core problems of drug arrests and street violence, the United States might even be said to have solved its notorious prison problem. Is such an ambitious goal possible? While it might sound too good to be true, the HOPE-style thinking about deterrence offers a promising road map for addressing all these challenges.

Although he acted on his own, Judge Alm did not design the HOPE program without inspiration. In the mid-1990s, when he was a U.S. attorney in Hawaii, Alm heard a presentation by David M. Kennedy, who is considered the patron saint of the new thinking about deterrence. Kennedy, who now teaches at John Jay College of Criminal Justice, spoke about Operation Ceasefire, a program he was designing to reduce youth violence in Boston. Along with his colleagues Anne M. Piehl and Anthony Braga, Kennedy worked with the head of the Youth Violence Strike Force, a division of the Boston Police Department. The police officer explained that while conventional deterrence hadn't worked, he had begun to persuade gangs to behave by issuing a credible threat: namely, that when a gang attracted attention with notorious acts of violence, the entire gang—all of whose members likely had outstanding warrants or probation, parole or traffic violations—would be rounded up.

Kennedy recalls this today as a breakthrough moment in his thinking. Ever since the days of Cesare Beccaria, the 18th-century philosopher and death-penalty opponent, classical deterrence theorists had focused on credibly threatening individuals; Kennedy's first innovation was to focus on increasing the legitimacy of law enforcement in the eyes of groups. "The legitimacy element has risen in my mind from being an important element of the strategy to the most important element," Kennedy told me. Convinced that the best way to increase legitimacy was to enlist what he calls the "community's moral voice," Kennedy set out to deter the most dangerous young gang members by persuading their friends and neighbors to pressure them into obeying the law.

In May 1996, Kennedy, Piehl and Braga helped to design the first of what came to be known as "call-in" sessions, intended to put gangs on notice that they would face swift and certain punishments. Working with Kennedy, probation and parole officers ordered gang members to attend face-to-face meetings with the police. The gang members were given three warnings. First, they were told that if anyone in their group killed someone, the entire group would suffer consequences. Second, the gang members were told that if they want to escape from street life, they could get help and job training from social service agencies and churches. And finally, they heard from members of their community that violence was wrong and it had to stop. The results of the forums were striking and immediate. Within two years, youth violence in Boston fell by two-thirds and city homicide rates by about half.

Why was Operation Ceasefire so effective? One reason was that the warning hearings gave the gang members a sense of what to expect. Increasingly draconian sentences don't always reduce crime, and sometimes increase it. (After increasing in the 1980s, crime fell by 25 percent in the 1990s, but states that put more people in jail had a smaller decline than states that imprisoned fewer.) In part, this is because many people actually don't know the punishments they face.

In addition to offering knowledge, Operation Ceasefire provided certainty. The small numbers of gang members singled out meant they could trust that the police would be able to follow through on their threats. "If you can get people to behave by threatening them credibly, you'll need less actual punishment than if you let them run wild and punish only occasionally," says Mark A. R. Kleiman, author of the new book "When Brute Force Fails: How to Have Less Crime and Less Punishment." Kleiman, whom Alm consulted soon after initiating the HOPE program, became interested in swift, certain and moderate punishment when he was a colleague of Kennedy's years before. Lastly, Operation Ceasefire gave gang members an incentive to obey the law by promising that they would get positive reinforcement from their families and neighbors for changing their behavior.

In all of this, Kennedy's insights were supported by a variety of recent research suggesting that people are more likely to obey the law when they view law enforcement as fair and legitimate. Tom Tyler, a psychology professor at New York University, has found that compliance with court orders is highest for offenders who perceive that they have experienced a fair process. And in a recent book, "American Homicide," the Ohio State University historian Randolph Roth argues that throughout American history, the homicide rate has decreased when people trust that the government is stable and unbiased and believe in the legitimacy of the officials who run it. Similarly, the legal scholar Paul Butler argues in his new book, "Let's Get Free: A Hip-Hop Theory of Justice," that widespread incarceration in the 1980s and '90s undermined the legitimacy of law enforcement in the eyes of the affected communities by converting a prison term into something heroic rather than stigmatic.

After Operation Ceasefire, Kennedy turned his attention from gangs to open-air drug markets. He set out to change how the criminal-justice system was viewed from the perspective of the offenders and their communities—and how the offenders and their communities were viewed by the police. As Kennedy told me, "I saw law enforcement believing plausible but untrue things about the communities they police"—namely, that the communities were corrupt and didn't care about the violence that was destroying them—"and the communities believing untrue things about the police"—namely, that the cops were part of a racist conspiracy to lock up black offenders while overlooking white ones.

To correct what he calls a "corrosive and tragic mistake," Kennedy came up with the idea of a kind of truth-and-reconciliation commission in which offenders would talk to the police accompanied by the people they trusted the most: their mothers. In 2003, working with James Fealy, the police chief in High Point, N.C., Kennedy arranged some preliminary meetings. Although Fealy had been shocked to learn that the community thought he and his officers were almost as bad as the drug dealers, Fealy, in turn, surprised community members by declaring that no one in law enforcement thought the drug war could be won.

These meetings prepared the groundwork for the strategy that followed. After identifying 16 active drug dealers, Fealy arrested four and then prepared warrants for the other 12 that could be signed whenever the police chose. He then called in the other dealers, nine of whom arrived accompanied by their mothers and other "influentials" like grandmothers, and delivered the following message to them as a group: "You could be in jail tonight. We don't want to do that, we want to help you succeed, but you are out of the drug business." The mothers and grandmothers, seemingly impressed by the decision not to arrest, cheered on the police. In subsequent meetings, the "influentials" shouted down naysayers, including a conspiracymonger who accused the C.I.A. of having created the crack epidemic to oppress black people. The drug market in the area dried up.

In addition to influencing Judge Alm's probation reform, Kennedy's efforts to rethink deterrence have also inspired one of the most powerful recent models for national parole reform, which comes from Tracey Meares, a law professor at Yale. (Unlike probation, which involves a sentence instead of prison, parole involves supervision after part of the prison sentence has been served.) In 2002, Meares, who was then a law professor at the University of Chicago, was asked by the U.S. attorney in Chicago, Patrick Fitzgerald, to analyze how best to address crime in the city. She concluded that they should begin on the West Side, in West Garfield Park and the surrounding area, where rates of murder and gun violence were more than four times the city average. Fitzgerald suggested that they might implement a version of Project Exile, a controversial program in Virginia that sought to deter gun violence by threatening federal prosecutions—and a five-year mandatory minimum sentence—for repeat offenders convicted of illegal gun possession. But Project Exile had experienced only mixed success: federal prosecutors could prosecute only a small proportion of the gun cases submitted by the Richmond police. The threat of a severe sentence was, in effect, something of a bluff.

Meares told Fitzgerald that threats of zero tolerance wouldn't work because they simply weren't credible. Instead, Meares argued that law-enforcement officials should concentrate on specific groups of wrongdoers in ways they could accept as both reasonable and fair. Using Operation Ceasefire in Boston as a model, Meares identified everyone who had committed violent or gun-related crimes and had been released from prison and recently assigned to parole. She gathered them in random groups of no more than 20 for call-in sessions in what Meares calls "places of civic importance"—park buildings, local schools and libraries—where they sat at the same table as the police in order to create an egalitarian, nonconfrontational atmosphere. They then heard a version of Kennedy's three-part presentation. The results of the program were drastic: there was a 37 percent drop in the average monthly homicide rate—the largest drop of any neighborhood in the city. Violent crime in Chicago today is at a 30 year low. "All these strategies are a way of signaling to groups of people that government agents view them with dignity, neutrality and trust, which is the best way of convincing them that the government has the right to hold them accountable for their behavior," Meares told me.

From Kennedy and Kleiman to Alm and Meares, the judges and scholars developing new deterrence strategies are changing the way we think about parole, probation, gang violence and drug markets. But the strategies also present a rare opportunity to persuade the nation's policymakers that the most urgent case for prison reform is not only economic but also moral and practical. Yes, it's an outrage that the United States locks up citizens for so long with such uncertain effect; but it's also self-defeating, because long sentences give rise to a crisis of legitimacy that can lead to more crime, not less.

A crisis of legitimacy may sound like a huge, perhaps intractable problem, but the tantalizing promise of the new deterrence thinking is that the crisis can actually be solved, practical step by practical step. The relative simplicity of the solutions, it turns out, is at the core of their radical potential.

Critical Thinking

1. How would you explain the HOPE program?
2. What is Operation Ceasefire?
3. Why have both programs been effective?

Jeffrey Rosen, a law professor at George Washington University, is a frequent contributor to the magazine. He is at work on a book about Louis Brandeis.

Article 44

Addressing Gender Issues among Staff in Community Corrections

KELLI D. STEVENS

Gender-responsiveness research in the criminal justice field has increased during the past decade as professionals learn more about differences between male and female offenders: their unique pathways to crime, their varying needs and gender-specific strategies to reduce crime. Gender responsiveness is also relevant to female professionals in community corrections because organizations need to recognize and address the needs of women in the workplace. While community corrections organizations are actively addressing the needs of female offenders, they are still struggling to meet the needs of female professionals working in the field.

Female Offenders in the System

The number of women under correctional supervision has increased significantly during the past several decades, but the policies addressing the criminality of women and how they are treated in the criminal justice system have not kept pace. Researchers have explored "gendered justice" and found most women in the criminal justice system are charged with nonviolent offenses and do not pose a serious risk to public safety.[1] The increase in the incarceration rate of women has been influenced by structural and social causes of crime that have been largely ignored, while focusing on risk models based on male characteristics and male criminality.[2]

Meda Chesney-Lind found that women have a high rate of technical violations while under community supervision, but strategies for dealing with technical violators are based on male criminality and do not generally take into account the needs of women.[3] Ann Jacobs proposes a matrix model of addressing the needs of women under community supervision that includes recognizing challenges women face (poverty, substance abuse, homelessness, at-risk children and chronic physical and mental illness); developing a life plan within the domains of subsistence, residence, children and family, health, mental health and sobriety, and criminal justice compliance; and taking into consideration the degree of functionality of the individual.[4]

Prominent researchers in the field of gender issues in the criminal justice system developed six guiding principles to help organizations effectively supervise female offenders:

- Acknowledge that gender makes a difference;
- Create an environment based on safety, respect and dignity;
- Develop policies, practices and programs that are relational and promote healthy connections to children, family, significant others and the community;
- Address substance abuse, trauma and mental health issues through comprehensive, integrated and culturally relevant services, and appropriate supervision;
- Provide women with opportunities to improve their socioeconomic conditions; and
- Establish a system of community supervision and reentry with comprehensive, collaborative services.[5]

Gender issues, however, do not only apply to the inmates; community corrections agencies also need to consider the gender issues that may be affecting their staff.

Women in the Work Force

Women continue to face sexual harassment and gender discrimination, including disparity in pay—a phenomenon known as the "motherhood penalty"—and lack of promotional opportunities.

Sexual Harassment

Sexual harassment is defined as "unwelcome sexual advances, requests for sexual favors, and other verbal or physical conduct of a sexual nature."[6] Examination of gender proportions on sexual harassment situations in the workplace has shown sexual harassment is more common in workgroups where males are the majority because these contexts reinforce traditional sex roles.[7] The sex-role spillover theory explains that men are more likely to behave in a manner consistent with their social roles of being aggressive when they are in male-skewed workgroups than when they are in female-skewed workgroups.[8] As more women have entered the field of community corrections and provided a balance in the workgroup composition, sexual harassment complaints have decreased and working conditions seem to have improved during the past several decades. However, problems still exist.

Gender Discrimination

Women continue to experience gender discrimination in the modern workplace. According to the U.S. Department of Labor, the average weekly salary of women in 2008 was only 81 percent of that of men.[9] Despite the fact that 43.6 percent of women comprised the full-time work force in 2005, women made up only 31 percent of workers in the highest earnings category. Scholarly research supports the "motherhood penalty," which posits mothers earn less than their male counterparts. Having two to four children can decrease a woman's wages from 4 percent to 8 percent.[10] The opposite—the "fatherhood premium"[11]—has been shown to be true for males.

In light of the U.S. Department of Labor statistics regarding the disparity in pay between men and women in similar positions, and a plethora of empirical research supporting gender discrimination regarding pay scales and promotional opportunities, community corrections organizations need to examine their current compensation structures and promotional processes to bring those in line with current gender-responsive strategies.

Commitment

Gender biases are manifested in a variety of contexts within organizations. Research has shown that gender bias is present in perceptions of commitment to the organization.[12] Commitment has been associated with lower absenteeism, lower turnover rates and increased intention to stay with the agency.[13] However, when examining these issues as they pertain to women employed in community corrections organizations, problems become evident. Women may often be the primary caregiver for their children, parents or other family members, which can explain absenteeism, but does not mean they are less committed to their jobs than their male counterparts. Because of the nature of community corrections and requirements for supervising offenders, when an employee is absent, the absence impacts his or her co-workers more so than a traditional office job. Turnover rates and perceived lack of intention to remain at one community corrections agency throughout their entire career does not translate into women being less valuable to the organization. Rather, an array of other social and structural factors could be at play. The increase in the number of single parents, increase in costs for child care, lack of child care options, and lack of equal pay and opportunities for women are explanations largely ignored.

The Glass Ceiling

The glass ceiling effect refers to a form of inequality where artificial obstacles hinder the advancement of women and minorities, and where the obstacles are more severe at higher occupational levels.[14] Women may be in positions close enough to the top levels of administration in community corrections organizations, but still more men than women are in top-ranking positions. Advancement opportunities have improved for women in community corrections, but organizations should continue to strive toward global gender-responsiveness strategies.

Organizational Politics

Organizational politics play a key role in power structures and even in informal interactions. Women in community corrections organizations can, and do, experience gendered organizational politics. Although not always overt, these politics can be masculine in nature, which can act as a barrier to their careers due to political activity being "linked to the performance, achievement and maintenance of power."[15] Formal internal policies, procedures and practices of an organization can create separations along gender lines, vertically and horizontally, whereby men hold the majority of top positions of power; the language used within the organization can promote gendered divisions (men as actors, women as supporters); and employees might accept these divisions as part of the organizational culture.[16]

These divisions become useful for men in the arena of promotions and career advancement, as there tends to be more informal and formal mentorship for male employees through the organizational politics of some community corrections organizations.

Improving Institutional Practices

The term "evidence-based practices" is used quite frequently today by community corrections professionals, but how many organizations are actually implementing and breathing life into this concept? Community corrections agencies at all levels—federal, state and local—have provided and continue to provide training to staff regarding evidence-based practices in relation to supervising the offender population. Additionally, community corrections organizations have recognized the importance of implementing programs and services grounded in empirical research to improve offender outcomes. However, it is yet to be determined how this principle has migrated into other aspects of operating a community corrections organization: hierarchical structures, communication practices, organizational culture, recruitment practices, training and on-boarding of new staff, retention of current staff, management and leadership practices, and gender responsivity.

Community corrections has placed importance on evidence-based practices and understanding what motivates offenders. The empirical research discussed throughout this article and the proposed guiding principles for implementing gender-responsive strategies for female offenders also can be applied to address gender issues for female professionals in community corrections.

Gender Matters

Agencies need to analyze their recruitment and hiring procedures, written policies and procedures, informal policies and practices, mentoring programs for staff and promotional opportunities as they relate to women. For example, do written policies default to using gender-specific descriptors (e.g., he or his), where the majority of employees are women? Or are job descriptions gender-neutral, excluding overall gender biases and gender-biased language? Staff retention and succession planning are critical issues in recruiting, developing and retaining experienced employees, so it is time to address gender issues in the community corrections work force.

Gender and Organizational Environment

Create an environment based on safety, respect and dignity. Are policies relating to the safety of female officers gender biased? Does the agency's policy relating to field work only allow for female officers to conduct home visits on female offenders, and male officers to conduct home visits on male offenders? Or do women have to take a field partner with them while doing field work? In some situations this is appropriate, but blanket policies such as this are discriminatory. A less discriminatory policy would be to account for the safety issues through self-defense training, nonlethal weapons training and ethics policies rather than limiting the jobs based on gender.

Another recommendation in this area is to provide all employees with clear sexual harassment policies and take appropriate action when such complaints are made. Considering that one out of four girls will suffer from sexual violence during their lifetime,[17] this means that a portion of the female community corrections professionals have suffered sexual abuse. Employers have a responsibility to ensure they are providing appropriate work environments for all employees and understand sexual harassment in the workplace could further traumatize victims of sexual abuse.

Relationships

The organizational culture should be inclusive of informal networking opportunities and formal mentoring programs for women wanting to advance in the organization—absent of masculine-oriented organizational politics. The "relational principles women bring to the environment can have mutually beneficial consequences for multiple stakeholders"[18] (including probationers, victims, judges and the community). Because women place high importance on relationships, community corrections organizations should allow for flexibility to maintain important relationships so as not to penalize staff for maintaining these relationships. This will maximize benefits for employees and the organization.

A System of Community and Collaboration

Does the organization have a fair representation of women on important committees tasked with making important decisions or recommending substantial changes within the organization? "Because women in the workplace help build connections rather than hierarchies,"[19] fostering collaborative relationships will improve organizational functioning.

Community corrections organizations that truly embrace evidence-based practices should turn to the research available on gender responsivity not only regarding effectively managing their female offender populations, but also to glean ideas for how to appropriately respond to the needs of women in the workplace. Some strides have already been made in this area. For example, there has been an increase in the number of special trainings regarding gender-responsiveness strategies for female offenders, professional organizations sponsoring focus groups and publications dedicated to women's issues, and leadership training for women.

Notes

1. Greenfeld, L.A. and T.L. Snell. 1999. *Women offenders.* Washington, D.C.: Bureau of Justice Statistics.
2. Covington, S.S. and B.E. Bloom. 2003. *Gendered justice: Women in the criminal justice system.* Durham, N.C.: Carolina Academic Press.
3. Chesney-Lind, M. 1998. The forgotten offender, women in prison: From partial justice to vengeful equity. *Corrections Today,* 60(7):66–73. Alexandria, Va.: American Correctional Association.
4. Jacobs, A.L. 2005. Improving the odds: Women in community corrections. *Women, Girls & Criminal Justice,* 6(5):65–80. New York: Women's Prison Association.
5. Bloom, B., B. Owen and S. Covington. 2003. *Gender-responsive strategies: Research, practice, and guiding principles for women offenders.* Washington, D.C.: U.S. Department of Justice, National Institute of Corrections.
6. Equal Employment Opportunity Commission. 1980. Guidelines on discrimination because of sex. *Federal Register,* 45:74676–74677. Washington, D.C.: U.S. Equal Employment Opportunity Commission.
7. Burian, B.K., B.J. Yanico and C.R. Martinez. 1998. Group gender composition effects on judgments of sexual harassment. *Psychology of Women Quarterly,* 22(3):465–480. Hoboken, N.J.: John Wiley & Sons Inc.

   Fitzgerald, L.F., F. Drasgow, C.L. Hulin, M.J. Gelfand and V.J. Magley. 1997. Antecedents and consequences of sexual harassment in organizations: A test of an integrated model. *Journal of Applied Psychology,* 82(4):578–589. Washington, D.C.: American Psychological Association.

   Gutek, B.A. 1985. *Sex and the workplace.* San Francisco: Jossey Bass.

   Gutek, B.A., A.G. Cohen and A.M. Konrad. 1990. Predicting social-sexual behavior at work: A contact hypothesis. *Academy of Management Journal,* 33(3):560–577. Briarcliff Manor, N.Y.: Academy of Management.
8. Goldberg, C.B. 2001. The impact of the proportion of women in one's workgroup, profession, and friendship circle on males' and females' responses to sexual harassment. *Sex Roles,* 45(5–6):359–374. New York: Springer.
9. U.S. Department of Labor. 2009. *Highlights of women's earnings in 2008.* Washington, D.C.: U.S. Bureau of Labor Statistics.
10. Glauber, R. 2007. Marriage and the motherhood wage penalty among African Americans, Hispanics, and whites. *Journal of Marriage and Family,* 69:951–961. Malden, Mass.: Blackwell Publishing.
11. Glauber, R. 2008. Race and gender in families and at work: The fatherhood wage premium. *Gender and Society,* 22:8–30. Kingston, R.I.: Sociologists for Women in Society.
12. Bailyn, L. 1993. *Breaking the mold: Women, men and time in the new corporate world.* New York: The Free Press.

    Voydanoff, P. 1987. *Work and family life.* Newbury Park, Calif.: Sage.
13. Angle, H. and J. Perry. 1981. An empirical assessment of organizational commitment and organizational effectiveness. *Administrative Science Quarterly,* 26(1):1–14. Ithaca, N.Y.: Johnson Graduate School of Management at Cornell University.

    Mowday, R.T., L.W. Porter and R.M. Steers. 1979. *Employee-organization linkages: The psychology of commitment, absenteeism, and turnover.* New York: Academic Press.
14. Maume, D.J. 2004. Is the glass ceiling a unique form of inequality?: Evidence from a random-effects model of managerial attainment. *Work and Occupations,* 31(2):250–274. Thousand Oaks, Calif.: Sage Publications.
15. Davey, Kate Mackenzie. 2008. Women's accounts of organizational politics as a gendering process. *Gender, Work and Organization,* 15(6):650–671. Malden, Mass.: Wiley-Blackwell.
16. Acker, J. 1998. The future of "gender and organizations": Connections and boundaries. *Gender, Work and Organization,* 5(4):195–206. Staffordshire, United Kingdom: Wiley-Blackwell.
17. Centers for Disease Control and Prevention. 2007. *Understanding sexual violence fact sheet.* Retrieved from www.cdc.gov/ncipc/pub-res/images/SV%20Factsheet.pdf.
18. Fletcher, J.K. 1999. *Disappearing acts: Gender, race and relational practice at work.* Cambridge, Mass.: Massachusetts Institute of Technology.
19. Ibid.

Critical Thinking

1. When supervising female offenders in the community, how does their gender make a difference?
2. How does gender affect women who work in corrections?

Test-Your-Knowledge Form

We encourage you to photocopy and use this page as a tool to assess how the articles in *Annual Editions* expand on the information in your textbook. By reflecting on the articles you will gain enhanced text information. You can also access this useful form on a product's book support website at www.mhhe.com/cls.

NAME: DATE:

TITLE AND NUMBER OF ARTICLE:

BRIEFLY STATE THE MAIN IDEA OF THIS ARTICLE:

LIST THREE IMPORTANT FACTS THAT THE AUTHOR USES TO SUPPORT THE MAIN IDEA:

WHAT INFORMATION OR IDEAS DISCUSSED IN THIS ARTICLE ARE ALSO DISCUSSED IN YOUR TEXTBOOK OR OTHER READINGS THAT YOU HAVE DONE? LIST THE TEXTBOOK CHAPTERS AND PAGE NUMBERS:

LIST ANY EXAMPLES OF BIAS OR FAULTY REASONING THAT YOU FOUND IN THE ARTICLE:

LIST ANY NEW TERMS/CONCEPTS THAT WERE DISCUSSED IN THE ARTICLE, AND WRITE A SHORT DEFINITION:

NOTES

NOTES

NOTES

NOTES

NOTES

NOTES

NOTES

NOTES